Wovoka and the Ghost Dance

EXPANDED EDITION

Researched, Compiled, and Written by Michael Hittman

Edited by Don Lynch

University of Nebraska Press
Lincoln and London

⊖ The paper in this book meets the minimum requirements of American
National Standard for Information Sciences—Permanence of Paper for
Printed Library Materials, ANSI Z39.48-1984.

First Bison Books printing: 1997.
Most recent printing indicated by the last digit below:
10   9   8   7   6   5   4   3   2   1

Library of Congress Cataloging-in-Publication Data
Hittman, Michael.
Wovoka and the ghost dance / researched, compiled, and written by
Michael Hittman; edited by Don Lynch.—Expanded ed.
p.   cm.
ISBN 0-8032-7308-8 (pbk.: alk. paper)
1. Wovoka, ca. 1856–1932. 2. Ghost dance. 3. Paiute Indians—Biography.
I. Lynch, Don. II. Title.
E99.P2W617   1998
973′.049745—dc21   97-22025   CIP

First edition published in 1990 by the Grace Dangberg Foundation, Inc.,
Carson City, Nevada.

CONTENTS

LIST OF ILLUSTRATIONS

FOREWORD

Wovoka, also known as Jack Wilson, was one of the most important and influential leaders of the American West. A Northern Paiute Indian born near Yerington, Nevada, about 1856, Wovoka gained his greatest renown as the messiah or prophet of the 1890 Ghost Dance movement.

On New Year's Day 1889, while ill from a fever, Wovoka had a religious revelation wherein he "died" and went to heaven. There God gave him a dance and a message of peace to share with all people.

Word of the movement spread like a prairie fire among the Indians of the Great Plains, and by 1890 the Ghost Dance ceremonies were practiced by the Sioux, the Cheyenne, the Comanche, the Shoshone, the Arapaho, the Assiniboin, and other tribes of the Trans-Mississippi West.

Variously described as a "revitalization movement" and as a "crisis cult," the teachings of Wovoka were eagerly accepted by a people who had recently suffered ruinous cultural problems — military defeat, the destruction of the buffalo, confinement on Indian reservations, and epidemics of strange and frequently fatal diseases.

By the summer of 1890, Wovoka's Great Plains followers had worked themselves into a frenzy of excitement, and the whites feared an Indian uprising. The situation was especially tense on the Pine Ridge Reservation in South Dakota, and in December 1890 Colonel James Forsyth of the U. S. 7th Cavalry Regiment — Custer's old unit — attempted to disarm Chief Big Foot's band of Miniconjou Sioux, who were camped on Wounded Knee Creek. On December 29, shooting broke out at Wounded Knee, killing at least 146 Indian men, women and children.

The Battle of Wounded Knee ended almost three hundred and fifty years of Indian warfare in North America, and also effectively ended the Ghost Dance movement as well.

In *Wovoka and The Ghost Dance*, Michael Hittman has made an invaluable contribution to the literature of the American West. However, Hittman's work has an even broader significance to the study of comparative religions and culture. His collection of primary sources relating to the Paiute prophet, presented together with his extensive and thoroughly-researched notes, gives us the most full and accurate portrait of Wovoka ever presented to the world.

The richness of detail of *Wovoka and The Ghost Dance* is truly impressive. Every known first-hand account of the Paiute shaman's life, published or unpublished, has been collected and collated for this book. The story is a fascinating one. The reader is drawn into the magical work of the Indian messiah. Hittman's text features eyewitness accounts of the career of the weather prophet, rain-maker and miracle worker, omitting nothing.

The Grace Dangberg Foundation is proud to have the honor of publishing *Wovoka and The Ghost Dance*.

David Thompson
President, The Grace Dangberg Foundation
Reno, Nevada
December 24, 1990

Preface to the Expanded Edition

Since 1990, the Yerington Paiute Tribe has diligently sold the first edition of this book, conceived as a vital part of the centennial celebration of the 1 January 1889 Great Revelation by Wovoka. The Wovoka Project, launched in 1986 by its tribal council under the dynamic leadership of chairperson Linda Howard has seen three of four goals realized: (1) the commissioned research of this biography of Wovoka, whose first five hundred copies were sold by Grace Dangberg Press, under an agreement that it would turn over all subsequent publishing rights to the Yerington Paiute Tribe; (2) the sale of a poster of the 1890 Ghost Dance prophet by the Tribe; and (3) the Tribe's hosting of a Wovoka Centennial Powwow on Campbell Ranch Reservation, Nevada, on 25 August 1989. Only a U.S. postage stamp of the great visionary and man of peace, Wovoka, a.k.a. Jack Wilson, remains to be achieved.

Reprinting *Wovoka and the Ghost Dance* allows it to reach a wider audience and its author to introduce new materials about the famous Northern Paiute (Numu) prophet that were collected while researching a subsequent book (Hittman 1996a). This expanded edition also permits a reconsideration of conclusions, as well as an opportunity to correct certain errors, both prompted by awareness of publications missed during the initial writing and material published since then.

The newly discovered information includes several audiotapes that are now available for purchase; additional newspaper articles as well as government correspondences stumbled upon during the aforementioned unrelated archival research; and various unpublished manuscripts (fieldnotes of Willard Z. Park, in possession of Catherine Fowler). But, as stated, there are also published materials bearing critically on Wovoka and the 1890 Ghost Dance he founded, which either appeared in print too close to or after the publication of the first edition (e.g., Kehoe 1989, Vander 1997) or whose significance or existence was entirely missed by the author (Moses 1987, Ewers 1964). New information is presented in Chapter 10, "More about Wovoka." In the spirit of the first edition, some of the new data will be reproduced *in toto* in appendices, including a taped interview with Edward A. Dyer, in which Wovoka's amanuensis and business partner discusses (among other things) his meeting with and work as an interpreter for Mooney; "Alice Wilson Vidovich, Andy Vidovich and Peg Wheat Discuss Paul Bailey"; and "Eileen Kane's 1964 Field Notes on Wovoka." A supplementary bibliography has also been added.

The aim of this book, therefore, remains unchanged: it is an ethnohistorical biography of the founder of the last important Native American millennial movement of the nineteenth century, containing its source materials so that the general reader or specialist can not only trace this author's arguments but continue to disagree, correct, amend, or reinterpret them.

Once again I have the opportunity to express my gratitude to everyone mentioned in the original preface. Special recognition should now go to the dedicated archivists and librarians whose prodigious and generally unrecognized labors led me to most of the new materials discussed in Chapter 10: Kathleen O'Connor of the Leo J. Ryan Federal Archives Building, San Bruno, California; Susan Searcy and Linda Perry of the Special Collections Department,

University Library, the University of Nevada–Reno; and Phil Earl, curator extraordinaire, of the Nevada Historical Society (Reno). An additional, special acknowledgment, however, needs to be extended to Ms. Stacy Stahl of the Yerington Paiute Tribe. As its chairperson, this young, savvy, emerging Numu political leader was first of all able to convince the Council to allow my book to gain this second life. She then coordinated talks between tribe, tribal attorney, author, and publisher. Thanks, Stacy!

Michael Hittman
February 17, 1997
Eric's Place, Shelter Island, NY

PREFACE TO THE FIRST EDITION

Anthropologists are trained to observe rather than influence or change other cultures. Nevertheless, after more than two decades of a professional relationship with the Yerington Paiute Tribe of Nevada, I appeared before their Tribal Council on October 12, 1986 to propose that the 100th anniversary of the Great Revelation of Jack Wilson, or Wovoka, the 1890 Ghost Dance Prophet and their native son, be officially recognized by them.

My suggestion was that (1) we undertake a national campaign to collect letters of support (in order to petition the United States Post Office) for the issuance of a stamp by the U.S. Post Office to commemorate this centennial; (2) a commercial artist be hired to produce a poster of Wovoka for sale as tribal income; (3) any and all photographs of the 1890 Ghost Dance Prophet be purchased for the purpose of mounting a comprehensive exhibit; (4) the Tribe host a one-day powwow, preferably in the ghost town where Wovoka originally had his fateful meeting with God; and, finally, (5) I write a biography of the 1890 Ghost Dance Prophet, all proceeds going to the Yerington Paiute Tribe. Thus was born the Wovoka Project.

Happily, three years later I can report that all phases of the Wovoka Project are complete. After a generous outpouring of support, the stamp proposal currently sits in Washington, D.C., pending approval. A handsome poster of Wovoka, done by Kathy Cimis of the Graphic Arts Department of Cooper Union College of New York, went on sale in August of 1989 and is available through the business office of the Yerington Paiute Tribe. Photographic exhibits were held in May 1989 at the Lyon County Museum, Yerington, Nevada. In June, at the Stewart Indian Museum, Carson City, Nevada (the latter under Ed Johnson's gracious auspices), "Wovoka Day," a centennial celebration, was attended by several hundred people. Later that year, on August 26, another Wovoka centennial celebration was held at the Campbell Ranch and received local coverage as well as being filmed by WCBS-TV. Since it would be virtually impossible to acknowledge every individual who contributed to the realization of the Wovoka Project, I will focus instead only on those intimately associated with *Wovoka and The Ghost Dance,* the last leg of the project.

Michael Hittman

ACKNOWLEDGEMENTS

To begin with, I express my appreciation to the staff of the Inter-Tribal Council (ITC) of Nevada (Reno), where I began my archival work. Special Collections at the University of Nevada Library (Reno) gave permission to reproduce the unpublished Edward S. Dyer Manuscript, lengthy sections from the Margaret Wheat Papers, and the photograph of Wovoka appearing on the cover of this book as well. For the many small courtesies and constant helpfulness of its staff, I am grateful. I also offer my appreciation to the Nevada State Historical Society (Reno) and, in particular, its curator Phillip Earl. Phil directed me to the Wier Notes and to Grace Dangberg's Composition Notebook, both of which contained useful information about Wovoka. I would also like to acknowledge the staff at the Federal Archives, San Bruno, California, where I read and photocopied much of Special Case 188 (SC 188), Volumes 1 and 2 of the Ghost Dance file, available there on microfilm.

The Nevada Humanities Committee of the National Endowment for the Humanities awarded a grant (NHC No. 87-33) to the Wovoka Project in 1987. The money not only covered my travel expenses from New York City but allowed for the reimbursement of Yerington Paiute elders who were willing to serve as informants. I single out the executive director of NHC, Judy Winzeler, for her genuine interest and strong support throughout all phases of the Wovoka Project, and also her friendship to me.

Anthropologist Ron McCoy graciously lent permission to use the photograph of Wovoka on the poster and to quote from the transcript of his tape-recorded interview with his father Tim McCoy. Jay Miller was kind enough to read an early draft of my study and offer some critical comments. His own research on Native Americans continues to stimulate my anthropological thinking. Alice Lopatin edited an early draft of this book and has taught me more about writing than perhaps she realizes. Peggy Lee was hired by the Yerington Paiute Tribe to edit my final draft, however, and was instrumental in bringing additional light to the dark tunnel of my writing. I, of course, assume full responsibility for any errors contained within.

I wish also to acknowledge Marion Edwards, secretary of the Anthropology and Sociology Department of Long Island University, where I teach, for innumerable assistance throughout the Wovoka Project. Several colleagues also need to be singled out. Peter Strodl, of the Bilingual Education Department, was kind enough to run a desk-top publishing layout of the text. Stuart Fishelson, of Media Arts, reshot the photographs of Wovoka found in this book and made slides so that I could deliver public lectures on the subject. Cynthia Dantzic, of the Art Department, volunteered to do the cover of the book.

On the home front, my wife Meryl encouraged me (as she always does) to strive for excellence. My love for her only deepens.

Any number of individuals from Smith and Mason valleys, Nevada, were helpful during the course of field investigations: Mary Ann Cardenale, Roy Wittacre, Walter Cox, John McGowen, Alex Miller, Joe Tibbals, Tony Howard, Velma Ford, and the entire staff of the Lyon County Court House, where I read old newspapers.

Then, of course, there are the Prophet's descendants. Being asked to dredge up the past was not at all easy, so I express both my deepest appreciation and apologies to Yerington Paiutes who volunteered to surrender information about their famous Prophet: Irene Thompson, who helped me reconstruct Wovoka's family; Howard Rogers, masterful raconteur; Lena Rogers; Russell Dick, whom I call "uncle," and who proves that it is not age alone which bestows cultural knowledge upon an informant; Mary Stevens; Ernie Conway; and Chester Smith; as well as Numus who are no longer living — Corbett Mack, Hazel Quinn, Andy Dick, Nellie Emm, and Rosie Brown, who were also my Wovoka teachers. To Ida Mae Valdez, I publicly wish to acknowledge that being welcomed as a son in your house since 1965 has influenced not only how I think but the very way in which I live my life.

As for the staff of the Yerington Paiute Tribe — Bernie Giron, Becky Boatwright, Barry Barredo, and Fawn Lewis — you facilitated my every working moment in Yerington, and I do not see how this book or the Wovoka Project could have been accomplished otherwise. Similarly, the Yerington Paiute Tribal Council must be singled out for special kudos. During the fiscally lean Reagan years, the Yerington Paiute Tribal Council thought highly enough of the Wovoka Project to launch my work with a modest grant; but without its chairperson, nothing would have come to fruition. Linda Howard provided stability and continuity throughout. She was diligent in seeking funding for the Wovoka Project and, in fact, wrote the proposal to The Grace Dangberg Foundation, who agreed to publish this book. The mixture of her keen business sense with passionate commitment to education should serve as a model for political leaders everywhere, and I am proud to call her my pune'e, my sister.

Finally, I mention Gunard Solberg. In August of 1988 I sat down in the California home of this Wovoka scholar to discuss my subject; and, nearly twenty-four hours later, we were scheming how to bridge the continent for another occasion to meet. Gunard was kind enough to offer many useful criticisms of this book. I wish to thank him for sharing his voluminous information about Wovoka and his many photographs of the Prophet. I dedicate *Wovoka and The Ghost Dance* to him.

Michael Hittman

"Andy, it's a great responsibility to me, too. It's like having a knowledge you didn't know what to do with. I try to be very careful.... One thing, I will try never, never to do is to write or make public something that will hurt someone else."

"To hurt somebody else. I don't like that either. That's a terrible thing. That's what hurt Alice and me. Poor old Wavoka [sic]. They run him down. They didn't know the concrete of the thing.... What I'd like to do is to have it put out rightfully."

(Conversation between Peg Wheat and Andy Vidovich. Margaret Wheat Papers, Special Collections, University of Nevada Library, Reno. Tape 100:1)

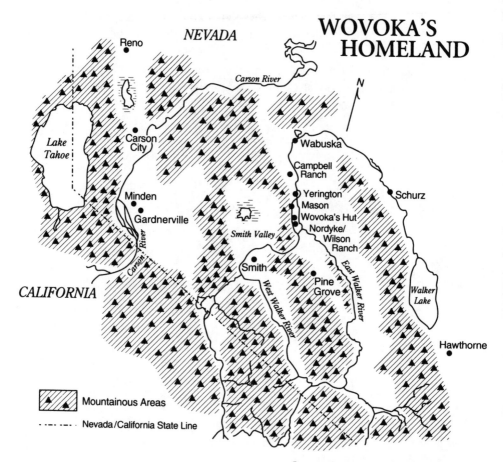

WOVOKA'S HOMELAND

NEVADA

Reno

Carson River

N

Lake
Tahoe

Carson
City

Wabuska

Campbell
Ranch

Yerington
Mason
Wovoka's Hut
Nordyke/
Wilson
Ranch

Schurz

Minden

Gardnerville

Smith Valley

Smith

Pine
Grove

*Walker
Lake*

CALIFORNIA

West Walker River

East Walker River

Hawthorne

▲ Mountainous Areas

- - - - Nevada/California State Line

Courtesy Jim Bean Consulting Associates

Introduction

"...it is nevertheless deplorable that no straightforward account of this 'prophet' has been written by a person whose aim is not the marketplace but the service of truth" (Dangberg 1968:25).

The 1890 Ghost Dance Religion began in Smith and Mason valleys, Nevada, with the Great Revelation of Jack Wilson, or Wovoka, **Numu** (Northern Paiute). Numerous studies of this messianic movement exist. "Ghost Dance" has joined potlatch, wampum, powwow, totem pole, guardian spirit, and the vision quest as enduring contributions of the Native American, both to the English language and Euro-American culture. But although a century has passed since "The (Wood) Cutter" proclaimed his stirring message of salvation, basic questions about the religion Wovoka founded remain:

What was the original message of the 1890 Ghost Dance Prophet?

Did Wovoka urge militancy or pacifism?

Did he alter the Ghost Dance message after the Wounded Knee massacre?

Did Wovoka prophesy an earthly paradise in which the dead would be resurrected, or were the living to reunite with their lost loved ones in the afterlife?

And what was the place of **Tibo'o** (whites) to have been in all this? Moreover, the most elementary questions about the 1890 Ghost Dance Prophet have yet to be asked:

Who were his parents?

Did Wovoka have any brothers and sisters?

What is known of the Prophet's early life?

Who was his wife?

Did the Prophet have children or grandchildren?

What were the 1890 Ghost Dance ceremonies like in Nevada?

What were the significant religious influences upon Wovoka's early life?

What miracles and prophecies were attributed to Wovoka in his homeland?

What became of him after his influential religious movement ended?

And how is the Prophet remembered today by his descendants, the Yerington Paiute Tribe of Nevada?

Even if these questions could be answered, it is doubtful that a satisfactory biography could ever be written. The 1890 Ghost Dance Prophet Wovoka refused to give interviews after the infamous Wounded Knee massacre in 1890. Since he neither read nor wrote, there are no personal diaries or journals that lie hidden awaiting the research efforts of future scholars. But even if Wovoka had been literate, retrieval of such treasure troves would seem unlikely since personal belongings of the dead were traditionally buried or destroyed by Numus. Moreover, research into this prophet's life becomes increasingly difficult with the passage of time and ensuing deaths of those who knew him best. "Ghost fright" (Whiting 1950), too, can be cited as another impediment because the older the Numu the less inclined he or she was to discuss deceased relatives. "Who, Jack Wilson? He's dead a long time!" This was the most frequently heard response to biographical inquiries about the past and the 1890 Ghost Dance Prophet in particular. Then there is the problem caused by Wovoka's international fame.

Because his career was that of a visionary and miracle worker, Numus as well as Tibo'o emphasized this aspect of Wovoka's which has resulted in the creation of the Prophet's "mythic" personality (Olofson 1979:14). Yet another obstacle to biographical research into the life of Wovoka can be cited. Aware of the ridicule that has been heaped upon their great Prophet by outsiders, many Yerington Paiutes were reluctant to discuss him; i.e., lest old prejudices resurface in yet another study of Wovoka. Moreover, since much of the traditional culture has been lost, and the majority of Yerington Paiutes are Christians, another difficulty can be said to derive from the influence of fundamentalist preachers, who have besmirched the good name and reputation of the 1890 Ghost Dance Prophet by branding Wovoka a "false prophet" and worse.

As Yerington Paiutes struggle to assume their rightful place in mainstream America, the knowledge of Wovoka they might otherwise have acquired at home tends to be replaced with what is taught and written in the published texts and curricula adopted by the public school system — information which is sketchy and often inaccurate or misleading. With so many provisos, why even attempt this study?

Certainly the occasion alone merits such effort. 1989, after all, marks the Centennial of Wovoka's Great Revelation, and the fact remains that no single comparable treatment of this Numu has even been attempted. Since "Ghost Dance" in the minds of most readers is too freely associated with the Wounded Knee massacre which took place in South Dakota, almost any reconstruction of the religion Wovoka founded would be a contribution in itself. Moreover, the discovery of new and relevant information about the Prophet's life can be said to warrant this study.

Field work conducted among Yerington Paiute Tribal members since 1965 has resulted in the compilation of many important, first-hand remembrances of the 1890 Ghost Dance Prophet. Second, certain archival documents have either been ignored by scholars or too lightly utilized. The Wier Notes are an example. Jennie Elizabeth Wier was Professor of Political Science at the University of Nevada-Reno and founder of the Nevada Historical Society. Wier went to Mason Valley about 1910 to interview members of the Tibo'o family on whose ranch Wovoka had lived as a youth and subsequently worked when grown. Edward C. Johnson, in 1975, made use of the Wier Notes in a chapter about the Prophet in his important history of the Walker River Reservation; however, the Numu historian did not completely exhaust this source. Similarly, I cite the Dangberg Composition Notebook. Grace Dangberg, a Berkeley-trained historian, whose family owned vast acreage in Carson Valley, conducted field work on the life of Wovoka in Smith and Mason valleys. Although this resulted in the publication of two monographs about the 1890 Ghost Dance Prophet, pertinent and even vital data from her field notebook did not reach the printed page.

Two additional sources of information have gone untapped. They are the Vidovich-Wheat Tapes and the McCoy-McCoy Tapes. The taped and transcribed conversations of the Vidovich-Wheat Tapes were held between Wovoka's son-in-law, Andy Vidovich, and Margaret "Peg" Wheat of Fallon, Nevada. The unpublished Vidovich-Wheat Tapes offer essential biographical data about Wovoka, as well as stunning texts on his miracles and prophetic powers. The McCoy-McCoy Tapes are material from the famous silent movie star, Tim McCoy, and his anthropologist son, Ron McCoy. The McCoy interviews serve as the material for Ron McCoy's 1977 book, *Tim McCoy Remembers The West*. These original tapes contain much useful biographical information about the Prophet, but much information was not included in the book.

Certain theoretical developments in the social sciences also shed light upon the life of the 1890 Ghost Dance Prophet. I mean here the literature on "revitalization" (Wallace 1956) and "social movements" (Aberle 1966), as well as recent psychological studies of Altered States of Consciousness (La Barre 1970) and Near-Death Experiences (Ring 1984).

I wrote this book, *Wovoka and the Ghost Dance*, as a source book because nearly half its pages contain the most important published and unpublished materials about the life of the prophet and the religious movement he founded. I employ ethnohistory: melding ethnographic information gained through participant-observation with historical data from the local newspapers. Although much of this information will be incorporated into the body of this biography, it was both my original intention and hope that by reproducing it separately in this study, future Ghost Dance scholars will benefit from having the corpus in a single source.

Part I

Chapter 1

The Four
Primary Sources

"The prophet is nothing without his people"
(Heschel 1962:362).

ARTHUR I. CHAPMAN

Find and interview the "Indian who impersonated Christ!" With these orders from Brigadier General John Gibbon, commander of the Military Department of the Pacific, Arthur I. Chapman, Indian scout, left San Francisco on November 28, 1890 for the Walker River Reservation, Nevada. Chapman arrived two days later at the reservation townsite of Schurz, only to have James O. Gregory, farmer-agent in charge, correct a misconception. He said the name of the Numu who preached to all the Indians was not John Johnson but Jack Wilson. Jack Wilson claimed to be the new Messiah and had been preaching for the last two or three years, since 1887. Furthermore, Gregory related that ceremonies were being held in different places at intervals of about three months. Chapman also learned from the farmer-agent that attendance had been swelling of late. The ceremonies were becoming more frequent, as a great many strange Indians from a great way off were now traveling to western Nevada to participate in Jack Wilson's new religion — including Cheyenne, Sioux, and Bannocks, the latter as recently as March of 1890. "The new Messiah" had been "mostly raised" by a white man in Mason Valley, 50 miles from the reservation, or so Gregory told the Indian scout. And Jack Wilson had a "good name," as well as a reputation among whites for being an "honest, hard-working Indian."

Chapman then reported that Gregory introduced him to a Walker River Reservation Numu named James Josephus, a "Captain" of the reservation police force. Josephus stated that he was born at the Carson Sink 48 years prior and had served in the past as an "interpreter for the Government." Josephus then proceeded to narrate for Chapman our earliest recorded account of the 1890 Ghost Dance Religion in its homeland.

Quoitze Ow was the Prophet's name, Captain Josephus related. Born of a poor family at Walker Lake, Quoitze Ow (Wovoka, Jack Wilson), when quite a large boy, had moved to Mason Valley where he worked for Dave Wilson, a white rancher. At 20, the future Prophet married. He and his bride continued to live and work on the Wilson ranch: "About three years ago [1887]," Josephus stated, "while cutting wood in the mountains for the Wilsons," Quoitze Ow [Wovoka] heard "a great noise which appeared to be above him on the mountains." Startled, the Numu "lay down his axe" and "started to go in the direction of the noise when he fell down dead." God thereupon lifted Quoitze Ow to Heaven. "It was the most beautiful country you could imagine," Josephus told Chapman, a land "nice and level and green all the time; there were no rocks or mountains there, but all kinds of game and fish." And God "showed him [Wovoka] everything there. Both Indians and whites, who were all young.... God told him that when the people died here on this earth, if they were good, they came to heaven, he made them young again and they never grew to be old afterwards." Moreover, the dead in Heaven were said to be "dancing, gambling, playing ball and having all kinds of sports." According to Josephus, the Prophet returned to his camp upon awakening and apparently said nothing about the experience to members of his family. Later that night, however, God came to Quoitze Ow again while he slept.

"Tell all the people that they must not fight, there must be peace all over the world," God instructed him. And it was during this second revelation, according to Josephus, that the 1890 Ghost Dance Prophet learned the precepts of the new religion:

1. "All men were brothers," so "people" should "be good to each other."

2. Thou shalt not steal.

He "would come after him again," God further revealed, though only upon the successful completion of Quoitze Ow's ministry on earth. Afforded a second glimpse of Paradise within 24 hours, the new Prophet once again saw both Numus and Tibo'o "who had died heretofore." With their youth restored, the deceased members of both races appeared to be well-fed, prosperous, and happy. Curiously enough, Quoitze Ow even described having seen his own dead mother in Heaven, despite the fact that she was alive in 1889. In any event, Josephus went on to relate to Chapman how God next directed the Numu Prophet to return to earth again to tell "his people" that they "must meet often and dance five nights in succession and then stop for three months." Thus the "new messiah," as Captain James Josephus called Quoitze Ow, received "great power and authority to do many things." Including the ability to "cause it to rain or snow at will."

At this point, however, the Walker River Reservation Numu policeman (Josephus) confided to the Indian scout Chapman that he originally was not a true believer in the powers of the 1890 Ghost Dance Prophet. Josephus's conversion had taken place during the blistering drought of the previous winter. Because Walker River Reservation Numu crops were so severely threatened, Josephus related how he traveled to Smith Valley, or to Mason Valley, in order to personally petition the "new messiah" to employ his much vaunted "power over the elements" on their behalf. Wovoka "sat with his head bowed but never spoke a word during all this time," according to Josephus. The hour must have been late, for the Prophet went directly to bed without answering his plea. "Early in the morning," though, Wovoka was said to have approached Josephus's bed and delivered the following prophecy: "You can go home, and on the morning of the third day, you and all the people will have plenty of rain."

The rains did indeed come. The Walker River flooded its banks, and the severe drought of 1888-1889 ended exactly within that specified or prophesied time — three days, the Christian integer, not the Northern Paiute sacred numbers of four and five. When this prophecy came to pass, Captain James Josephus became a "strong believer" in the "unnatural powers" of the "new Christ," or so he stated to Arthur Chapman. In his December 6, 1890 report, which Chapman subsequently filed with the Department of War from San Francisco, the Indian scout wrote that another "captain" of the Walker River Reservation police force, Ben Ab-he-gan, happened to be present during his interview with James Josephus and "corroborated every word spoken."

Yet, the new Prophet also had his "distractors [sic]," Chapman stated. Besides James O. Gregory and another reservation employee named Peas, who would not credit the recent rains to Quoitze Ow (Wovoka), there were Numu doubters as well. Because some even viewed him as an "impostor," the 1890 Ghost Dance Prophet reportedly had "sent them word to come and see him and hear him talk and he would convince them." This was at the recent ceremony at Walker Lake which farmer-agent Gregory had already told Chapman about — a gathering attended by 1,600 Indians including Cheyennes, Lakotas, Arapahos, Utes, Navahos, Shoshones, and Bannocks, and "a tribe to the south of them that they called the Umapaws."

With Captain Ben Ab-he-gan as his interpreter, the Indian scout

Chapman set out for Mason Valley where "Jack Wilson, the Messiah," was said to be living. However, in Mason Valley, located twenty or so miles north and west of the Walker River Reservation, Chapman learned that Wovoka was elsewhere; so he and Captain Ben left at once for Desert Creek in the adjoining valley — Smith Valley, thirty miles south and west. On December 4, 1890, in the tiny rural hamlet of Wellington, Nevada, on the west fork of the Walker River, the very first recorded interview with the 1890 Ghost Dance Prophet took place. Because it was "raining and snowing alternately...I sent for Jack Wilson to come down to Mr. [Zadok] Pierce's house, as the weather was not suitable for holding outdoor meetings," Chapman begins. When Wovoka finally "put in his appearance," Captain Ben introduced the two men, who shook hands, "Jack Wilson remarking that he was glad to see me." In the interview we learn the following about the 1890 Ghost Dance Prophet: He was about 30 years of age; the father of this "new Christ" was still living; Wovoka had three brothers, all younger; and he stated that he had never been away from his "own country."

> Chapman: Are you a chief?
>
> Wovoka: Yes; I am chief of all the Indians who sent represen-
>   tatives to me.
>
> Chapman: When did you commence to preach to the Indians?
>
> Wovoka: About three years ago.

A reiteration of most of what Chapman had previously learned from Captain Josephus follows, interspersed with these addenda: Yes, he had been visited by God, and "many times since," Wovoka stated. God urged him to "tell the Indians that they must work all the time and not lie down in idleness," as only "the people who had been good heretofore were to be made over again." Such was Wovoka's utter lack of temerity that he could tell Chapman of his "power to destroy this world and all the people in it and to have it made over again" — a statement remarkable in itself, and all the more so considering he must have known that he was being interviewed by a War Department representative!

"This country was all dry early last spring," Chapman quoted the 1890 Ghost Dance Prophet as saying:

> There was nothing growing, and the prospects for the future
> were very discouraging to both the Indians and the whites, and

they came to me and asked for rain to make their crops grow. I caused a small cloud to appear in the heavens, which gave rain for all, and they were satisfied.

At this point in the interview a pecuniary note was sounded: "I think that all white men should pay me for things of this kind, some two dollars, other(s) five, ten, twenty-five, and fifty, according to their means." And, according to this primary source, the 1890 Ghost Dance Prophet was also plainly outspoken in his resentment toward Tibo'o (whites). Paraphrasing Wovoka's words, Chapman thus related:

> ...that the people [whites] of this country do not treat him and his people right; that they do not give them anything to eat unless they pay for it. If the whites would treat him well, he would have it rain in the valley and snow on the mountains during the winter, so that the farmers would have good crops.

Wovoka further told Chapman that he knew he had enemies among his own people. Two in particular — Captain Sam and Johnson Sides, from Reno — were "telling all over the country that the soldiers are coming to take him and put him in a big iron box, and take him out to sea on a big ship and sink him in the ocean."[1] Nevertheless, the Prophet wanted Chapman to know that it was his sincerest desire to have his enemies stop talking against him, and that they should "not be afraid but come and talk to him." Wovoka also wanted it to be known that he "hired out to white men to work all the time. That he liked to work."

Chapman: Did you tell the Indians if they got into trouble with whites that they must not be afraid, that you would protect them against being hurt?

Wovoka: That was my dream. It has not come to pass yet.

Chapman: What about the time you asked your own brother to shoot at your calico shirt while you stood on a blanket ten feet away just to show off that you were bullet-proof and the ball struck your breast and dropped to the blanket?

Wovoka: That was a joke.

Wovoka finished, "I heard that soldiers were coming after me. I do not care about that; I would like to see them. That is all I care to talk now.

We are going to have a dance next Saturday."

But was this new religion peaceful or warlike? Arthur I. Chapman, United States Army Indian Scout — who no doubt knew what fear Wovoka's 1890 Ghost Dance Religion had been arousing among Tibo'o throughout the state of Nevada (Johnson 1975, Zanjani 1988) and the entire West (Utley 1963) — nevertheless ended his report with these revealing words: "Only a few of the [local] white men...[were] suspicious of Wilson's doctrines." In attributing the following words to Wovoka — which I deem critical for any interpretation of the 1890 Ghost Dance Religion — Chapman also related: "I told all the headmen who came to see me (meaning the representatives of other tribes) that when they went home to say to their people that they must keep the peace." To which the Indian scout commented, "If they [Native Americans who were not Numus] went to fighting that he [Wovoka] would help the soldiers to make them stop."[3]

Two years later, in 1892, James Mooney recorded a version of Wovoka's religion which substantially agrees with Chapman's.

JAMES MOONEY

According to his biographer, L. G. Moses (1984), the "Indian Man" — as Mooney was known within the Bureau of American Ethnology — began field investigations into the so-called "Messiah Craze" while war clouds were beginning to hover over South Dakota. In November 1890, Mooney left Washington, D.C. for the Indian territory in Oklahoma to complete his Kiowa studies. He reached the Cheyenne and Arapaho agency in Darlington, Oklahoma about the time that deadly Hotchkiss guns, belonging to the 7th Calvary, were being positioned against Big Foot's Minniconjou band of Lakota at Wounded Knee Creek on the Pine Ridge Reservation. While there, Mooney "participated in Ghost Dances...[took] many photographs of the ceremony, began a linguistic study of the Kiowas, and most important had learned the identity of the Indian messiah, something that for months had eluded investigators from the Indian Bureau, the War Department, and numerous newspapers" (Moses 1984:60). This former newspaper man from Indiana returned to the nation's capital one and a half months later to work on the Columbian Exposition, copying official documents relating to the "Messiah Craze" in his spare time from August through October of 1891. Apparently it was C. C. Warner's reply to an inquiry Mooney made about the new religion that catapulted Mooney back into the field again. Warner, who replaced Walker River Reservation Agent S. S. Sears on December 12, 1890, wrote from his headquarters at

Pyramid Lake that he was "pursuing the course with him [Wovoka] of nonattention or a silent ignoring" (Mooney 1896:767n1; cf. Appendix E). "Here is an agent...[who] pursues the course of nonattention," Mooney (ibid.) uncharacteristically savaged Warner.

> [He] has under his special charge and within a few miles of his agency the man who has created the greatest religious ferment known to the Indians of this generation, a movement which has been engrossing the attention of the newspaper and magazine press for a year, yet he has never seen him; and while the Indian Office, from which he gets his commission, in a praiseworthy effort to get at an understanding of the matter, is sending circular letters broadcast to the western agencies, calling for all procurable information in regard to the messiah and his doctrine...the agent at the central point of the disturbance seems to be unaware that there is anything special going on around him and can "silently ignore" the whole matter.

Determined to personally interview the 1890 Ghost Dance Prophet himself, James Mooney left the nation's capital for the field once again; this trip beginning in the middle of November 1891.

His first stop was Nebraska. There Mooney learned that Omaha and Winnebago Indians had recently rejected Wovoka's new religion (Moses 1984:63). In South Dakota he was deeply affected by the mass grave containing scores of victims of the December 29, 1890 Wounded Knee massacre and the wooden scaffolding constructed at the grave by mourning Lakotas: "The survivors had fenced off the trench and smeared the posts with paint made from the clay of western Nevada given to Sioux delegates by Wovoka" (Moses ibid.). Since Lakotas were either unwilling or unable yet to discuss their recent tragedy — "The dance was our religion, but the government sent soldiers to kill us on account of it. We will not talk any more about it" (Mooney 1896:1060) — Mooney repacked his bags and continued west.

In Reno, Nevada, Mooney spent Christmas Eve in a hotel across from the railroad station. The very next day he boarded the train for Schurz, on the Walker River Reservation, where he immediately sought out the Prophet's uncle, Charley Sheep. "Wovoka found the visits (by foreign delegations) to be increasingly annoying, particularly since the American government branded the religion dangerous and inimical to order and progress," or so Sheep warned the government ethnologist (Moses 1984:65). To ingratiate himself with the Numu, Mooney displayed photographs that he had taken of Arapaho and Cheyenne visitors to the 1890 Ghost Dance ceremonies in Nevada. With the ice broken, Mooney (1896:768) related how he spent a solid week inside Charley Sheep's house on the Walker River Reservation, interviewing him. They talked about "the old stories and games, singing Paiute songs, and sampling the seed mush and roasted pinions," even as a Numu shaman was curing a sick child across from their very fire! Feeling at last that he could broach the aching question, Mooney wrote: "I then told Charley that, as I had taken part in the dance, I was anxious to see the messiah and get from him some medicine paint to bring back to his friends among the eastern tribes." Wovoka's uncle consented. Mooney wrote: "He spoke tolerable — or rather intolerable — English, so that we were able to get along together without an interpreter, a fact which brought us into closer sympathy, as an interpreter is generally at best only a necessary evil" (Mooney ibid.). Even so, Mooney decided to hire an additional translator. He and Charley Sheep rode the Carson and Colorado Railroad from Schurz to Wabuska, in Mason Valley, and the overland stage another eight miles to Dyer's Dry Goods in Greenfield (formerly Pizen Switch and today Yerington), whose proprietor, Ed Dyer, was "well acquainted with Jack Wilson" (Mooney 1896:768). Indeed, Dyer immediately demonstrated his usefulness by telling Mooney "that the messiah was about 12 miles farther up the [Mason] valley, near a place called Pine Grove." A wagon and team were contracted, and Mooney and his entourage set out for the mining community in the mountains, 23 miles south of Greenfield, on New Year's Day 1892.

The snow was deep on the ground, which Mooney stated was "a very unusual thing in this part of the country and due in this instance, as Charley assured us, to the direct agency of Jack Wilson." After crossing a Ghost Dance ceremonial ground — "with the brush shelters still standing" — they encountered the Prophet. Ed Dyer saw him first. Charley Sheep called Wovoka over. Wovoka shouldered his shotgun — he had been jackrabbit hunting — and approached their wagon and team. A formal exchange of introductions followed. Mooney (1896:769) wrote that Wovoka "took my hand with a strong, hearty grasp, and inquired what was wanted." With his uncle explaining the purpose of the visit, the 1890 Ghost Dance Prophet "after some deliberation said that the whites had lied about him and he did not like to talk to them; some of the Indians had disobeyed his instructions and trouble had come of it, but as I was sent by Washington and was a friend of his friends, he would talk with me" — after he had finished hunting.

According to this primary source Mooney, Dyer, and Sheep visited the "nearest ranch" [Zadok Pierce's?] to wait until nightfall for their scheduled visit with the 1890 Ghost Dance Prophet. It was a freezing January night when they set out again and Mooney (1896:769-70) stated that because Sheep's eyesight was failing, they got lost in the snowy darkness and nearly froze to death. Charley Sheep also admitted to Mooney that it had been nearly two years since he had visited his nephew Wovoka's campsite in East Walker country. Many false trails later, they spotted a shower of sparks against the black starry sky, indicating a Numu encampment, which luckily enough proved to be the Prophet's.

James Mooney (1896:770) described Wovoka's traditional encampment as "three or four little wikiups [sic], in one of which we were told the messiah was awaiting our arrival." Sitting or lying around the fire were half a dozen Numus, including the messiah and his family, Wovoka's "young wife, a boy of four years of age, of whom he seemed very proud, and an infant." A family man himself, Mooney was led to conclude by the Prophet's conduct toward his young son that he was a "kind husband and father," which he also remarked was "in keeping with his reputation among the whites for industry and reliability." Wovoka and his uncle, Charley Sheep, "entered into a detailed explanation [of Mooney's visit]...which stretched out to a preposterous length, owing to a peculiar conversational method of the Paiute." The exasperated government ethnologist wrote:

> Each statement by the older man was repeated at its close, word for word and sentence by sentence, by the other, with the same monotonous inflection. This done, the first speaker signified by a grunt of approval that it had been correctly repeated, and then proceeded with the next statement, which was duly repeated in like manner (Mooney 1896:770-71; cf. Liljeblad 1986:650).

This done, the historic interview between the "Indian Man" and the 1890 Ghost Dance Prophet began.

To Mooney's opening query about his age, Wovoka pointed to his son, indicating that he was "about the size of his little boy" at the time of the Pyramid Lake War of 1860. Mooney estimated the boy's age at "about 4 years" and suggested 1856 or 1857 as the Prophet's birth date. Furthermore, Mooney learned that Wovoka's father's name was **Tavibo**, a name which Dyer, "with whom he [Wovoka] seemed to be on intimate terms," translated as "White Man" (Mooney 1896:771). Mooney even suggested an etymology for Wovoka's father's name. It derived from the Northern Paiute word for "sun" or "sunrise," **taba**, he wrote, adding that Tavibo was a "capita" or "petty chief" and not a headman, a "dreamer" who additionally was "invulnerable." As for the name "Wovoka," the 1890 Ghost Dance Prophet himself told Mooney that he acquired it in boyhood. Of late, however, the Prophet was said to have assumed the name of his paternal grandfather, **Kwohitsauq**, "Big Rumbling Belly." "Jack Wilson," or so Mooney (ibid.) recorded, was a name acquired from the family of whites whom the Prophet worked for, though only used after Tavibo's death. Mooney (1896:765), in fact, "noticed" eleven names for him in all: "**Wo'voka**, or **Wu'voka**," which he wrote could "provisionally be derived from a verb signifying 'to cut'"; **Wevokar**, **Wopokahte**, Kwohitsauq, **Cowejo**, **Koit-tsow**, **Kvit-Tsow**, Quoitze Ow, Jack Wilson, Jackson Wilson, Jack Winson, and John Johnson. And these did not include such honorifics as **Tamme Naa'a**, "Our Father," and "Messiah."

Mooney (1896:771) also could state with certainty that the Prophet was full-blooded. "The impression that he is a half-blood may have arisen from the fact that his father's name was "White Man" and that he has a white man's name." In other words, the government ethnologist disputed both rumor and the sworn testimony of Plains Indian visitors to Nevada that Jack Wilson/Wovoka, "Messiah" or "Indian Christ," was light or white skinned. Mooney wrote that the Prophet "spoke only his own Paiute language, with some little knowledge of English," and "is not acquainted with the sign language, which is hardly known west of the mountains."

In spite of Wovoka's reiteration that he had never been away from Mason Valley, Mooney, in contrast to Chapman, remained dubious. After all, these stunning coincidences had to be reckoned with: (1) the fact that members of Wovoka's tribe used to forage at the watershed of the Columbia River; (2) a report that Numus from Warm Springs, Oregon, had visited him; and (3) the story told by Pacific Northwest Shakers about "a young man to whom they taught their mysteries, in which he became such an apt pupil that he soon outstripped his teachers, and is now working even greater wonders among his own people" (Mooney 1896:763). Thus, James Mooney (ibid.) was led to conclude that "this young man can be no other than Wovoka, the messiah of the Ghost dance, living among the Paiute in western Nevada." He concluded that Wovoka must have traveled into central Oregon where he learned the Shaker religion originated by John Slocum (Barnett 1957), and this influenced the Nevada Prophet's own syncretic religion.

Mooney, however, did not discuss the "great noise" that Josephus told Chapman had a triggering effect upon Wovoka's Great Revelation, or

Chapman's statement that the 1890 Ghost Dance Prophet had seen his own dead mother in Heaven, or the existence of Tibo'o in Heaven. On the other hand, Mooney could concur with Chapman that it had been about "four years since he [Wovoka] had taught the dance to his people" (Mooney 1896:771). As for the Great Revelation:

> On this occasion "the sun died" (was eclipsed) and he fell asleep in the daytime and was taken up to the other world. Here he saw God, with all the people who had died long ago engaged in their oldtime [sic] sport and occupations, all happy and forever young. It was a pleasant land and full of game. After showing him all, God told him he must go back and tell his people they must be good and love one another, have no quarreling, and live in peace with the whites; that they must work, and not lie or steal; that they must put away all the old practices that savored of war; that if they faithfully obeyed his instructions they would at last be reunited with their friends in this other world, where there would be no more death or sickness or old age. He was then given the dance which he was commanded to bring back to his people. By performing this dance at intervals, for five consecutive days each time, they would secure this happiness to themselves and hasten the event. Finally God gave him control over the elements so that he could make it rain or snow or be dry at will, and appointed him his deputy to take charge of affairs in the west, while "Governor Harrison" would attend to matters in the east, and he, God, would look after the world above. He then returned to earth and began to preach as he was directed, convincing the people by exercising the wonderful powers that had been given him (Mooney 1896:771-72).

Wovoka's Great Revelation occurred simultaneously with a total solar eclipse; and James Mooney (1896:774), on the basis of information received from the Nautical Almanac Office, even ventured to date it at January 1, 1889. "Cataleptic seizures" and "self-hypnosis" were the explanations Mooney (1896:929-32) gave for Wovoka's vision. By relating a local rancher's account of the high fever that had bedridden the Prophet at the time of his Great Revelation (Mooney 1896:773), Mooney, by half a century, anticipated research on the bearing of Altered States of Consciousness (cf. La Barre 1970:54-61) and Near-Death Experiences (Ring 1984) on the rise of prophets and religious movements in general. As for the notorious "Ghost Dance shirts," those dyed and painted, fringed muslin or buckskin outer garments, which Plains Indians tragically came to believe would render them invulnerable, Mooney (1896:772) reported that Wovoka disclaimed any responsibility for them. More fruitful cross-cultural comparisons, he wrote, would be made with Millerite "ascension robes" and, in particular, with the "holy garments" worn by Mormons.

"Are you The Christ, the Son of God, as has been so often asserted in print?" Mooney (1896:773) pointedly asked. Wovoka's reply: "[Only]...a prophet who has received a divine revelation." We also learn in this primary source that Wovoka explicitly denied any Numus had ever experienced ecstatic seizures, an assertion Mooney (1896:772) stated he independently confirmed with neighboring ranchers who were eyewitnesses to 1890 Ghost Dance ceremonies. "His religion was one of universal peace," the government ethnologist thus could conclude with Chapman. Which direction should Native Americans take in the future? "Follow the white man's road," Wovoka answered him, and "adopt the habits of civilization." And what reward would they reap for this? "They would at last be reunited with their friends in this other world," Mooney (ibid.) was told.

Concluding how, on the whole, Wovoka "seemed honest in his belief and his supernatural claims," Mooney (1896:773) nevertheless wrote that he was forced to accept the Prophet's assertions "with several grains of salt." For one, Mooney wrote that he learned Wovoka was rumored to be "an expert sleight-of-hand performer," someone who on occasion would resort to "cheap trickery to keep up the impression of his miraculous powers." In addition, he cited James O. Gregory's statement to Chapman regarding the Prophet's request to Gregory (when he was the farmer-agent in charge of the Walker River Reservation) to draw up and forward to the President of the United States a document averring Wovoka's supernatural claims, including the binding agreement that if he, Wovoka, were to receive a regular stipend from the government, he "would take [up] his residence on the reservation and agree to keep Nevada people informed of all the latest news from heaven and to furnish rain whenever wanted." With apparent relief, Mooney erroneously reported that this letter had never been sent. The pecuniary side of the 1890 Ghost Dance Prophet also surfaced in Mooney's famous interview with Wovoka.

After his request for some token demonstration or "sign" of Wovoka's supernatural **bbooha** or power had been refused, Mooney proposed to photograph the Numu Prophet. Wovoka's reply was that no man had ever before been granted the privilege. When Mooney offered to pay, Wovoka promptly countered that someone once had offered him $5.00 for his photograph. Haggling proceeded apace, and when a price was finally agreed upon Mooney (1896:774-75) would pay $1.00 — his standard fee to informants. The result was the famous photograph of Wovoka seated in a chair alongside his uncle, Charley Sheep, taken with "Kodak and tripod." It appears on page 764 of Mooney's classic study and is reproduced and appears, along with a charcoal drawing, in this book. At the conclusion of the photography session, Wovoka handed Mooney several items to carry back to the Prophet's friends from the Indian Territory of Oklahoma, who had visited him in Nevada: "A blanket of rabbit skins, some pinion nuts, some tail feathers of the magpie...and some of the sacred red paint, which plays so important a part in the ritual of the Ghost-dance religion" (Mooney 1896:775). "Thus with mutual expressions of good will, we parted," wrote James Mooney (ibid.), "his uncle going back to the reservation, while I took the train for Indian territory."[3]

EDWARD A. DYER

As a small boy, Dyer was brought to the Comstock by his parents in 1875. Dyer wrote that he reached manhood in Mason Valley where, since 1880, he lived the major part of his life. "As a child and adult" Dyer stated that he "mingled with the Pahute [sic] Indians" and "learned their language fluently." Jack Wilson was a "man I deemed my friend once long ago," Dyer recalled for his son when he was 86. They met when the Prophet "was a grown man somewhat older than I, when in my teens I started a store in Yerington." Regarding Wovoka's formative years, Dyer wrote that he gained this information from his wife, who was born in the mining community at Pine Grove, where for a time Dyer also owned a dry goods store. And David Wilson had only a "partial hand" in raising the Prophet, Dyer claimed. A view which somewhat contradicts both Chapman and Mooney.

The Wilsons of southern Mason Valley (Nordyke was the post office address) and later of Pine Grove "were of devout turn of mind," he wrote, and "it was at this ranch, where some of [Wovoka's]...relatives were employed that the Indian Wilson spent much of his youth." The Wilsons not only named the young Numu "Jack Wilson" but invited him into their household for meals as well, and this constituted Wovoka/Jack Wilson's exposure to Christianity, to "religious teaching through family Bible readings, evening prayers, grace before meat, and similar family devotions." Though Wovoka "may not have thoroughly understood all he heard," Dyer suggested that "some particular effort was made by the lady of the house to read to the boy some of the better known Bible stories." But which Bible stories? Because Dyer felt that his Numu friend had "fashioned himself as some sort of an Indian version of an Old Testament prophet," a case will be made in Chapter Five that Hebrew prophets, Elijah in particular, might have carried as much formative weight in Wovoka's own career as the Gospel stories that may have been read to him by the Presbyterian Wilsons.

Jack Wilson then "drops out of sight for a time," Ed Dyer wrote. Because he was said to have "never [been] loquacious about his travels," Dyer's view that the 1890 Ghost Dance Prophet "perched atop the railroad's handy boxcars" with Walker River Paiutes and took "seasonal trips...to northern California for the purpose of picking hops" hopefully constitutes what he knew, rather than mimicry of what Mooney wrote. In contrast to Mooney, however, Dyer does not invoke Shakerism of the Pacific Northwest as the spark allegedly igniting Wovoka's religion.

Dyer wrote that it was only after the Numu's "start in his endeavors to make of himself a personage among the Indians" that the two men initially met. Ed Dyer reported that Wovoka "didn't aspire to be a chief," nor was "the role of medicine man...for him either." But he did claim pretensions to "some facility in the matter of prophecy." "He could describe the delights of the Happy Hunting Grounds from personal observation — he'd gone there on short trips," related Dyer. Met then with skepticism, Wovoka "eventually had to demonstrate or shut up." And so it was on that hot day in July that the 1890 Ghost Dance Prophet caused ice to fall from the sky and perfected the art of trances.

"Doo-mur-eye" was the title of Ed Dyer's memoirs — the Northern Paiute word, **tumurai** ("accent on second syllable"), or **mamuaka,** for legerdemain — and in relating how Wovoka had prophesied to a group of Numus that a block of ice would fall from the sky, Dyer would comment cryptically: "Not too difficult a feat if one possesses some ingenuity and a supply of ice." Nevertheless, Dyer indicated that, to his Numu audience, Wovoka was believed to have accomplished a modern-day miracle. Regarding what Paul Bailey would debunk as a second or separate miracle of ice floating down the Walker River — also on a hot summer day — Dyer indicates he either missed this altogether, or more likely, it was some "distortion of what I witnessed."

On the other hand, Jack Wilson's "alleged acts of wizardry" were positively impressive, wrote Dyer. In one such instance, which Dyer personally witnessed, the 1890 Ghost Dance Prophet was said to have entered a trance-state in which he "remained for as long as two days."

He wasn't shamming. His body was as rigid as a board. His

mouth could not be pried open and he showed no reaction to pain inducing experiments.... The whole matter is one to which I still confess considerable puzzlement.

As a result of the above, Numus of Smith Valley and Mason Valley began calling Wovoka "**Numu-naa'a**," or "Indian father," wrote Dyer, whereas "**Coo-ee-jah-o**" ("accent on the third syllable") had formerly been his Northern Paiute name. Dyer's description of Wovoka's invulnerability will be presented in Chapter Five, here we need to note that the Prophet's claim that he "couldn't be killed by a gun" was as much responsible for his "universal acceptance among the Indians" as was his "declaration that better and happier times for Indians were coming soon." These twin declarations "eventually led to considerable trouble for Uncle Sam." For in relating how he and his brother had witnessed "many dances" hosted by Jack Wilson, Ed Dyer observed that "a sort of religious fervor was generated." With "the belief built up that the Indian peoples had something at long last," Native Americans, and especially Plains Indians, flocked to Mason Valley to see Wovoka, who came to be regarded as a "veritable Messiah come to punish the Whites." How did the Numu handle this notoriety? "His fellow Indians...ran off with the ball...[while] he was content merely to bask in the adulation and veneration," or so Dyer wrote.

It was at this point that Dyer became a "sort of confidant" to the 1890 Ghost Dance Prophet. Dyer "functioned as his secretary," he wrote, sharing the duty with J. I. Wilson of Yerington, the second of three sons born to David and Abigail Wilson, and a childhood playmate of Wovoka as well. Letters addressed to the Prophet as "Dear Father" would arrive at the Greenfield Post Office. They contained money and requests for specific gifts, "particularly shirts." Dyer would read them, and pending Wovoka's instructions, forward "magpie feathers, red ocher for paint, clothing that he [Wovoka] had worn."

A summary of the Lakota reinterpretation of Wovoka's Great Revelation is given next in the Dyer Manuscript. In contrast to the impression gained by Mooney, Dyer concluded that because of Wounded Knee, his Numu friend and business associate "was not exactly hiding nor had he run away" at the time of the government ethnologist's visit; rather, Wovoka had "prudently...remove[d] his camp to the south end of the valley...in a brush big enough to hide from the casual observer." And as for his contribution to Mooney's 1892 interview with Wovoka, Ed Dyer immodestly proffered: "Wilson was known to have a good working knowledge of English but not quite up to explaining obscure points of Indian theology."

In Dyer's judgment, the Wounded Knee massacre brought an end to Wovoka's "wizardry." Besides selling healing articles, the 1890 Ghost Dance Prophet, on Dyer's advice, thereafter reportedly traveled to Oklahoma, where not only was he lionized but returned home laden with "presents of money." Dyer, 20 years later, could state that Wovoka "still wore some of those vests and moccasins." He remained a "personage until the end," Dyer could thus conclude. And contrary to Biblical wisdom, the former 1890 Ghost Dance Prophet even received honor at home; for example, riding on a wagon to communal rabbit drives at which he never was required to carry a gun, or hunt, because "every Indian contributed generously of his kill to swell Jack's share." The 1890 Ghost Dance Prophet could also demand and receive a discount on jackrabbits sold to Numus living at the Yerington Indian Colony by Dyer's own two sons.

Was the religion Wovoka founded a threat to the local non-Indians? Ed Dyer, who at 18 joined Company I of the state militia (eventually attaining the rank of lieutenant) which formed in 1890 in response to statewide panic regarding the 1890 Ghost Dance, opined that "violence was contrary to his very nature." "On the other hand," Dyer also wrote, "it should be said that there is no evidence to show that he tried to restrain over-zealous followers. In a way, once started, he was riding a tiger. It was difficult to dismount."

Finally, Dyer's concluding paragraph insinuates that the brief life and heroic death of Jack Wilson's grandson, World War II pilot Harlyn Vidovich, constituted "services paid in full" for the 1890 Ghost Dance, a religious movement begun ingenuously enough by its prophet, yet one in which Wovoka demonstrated "a very real regard of what had happened."

PAUL BAILEY

The fourth and final primary source considered in this chapter is Paul Bailey's book, *Wovoka, The Indian Messiah*, which has been praised by Robert Utley (1963) in his excellent history of the 1890 Ghost Dance Religion among the Lakota as a "highly useful" biography.

A great man and a fake was western writer Paul Bailey's paradoxical view of Wovoka, which he stated was influenced not only by Mooney but the following sources: conversations with Ed Dyer, who was living in Fallon, Nevada, in the 1950s, the time of Bailey's research; Colonel Tim McCoy who personally knew Wovoka; the Prophet's daughter Alice and her husband, Andy Vidovich; and with non-Indians living in Smith Valley and Mason Valley (Bailey 1957:13-14).

According to Bailey (1957:20-21), the 1890 Ghost Dance Prophet was remembered "only as Jack Wilson" by Numus in his home area. The name "The (Wood) Cutter," Bailey wrote, was received from his father, "Tavibo" or "White Man," who died in 1870. Born on the Walker River in Mason Valley in 1858, Wovoka was said to have been an only child (Bailey 1957:23). Orphaned at 14, the future Prophet was raised in the Mason Valley household of the Wilsons, "devout (United) Presbyterians who cared nothing about his dreams or his thoughts."

> They taught him how to brand a calf, how to pitch hay, how to clean a stable, and how to handle a plow. They took him out of his rabbit-skins, and put him into white man's jeans. They cropped his hair to shortness, and commanded him in the white man's language, which he quickly learned. They taught him to sit on a chair when in their house and not to squat on his hams on the floor. They gave him a white man's name — "Jack." And, since he now was white man in everything but color, and since he was Wilson's in everything but soul, he accepted the captivity by accepting the name. From that time forward he answered to "Jack Wilson" (Bailey 1957:23-24).

Wovoka, accordingly, was befriended by the Wilsons' three sons, wrote Bailey (1957:25): "Billy" or James William Wilson (1857-1930), "Joe" or Joseph Isaac Wilson (1859-1954), and George Washington Wilson or "Uncle Mack" (1863-1927). One day the oldest Wilson boy invited him to become a blood brother. The ceremony, as recounted by Bailey (1957:35-46), took place on Mount Grant, locale of the Numu Creation Story, whose version in Bailey (1957:28-31) is entirely unlike what Hittman (1984) and others (cf. Mooney 1896:1050-51; Johnson 1975:15-16) have recorded. Mount Grant, incidentally, was also the source of the red "paint" that Wovoka subsequently would sell to Native Americans. In any event, we read in Bailey that blood brotherhood between Wovoka and Billy Wilson was absolutely pivotal to the Numu's development as a prophet, if only because the residual scars were perceived by visiting Native Americans in 1889 as the Stigmata (Mooney 1896:795).

"He wished he were a white man and could go to the white world," is how Paul Bailey (1957:33) psychologized an even deeper laceration allegedly experienced by Wovoka. And Bailey (1957:51), like Chapman, might have picked up Mooney's contention that the 1890 Ghost Dance Prophet rode the trains over the high Sierras with fellow Numus to pick hops in California, Oregon, and Washington. For it was in the Pacific Northwest where Wovoka first gained exposure to the Indian Shaker Religion, Bailey (1957:657) wrote. The Prophet returned to Nevada in 1887, and upon meeting a Walker River Reservation girl at the train depot in Reno, Wovoka was said to have renamed her Mary, in honor of his employer's wife (Bailey 1957:56), whereas I recorded Abigail Jane Butler (1836-1910) as the name of David Wilson's wife. The newlyweds, in any event, went to live and work on the Wilson Ranch.

And so it was that, according to Bailey (1957:47-61), Wovoka, with his "incipient hatred of the White man," surrendered his "shack" on David and Abigail Wilson's ranch for the traditional **kane** in which he commenced his career as a prophet, "staging" Shaker-type "seances" in this tule house. Nor would mere legerdemain, learned from his father, satisfy the burgeoning prophet's ego. For there were two "false miracles" — the first being Wovoka's prophecy that ice would float down the Walker River at high noon during the hot summer month of July, the second, Wovoka's prophecy that a block of ice would drop to earth from Heaven, also in the summertime (Bailey 1957:71).

In agreement with Mooney, Bailey wrote that he felt Mormonism had contributed heavily to 1890 Ghost Dance ideology. Visits by Mormon proselytizers led to the Prophet's interest in a single article of The Church of Jesus Christ of Latter-Day Saints' faith, the Endowment Robe worn by married couples, or so Bailey (1957:77) wrote. Bailey felt that the decorated "holy undergarment" of Mormon faith was the ultimate source of Wovoka's claim of invulnerability.

Bailey (1957:80) wrote that Wovoka's first trance lasted two days. The five night "dance" in southwest Mason Valley followed, after which the Prophet ordered Numu dancers to bathe in the Walker River. Nor does Bailey record any presence of Tibo'o in Heaven in his rendition of Wovoka's mystical flight. Rather, the 1890 Ghost Dance Prophet was said by Bailey (1957:82) to have seen only the Indian dead "all alive again":

> Go back, and tell your people the things that you have seen, and the things that you shall hear. You must teach that Jesus is upon the earth. That he moves as in a cloud. That the dead are all alive again. That when their friends die they must not cry. That they must not hurt anybody or do harm to anyone. They must not drink whiskey. They must not fight. They must do right always. They must not refuse to work for the Whites, and not to make troubles any more with them. You must take the dance we will show you back to earth. It is the dance of goodness. It comes

from heaven. It has a purpose. It will make your people free, and it will make them glad.

Two years after this vision, Wovoka was hired by the Wilsons to cut timber in Pine Grove, we learn in this primary source. One day in the mountains his face became "red with a white man's disease." The Prophet subsequently "died," Bailey wrote, and assisted by Charley Sheep, Mary Wilson had to haul her husband down from the Sierra Nevada mountains. But "days later," Wovoka spontaneously revived. And since his recovery took place during a total solar eclipse, Wovoka was perceived by Numus as having prevented the moon from "devouring" the sun. In other words, according to Bailey (1957:86-87), the 1890 Ghost Dance Prophet achieved much of his fame on account of the Numu belief that he saved the universe from ending, as Mooney previously had argued.

Using Mooney's January 1, 1889 date for the Great Revelation, Paul Bailey (1957:93-96) reported that God had instructed Wovoka as follows: The "earth shall die," but Northern Paiutes "must not be afraid" because the "earth will come alive again." And not only would the animals return and non-Indians be destroyed, Indian skeptics as well were to be excluded from the Millennium. Thus Wovoka acquired weather-control powers from his empyrean journey, or so Bailey (1957:103) reported. Foreign delegations of Indians began arriving in Smith Valley and Mason Valley at this point: Porcupine, a Cheyenne; Short Bull and Kicking Bear, Lakotas, in November of 1889; followed by a second delegation consisting of Good Thunder, Cloud Horse, Yellow Knife, and Short Bull, Lakotas, one year later (Bailey 1957:104-115). Because Tibo'o attended these ceremonies, Bailey further opined that Wovoka necessarily altered his original message, which was anti-white. The 1890 Ghost Dance Prophet also began "faking" other self-professed powers. Bailey (1957:125) suggested that the claim of invulnerability, like the "staged" demonstrations with the blocks of ice, was the desperate effort on the part of the fledgling Prophet not only to settle tormenting inner doubts about the new religion he founded, but also was intended to impress out-of-state Indian visitors.

According to Bailey (1957:178), Wovoka also had to be "summoned" to meet the Indian scout, Arthur Chapman. In Chapman, recall, we read of an "invited" subject who amenably cooperated. The 1890 Ghost Dance Prophet, in any event, headed immediately for the mountains following Chapman's departure; and after much deliberation, decided once and for all to become secretive about the new religion (Bailey 1957:175). Because he went underground, Bailey (1957:181-82) wrote that when Ed Dyer became his business partner, Wovoka would sneak into the grocery store at night, where letters from Native Americans were read to him so that he could instruct Dyer as to which medicines were to be packaged and mailed in response.

And the Prophet was not hunting jackrabbits along the East Walker River when James Mooney arrived at the beginning of 1892 to interview him, at least according to Bailey (1957:188). Rather, Wovoka was then still in hiding. We also read of three daughters subsequently being born to Jack and Mary Wilson — Daisy, Ida, and Alice, the Prophet's last child, or so Bailey (1957:206-207) mistakenly argued, being their only child to survive into adulthood.

"His [Wovoka's] one great mistake" was in prophesying that the Apocalypse would take place in Spring of 1891, Paul Bailey (1957:210) concluded. Bailey would have us believe that Wovoka deemed it was interference on the part of American soldiers which caused this targeted prophecy to fail. Even so, he reported that Wovoka was subject to trances until the end of his life, "occasionally" even giving forth "thunderous prophecies" (Bailey 1957:203). And whether an "opportunist," a "faker," or a "divinely inspired prophet," Wovoka nevertheless founded what must be "rated as one of the world's great religious movements," wrote Paul Bailey (1957:208). For he "succeeded where Christians had collectively failed" because his "doctrine was Indian in origin and Indian in concept, in spite of its vague Christian framework" (Bailey 1957:210).

ENDNOTES

1. "Captain Sam was a "Chief" from Dayton, Nevada. Johnson Sides, called "The Peacemaker," was a former government interpreter from the Walker River Reservation. Cf. "...Johnson Sides, a Paiute, living near Reno, Nevada, seems to have attained what he considers an unenviable notoriety in connection with this matter, several papers having printed descriptions of him, in which he figures as a claimant to the Messiahship of his people. Sides is in truth a reasonably sensible and well-informed old coffee-cooler, who claims that Kvit-tsow [Wovoka] is crazy, and he, together with Lee Winnemucca, who is a brother of Sarah and a son of the original Winnemucca, loses no opportunity to combat what they consider a most pernicious doctrine" (Phister 1891:107).

2. According to Moses (1984:69), although Chapman's report reached the Secretary of War and helped to dispel most nagging questions about the Prophet, oddly enough it was omitted from Special File #188, "The 1890 Ghost Dance Religion," which was kept at the Indian Office in Washington, D.C.

3. Mooney ran afoul of superiors at the Bureau of American Ethnology for daring to compare Native American religious movements with instances from Judeo-Christian -Islamic civilizations. As a consequence, the following caveat emptor was inserted into his great study: "...caution should be exercised in comparing or contrasting religious movements among civilized peoples with fantasies as that described in the memoir; for...red men and white men are separated by a chasm so broad and deep that few representatives of either race are ever able clearly to see its further sides...." (Moses 1984:91-92).

CHAPTER 2

Family

"Prophecy is the voice that God has lent to the silent agony, a voice to the plundered poor, to the profaned riches of the world" (Heschel 1962:5).

That Wovoka was born either in the Colony District of Smith Valley, as one informant suspected, or in Mason Valley receives ample testimony. The 1890 Ghost Dance Prophet, then, was a **Toboose tukadu**," a "Taboosi-eater," the food-name applied to Numus who frequently harvested *Brodiaea capitatum*, or "grass-bulb nuts," along the banks of the Walker River (Stewart 1939:142-43).1 Mooney calculated his birth date to be 1856. Tim McCoy (1977), the cowboy actor who befriended Wovoka in the 1920s, quoted the Prophet's statement that he was born "around the time of the treaty of Fort Churchill," a Peace and Friendship accord signed by Numus in 1863 (Clemmer and Stewart 1986:526). Genealogical work among Toboose tukadu descendants corroborates the 1856 to 1863 birth date. In Hittman (1973a), I concluded on the basis of an obligatory terminological distinction between older and younger siblings made in Northern Paiute that Wovoka had to have been born at or near the head of an 1860-1884 birth cohort.

One additional support for this birth date can be mentioned. While I was hunting for unpublished photographs of Wovoka, Mary Ann Cardenale, former owner of Hoye's General Store in Smith Valley, generously volunteered the print that appears as Plate B in this study. On the back it reads, "Levoka at 16." The print's identification, Mrs. Cardenale stated, was made by Laura Miller of Smith Valley, the original owner of the photograph. I obtained independent confirmation from both Mrs. Miller's husband, Alex, as well as Cora Sayers (b. 1897), the daughter-in-law of Smith Valley's first white settler, T. B. Smith. Since Wovoka grew to six feet at maturity and "Levoka at 16" is not any taller than Hoye Store's owner, Annie Kingsdale Hoye, or her two nieces who stand alongside her on the front porch of the general store, this indicates that the 1856 - 1863 birth date must be correct. Of note, too, is the fact that 17 years before Mooney's famous photograph (Plates A.1 and A.2), the teenaged Numu

PLATE B. "Levoka at 16." Standing on the Hoye Store front porch, Smith Valley, circa 1875. *Photo courtesy of Mary Ann Cardinal.*

was already wearing a feather (eagle?) above his left ear, and also that Wovoka's hair at age 16 was already coiffed as Mooney (1896:769) described it at 30, "cut off square on a line below the base of the ears."

PARENTS

Mooney (1896:701) wrote that the Prophet's father was named "Tavibo," that he died around 1870 and may have been the founder of an earlier Ghost Dance Religion in the Walker River area. Since "Waughzeewaughber" was yet another name reported for the earlier Ghost Dance Prophet, Mooney (1896:703) reasoned that either it was Tavibo's additional name, or, more likely, that "Waughzeewaughber" was Wovoka's father's disciple. To Cora Du Bois (1939:4) goes credit for putting the ethnohistorical record straight. She showed that the founder of the 1870 Ghost Dance Religion was **Wodziwob**, and Hittman (1973b) suggested that his name meant "Grey Head," that he was from Fish Lake Valley, California, and was also called "Fish Lake Joe" and "Hawthorne Wodziwob."2 Wovoka's father's name was **Numu-tibo'o**, "Northern Paiute-White Man." Neither Wodziwob nor Numu-tibo'o had died in 1870, they both lived well past the turn of the century. Although the exact role in the 1870 Ghost Dance played by Wovoka's father has yet to be determined, useful information about him exists.

Corbett Mack (b. 1892), my primary Toboose tukadu informant, could recall having seen Numu-tibo'o alive during visits to the Prophet's camp in Mason around 1910. Beth Wilson Ellis (b. 1891), the daughter of J.W. Wilson, told Grace Dangberg (1968:5) much the same. In fact, in the Bicentennial Edition of the *Mason Valley* (13 August 1976), she stated that Numu-tibo'o did not die until circa 1915, recalling seeing Wovoka's "blind father" alive in the Prophet's camp in Mason at that time. On the authority of J. I. Wilson, Dangberg herself recorded that Numu-tibo'o "died at 95 or 100." Since Dangberg's field investigations were conducted in the 1920s, J. I. Wilson's statement to her that Wovoka's father had died "only a few years ago" solidifies this argument. And if Andy Vidovich's memory is correct, we might even know the exact year of Numu-tibo'o's death. For in characterizing a visit to his father-in-law's camp in Mason Valley, where Wovoka was said to have been working either for a Nordyke farmer or at the Wilson Ranch, the Prophet's son-in-law recounted how Wovoka that night decided to take his family to the Yerington movie theater. On returning home, they found the aged Numu-tibo'o dead (Vidovich-Wheat Tape 100:3-4).3 Andy Vidovich gave 1914 or 1915 as the year of this death, and com-

PLATE A-1. Wovoka (seated) with Charley Sheep, January 1, 1892. *Photo courtesy Smithsonian Institution.*

mented that his grandfather-in-law was buried "southwest of Nordyke," "south of Yerington," or "near the twist in the [motor] road." Unfortunately, the derivation of Numu-tibo'o's name is unknown.

Jennie Wier was told by Angus McCloud that Numu-tibo'o was very old when he came here, whereas Corbett Mack suggested that he was from Smith Valley or Mason Valley. The name "Northern Paiute-White Man," Corbett felt, was the result of his having been "taken away" or captured by solders following the "Big War," the Pyramid Lake War of

PLATE A-2. Detail — Wovoka seated, January 1, 1892. Drawing in charcoal. *Courtesy Smithsonian Institution.*

1860. Does this suggestion receive confirmation in the Vidovich-Wheat Tapes (100:3-4)? There we read, "his [Wovoka's father] name was given during the time that Winnemucca [**Tonadu**] and that bunch was having that fight over there." And if the "Big War" was indeed the Pyramid Lake War of 1860, then Ferol Egan's (1972:261) statement that Colonel Lander took "five Paiute prisoners who were purchasing percussion caps and ammunition from a wagon train" might very well apply here. Or perhaps Numu-tibo'o had fought in the Bannock War of 1875 - 1878, when "many of the Nevada and Oregon Paiutes, as well as some Bannocks, were interned at the Malheur Reservation in Eastern Oregon" (Egan 1972:277). Regarding this skirmish:

> [Numus were] kept at Fort McDermitt, Nevada. Others were sent to the reservation at Yakima, Washington, and were promised that they would be transferred from this overcrowded and very poor reserve to their own homes. But after several years, the transfers had not arrived. The Indians decided that escape and flight was better than incarceration. Thus in 1883, they forgot about long overdue promises, broke out of the Yakima Reservation and headed for their Nevada home (Egan 1972:278).

If Numu-tibo'o was taken captive by American soldiers during the earlier period of hostilities in the Great Basin, another question must be asked: How long was the Prophet's father absent from Smith and Mason valleys? In broad psychohistorical terms one might speculate about the Prophet's formative years. For example, can Wovoka's apparently closer identification with his mother be explained by Numu-tibo'o's absence? Similarly, can we relate Numu-tibo'o's apparent hostility to working for Tibo'o ranchers and farmers in contrast to Wovoka's mother's dependence upon wage labor? Can both be related to the Prophet's own attachment to the Wilson Ranch and Protestant-type work ethic characterizing his Great Revelation? Both the Wier Notes and Dangberg's Composition Notebook do, however, contain invaluable descriptions of Wovoka's father.

Maurice Snyder, on the one hand, related to Wier that Numu-tibo'o was a "real prophet. [He] could make it rain, etc." Angus McCloud, on the other hand, another Mason Valley rancher, stated that Numu-tibo'o was "only a common Indian." Wier also quoted "Mr. Plummer," who was either George Plummer, Sr. (1849-1921), the husband of David Wilson's daughter, Luisa (1855-1890), or George Plummer, Jr. (1877-1935), their adopted son. This Mason Valley rancher's comment was that Wovoka's "father [was] wild and quarrelsome. Never knew him to drink. Would steal cattle and horses. Medicine man." Plummer even speculated that "perhaps he [Wovoka] got some of his ideas from him [Numu-tibo'o]." While in the Dangberg notes, we learn Wovoka's father's English name.

"[Wovoka's] Father [was] Buckskin a medicine man," Bob Dyer, Ed's bilingual brother, told Dangberg. (Bob Dyer, incidentally, married a Mason Valley Numu and fathered several children.) J. I. Wilson independently confirmed this, adding the following to Numu-tibo'o's profile:

"Buckskin - father of J. [Jack Wilson was] mean and treacherous. Had three wives. Could run down a deer. He was rather a chief of at least this [southern] end of the valley. Head of councils." Numu-tibo'o, known as Buckskin, according to J. I. Wilson, was also said to have been the "biggest doctor too besides big chief. Whenever [a] Dr. lost three patients [he was] killed. Buckskin [was] never executed because [he was] a chief, too." Moreover, "Buckskin was unprincipled. Steal, etc., and was not trustworthy." Andy Vidovich (Tape 90:15), however, offered quite a different view. "A wonderful man," he recalled, someone who "stopped his people from killing the settlers."[4]

I suggest, then, the following composite portrait of Numu-tibo'o or Buckskin, the 1890 Ghost Dance Prophet's father: like so many other Native Americans in the Great Basin, Numu-tibo'o was initially friendly to fur trappers and emigrants. Born in 1835(?), Wovoka's father, however, responded to continual encroachment upon Numu lands and to the many flagrant actions of Tibo'o settlers by joining one of the many equestrian bands that formed for defensive purposes in the 1850s (cf. Steward and Wheeler-Voegelin 1974:221). Perhaps Numu-tibo'o belonged to the band led by **Hadsapoke**, "Red Horse," or to **Yurdy's** band, or the band led by **Wahi** ("Fox") on the Carson River, or even to the band led by Chief Winnemucca (Tonadu) at Pyramid Lake (cf. Stewart 1939). If so, then in all probability Numu-tibo'o had fought in either the Pyramid Lake War of 1860 or the Bannock War of 1878 (Clemmer and Stewart 1986), perhaps even the Owens Valley War of 1863 (Steward and Wheeler-Voegelin 1974:273-79). And if captured and interned - as Corbett Mack suggested -Numu-tibo'o would have been absent from Smith and Mason valleys during at least some portion of his son's early life.

Described as a **poenabe** or "good talker" ("chief"), Wovoka's father was also said to have possessed bbooha or "power." "Jack Wilson's father [was] a medicine man," we read in the Wier Notes. Corbett Mack (Appendix K) related how his father, Big Mack, a contemporary of Wovoka, suspected the Prophet's father of being a witch after he treated Big Mack's sister who died. And according to what Wovoka himself had told Mooney, Numu-tibo'o was also bulletproof. If he were living in the Walker River area in 1869, no doubt Numu-tibo'o participated in the 1870 Ghost Dance Religion, a revitalization movement that erupted at the Walker River Reservation in 1869. Because the Wier Notes and the Dangberg notes separately indicate that Wovoka's father was "wild," "quarrelsome," and "unprincipled," one wonders if this was hostility expressed toward the early Tibo'o settlers of

PLATE C. Numuraivo's house at Pine Grove, circa 1880. *Photo courtesy Nevada Historical Society*

Smith Valley and Mason Valley? For certainly there is no evidence that the father of the 1890 Ghost Dance Prophet bore even a smidgen of either his wife's or his son's reputation as a hard working field and ranch hand. Plate C, in any event, has been identified as Numu-tibo'o's home in Pine Grove, circa 1880. The only other datum about him that can be added at this time is Nellie Emm's hoary recollection: "Wovoka's father was alive when I began to know things," this Yerington Paiute elder stated. "He used to tweeze his beard with two nickels."

Hazel Quinn (b. 1899) volunteered the name of Wovoka's mother, **Tiya,** which she said she was unable to translate. Unless the Prophet in 1889 had envisioned his aged mother turned young again, Mrs. Quinn's statement that Tiya had died two to three years after her husband, about 1920, makes Chapman's rendition of the Great Revelation, which has Wovoka seeing his own dead mother in Heaven, puzzling indeed. Corbett Mack suspected that although Tiya was a Numu, she definitely was not a Toboose tukadu. Rather, Wovoka's mother had come to live in the Walker River area with her husband, Corbett suggested, following Numu-tibo'o's incarceration. The fact that no informants could trace kinship with her (nor with Numu-tibo'o for that matter) strengthens Corbett's claim and lends support for Bailey's contention of Wovoka's early orphanage.

In describing the Prophet's mother, J. I. Wilson also told Dangberg that she was a "...typical squaw. Very intelligent ...." In contrast to her husband "Buckskin," Tiya was said to have been entirely "trustworthy."

This same Wilson also told Dangberg that "Jack's disposition [was] like [his] mother." And in the Wier Notes, too, "Dave Wilson," whom we can assume was David Wilson, the founder of the Wilson Ranch, stated that "Jack [was] like his mother, not so wild as his father."

Because of this characterization of Tiya, we might infer that the Prophet's mother worked steadily for Tibo'o ranchers and farmers in Smith Valley and Mason Valley. If so, then the Protestant-type work ethic, which was at the core of her son's religion, might mean that Tiya's maternal influence bore acculturative fruit in the ideology of the 1890 Ghost Dance.

SIBLINGS

Chapman in 1890 wrote that Wovoka had three brothers; however, my oldest informants could recall only two, Pat Wilson and **Toyanaga-a**, both younger than the Prophet.

Pat Wilson was the middle brother. His name was **Honocha-yu**, which Yerington Paiutes suggest might mean "Ground Flour." According to their naming principle, Honocha-yu could have been inspired by some statement or exaggerated action made in childhood, for example, while his mother was grinding seeds. Born about 1870, Honocha-yu was described as being neither tall nor nice-looking. He was an excellent horseman, and he worked all his life as a ranch hand in the Colony District of Smith Valley. A "nobody," was how one informant contrasted Pat Wilson's anonymity with his older brother's national fame. He belonged to that birth cohort (1885-1909) of opiate addicts whom I unhappily described in my doctoral dissertation (Hittman 1973a). However, Yerington Paiutes suspected Pat Wilson possessed power in his own right, as his "mind" (**soonamme-ggwitu**) was said to "always be working." He was married to Annie Bennett, or **Yadobe**, the daughter of the nonpracticing shaman, Dick Bennett. She was named for the mica-studded black mineral pigment that medicine men would sprinkle on the heads and faces of patients to frighten away sickness or bad dreams. She and Pat Wilson had seven children in all: a son who died in infancy; Amy "Pumpkin" Wallace (1896-1960?), who married several times and was the mother of Jane Wallace Sam and an infant son who died in Smith Valley; Sadie Wilson Dick (1908-1964?), who was married to Johnson Dick of Coleville, an Antelope Valley Paiute peyote user, and was the mother of Frieda and Hubert Dick; Emma Wilson (b. 1910?) and who "died young"; Eva Dick (1911-1941?), a peyote user, who followed the Numu custom of marrying her sister Sadie's husband's brother, Streeter Dick, lived in Coleville, California, and was also the mother of two daughters, Verdina and Ruby, and two sons, Elmer and Wesley; Woodrow Wilson, born January 10, 1914, decorated W.W. II veteran; and Willie Wilson, who died of tuberculosis as a youngster at Stewart Institute in Carson City. Interviewed in the summer of 1988, Woodrow Wilson, who worked for the Fulstones in Smith Valley for 35 years and was then residing with his second Washo wife in Woodfords, California, told me that his father, Pat Wilson, died at the Yerington Indian Colony of a ruptured appendix that Wovoka had unsuccessfully attempted to doctor. The Lyon County coroner, on August 18, 1931, gave "intestinal obstruction" as the cause of Pat Wilson's death, and the Prophet's younger brother was buried at the Yerington Indian cemetery near his wife Annie, who died on November 8, 1938.

The name of Wovoka's younger brother, Toyanaga-a, as one informant suggested, sounded like **toniga-a**, "to plug up a hole." Born about 1880, Toyanaga-a was married to **Apima-a** or **Api**, "Happy, Effie, or Eppie," who appears to have been a "cousin-sister" of Pat Wilson's wife. Childless, Wovoka's younger brother used neither drugs or alcohol and was said by Corbett Mack to have "died young" in Smith Valley, about 1907, perhaps of "clap."

The Prophet himself was married once and raised three daughters, two of them his own.

THE PROPHET'S WIFE

Although Bailey stated that Wovoka married an **Agi tukadu**, or Walker River Reservation "Trout-eater" in 1887, immediately upon returning from the Pacific Northwest, Hazel Quinn thought Wovoka's wife was Pit River. Irene Thompson (b. 1911), on the other hand, thought she was Bannock, reasoning that this explained why so many Idaho Bannocks attended the dances "put up" by Wovoka. Mary Wilson's Northern Paiute name was **Tumma**, the word for the closely woven, heart-shaped basket used in processing pine nuts (Fowler and Dawson 1986:722). Cultural geographer Earl Kerstein (Ms.) reported that, around 1904, Wovoka's wife worked alongside her sister at a hotel owned by the Wilsons in Pine Grove. One of Wier's informants was Mrs. Wilson, whom Gunard Solberg (Personal Correspondence) suspects was Genevieve Chapin (1888-1971), the daughter of J. I. Wilson. Mrs. Wilson stated that "Jack's wife [was] now [1910] working in [a] hotel at Mason," the townsite on the Walker River which threatened to replace Yerington as Lyon County's capital. We also know that in 1919, when a labor strike closed the Thompson Copper Smelter and the town of Mason precipitously declined, Mary and Jack Wilson were reported to have abandoned their camp along the Walker River. They moved directly onto the recently purchased 10-acre Yerington Indian Colony in Mason Valley, where the Prophet's wife secured employment at the Lyon County Hospital.

Regarding their married life, Dangberg notes "M. Wilson's" [J. W. Wilson's?] statement that "long after [Wovoka] had a family, [he] quarreled with Mary. [He] Went to S [Smith] Valley [as a result] and got another woman, but only lived with her [a] short time." The Wier Notes also reported that the Prophet once "stole" the wife of a Virginia City Numu. Genevieve Chapin told Wier that Wovoka "went to Virginia [City] and stole another man's wife.... [He] was already married to Mary when this happened."

"M. Wilson" [J. W. Wilson?] was quoted by Dangberg as saying that before "Mary [was his] first wife...[Wovoka] stole [the] wife of Virginia City man [who] hunted him for days." This same informant also stated in the Dangberg notes that, "He [Wovoka] kept [the] woman and finally gave her up." And, finally, J. I. Wilson called the Numu woman from Virginia City "a beautiful Eve" (Dangberg Notes), while his brother, J. W. Wilson, recalled how their father had "supplied food for the truants...[where Wovoka] was hiding with V. City woman." Apparently Wovoka was teased about this by the Wilsons, for we also read in these sources the following rejoinders attributed to the 1890 Ghost Dance Prophet: "[Jack Wilson] Said he no steal a woman, woman steal him," Mrs. Chapin told Wier. While in J.I. Wilson's version (Dangberg Notes), "Me no stealin' woman. I no steal that woman. That woman she steal me." As a discussion of humor will be reserved for Chapter Six, here I note only the comment made about Mary Wilson to Grace Dangberg by one of the three Wilson sons: "Mary [was] not untrue to Jack before his adventures.... Some of Mary's children [were] half-breeds." The inference being, of course, that there were sexual politics in the marital life of the 1890 Ghost Dance Prophet.

Yerington Paiutes today recall Tumma, or Mary Wilson, as a "short, quiet lady." She spoke their dialect but was definitely not a relative. The Prophet's wife did not use opiates nor did she drink, they said, and seemed atypical for her generation because she was a woman who "kept away" from others; that is, she did not gamble. Tumma, or Mary Wilson, died in August of 1932 and was buried in Schurz, a month before her husband.

CHILDREN

Genevieve Chapin told Wier that Wovoka "never could raise a boy," while Ed Dyer's brother, Bob, told Dangberg, "Every boy they had (6) developed epilepsy and died." The only one of these sons we can speak of with fair certainty is "Bill Wilson," as an informant rendered the boy's name. He, according to Bailey, was named after the Prophet's blood brother, J. W. or "Billy" Wilson, and may have been the 4-year-old seen by Mooney in 1892. Numus today report that the Prophet's son was killed in a horse and wagon mishap during a Pine Nut Festival in Pine Grove or at the Walker River Reservation. Hazel Quinn stated that Bill Wilson was a **nana'a** at the time of his death - a "young boy just turning into a man." Grief-stricken, Wovoka was said then to have unleashed torrential rainstorms, which either were intended to efface the boy's tracks on this earth or those belonging to the burying party. As will be seen, this prophet-driven rainstorm is entirely consistent with the significance of weather control seen in this study for the beginnings of the 1890 Ghost Dance Religion.

Wier quoted Mrs. Chapin's statement about the death of a daughter, "When Jack's daughter died, Mary lay in the dust for five days...." Numu mourning customs (cf. Stewart 1941:412) also involved blackening their faces. We learn, as well, in the Wier Notes, that "Jack would not talk about it [his daughter's death]," which also was in conformity with the traditional culture. My own informants were not old enough to recall this death; they, however, knew Mary Wilson's three surviving daughters.

The oldest was named **Zohoona** or "Grinding Flour." More commonly known as Daisy or Josie or Lucy or Emma, she was born around 1885 and was characterized as being "real comical." "She acts and says anything crazy," as one informant stated. Zohoona, like her parents, was entirely abstemious; she neither used opiates nor alcohol. The Prophet's oldest daughter was married to Pete Penrose (1860?-1934) and had three children: Andrew (1902-1955?), Archie (1907-1958?) and Ina (1915-?). Andrew Penrose was an opiate addict. In and out of prison, this Numu had an unsavory reputation and is recalled as a "mugger" (of fellow Numus), as someone who did not work, and as having almost killed his brother once for drug money. One informant recalled his having once stolen Wovoka's harvest of pine nuts for opiate money. Married twice - to Florence Waterson, a Yerington Numu, and subsequently to Ida Dick — this grandson of the Prophet acted in the Nelson Eddy-Jeanette MacDonald film, "Rosemarie," shot at Lake Tahoe. Andrew Penrose's younger brother Archie was also in that film. Archie Penrose was married twice — first to Julia Benjamin of the Walker River Reservation, then to her sister, Josie. He

Plate D. Wovoka's daughter (left), Ida Wilson Bender. *Photo courtesy of Inez Jim*

did not use opiates and apparently did not drink either. Childless, Archie Penrose died around 1958 in Chester, California, and was buried in Schurz. His sister, Ina, attended Stewart Institute. She married a Walker River Reservation Numu named Dave Sharp. Together they had three children: Dora, who was married to a Pyramid Lake Reservation Numu named Green and died relatively young; Inez (b. 1927), the mother of two children; and Evelyn (b. 1929), who was childless. These latter, retired Public Health nurses, today live on the Walker River Reservation.

On Zohoona's, or Daisy Wilson's, death certificate (July 7, 1920) the occupation of "Washerwoman" was given. Although her cause of death was omitted, the Lyon County coroner did note that the Prophet's oldest daughter was in the care of a **poohaguma,** or medicine man, at that time. Yet oddly enough, Zohoona's age was given on this document as 20. Irene Thompson of Smith Valley told me that Zohoona, or Lucy Penrose nee Wilson, had "died young," and Corbett Mack added that she was a suicide. "Jack's daughter committed suicide," we read in the Wier Notes. Mrs. Chapin was the speaker, but Wier for one reason or another penciled a line through "daughter" on her page and superimposed "brother" above it. If Chapin had meant the Prophet's youngest brother, Toyanaga-a, and not his oldest daughter, Zohoona, the subsequent entry does not logically follow: "Jack has (her) children of dead daughter." One suspects, therefore, that Wier recorded it correctly the first time. Thus it should read, "Jack's daughter [Zohoona] committed suicide," followed by, "Jack has (her) children of dead daughter." And there is supportive evidence for this. For example, Chester Smith (b. 1917), former chairman of the Yerington Paiute Tribe and a life-long resident of the Yerington Indian Colony, stated that his mother's second husband, Archie Penrose or Zohoona's son, had "lived with" the Prophet as a small boy, hence was "raised by" Wovoka.

Ida Wilson was the name of his second daughter (Plate D). "A 24 year old named Ida, the mother of two sons," or so Mrs. Chapin commented to Wier around 1910. Informants described Ida Wilson as a "tiny lady with a voice that sounds like she's whispering all the time, not hoarse." Ida or _aydi Wilson was married to a Walker River Reservation Numu named Hank, or Richard Bender (**Sigi** in Northern Paiute, "Quail") who died on November 7, 1923 as a result of poisonous homemade wine sold to him in direct retaliation for having turned in a Smith Valley Italian bootlegger during Prohibition. Because her husband was an opiate addict, Ida Bender nee Wilson was said to have acquired the habit. She is buried in the Numu cemetery in Mason Valley closest to Yerington. Her offspring were Dennis

PLATE E. Wovoka and Dennis Bender at Walker River, Nevada. *Courtesy Inter-Tribal Council of Nevada*

(1909-1964) and Elizabeth Bender (1918-1933), and a half-brother named Robert Minkey, who, informants felt, had been fathered by a Japanese or Chinese resident of Smith Valley and Mason Valley.

On the basis of his crossed eyes, informants positively identified Dennis Bender as the 5-year-old boy standing alongside Wovoka in the 1914 photo taken outside the Baptist church building at Stewart Institute by Matr late E). Tim McCoy mentioned the Prophet's grandson during his 1924 visit to the Yerington Indian Colony and must have been referring to Dennis Bender. Isabelle Creighton, a neighbor of Wovoka's in Mason in 1915, gave Gunard Solberg this following description of Bender, whom she apparently confused with the Prophet's son Bill:

> Dennis, was built rather on the heavy side, would no doubt have been a big man like Jack, had he lived. Had coal black hair, worn short, and always neat and clean. He was about nine years old, when we kids played hide-and-seek so much. He loved that, and I am afraid we kids were rather mean to Dennis. Since he could not see well, if he was it, we made him run and work harder to find us. Or would hide where he could not see us.... Dennis, was always rather slow, and real quiet, but he had a wonderful smile, when you were kind to him, and I repeat how he loved to have the funny papers read to him. He absorbed every word, so no doubt the eyesight had much to do with his quietness. When we asked what was the matter with his eyes, the answer the Indians gave was snow blindness, which when we asked what that meant,

we got the reply that it was because when snow was on the ground, he had looked at the sun too much, reflected on the white snow, and had gone blind. After I was older, and became aware of how many other Indians, both adults and children (as I always kept up with my former playmates after they came home in the summer time from Stewart) had eye problems, we concluded that no doubt there was something else wrong, instead of snow blindness as they termed it. Dennis, was sick much more often [than] Alice [the Prophet's youngest daughter], and sometimes a week would go by when he wouldn't come to play at my house. I have always been under the impression that he sickened and died. I do not remember anything about a runaway. One day he was with us, and the next thing we know he was gone (Gunard Solberg - Personal Correspondence).

Dennis Bender became the first chairman of the Yerington Paiute Tribe (1936-1937). He was married to Catherine Decroy (1914-?), and they had six children: Gerdie or Gertrude Williams, deceased; Charlotte, who married a Pyramid Lake Reservation Numu, has three daughters, and was living at Campbell Ranch in Mason Valley in 1988; Cathy, who resides with her large family in Wyoming; Mary Alice, who died of a burst appendix at age 8; Loren, who lives in Reno; and Kenneth Bender, an employee of the Yerington Paiute Tribe in 1982 when I knew him, and who bears a most uncanny resemblance to the 1890 Ghost Dance Prophet. It was in Dennis Bender's house at the southeast end of the Yerington Indian Colony that the Prophet died. Wovoka's grandson was himself killed at the Colony in a brawl involving his wife in 1964. His sister, Elizabeth Bender, "died young" of tuberculosis. She was living at Nixon at the time, and her body had to be shipped home to Yerington for burial in Schurz. Their half-brother Robert Minkey was said to have relocated to Portland, Oregon, following military service, where he died in the 1970s.

The Prophet's third and youngest daughter was not fathered by him. "Jack Wilson has two living daughters: A 24 year old named Ida, the mother of two sons, and a ten year old named Alice," stated Mrs. Chapin in the Wier Notes. She was called a **namooggwitu** by Corbett Mack, a "stolen" child; and informants, with their keen interest in paternity, reasoned that because Alice "looks like George [Simpson] when she smiles," she must have been fathered by the married son of Desert Creek Ranch's founder, Dan Simpson of Smith Valley. The Prophet's illegitimate daughter was born in 1903. Since Dan Simpson was described as being a strong believer in Wovoka's ability to predict rain, it is only reasonable to assume that Jack and Mary Wilson were either working for the Simpsons at the time of Alice's conception or nearby. Warren Emm's investigation into the shooting death of his maternal grandmother, Mae Jim, on the Simpson Ranch also has a bearing on this. This Numu woman was killed in 1896 when a rifle accidentally discharged in the Simpson house, the bullet striking her from two rooms away. Emm learned that the Simpsons had paid Jack and Mary Wilson to look after Mae Jim. The proximity of that date, 1896, to Alice Wilson's birth date in 1903 confirms that Wovoka was closely associated with the Simpsons in those years.

Corbett Mack, a namooggwitu himself, and someone who suffered deeply because of his Numu father's rejection of him on the basis of his own illegitimacy, once remarked about Wovoka's youngest daughter: "Even though she's stolen, Jack claimed her. He called Alice his **baadu**, 'daughter.'" Envy? Maybe. Beth Ellis nee Wilson, in any event, told the *Mason Valley News* (13 August 1976) that Wovoka took the name "Alice" from her own daughter. Yerington Paiutes volunteered **Pozi-niyu** (**Pozunna?**), or "Patchquilt," as Alice Wilson's Numic name. This was explained by Irene Thompson as follows:

> A long time ago, you know, people used to have a hard time. So I guess her mother, she must have a lot of left-over goods that a White lady gave her. So she cut them like a quilt and she sewed them all together, and she [Alice] used to wear it. That's the way they used to call her Pozi-niyu. It means in Indian "quilts."

Attendance at the boarding school established in Carson City at the time of the 1890 Ghost Dance was not voluntary. "Twenty-six Indians were taken to the Indian School at Carson last Thursday, washed and properly cleaned to enter the school. Superintendent Gibson has agents all over the State on the hunt, and expects to have over 100 on the grounds before next month," *Lyon County Times* (20 December 1890) — yet Arthur Chapman nevertheless could report that Wovoka was an advocate of Western education. And, in fact, of his three children, it was the Prophet's illegitimate daughter who went to school. Alice Wilson attended the Carson Industrial School (or Stewart Institute), which opened its doors to Numus, Shoshones, and Washoes in 1890; and Ed Johnson, who is writing a long overdue and greatly anticipated history of this recently closed institution, told me that Wovoka would occasionally appear at graduation and other ceremonial functions. The Prophet's youngest daughter met her future husband there. Andrew Vidovich was a Death Valley Shoshone who worked

PLATE F. Alice and Andy Vidovich receiving posthumous award for son, circa 1945. *Photo courtesy of Inez Jim*

as a railroad employee, carpenter, and for a time, was also the specially-deputized Treasury Department officer during the narcotics scourge among Walker River Numus. Although he maintained that the Prophet had had a close relationship with Alice as a child — "The old man used to take her out hunting and fishing, you can't beat her fishing" (Vidovich-Wheat Tape 96:7) — Vidovich, on the other hand, told Peg Wheat how his wife as a young girl had lived with her aunts, "two sisters." The explanation he gave for this is revealing: Alice's "mother wasn't well at the time."

I would venture to suggest, however, that "illness" was not the reason. Mary Wilson may have surrendered her youngest child to close relatives for a time in the interest of marital harmony. Recall the Prophet's dispute with his wife over another woman. Also there was the statement in the Wier Notes that Mary Wilson had delivered "half-breeds" in direct re-taliation for Wovoka's perfidy. In my own field notebooks I record a high incidence of resentment occasioned by the births of so-called "stolen" children, and how these sometimes would lead to domestic violence, even when the genitor was himself a Numu. Andy Vidovich might have implied as much when he commented that his wife's aunts used to cover Alice's hair all the time with a cap or scarf because "it didn't look like an Indian's hair" (Vidovich-Wheat Tape 96:8). One final evidence can be adduced. Beth Wilson Ellis, the daughter of J. W. Wilson, told Gunard Solberg that "Jack tried to kill Alice when she was born" (Gunard Solberg - Personal Correspondence).

Alice Vidovich declined my invitation for an interview in 1968; and Mary Aizzi, a reporter for the *Mason Valley News* at the time, told me that a piece she had written about Wovoka had to be pulled at the very last minute on account of an objection raised by the Prophet's step-daughter. ("In some instances material was not used at the request of living relatives, such as was the case of the very colorful figure, Jack Wilson, the 'Indian Messiah,'" *Mason Valley News*, 2 June 1961.) And while the ghost perceived drubbing done to her famous father by Paul Bailey has been given as the standard explanation among Yerington Paiutes for Alice Vidovich's reticence to discuss Wovoka, Bailey in all this might only be a convenient scapegoat. Twenty years earlier, the *Reno Evening Gazette* (4 October 1932) in reporting Wovoka's death (the *Mason Valley News*, whose byline is "The Only Newspaper In The World That Gives A Damn About Yerington," did not even mention the Prophet's passing) indicated that Alice Vidovich "did not wish to discuss her father's life or powers." And six years later, Nevada Superintendent Alida C. Bowler would write to John C. Harrington of the Bureau of American Ethnology expressing that she doubted "very much if a person could obtain much information from her" (Appendix J). Alice Vidovich nee Wilson "never liked to talk about things like that," Ms. Bowler relayed in 1938, something she apparently had learned about the 1890 Ghost Dance Prophet's youngest daughter from Jerry Vidovich, Alice's brother-in-law. Alice Vidovich, in any event, owned a diner attached to her brother-in-law's auto service station on the Walker River Reservation and was renowned for her home baked pies. She died of viral pneumonia in 1971 and was buried in the family plot in Schurz. "Staunch members" of the Mormon church was how Paul Bailey (1957:212n10) characterized both Alice and Andy Vidovich (Plate F), whose only child, as we shall see, figures prominently in Wovoka lore.

ENDNOTES

1. Also called "cyprus bulbs," these tiny coconut-like nuts with a hairy exterior and milky center were an important food for Walker River area Numus. Regarding the identity of the Toboose tukadu, although Omer Stewart (1939:142-43) called them a "band," Steward and Wheeler-Voegelin (1974:102) wrote that they were the most confused of the three (bands) that Stewart outlined for the [Walker River] area. The importance of residence in determining Numu identity is well illustrated by Walter Vorhees' testimony before the Indian Claims Commission. In answer to a question about his mother's

"band name," this Walker River Reservation Numu stated: "Well, that would depend on the question because at that time when she was living at Walker River she would be known as an Agi tukadu, but you could continue with that and say her grandparents, rather than her parents, were from the Mono Lake group" (Steward and Wheeler-Voegelin 1972:292).

2. G.W. Ingalls (Davis 1913) quoted Warren Wasson's early report on the 1860 death and resurrection of "Chief Waz-zda-zo-bah-ago" of the Mono Lake band of Paiutes. According to John Wesley Powell (Fowler and Fowler 1971:233): "In the Walker River gens the chief has always been called Wat-su-wab."

3. Mrs. Velma Ford told me in 1988 that Yerington Theater movie-goers were sent home after the last picture show, either to Wovoka's face on the screen or that of a Chinese man.

4. However, Gunard Solberg feels that Vidovich probably was discussing Chief Winnemucca (Gunard Solberg - Personal Correspondence).

CHAPTER 3

The Early Years

"The prophet is a lonely man. His standards are too high, his stature too great, and his concern too intense for other men to share. Living on the highest peak, he has no company except God" (Heschel 1962:100).

Although Chapman recorded Quoitze Ow as the 1890 Ghost Prophet's earliest name, Mooney gave it as Wovoka, "The (Wood) Cutter," transcribing Quoitze Ow as Kwohitsauq, "Big Rumbling Belly" (colic?). Mooney stated that the name Wovoka belonged to the Prophet's paternal grandfather and, in 1892, had only recently been taken. Ed Dyer, on the other hand, recalled Cowejo as his earliest name, stating it to be a "corruption" of Quoitze Ow. In the Wier Notes, however, we read that Wovoka, too, was called by his father's English name, "Buckskin."

"Later [the Prophet was called] 'Buckskin,'" David Wilson stated. "[But he] Does not like it. Wants to be called 'Dr. Johnny' [instead]." The name "Dr. Johnny," interestingly enough, appears in the 1880 Census tracks for the Walker River area. On June 17 and 18, 1880 we find the following entry: "Piute [sic] Dr. Johnny. Age 49. Smith Valley. Married to Maggie. Age 34. Father of three children, a 14 year old daughter named Leanna, a 4 year old son named Pat, and a baby boy, age 2." The very next entry reads "Piute [sic] Jack. Age 30." And, "Piute [sic] Jack" was said to be a "laborer" who was married to Maggie, age 30. Her occupation was listed as "keeping house." Their offspring included: a boy named Fol (age?), another boy named Jim (2), and a one month old infant whose gender was not indicated. Were these the respective families of Numu-tibo'o, known as Buckskin, known as "Dr. Johnny," and his son, "Piute [sic] Jack," known as Buckskin, as well as Wovoka et al., the 1890 Ghost Dance Prophet?

Yerington Paiutes could only recall Numu-tibo'o with a single wife. Nor is there evidence that the 1890 Ghost Dance Prophet's father was ever called "Piute Dr. Johnny," or "Buckskin" for that matter. But certainly the ages of those Numus given in the 1880 Census tracts correspond well with the birth cohorts proposed in a previous study (Hittman 1973a): Numu-tibo'o, belonging to the 1835-1859 cohort, would have been about 45 in

1880; while his famous son belonged to the 1860-1884 birth cohort and would have been about 20 in 1880. "Pat," age 4, could very well have been Pat Wilson, whose birth year was about 1870. Since the Prophet and Mary Wilson were said to have lost a succession of sons to epilepsy, three of them arguably could have been recorded in that 1880 Census.[1] The argument, then, is that the 1880 Census taker not only documented the presence of these two families in Smith Valley in June of that year, but also in recording them successively, he demonstrated the importance of extended family living. These are "kin cliques," as Don Fowler (1966) characterized Numu traditional society — well into the post-contact period. There is abundant testimony that Wovoka always established his home close to his father's.

I record, however, one additional name for him, **Moohoo'oobit**. Corbett Mack reported it, and I suggest the name derived from all-too-frequent requests made by suffering opiate addicts to the relatively affluent 1890 Ghost Dance Prophet for loose change — **bit** — to purchase **moohoo'oo** or "**yen shee**," a narcotic whose addiction afflicted even the Prophet's own brother and daughter. Unfortunately, Yerington Paiutes no longer retain the earlier names by which the Prophet was known. Most admitted that they had not even heard the name "Wovoka" until after his death, indicating that, as Paul Bailey (1957:21) earlier wrote, they knew "Jack Wilson, the name white men gave him, the name by which he answered to them." Since "Wovoka" and "Jack Wilson" so translucently give context to the life of the 1890 Ghost Dance Prophet, we turn directly to them now before discussing his early years.

WOVOKA

Mr. and Mrs. Howard (b. 1903) and Lena (b. 1904) Rogers of Campbell Ranch, on the Yerington Paiute reservation in Mason Valley, explained "**wovoka-a**" as follows. It means "cutting" or "sectioning" something into many pieces, they stated, as in "lots of wood," from **wika**, "one," **wivika**, "more than one." **Su wivi_qa-a**, "someone who cuts more than one piece of — [wood]." According to Ari Poldervaart (1987), Wycliffe Bible translator and author of the *Yerington Paiute Language Grammar*, the name Wovoka should be read from its constituent morphemes: **wi** — "the edge [of an axe]," **xi** — "break," **ri-i** — "to shoot out or to go out." Wovoka, then, derived from the Prophet's handiness with an axe. "As a woodcutter he was a man," Andy Vidovich (Tape 90:15) related. "Some days he lived by cutting wood for the mines, the mills and everything. The power was made by wood." Mooney's claim, therefore, that Wovoka had been the Prophet's name since childhood makes little sense, unless "The (Wood) Cutter" was obtained as a result of some preternatural childhood play with axes. However, there are no stories of Bunyonesque strength attributed to the Prophet, so the safest conclusion can only be that Wovoka was acquired when he was a good-sized young man, and was not his earliest name.

OCCUPATIONS

Regarding this occupation, we know that Numus were hired by Tibo'o, early in their acculturation, to chop cedar and pinion pine trees for mining shafts and for charcoal in smelting purposes, as well as to cord wood for fence posts and winter fires (Lanner 1981). Contrary to Mooney (1896:809), who reported that cedar was used as the center pole of Plains Indian Ghost Dance ceremonies because of its "mystic sacredness...from its never-dying green, which renders it so conspicuous a feature of the desert landscape; from the aromatic fragrance of its twigs, which are burned as incense in sacred ceremonies," no evidence exists that cedar (**waape**) poles were employed in Wovoka's ceremonies in Nevada. Nor, in fact, does cedar appear to be sacred in Numu cosmology. In the Numu Creation Story, for example, thick groves of cedar come to dot the surrounding mountainsides because of Trickster Coyote's profane action: he swallows the watered-down pine nut soup (**paape**), which the Animals have stolen from the People of the North, and upon returning home to the Walker River area, wherever Coyote spits, *Juniperus* took root instead of the desirable *Pinus monophylla,* or pinion pine. Assuming Wovoka's activities as a woodcutter involved the cutting down and cording of pinion pine trees, whose nutritious seed, **tuba,** was vital to Numu survival, and which can be considered sacred to Numus, the following question must be raised in any biography of the 1890 Ghost Dance Prophet: What was the personal meaning of Wovoka's occupation as a woodcutter and to the Numus living in the Walker River area at that time?

"So important were pinion resources that groves of trees were considered family property in several locations," Catherine Fowler (1986:65) has characterized the traditional economy. Pine nuts were so vital for winter survival that tons of them were buried in caches, or until fish and other valued food resources could be obtained in the springtime. Moreover, this staple was harvested with much ceremony every fall. Eugene Hattori (1975:16) discussed its corresponding value to non-Indian settlers during those early years of Numu acculturation: "The pinion is considered the most valuable firewood, being a

PLATES G1, G2, G3. David, Abigail and J.W. Wilson. Drawings in charcoal. *Courtesy Mason Valley News.*

hard, resinous fine grained variety growing 10 to 30 feet in height, and commands about $2 per cord more than cedar." How deleterious, then, to this vital, if not sacred, food resource were those silver and gold mines that sprang up in the Sierra Nevada Mountains in the 1850s? And what might the initial Numu reaction to its floracide have been?

On the Comstock, an estimated 568 cords of firewood were said to have been used daily in 1867, resulting in an annual consumption of 120,000 cords (Hattori 1975:15). Ronald Lanner (1981:118) wrote that, by 1868, pinion pine had to be "packed in on mules from inaccessible areas back in the mountains" because the local supplies were already "entirely exhausted;" and that "pinion was selling for sixteen dollars a cord, most of the cost going for transportation." At least one Numu's reaction to the desecration of the staple crop has been preserved. **Numaga**, "Young Winnemucca," the son of Chief Winnemucca stated: "Pine nut groves were the Indian's orchards and they must not be destroyed by the whites" (Hattori 1975:16-17). Assuming Numaga's sentiment was in some ways reflective of widespread Numu opposition to the desecration of their groves of pinion pine (and cedar) trees, we can speculate that Walker River Numus shared the sentiment. And if there was resentment toward Wovoka's occupation, did the members of the 1835-1859 birth cohort, especially those who fought in the early wars to protect Numu lands against usurpation by Tibo'o, resent fellow Numus who went to work as woodcutters in the mountains for Tibo'o miners, ranchers, and farmers? One might even suspect that a rift occurred between the 1890 Ghost Dance Prophet and his father Numu-tibo'o as a result of Wovoka's occupation. Could this, then, have fueled Wovoka's "ambition" to become "more" than a medicine man? The allegation by Ed Dyer, which was repeated by Paul Bailey, that Wovoka felt driven to achieve some unique type of personal recognition in the 1880s, to become more of a personage than Numu-tibo'o?

Furthermore, one might wonder whether or not Wovoka was filled with guilt or inner conflict as a result of his signifying occupation — similar emotions to those which afflicted other prophets such as Handsome Lake (Wallace 1970), the alcoholic Seneca who trampled upon his Iroquois religion while inebriated; or the Hebrew prophet, Moses, who was forced to hide in the Sinai Desert after having murdered a fellow Egyptian. If the 1890 Ghost Dance Prophet suffered remorse on account of his chosen occupation, then psychologically speaking, couldn't guilt or conflict or self-doubt have been the deus ex machina which lie behind the Great Revelation? Unanswered as these questions remain, one can glean from photographs his sheer physical size and power in order to imagine the prodigious number of pinion pine and cedar trees that the 1890 Ghost Dance Prophet in his day would have been able to chop down!

JACK WILSON

The name "Jack Wilson" also has to be considered within the context of Tibo'o settlements of the Walker River area, for it, too, directly links the Prophet with the Wilson family of Mason Valley.

David Wilson (1829-1915) was of Scotch and English ancestry (Plate G.1). Born in Harrison County, Ohio, Wilson moved to Missouri in 1837 with his family, which was engaged in farming and stock raising. After some time spent in Illinois and Wisconsin, the lure of the Gold Rush beckoned him. David Wilson crossed the country in 1850 to placer mine on the South Yuba River and at Mound City, California. Returning to Missouri three years later, to care for his dying father, Wilson fought in the Union Army. After receiving an honorable discharge in 1863 (sunstroke during the Battle of Athens), he, along with his bride, Abigail Jane Butler (1836-1910) (Plate G.2), and brothers, James and William (1826-1912) Wilson, headed west again. They eventually settled "Missouri Flat," the lower or southern end of Mason Valley, where the upper or northern end had already been claimed by N. H. A. "Hoc" Mason, for whom the valley was named (Ford 1976). In what the *Mason Valley News* (2 June 1961) called the "first agricultural transaction recorded" in Esmerelda County, the Wilsons purchased 220 acres of scrub land from the Wheeler brothers, Mormons called back to Utah. Three years later, in 1866, David Wilson's younger brother, William, discovered gold in the Sierra Nevada Mountains. The booming settlement of Pine Grove, California, appeared overnight. In its heyday it boasted a population of over 1,000, three double-storied hotels, five saloons, three blacksmith shops, one variety store, a Wells Fargo agent, a large general store (owned by Ed Dyer), a hardware store, a boot maker, a shoe shine parlor, dance hall, public school, post office, one doctor, one notary public, and a Justice of the Peace (Anonymous, "The Early History of Smith and Mason Valley," Lyon County Public Library, Yerington). Besides the Wilson Mine, two other mines were operative in Pine Grove, revenues being in the tens of millions. Considering that the Wilson Mine alone was 200-feet deep and worked by 40 men, one can only begin to imagine the vast number of trees that were required to sustain their combined operations. Wovoka's contribution as a woodcutter, in other words, would not have been inconsiderable.

The derivation of the Prophet's first name, however, is unknown. The name "Jack" was common enough among Tibo'o. As shown in the Tenth Census, nearly every Numu man and woman reported living in Smith Valley, Mason Valley, Pine Grove, and Sweetwater Valley in 1880 carried English names such as Jack, Tom, Dick, Jennie, and Sadie. Nor was Wovoka's close attachment to a Tibo'o family atypical. Genealogies collected among Yerington Paiutes reveal that all Numus who found steady and gainful employment on the farms and ranches of the Walker River area took or were given their employers' names: Penrose, Wright, Rogers, Wheeler, Bennett, McCloud, Reymers, etc. Indeed, a Bodie or Sweetwater Numu even carried the name "Jim Mooney," though the circumstances which related him to the famed 1890 Ghost Dance scholar were not recalled.

THE PROPHET'S CHILDHOOD

Information regarding Wovoka's earliest years significantly locates him on the Wilson Ranch. Genevieve Chapman (1888-1971), J. I. Wilson's daughter and David Wilson's granddaughter, told Dangberg (1968:26) the following: "Some of Jack's people worked for him [David Wilson] and they always brought all the children to be fed as food was scarce. Jack began playing with Billy and Joe .... There were no other playmates."[2] That year was 1864, and Dangberg gave the Prophet's age as 8. Continuing in this vein, Dangberg also quoted Mrs. Chapman's statement that "their play consisted in climbing trees, hunting bird's nests, fishing and swimming in the river. And when they were a little older [there was] the playing of pranks of which Billy was a past master." In the Dangberg notes, too, we read the statement by J. I. Wilson characterizing Wovoka's boyhood as "very normal. No epilepsy." "M. Wilson," believed by Gunard Solberg to be J. W. Wilson (Gunard Solberg — Personal Correspondence, cf. Plate G.3), also characterized the Prophet then as a "jolly young fellow...with [the] Wilson boys ...[they] went swimming together — worked, played marbles." Wovoka, J. I. Wilson further revealed, was their close friend, if only because "Indians [were] about [our] only playmates."

As the Wilson boys grew older, however, "Jack, Joe, and Billy Wilson took on the chores of chopping wood for the fires, milking cows, and general ranch chores" (Mrs. Chapin, Dangberg Notes). I suggest "chores" are important for our understanding of Wovoka's entire life. If his father did indeed resist wage labor, the Prophet, as we know, most certainly did not. "He hired out to white men to work all the time; that he liked to work," Chapman quoted him saying. And in Mooney's version of the Great

Revelation, Wovoka was again quoted as saying that Native Americans "must work." Even in the so-called Messiah Letter, which Mooney claimed the 1890 Ghost Dance Prophet had dictated in Nevada to a disciple who then mailed it to Plains Indians, there is this insistence upon manual labor: "Do not refuse to work for the whites" (Appendix F). How vital was Numu labor to the welfare of early settlers of the Walker River area? Timothy B. Smith (1911-1912:226), who in 1859 drove cattle back from California into the adjoining valley to Mason Valley which today still carries his name, recalled his first years among the Toboose tukadu:

> In justice to the Piute [sic] Indians, it must be said that during the first years we were among them, though we would gladly have seen them leave the country because of the anxiety and annoyance they caused us, yet a few years later I do not see how we would have managed without their assistance. In the harvesting of our large crops of hay as well as in some other lines of work, what they did was generally pretty well done. As hay stackers and in the use of the horse fork they excelled.

Toboose tukadu response to Tibo'o occupation of their lands resembled other Great Basin Indians (Steward 1938). After a short-lived period of defensive hostilities, they, too, eagerly sought Euro-American foods, clothing, and assorted technologies. The 1875 photograph of Wovoka on the front porch of Mrs. Hoye's General Store in Wellington, Smith Valley, well illustrates this dramatic transformation (cf. Plate B); for, at 16, the Prophet is already wearing a tailored winter jacket and Stetson hat, his trouser knees appear to be scuffed, as though from work. By 1880, the following occupations were given alongside the names of the 500 or so Numus living in the Walker River area: men — farming, chores, and "labor"; women — washing, gardening, general housework. Remarkably, too, Walker River area Numus were anxious to operate their own farms and ranches early on. Numaga's words again can be taken as representative. This impressive Numu, who in the 1860s demanded $16,000 from the settlers of Honey Lake for occupation of his people's land in California, told Captain Weatherlow that he wished "to learn to till the soil and live like a white man" (Egan 1972:74). Annual reports to the Commissioner of Indian Affairs also evidenced the early Numu interest in farming on the Walker River Reservation (Hittman 1973b, Johnson 1975). But Numus living in Smith Valley and Mason Valley did not obtain reservation lands for farming and ranching until 1936. Defined as "off-reservation" Indians, their general lot in 1890 was revealed by the Eleventh Census (1894:395):

The Indians off reservations are congregated in the mining towns and the towns along the railroads of the state and maintain themselves and their families by working at odd jobs, such as cutting wood, hunting stock, and by general chores. The women wash, iron, scrub, and do general kitchen work and house cleaning.... Those that reside in the valleys among the ranchers and stockmen are a more moral and industrious class of Indians. They live in groups in tents and willow wickyups [sic] in the valleys where they work. Many of them have little patches of ground which they cultivate, and some have a little stock, chiefly ponies. They all seem very anxious to have an assignment of land, where they can build houses but do not want to go on the reservation.

Because Debbie Hanson ("Early History," Lyon County Public Library, Yerington, Nevada), wrote that "before his fame the Indian Messiah Jack Wilson" worked at the Henry S. Morgan Ranch on East Walker (the Flying M Ranch today), we can assume that in addition to cutting wood, Wovoka performed all the chores associated with hay-growing in the Walker River area — grubbing sagebrush, leveling lands, planting, irrigating, harvesting, stacking hay, etc. Ranching was yet a second component in the regional economy (Kerstein 1961), but whether or not the Prophet ever broke horses and drove cattle to and from summer pasture as a **pakeada'a** or "cowboy" is unknown. Kerstein (Ms.), however, did learn that he "was proud of his knowledge of horses," although this simply could refer to the animals Wovoka owned for transportation in his buggy.[3] And when around the turn of the century northern Italians from Lucca introduced row crop culture of potatoes, onions, and garlics, which came to rival the alfalfa, cattle, and sheep industries in Smith and Mason valleys, the suspicion is that Wovoka also performed those back-breaking labors. Yerington Paiutes, it should be noted, were of little help in this regard. "Who, Jack Wilson? Never seen him do a day's work in his life!" A perception, however, which dates from the post-1890 Ghost Dance years, or when the Prophet's shamanic practice and sale of thaumaturges were primary sources of livelihood.

EARLY RELIGIOUS INFLUENCES

Since Numu-tibo'o was a medicine man, Numu shamanism had to have influenced the Prophet. But so too did the Wilsons. They were "strict" or devout United Presbyterians. What impact, and how, did their brand of frontier Protestantism have upon the young Numu Prophet, who not only worked on their ranch but took meals with them as well?

"When Jack or his family worked for Mr. Wilson," Genevieve Chapin told Dangberg (1968:26-27), "they all came for breakfast. Mr. Wilson was a devout Christian and every morning after breakfast he would read a few chapters from the Bible aloud before they started to work." In the Dangberg Notes, J. I. Wilson even outlined those theological discussions: "Mr. Wilson talked to him [Wovoka] about religion. [Wilson] Was a United Presbyterian. [He] Told Jack about Jesus — resurrection, etc. Not to steal or lie — [and also the] doctrine of peace." And in yet another entry, "M. Wilson" (J. W. Wilson?) was quoted by Dangberg as stating that Wovoka "didn't get [the] Messiah idea from [the] Wilsons" (cf. Dangberg 1968:27). Rather, Wilson felt that it came as a result of the Prophet asking David Wilson "about life after death, happy hunting ground. [He used to] Talk to them a lot about that." This same source also contrasted Wovoka's temperament as a youth with that of his brothers, who were said to be "not religious themselves, [but were] pretty devilish, mischievous." In light of their historical linkage with the 1890 Ghost Dance Prophet, any defensiveness on the part of Wilson family members — "the most famous Wilson so far" was how J. W. Wilson evaluated Wovoka (cf. Appendix E) — would readily be understandable. Grace Dangberg's (1968:6) conclusion on the basis of interviews with Wilson family members in the 1920s, therefore, is important:

> It is probable that the attendance at the Wilson family devotions was merely perfunctory, that Wovoka and his playmates J. W. Wilson and J. I. Wilson were uneasy, restless listeners to the Biblical stories in archaic English and that they rushed from the readings and prayers to the outdoors where they could play pranks and where Wovoka taught the lively Wilson boys to speak Paiute. It is quite natural that anyone failing to distinguish some of the elemental concepts common to all, or most, prophecy would make an effort in this instance to link the prophet living on the Walker River and in the Walker Lake area to men or to a single divine person, who led his people two thousand years ago on the banks of the Jordan and the shores of the Sea of Galilee.

"Archaic English" no doubt refers to the 1611 King James Bible used by 19th century Presbyterians, but which chapters and verses were read in the young Numu's presence is unfortunately not known. We do know, however, that it was the so-called "Princeton Theology of the Old School" which dominated Presbyterian intellectual life in the 19th century. Joseph H. Hall (1987:5) described its belief system as the "salvific work of

Christ's grace through faith," and Michael C. Coleman (1985:81) recently remarked the following about frontier American Presbyterianism:

> Their Calvinistic Protestantism was monotheistic and exclusive. It was centered on a sovereign God who was first cause of all things... requiring the free allegiance of all men, and decreeing that those who rejected him should fall to hell for all eternity.

The discussion by Coleman (1985:10) about its social ethics is especially pertinent for this study.

> ...its activities included antislavery agitation, black colonization, female moral reform. Bible and tract distribution, Sunday schools, temperance, the suppression of vice and the promotion of good morals, anti-tobacco reform, and home, foreign, and Indian missions.

None of these injunctions belonged to 1890 Ghost Dance ideology. However, the Prophet himself did not drink and was involved in a local Baptist Temperance Society in his middle years. And since we have no evidence whether or not the Wilsons demonstrated Missouri Presbyterian opposition even to "the acceptable social amenity of taking a social drink when offered (Hall 1987:8-9), their abstinence can only be hypothesized as having impacted upon Wovoka. Like Numu shamans, who used wild tobaccos during cures, the 1890 Ghost Dance Prophet also then smoked; unlike them, however, he abstained from recreational smoking. Here again, then, the same questions as before must be asked: (1) Did the Wilsons smoke? (2) If not, was this out of religious conviction? (3) Did they either directly or indirectly dissuade Wovoka from the habit?

Coleman (1985:42), furthermore, has remarked that frontier Presbyterian missionaries were also opposed to gambling, social dancing, Native American traditional religions, and in particular, syncretic religions such as the 1890 Ghost Dance.

There is but one reference to the Prophet ever gambling. "Jack got to gambling," Mrs. Webster, in the Dangberg Notes, remarked. "[When he] lost money, [Mr.] Webster [was] asked to get it back. Indians [then] said, 'He's not God, he's not Christ. No got to gamble, [because] if he gambles, he [should] win.' "[4] The implication here is that whether a sore loser or not, Wovoka quit gambling after his loss and the East Walker Valley rancher had refused to help him retrieve his money. Since Yerington Paiutes contrast their own strong appetite for gaming with their Prophet's abstinence, it is only reasonable to question whether or not Wovoka's seeming change of heart had anything to do with his exposure to Presbyterianism. Certainly there weren't any proscriptions against gambling in the 1890 Ghost Dance — compared, for example, with John Slocum's Shakerism (Barnett 1957).

As for social dancing, here again the evidence is wanting. Since a collective dance involving men and women was at the core of the religion Wovoka founded, the actual stance of the Wilsons toward 1890 Ghost Dance ceremonies, as well as to Harvest Moon Balls, New Year's Eve dances, and the like held in Smith Valley and Mason Valley, would be important to uncover. We might safely assume a modicum of strain in the friendship between David (and Abigail) Wilson and their "adopted" son, the Numu Prophet, if only because their "strict" Presbyterianism required opposition to any traditional form of Native American worship. Was this, then, the contributing element behind the Wilson cant that Wovoka was a "fake?" And given frontier Presbyterian opposition to new or syncretic religions invented by Native Americans following their exposure to Christianity (cf. Coleman 1985:81), we can, on principle, hypothesize Wilson family outrage with Wovoka on account of his creative attempt to blend the Judeo-Christian ethics they taught him with his own traditional Numu beliefs.

Education, however, was a positively championed value by early Presbyterians, despite its evangelical outlook. Hall (1987:19) discussed their recognition of a "great need of frontier education, [and for] making regular use of the newspaper media as a means of propagating its concerns." We have already seen in Chapman that the 1890 Ghost Dance Prophet favored schools and a Western education for Numus (cf. Plate E). Special Indian Agent Lafayette Dorrington also stated as much in 1917: "He sends his own relatives to the Carson Indian School and advises others to do likewise" (Stewart 1977:222). And as we shall see, one of the major prophecies attributed to Wovoka concerned the performance of his grandson, Harlyn Vidovich, in the public schools. Might we, then, not also attribute the Prophet's positive evaluation of a Western-style education to his exposure to frontier Presbyterianism?

Recall, too, the doctrine of racial equality in Chapman's rendition of the Great Revelation. Presbyterians, as Coleman (1985:139-170) so persuasively argued, stressed "grace, not race"; in other words, color this 19th century American religion ethnocentric but not racist, Coleman wrote. If "Heaven was for the white man, too," then by this shift in racial emphasis alone, the core of Wovoka's new religion can also be seen as possibly deriving from 19th century Presbyterian missionaries (cf. Coleman 1985:43).

Moreover, if the racial egalitarianism preached by Wovoka ("All [were] brothers and [we] must remain in peace") was yet another result of the Prophet's exposure to frontier Presbyterianism on the Wilson Ranch, one is also tempted to suggest a connection between the formal eschatology of the 1890 Ghost Dance Religion and that burning ambition of American Presbyterians. This ambition was for a "Christian civilization...this vision of a Godly American civilization...a millennial vision, driving them to cleanse their nation so that it could fulfill its awesome responsibility of leading the other peoples into the thousand-year Kingdom of Christ on earth" (Coleman 1985:33).[5]

Beyond these speculations, we do know for certain that the first Presbyterian church in Nevada was built in Carson City in 1861. By 1892, there were seven in the state, though none yet in Smith Valley, Mason Valley, or Pine Grove (Angel 1881:580-81). Perhaps this explains why Billy, Joe, and George Wilson were baptized on June 25, 1875 in the Methodist Episcopal Church (*Mason Valley News,* 18 July 75). Regarding the denomination, we read in the *Mason Valley News* (20 August 1876) that "in 1879 [the Methodist Episcopal Church had] approximately 35 members, the circuit was divided and the Yerington Church became part of the Mason Valley-Pine Grove circuit." The very first Methodist Episcopal Church was built in Yerington in 1880, interestingly enough, without Wilson financial support. Because the Wilson boys were baptized in 1875 by a Methodist-Episcopal missionary, and baptism may have figured prominently in Wovoka's religion, here is yet another possible intersection between the two religious traditions which blended to become the 1890 Ghost Dance. For Presbyterians practiced baptismal immersion, while Methodists favored sprinkling three drops (or "three waves") of holy water (Sockman 1963:129), and Wovoka had his followers bathe in the Walker River after the Miracle of the Block of Ice from Heaven. "Shortly thereafter, at Jack's order, the whole bunch stripped and plunged into the river," according to Ed Dyer. Did the 1890 Ghost Dance Prophet adopt this Pharisaic custom from the Wilsons? While this question, too, cannot yet be answered, Dangberg's Composition Notebook and the Wier Notes do contain valuable leads regarding Wovoka's religious acculturation.

In the Dangberg Composition Notebook, for example, there is this comment about Wovoka made by J. I. Wilson:

> Jack began to be prominent at 18 but old men did not honor the
> youngster's raving. He was so intimate with the David Wilson
> family that he often attended family prayers, morning and evening

and heard them read of the Bible. He also saw much of the honor, deference — money paid to [an] itinerant preacher. He sometimes attended the evangelistic meetings. When J. [Jack] was present at prayers, [he was] very reverent, respective. Never knelt however.

J. I. Wilson is referring here to "saddle-bag riders," those traveling evangelists who carried the Protestant banner to Tibo'o of the Walker River area. Jesse L. Bennett of the Methodist-Episcopal Church, for example, preached in Carson City as early as 1859 (Davis 1913:565), and the Rev. R. Carberry held services in Mason Valley for the United Community Methodist Church, which was part of the Walker River circuit and included Smith Valley, Pine Grove, and Antelope Valley. Gunard Solberg learned that yet another early Methodist circuit rider was Reverend Willis, the father of Carrie Willis, married to J. I. Wilson. These so-called "saddle-bag riders," or preachers, encouraged daily prayer and "concerts of prayer." Their revivals, as Hall (1987:27) wrote, took the form of "short, two or three day 'sacramental seasons,' which were usually held on weekends; they also favored the camp meeting and the local protracted church meeting." We previously heard the recollection by David Wilson's son of how his father used to talk to Wovoka about "religion...resurrection...not to steal or lie...[the] doctrine of peace." This same Wilson also told Wier that Wovoka not only witnessed revival meetings of "circuit riders [who] were here then," but was deeply "impressed" with them. J. I. Wilson observed in the Wier Notes: "Jack [believed he] could save Indians from hell fire," which further establishes the importance of Christianity in the making of the 1890 Ghost Dance Prophet and his religion. But still the question remains, which Bible stories did David and Abigail Butler Wilson read to their young Numu ward?

"It is highly likely that all of the mission teaching (to Indians) was 'strongly stamped with a Christian character,'" Coleman (1985:16) commented upon Presbyterian missionary efforts to the Osage, Omaha, Choctaw, and Nez Perce. According to Grace Dangberg (1957, 1968), the Gospels greatly impressed Wovoka — in particular, the miracles attributed to the messiah-magician from Galilee. That the cures and miracles attributed to Christ would have been entirely consonant with those tales of wonder heard by a Walker River area Numu in the 1880s can easily enough be assumed (Park 1938). More importantly, Wovoka would have been familiar with the latter, if only because his own father was a powerful medicine man. But why not tales of Old Testament prophets or miracle-workers as well? Why couldn't the Wilsons have read from Hebrew prophets, and these have been equally as formative in shaping Wovoka's missionary career?

"Young Indians studied [in the mission schools], or were required to study, the Scriptures, the *Shorter Catechism* of the PCUSA, psalms, and hymns, committing portions to memory," Coleman (1985:16) wrote about the Presbyterian foreign mission. Dyer, as we have seen, commented that Old Testament prophets heavily impacted upon the young Wovoka. Mooney (1896:929-30) himself wrote: "At Sinai, the Lord declares to Moses, 'I come up unto thee in a thick cloud....' Moses goes up into a mountain to receive inspiration like Wovoka of the Paiute." Although Mooney here was only thinking comparatively, his subsequent mention of another Hebrew prophet might be instructional. "As Wovoka claims to bring rain or snow at will, so Elijah said, 'there shall not be dew nor rain these years, but according to my word'" (Mooney ibid.). Elijah was the Tishbite who proclaimed the word of God during the wicked reigns of the Israelite Kings Ahab and Ahaziah and bodily ascended to Heaven. Elijah must return to resolve all world differences before the Messiah can appear, whereupon the dead shall be resurrected, and who executes God's command to slay Samael [Satan] and banish evil altogether (Ginzburg 1909:585-600).

The following parallels, I argue, evidence similarities enough with the miracles and prophecies of Wovoka to warrant consideration that David and Abigail Wilson might have read to the young Numu from Hebrew Prophets such as Elijah, in addition to the Glad Tidings of Jesus of Nazareth:[6] "But after a while the stream dried up, for the country had no rain (I Kings 17:7-8); "Please a little water in a vessel for me to drink" (I Kings 17:11-12); "Then he stretched out over the child three times, and cried out to the Lord saying, 'O Lord my God, let this child's life return to his body!'" (I Kings 17:21). Wovoka, too, as we shall now see, also brought rain during a drought, and was believed to have produced water magically in a tub or basket to satisfy the thirst of a large throng of assembled Numus. He became a healer, and, according to one source, anyway, the 1890 Ghost Dance Prophet similarly revived a dead child. Coincidences? Mere analogies? Clues might be gained by examination of the 1890 Ghost Dance Religion in its Walker River homeland.

ENDNOTES

1. Unless the Prophet had previously been married — i.e., the report of him living with a Virginia City woman and her children — Bailey's assertion that Wovoka had met Mary Wilson ("Maggie" in the

Tenth Census) in 1887 must surely be erroneous. It should also be noted that, in Smith Valley, a 20-year-old named "Piute Jack," reported to be married to a 26-year-old Numu woman named "Jenny" in 1880, was said to be the father of "Little Jimmie" (age 2) and a six-month-old baby. If "Piute Jack" was Wovoka, then either Mary Wilson's name was "Jenny" or the 1890 Ghost Dance Prophet had previously been married. Assuming the identifications made in Chapter Three are therefore correct, the listing of an 80-year-old "stepfather" named **Wachochi** and a 60-year-old Numu woman in Numu-tibo'o's household suggest the respective names of Wovoka's step-grandfather and grandmother.

2. George Wilson, as already stated, was the third Wilson son. There were two sisters as well: Louisa Wilson Plummer (1855-1889 or 1890) and Elizabeth Jane Wilson MacGowen (1881-1947). I wish to thank John "Frank" McGowen of Yerington at this point for supplying a photocopy of the David and Abigail Wilson family tree.

3. Numus, as a rule, did not work in the silver and gold mines which joined ranching and farming as the third major component of the Walker River regional economy (Kerstein 1961).

4. Numu Tom Mitchell owned a gambling house at the Yerington Indian Colony yet, according to those who knew him, Wovoka never went there to gamble, even though the 1890 Ghost Dance Prophet lived close enough by.

5. According to Coleman (1985:40-41), Presbyterian officials took credit for quieting the 1890 Ghost Dance on the Plains, "where missions had been novel or known, 'fanaticism, revolt and bloodshed had prevailed.' But...among those Sioux where missions have been longest established 'the Indians have stood like a rock, unmoved amidst the prevailing excitement and war.'"

6. Allen Chaves, Dean of Admissions at Long Island University, and a Presbyterian minister himself, informs me that frontier Presbyterianism would have drawn much inspiration from the Hebrew Bible, especially *Prophets*.

CHAPTER 4

The 1890 Ghost Dance Religion

"In a stricken hour comes the word of the prophet"
(Heschel 1962:23).

Although "Ghost Dance" is the name of the religious movement inspired by the Great Revelation of Jack Wilson or Wovoka, in Northern Paiute, as Mooney (1896:791) rightly observed, "it is called **nanigukwa,** 'dance in a circle.'" According to Angus McCloud (Wier Notes), a settler of Mason Valley who witnessed one of its early ceremonies, "Jack calls [it] the Friendship Dance of the Indian race." Unfortunately, Yerington Paiutes can only vaguely recall those "dances" Jack Wilson "put up;" so, before any reconstruction of the 1890 Ghost Dance can be attempted, some general points about this religion need to be summarized.

1.   The Prophet Wovoka probably experienced "minor" visions before his Great Revelation, which took place on New Year's Day 1889.

2.   On that date, while chopping wood in the Pine Grove Mountains he heard a "great noise." The Numu then lay aside his axe and headed directly toward its source, whereupon he fainted.

3.   Alternatively, Wovoka's Altered State of Consciousness was precipitated by a high fever, possibly scarlet fever.

4.   A Near-Death Experience was the result of the "great noise" he heard, his feverish delirium, or both. However long the Prophet remained comatose — "dead" — his awakening, or "rebirth," occurred during a solar eclipse.

5.   Numus living in the Walker River area interpreted the Prophet's spontaneous recovery on that date as his having "saved" the Sun, their principal deity; that is, Wovoka prevented the ending of this universe, an apocalyptic belief they held.

6.   Upon reviving, he announced that he had been to Heaven and conversed with "God."

7.   There, Wovoka saw "all the dead people," his own mother in-

cluded, and Tibo'o as well. Everyone was turned young again, well fed, dancing, and blissfully happy.

8. "God" then gave him power (bbooha) over the natural elements: 5 songs equaling 5 powers to make rain, snow, etc.

9. "You will now co-share the American Presidency with Benjamin Henry Harrison," God also told Wovoka. "Harrison will be President of the East, you, Jack Wilson, will be President of the West!" Or, quoting the words of Abraham Heschel (1962:xiv), this formerly obscure Numu wood-cutter from the Walker River area of Nevada had been chosen by God to become "a poet, preacher, patriot, statesman, social critic, moralist."

10. Other instructions to the new Prophet from On High included the injunction of certain Judeo-Christian apodictic laws: no lying, no stealing, no wars. Moreover, he was told that Numus should learn to get along with each other and with other tribes, and with Tibo'o as well, for whom they should additionally work.

11. Wovoka was also told by God that Numus, and probably other Native Americans who lived in the United States, were to perform a tra-ditional dance lasting three (according to Chapman) or five (according to Mooney) nights in succession. The Indian scout Chapman reported the ceremony should be repeated in three months.

12. Finally, the Numu Prophet learned of a reward awaiting the strict adherents of his "Great Revelation" — rejuvenated youth in Heaven. Thus, the so-called 1890 Ghost Dance Religion.

■ ■ ■

"Look out for the eclipse next Thursday." One week after the *Lyon County Times* carried this item on page 1 of its December 29, 1888 issue, the following account of the eclipse was given:

> Tuesday morning opened cold and cloudy, and everybody gave up the idea of seeing the eclipse, but the fog and clouds cleared away about 10 o'clock and the sun came out bright and clear. About the time the "moon began to eat up the sun," as the Mongolian put it, everybody in the community was on hand with a piece of smoked glass to witness the show. At 20 minutes past twelve the eclipse began, and at ten minutes of two it was total; at eleven minutes past three it had passed. At the time of totality, the thermometer low-ered from seven to eight degrees, and it was very cold. The darkness was so great that chickens sought their roost, and several stars were plainly visible. There were no scientific observations taken here (*Lyon County Times,* 5 January 1889).

Unlike the Shawnee Prophet Tenskwatawa, who predicted the 1806 eclipse (Mooney 1896:674), Wovoka apparently never claimed such powers. Yerington Paiutes today profess no memory at all linking his Great Revelation to the total eclipse of January 1, 1889. But neither do they recall Wovoka's sickness, which was emphasized by Tibo'o living in Smith and Mason valleys. Genevieve Chapin nee Wilson told Dangberg (1968:7n7a): "When Jack was a young man he had a terrible illness, a fever. He was in a coma and near death for days, and he believed he talked with God." Also in the Dangberg Composition Notebook we read: "Jack was not well. Men were chanting over him. Mr. Plummer stayed awhile. Soon after Indians said he died and came back."

In regard to this, we read in the *Lyon County Times* that on February 10, 1887 scarlet fever was raging in Reno, while on June 6, 1887 the same newspaper quoted Johnson Sides's statement that not since 1864 had smallpox and measles killed so many Numus. The following year, 1888, scarlet fever was said to have taken its toll on Numus living in Dayton and Reno, and on April 18, 1988, reporting these epidemics in Smith and Mason valleys, the *Lyon County Times* wrote: "There is hardly a buck, squaw or papoose that is not afflicted with the malady."

Part of this confusion, Mooney (1896:772) wrote, was that the Prophet might have had "different revelations...from time to time." Dangberg (1968:27-30), on the basis of David Wilson's son's comment, proposed 1879 as the year of Wovoka's Great Revelation, dating the earliest 1890 Ghost Dance ceremony seven years later in 1886. Mooney (1896:772) attempted to resolve the "discrepancy of statement" by stating that, although the Prophet's "death" had occurred "two or three years prior to his [1892] visit," the religion Wovoka founded probably began "four years" earlier, in 1888. By the same token, Mooney (1896:802) also wrote that the very first Ghost Dance ceremony was held on the Walker River Reservation in early January of 1889. Can the local newspapers help to resolve this confusion?

"The Mason Valley Piutes [sic] are having big dances every night now," or so the *Lyon County Times* stated on December 22, 1888. But how can one be certain that this was a "Ghost Dance" rather than another Numu ceremony? We can immediately rule out the Pine Nut Festival, the ceremonial occasion par excellence, when Numus came together to express their unity as a People (Steward and Wheeler-Voegelin 1974:48, Fowler and Liljeblad 1986:453), since these were held in the fall. Christmas celebrations are another possibility. However, Numus living in Smith and

Mason valleys were not yet Christians in 1888 and did not celebrate Christmas until the Yerington Indian Colony was founded in 1917, when a Roman Catholic mission was established (Hittman 1984). Yet a third candidate for these "dances held every night now" were celebrations held in honor of Numus departing for harvest work in the Sonoma and Mendocino County hop fields in California, except that these "departure" dances were held in August rather than December. If December 22, 1888, then, is the actual date of the start of 1890 Ghost Dance ceremonies, Chapman, Mooney, and Bailey were correct to distinguish between "Ghost Dances" held before and after the solar eclipse of January 1, 1889.

Unfortunately, the earliest account of any Numu's acceptance of the new religion was not recorded until December of 1890, when Captain James Josephus of the Walker River Reservation confessed to Chapman that he was not a follower at the beginning of Wovoka's ministry. Josephus's conversion, as we have seen, occurred after Wovoka had prophesied the end of a regional drought, which was adversely affecting Walker River Reservation Numu crops; he became a true believer in "the new Messiah" only when those rains came, and within the prophesied unit of three days time.

And we do, indeed, read of drought in those years in the local newspapers. The *Lyon County Times* on September 1, 1888 reported that "there is not a particle [of water] in the lower end of Mason Valley, and ranchers there have to dig wells to obtain water for stock." Snow was reported that winter; but by February 23 of the new year we learn that "much more snow is needed in the mountains to insure sufficient water next summer to run our milch and irrigate our ranches." Seven months later, however, the *Lyon County Times* (11 May 1889) indicated that farmers and ranchers had much reason to rejoice:

> The late storm has been of incalculable value to this State. Nearly every portion of the country has received a thorough soaking, and the amount of snow that has fallen in the mountains is sufficient for a good supply of water in the rivers until next fall.

By early August of 1889, conditions remained the same: "There is plenty of water in Mason Valley since the storm." On the other hand, the *Lyon County Times* correspondent who reported on Smith Valley could state that as of the tenth of that month of August, D. C. Simpson of Desert Creek Ranch was calling this "the driest season ever known in Nevada." The prognosis on September 21, 1889 was the same: "And still there are no signs of rain." A few months later, though, the drought fortunately ended:

> The terrible drought has at last been broken.... Taken all in all
> the weather conditions during October have been very favorable
> and farmers, cattle and milkmen are in consequence jubilant,
> the prospects being better at present than they have been for
> several months past (*Lyon County Times*, 23 November 1889).

It is important here to contrast the situation of the Toboose tukadu of Smith and Mason valleys with Walker River Reservation Numus, who were successfully farming since 1872 (Hittman 1973b). In discussing their history, former Walker River Reservation Tribal Chairman Ed Johnson (1975:62) wrote that around the time of Wovoka's new religion, "Crops of alfalfa were harvested and a good deal of farming was going on." Johnson (ibid.) implies just how devastating that regional drought would have been to Numu agriculture by quoting from the 1894 Annual Report to the Commissioner of Indian Affairs of the farmer-in-charge: "'[There were] 1,868 (more or less) acres under cultivation which is divided into 54 ranches and farmed by 63 persons.... [These] Indians have about 120 moderately good work horses.'" Unfortunately we do not know the exact date of Josephus's visit to the Prophet. Because the Numu policeman was appealing to Wovoka to employ his vaunted weather control powers, and the regional drought did not end until the following November, Josephus's conversion can safely be dated to have occurred after the Great Revelation. And the 1890 Ghost Dance Prophet's weather control powers were, of course, described by Mooney (1896:772-73):

> From his uncle [Charley Sheep], I learned that Wovoka has five
> songs for making it rain, the first of which brings on a mist or
> cloud, the second a snowfall, the third a shower, and the fourth
> a hard rain or storm, while when he sings the fifth song the
> weather again becomes clear.

By accurately prophesying rain, Walker River Reservation Numus with their crops saved would have been convinced that Wovoka had powers over the natural elements, just the sort of "spectacular demonstration" Charles Erasmus (1961) hypothesized is essential for audience acceptance of most innovators of change — the "sign," as Max Weber (1947) pioneered, of charismatic leadership. Certainly the 1890 Ghost Dance Prophet was always depicted in the local newspapers as a "Rain Maker" and the "Great Weather prophet."[1] Thus, under the heading "Rain Dance," the *Lyon County Times* on April 20, 1889 wrote: "The Piutes [sic] of Mason Valley had a big rain dance last week. Their big man who formerly brought rain when they desired it, died last summer, and therefore they have taken it upon themselves to pray for rain in their peculiar manner." Again, on August 3, 1889: "The great weather prophet is said to be a fine looking man, much resembling the late Henry Ward Beecher." The *Walker Lake Bulletin* on November 12, 1890 stated:

> This so-called Messiah first gained notoriety at the Walker Lake Reservation early last winter. The Indians wanted rain, and they assembled in conclave, and the Messiah appeared, and they asked for water — not fire water. The result was that the most severe storms of that stormy winter followed. After about a month of incessant rain and snow the Indians had enough, and again they sought the Messiah and asked him to let up. And lo and behold, the clouds rolled by, and soon the papers began blowing about the fine climate.

C. C. Warner, the Indian agent whose indifference to the 1890 Ghost Dance had so greatly aggravated Mooney, also reported the following about the new religion to the Commissioner of Indian Affairs from Pyramid Lake:

> Wovoka had obtained his notoriety by telling the Indians that he would invoke the Great Spirit and bring rain (after there had been a drought of two years)...and it so happened that his promised invocation was in the commencement of our severe winter of 1889 and 1890, during which time it stormed incessantly from October to April (Annual Report to the Commissioner of Indian Affairs 1890/1891:300).

Drought in the Walker River area a century ago was serious enough to have prompted the *Lyon County Times* editor, on October 3, 1891, to print a page 1 article evaluating the efficacy of "Rain Makers" in general. For our concern, however, it is more important to emphasize that Wovoka's powers over natural elements was rooted in traditional Numu culture and is also part of Wovoka's enduring legacy among contemporary Toboose tukadu descendants.

Practically every Yerington Paiute today could recall the following anecdote about the 1890 Ghost Dance Prophet. Numu men were either playing baseball or pitching hay, or the incident involved Tibo'o, in any event, Wovoka was walking along on that hot sunny day and one of them teasingly called out to him, "Hey, Rain-Maker, let's see if you can make it rain!" A cloud in that otherwise clear blue sky immediately appeared, and he had to be begged to "call off his powers," lest the baseball game or their crops be ruined. In yet another anecdote, Corbett Mack stated that Wovoka was replanting a tree for an employer in Smith Valley one day when suddenly it began to rain. Still he kept on working, the Prophet was neither frightened by the lightning and thunder, nor, miraculously, did he get wet at all. Irene Thompson of Smith Valley related what her mother, Sadie Brown (b. 1885?), had told her about the Prophet's weather control powers. How Wovoka could "start up" the wind simply by blowing on hot charcoal which, incidentally, he could apply to his bare forearms without burning himself.

But there were other spectacular demonstrations over the weather as well. We have already seen how bereavement associated with the death of his son led Wovoka to unleash such torrential rainstorms that the homes of Numus in Smith and Mason valleys were reportedly threatened with washouts. In variants of this story, Tom Mitchell, a powerful shaman in his own right, or Blind Bob Roberts, **tuneggwukeadu**, or "designated shamanic repeater and interpreter," had to beg the grieving Prophet to finally call off his bbooha before those rains actually ceased. And Wovoka was also said to be able to light his pipe by the sun and could form icicles in his hands (cf. Appendix K). "Wrapped in a blanket," Bob Dyer in the Wier Notes commented similarly, "[he went into a] trance, and when he came to [Wovoka] had ice in his hand." If Wovoka, then, was like the charismatic prophet Samuel (I Samuel 12:16-17), who was able to control thunder and rain during the harvest season, then, similar to Elijah and Jesus, he could also call for an empty receptacle in order to miraculously quench the thirst of indeterminate numbers of people — the so-called "Inexhaustible Cruise," a motif which is found in oral literature around the globe (cf. Gaster 1969). But Numus were not alone in believing that Wovoka could control the weather.

For example, Geraldine Webster, an East Walker River settler, told Dangberg (1968:27):

> Dan Simpson believed in Jack. One year during a drought (1887-1889), Jack went to Mr. Simpson and promised to make it rain if Mr. Simpson would give him three beeves. Mr. Simpson refused but later when his cattle began to die, he promised Jack one beef if he would make it rain. The storm came; even after this Mr. Simpson kept Jack in beef.

And we also read in the Dangberg Composition Notebook: "For five years [Wovoka] never missed a prophecy concerning weather and sun dogs ('86-'90)." Mrs. Webster, our source, additionally related to Dangberg how one spring day, when she had begun to clean house, the 1890 Ghost Dance Prophet appeared. "This [was] May of '91 or '92," she recalled, and Wovoka said to her: "'Thursday, Frid[Friday] and S[Saturday] and S[Sunday] [it] would storm [so] have the washing done.' [When the] storm came, [Wovoka said,] 'Look n.e. — sky. Jack make everybody know today he's God.'" To which Mrs. Webster added, "Mr. W[Webster] said he would use him for weather vane." "Jack accurately prophecied [sic] all storms," Grace Dangberg (1968:13) also argued: "It is generally conceded by residents of Mason valley that Wovoka correctly prophesied the 'hard winter' of 1889-1890; some claimed that he accurately foretold all storms occurring between 1886 and 1891 or 1892." While J. W. Wilson, in discussing Wovoka's reply to a written appeal from Plains Indians for spiritual guidance and healing amulets, gave this additional testimony regarding the importance of rainmaking to Wovoka's reputation:

> The letters to Jack were from Indians who were always asking Jack to make it rain more and to cure their people who were ill with diseases in imaginary diseases. Therefore, when Jack wrote a letter to the patient he would always insist that his own letter close with the statement that, "We have lots of rain here and my people are all very well and happy" (Dangberg 1957:285).

According to James Long, a quarter-blood from Oswego, Montana, Jack Wilson "sent his correspondents red paint with which to decorate themselves before a rain, and instructed them to stand out in the rain and let the drops wash it off" (Dangberg 1957:286). Finally, Andy Vidovich's conversation with Peg Wheat can be cited as solidifying the case that Wovoka, from the very beginning of his career, was perceived as a rainmaker or weather prophet both by Walker River area Numus and Tibo'o as well. Torrential amounts of rain had fallen in Pine Grove during pine nut gathering time, his son-in-law stated (Vidovich-Wheat Tape 90:6-7). Although not uncommon in that area, the storm that year caused their tents to leak and soaked their firewood through and through. When a group of Numus finally petitioned Wovoka to employ his weather control powers, he ordered them first to pile up their wet wood. Wovoka then asked for an eagle plume, about which Vidovich remarked, "It's part of the back feathers, it's so fine, it would quiver and shake with the slightest o' breeze." And in characterizing the Prophet's actions, then, he stated:

He was a big man, tall in that wind and rain and everything. He sticks up that eagle plume up there [in mid-air] as high as he could reach. He took it [his hand] [down] and that eagle plume stayed up there. Then he knelt down and waited a little while and then, maybe he hit two rocks together, I don't know what he did, anyway, a spark came and that wood began to burn. All that wet wood and everything.

"Everything," that is, except for the eagle feather that the 1890 Ghost Dance Prophet had borrowed, or so Andy Vidovich stated, it "turned the most beautiful color you ever see." And in quoting his father-in-law's words about that miracle, Vidovich also related:

Take from this fire to your tent, your tepee, build your fires. The rain will go on but your food will get dry and your tents will be dry, your tepees will be dry, and everything will be all right.

But in contrast to Walker River Reservation congeners, Numus living in Smith and Mason valleys did not yet own their own lands in 1889. Men found seasonal-to-permanent employment as cowboys, breaking mustangs, and driving cattle and sheep to and from summer pasture, and as farm hands who performed all the labor-intensive jobs associated with the alfalfa, barley, and wheat complex. (They received $1.25/day during harvest time and $1.50 for stacking hay, while Tibo'o earned $40/month and board and $60/month for stacking" (*Lyon County Times,* 31 May 1890). Numu women worked as cooks and secured additional wage labor by washing dishes and clothing on those same farms and ranches, and in the local hotels at Pine Grove, Mason, and Yerington. Wovoka's insistence in his Great Revelation that Numus always work industriously for their (Tibo'o) employers might therefore follow from this. It is also probable to note that the Prophet's God-given weather control songs would, in effect, have afforded him power over the entire Walker River area regional economy. For the moment, however, it is more important to note that the regional drought of 1888-1889 would have more diversely affected the Numus in Smith and Mason valleys with loss of jobs than Walker River Reservation Numus. However, because they were not yet landowners, their reasons for acceptance of the weather-control powers of Wovoka had to have been different from those of their kinsmen living at the Walker River Reservation. What, then, might their initial reasons for acceptance of Wovoka have been? Here again, perusal of the *Lyon County Times* becomes instructive.

Recalling Chapman's statement about the "great noise" which preceded the Prophet's original revelation, we find in the local newspaper on March 24, 1888 mention of "rumbling noises" in Smith Valley that sent Hinds Hot Springs 10 to 15 feet in the air. On June 16 of that same year we read of 40-mile-an-hour winds occurring most days that month, killing the fruit crop. Then, "a lunar eclipse was reported at eleven thirty at night on last Sunday," as reported on July 23, 1888. Also there were slight earthquake tremors in Smith Valley on August 18, 1888, followed by dense fog that struck on September 9, reportedly, the likes of which had never been seen before.

Mooney (1896:773) wrote that the January 1, 1889 eclipse caused grave alarm among the Numus in Smith and Mason valleys:

> On this occasion the Paiutes were frantic with excitement and the air was filled with the noise of shouts and wailings and the firing of guns, for the purpose of frightening off the monster that threatened the life of their god.

And while Ed Johnson (1975:47) feels that Mooney has probably stereotyped his people's reaction to eclipses, more than once I personally have observed attenuated alarm on the part of Numus living in Smith and Mason valleys during earth tremors. From Mammoth to Mono lakes, California, the entire area surrounding Smith and Mason valleys has been an active earthquake/volcanic zone for the past 2,000 years ("Science Section," *The New York Times*, 20 July 1982). And what fear an earthquake could engender among the local Tibo'o citizenry of the Walker River area is nicely revealed in an unpublished article by Edwin Ervin Webster, East Walker River settler (Lyon County Public Library, Yerington). Describing those sudden jolts which rocked Mason Valley for several months in the summer of 1874, Webster recalled that there were 6 to 8 shocks some days and at least one or more daily. They caused his cattle to jump to their feet and begin running helter-skelter, while his horses would stop on the trail to spread out their legs to prevent themselves from falling.

The suggestion here, then, is that those extraordinary climatological and geological events in the late 1880s, which culminated in the total solar eclipse of New Year's Day 1889, created a kind of angst for Numus living in Smith and Mason valleys, and the entire Walker River area. This created a stage onto which Wovoka stepped as shamanic manipulator of the weather, this being a traditional Numu social status.[2] It is important to note that Yerington Paiutes believe "ordinary" or powerless individuals can affect Nature. A woman can "call" or whistle for the wind to blow in the mountains late in the afternoon on a fall day during pine nut gathering season, when she wants to separate her seeds in the winnowing basket from empty shells. Similarly, one frequently hears the following admonition: "You don't want to make fun of the wind (or rain, or snow, etc.).[3] Yerington Paiutes also teach us never to tease a whirlwind or play near one because whirlwinds represent the souls of the dead, coupling this with the homily about a disobedient boy who did so and promptly died. One would no sooner trifle with the forces of nature than speak disparagingly of the amount of meat on a hunted deer carcass. Consider, then, the amount of control over the environment individuals who did possess weather bbooha would have been believed to exert.

The ethnographer, Willard Z. Park (1938:15), wrote that although shamanic weather control "is not usually exercised for the good of the community," certain individuals, "by waving a feather or by singing...may cause the clear sky to become cloudy, the wind to blow or rain to fall."

> They can also stop wind and rain or banish the clouds that they have brought. Although the predominant motive in weather-control is this exhibition of power, shamans have been known in the past to manipulate weather for the benefit of the community (Park ibid.).

Tom Mitchell told Park (1938:19): "The Indian doctors know the wind, clouds, and rain. A shaman talks to them. They are just like people, and they come. Anyone who makes fun of the thunder will be killed. One time a man at Schurz heard the thunder, and said, 'That is nothing. I am going to fight that thunder.' He went outside the house, and the thunder was heard overhead. He was hit by lightning and killed." I learned about a Toboose tukadu, **Pooggoo Mahanudu,** or "Horseman," who announced one day that the Hoye Store in Wellington would crumble when he rode past on his horse. (Presumably for slight, real or imagined.) So, after tying a feather onto his horse's tail, this powerful individual who, incidentally, was accused of being a witch and was killed with his own rifle by his grandson after a failed cure, then cantered past the general store. "Tibo'o came running outside the store because rocks were tumbling down the mountainside," more than one Yerington Paiute concurred. And in yet another example of weather control, during a forest fire in the Sweetwater Mountains, the father of **Naatse'ekwida's** ("Feces Boy") offered this prayer to the clouds: "I wish you would put the fire out." Rains, which immediately issued forth from the skies, extinguished the forest. Corbett Mack added parenthetically that, having personally seen the results of that forest fire, he felt Natsikwidi's father was more powerful than Wovoka.

A second anecdote involving this same "weather-control doctor," as Naatse'ekwida's father was called, concerned an eclipse. In Sweetwater Valley, California, when asked to intercede on behalf of his people who were then crying because they were freezing, Naatse'ekwida's father called for a gun, and with it prayed or "spoke" to the sun as follows: "I think I can turn you over." The shaman then fired, and the sun or this universe was said to have been saved. "That's why he's a very 'smart' [powerful] man," Corbett Mack concluded.

If Wovoka had had revelations prior to 1889, and the December 12, 1888 newspaper date records the very first 1890 Ghost Dance ceremony, then Numus living in Smith and Mason valleys might, like Josephus, have initially become true believers. This could have been based on their belief in the Prophet's having restored the Walker River area to "normalcy" during those climatological and geological anomalies of the late 1880s. Like those shamans mentioned by Park, who "manipulate[d] the weather for the benefit of the community," Wovoka achieved his early reputation as the master or shaman of unusual weather conditions and geological occurrences. In other words, with their belief in weather control doctors, he would have been perceived as having that power before the Great Revelation. Jay Miller's (1983) insightful discussion of bbooha is pertinent in this regard. Miller (1983:10), who calls this concept the "keystone" of Numu traditional religion, felt bbooha was "closely associated with water." Consider, then, the letter J. O. Gregory wrote to S.S. Sears about a 1890 Ghost Dance ceremony held on the Walker River Reservation in 1889:

> ...you will doubtless be amazed at the letter you will have received from Jack Wilson the prophet when this reaches you [sic] he has got the indians [sic] all wild at his wonderful command of the elements he claims that he alone is responsible for the storms of this season and they all firmly believe it. The letter he has written as he supposes to Washington is for the purpose of finding out if the government believes in him as a prophet. There was [sic] at least 200 Indians to say nothing of the squaws and papooses turned out yesterday in the face of a driving snow storm to see and hear him [sic] they took up quite a collection for his benefit fully $25 and they talk of nothing but Jack Wilson and the miracles he performs [sic] he would like to be allowed to come onto the Reservation to farm and guarantees the Indians that if the Government gives him permission to come he will

cause lots of rain to fall and they will never lose a crop again. They are expecting a reply to his letter and if you see fit to answer as in your judgement would be proper [cf. Appendix D].

One week and a half after the December 22, 1888 date, or what I argue were the first 1890 Ghost Dance ceremonies held, Wovoka's "death," or Near-Death Experience and Altered State of Consciousness, or Great Revelation occurred during the solar eclipse of January 1, 1889.

The intersection of the Prophet's sickness with the "loud noise" (i.e., those unusual weather conditions which he was believed to have controlled), was compounded by a regional drought, which led James Josephus to Wovoka's home to secure his self-advertised weather-control powers on behalf of Walker River Reservation Numus who were then farming. Wovoka's successful prophecy of spring rains in three day's time would have added yet another element into the new Prophet's swelling charisma. (Much as Thomas Overholt (1974) has analyzed the prophetic process as being a triadic "relationship of positive feedback" between the Supernatural, a charismatic individual, and his/her audience.) But there were also other powers demonstrated by Wovoka at social gatherings we call the 1890 Ghost Dance Religion: (1) the Miracle (or Prophecy) of the Block of Ice; (2) trances; and (3) the Prophet's invulnerability.

THE MIRACLE (OR PROPHECY) OF THE BLOCK OF ICE

"Regarding the ice episode," Ed Dyer wrote:

I can speak as an eye witness. My brother, Bob Dyer, who was also completely bilingual in Pahute [sic], and I became aware that some activity was going to take place which somehow concerned Jack Wilson. Upon learning the time and place we unobtrusively showed up to see what was afoot. The meeting took place along the river bank on a hot July day. A hundred or more Indians were present but there was no great excitement among them. Wilson was holding a sort of informal court at the side of a blanket spread upon the ground under a large cottonwood tree. Groups of Indians came up to talk to him and move away. Other small groups just milled around. We talked to some. They were distinctly not talkative to a white but we gathered that they expected Wilson to perform some miracle. Doo-mur-eye (accented on second syllable) they called it which means an act of wizardry. Suddenly a great outcry came from the group around Wilson. Every one rushed over to see what had happened. There in the center of the blanket lay a big block of ice some 25 or 30 pounds in weight. Wilson had caused it to come from the sky and the Indians explained to those who had their eyes turned the wrong way to see it for themselves.

Dyer commented that, "not being of my suspicious nature, Indians accepted the miracle in full faith." He also reported how Numus "ceremoniously" drank the melted water afterwards:

> It might have been sacramental wine judging from the solemnity. Shortly thereafter, at Jack's order, the whole bunch stripped and plunged into the river. It wasn't until years after that I realized that I had witnessed an aboriginal distortion of communion and baptism inspired by Biblical tales imperfectly understood.

In fact, Dyer scoffed at the entire episode:

> I was willing to believe it had fallen alright, but from no greater height than the top of that cottonwood tree, whose dense foliage would serve to hide the object until it sufficiently had melted to release it from whatever ingenious fastening Jack had fashioned to hold it for a time. That explained why the type of miracle was unspecified in advance. No Indian was likely to look up into the tree as he might if he were expecting ice from Heaven. It also explained the blanket. No Indian would stand on Jack's blanket and perhaps receive a pre- miracle icy drip, or worse, be beaned by the chunk itself.

Paul Bailey interviewed Ed Dyer, and Bailey's interpretation of this miracle appears to have been influenced by Dyer. While in the Wier Notes and the Dangberg Composition Notebook, Tibo'o comments run the gamut from viewing Wovoka as an innocent dupe of the Wilsons to a fun-loving "fraud." Genevieve Chapin nee Wilson, for example, was quoted in Grace Dangberg (1968:14n11) as follows:

> [Uncle] Billy was full of fun and played jokes on people all his life and Jack was smart and had a keen sense of humor and he played jokes on Billy and I firmly believe that in later life when Jack played some of the tricks on the Indians that the white people make so much of, trying to say that Jack was a fake, [they] were done with no intent to deceive or advance his greatness as a Messiah but because he had a sense of humor and did it for fun. He loved a joke and had a great wit. You will note in the story in Wovoka about the ice in the river in summertime

that Jack was assisted by Bill Wilson. They did it for fun in playing a practical joke. In later years it was construed to make it look like Jack did it to further his own cause.

Mrs. Chapin also told Wier, "Probably [Wovoka] got his ideas from them. Jack learned to play practical jokes by playing with the Wilson boys." An "awful fake but [I] wouldn't want to go on record as saying that," was the view of David Wilson's son expressed in Dangberg's Composition Notebook. The Wilson Ranch founder himself told Jenny Wier, "Jack is not capable of telling them things which are credited." George Plummer's statement (Wier Notes) is equally damning: "Jack Wilson told Mrs. D. [David] Wilson one day: 'I know there's nothing in it, but keep still. I get money from Indians.'"

But Yerington Paiutes take strong objection to these comments. "Whites made fun of him because he said he put ice in the river but I predict he did." "Yes, we believe him," another quite typically remarked. "If Jack Wilson said he was going to do it, then by God, he did! Why not? Because that was his power!" With his supernatural power over the weather, the Prophet could have produced ice in the summer they reasoned; prompting one, therefore, to imagine what kind and amount of faith their ancestors had in Wovoka at the time of the 1890 Ghost Dance. Be that as it may, the Miracle (or Prophecy) of the Block of Ice from Heaven logically enough suggests his weather control powers. And if the anonymous source quoted in Appendix H was correct about this miracle's date occurring on the Fourth of July, one gleans an aspect of the 1890 Ghost Dance which has previously been ignored in the literature: its political overtones. Not only did Wovoka with his divinely-revealed weather control powers implicitly gain control over all aspects of ranching and farming in the Walker River regional economy, the prophecy that ice would fall from the skies on that most important of all American holiday suggests a nascent attempt on this prophet's part to introduce a parallel ceremonial calendar.

TRANCES

"He went into trances in which he remained for as long as two days and when he awakened, announced that he had been to the Indian Heaven and was able to give a thorough-going description," Ed Dyer wrote. Dyer's brother, Bob, as we also have seen, told Dangberg that Wovoka "used to go into trance[s].... Wrapped in a blanket, trance, and when [he] came to [he] had ice in his hand." Continuing, Bob Dyer stated: "He went to Heavens through the Dipper or the Milky Way." And George Plummer told Wier that he once had seen Wovoka in a "supposed trance. Indians believed him to be in a trance. Only about one dozen [of] them then." Plummer's wife stated that "Jack's trances [were] not in connection with dance" (Wier Notes). "Several people [had] seen him in a trance this time," Dangberg (1968:27) concluded. The Prophet had been "ill with a severe fever; he was in a coma and near death for several days." And finally, Mrs. Plummer, the daughter of David and Abigail Wilson, recalled Wovoka's trances for Wier as follows:

> [It] started about a half mile west of here. Jack [w]as not well. Men chanting over him. Mr. Plummer stared awhile. Soon after Indians said he died and came back. All Indians believe that some Indians hold powers over others. Spirit power.

But in the Wier Notes "M. Wilson" (J. W. Wilson?) seems to be arguing that trances belonged to the phase of Wovoka's new religion corresponding with the arrival of visitors from Indian Territory:

> Messiahship — Big Dance — Indians from V. City, Bodie, Walker Lake — held in this [south] end of Valley. On Wilson Ranch. Biannual dances. All Indians lived in this end of Valley. Fall and Spring dances. Had a dance. Jack conceived the idea of being a prophet. Old fellows gathered in a circle and smoke a pipe — talk a little. Meanwhile others merry-making. Jack gave a big talk to whole trip [sic]. Proclaimed himself. Addressed whole trip [sic]. Unusual proceedings. Prophesied some things which came true. This a Spring dance. By Fall dance men came from Oklahoma. Didn't talk much. Less said the better for him. Big dance advertised for Fall. J. going into trance for the occasion. Many delegations.

> During dance went into 3 day trance. All Paiutes came. 2nd dance prophesied big wind and storm for three days. (Wind then storm) Plus shirt stunt. Prophesied trance then "came back" and told what he had seen. Even now in high repute [in] his own trip [sic].

Bob Dyer stated (Dangberg Notes) that the six sons born to Mary and Jack Wilson had died of epilepsy, but this disease can be ruled out as the source of Wovoka's trances because "M. Wilson," in the Dangberg Notes, related that "Jack never had epilepsy." James Mooney, on the other hand, explained them psychologically. He gave "catalepsy," "mental disturbance," and possibly self-hypnosis as their cause(s). Ignoring the ars magica of Numu culture as the possible source of Wovoka's trances, Mooney, who was followed in this regard by Bailey, further subscribed them to syncretic religions being developed by nearby Native Americans at the time — Smohalla's Dreamer Religion, and, in particular, Shakerism of the Pacific Northwest.

Smohalla was a Wanapum, from the Columbia River, who could enter trance states and was believed able to "control the sun" (Mooney 1896:718-19). After a remarkable journey which took him along the coast of California to San Diego and Mexico, Smohalla, called "The Shouting Mountain," was said to have returned home through Nevada. This, however, took place before Wovoka was born; and if we assume that the 1890 Ghost Dance Prophet had been contacted by one of Smohalla's disciples or learned of the Plateau religion — say while picking hops in the Pacific Northwest — opposition to farming, which was at the core of Smohallaism (Trafzer and Beach 1985), did not figure in the ideology of the 1890 Ghost Dance. Indeed, "Earth as Mother" would have found few adherents among Walker River area Numus, who, since the 1860s, strove to stand cheek to jowl with Tibo'o ranchers and farmers. Mooney felt that Shaker founder John Slocum's death and resurrection were more likely to have influenced Wovoka.

Pacific Northwest Shakers believed that the world would end on a Fourth of July (Mooney 896:749). Wovoka's miracle of the block of ice from Heaven in the summertime might have been deliberately given to coincide with American Independence Day. Furthermore, the comment by Mooney (1896:750) about Shakers practicing only the "strictest morality, sobriety, and honesty" could similarly be applied to Wovoka's new religion. However, Shakers doctrinally rejected whiskey, gambling, and horse racing also, and there is little or no evidence existing that the 1890 Ghost Dance Prophet ever spoke out against these vices.[4] Yet another seeming similarity between Shakerism and the 1890 Ghost Dance can be mentioned. A Shaker had declared himself to be "The Christ" and rode through the streets of Olympia, Washington, before being discredited (Mooney 1896:749), and the question exists whether or not Wovoka ever made the same claim. The Native American Presbyterian-like Shaker Church of the Pacific Northwest was "For Indians Only," whereas the 1890 Ghost Dance Prophet emphasized equality between the races, if not on earth then surely in Heaven. One might even speculate that Tibo'o were originally not excluded from Wovoka's ceremonies until a backlash of fear was generated by events on the High Plains. Were his trances then from Shakerism? "Quite a number of Piutes [sic] are going over the mountains to pick hops in California," the *Lyon County Times* on August 15, 1891 reported. And on November 12, 1892, "Our Indians [are] going every year to Sacramento to pick hops." And Homer Barnett (1957:45-46) noted "out-of-state" Indians who came over the Sierra Nevada Mountains from Nevada to pick hops and who attended Shaker ceremonies:

> There were annual congregations of all the tribes, from the Skokomish to the Puyallup, to celebrate the Fourth of July or to hold potlatches. In addition, there was a great amount of visiting between families on the different reservations who were related by blood or marriage. And above all, work in the hop fields at Puyallup each summer drew great numbers of Indians from all over the Puget Sound area, and even beyond from over the mountains. Reverend M. G. Mann, the Presbyterian missionary stationed at Puyallup, reported that some two thousand Indians were congregated around the fields there in 1881. The circumstances were therefore propitious for the diffusion of news, and it is quite probable that the story of John Slocum was widely told at these gatherings.

Yet Angus McCloud (Wier Notes) of Mason Valley wrote that Wovoka "never went to Oregon [and was] scarcely out of [the] valley." Mrs. Plummer even went so far as to state that his trances had nothing to do with the 1890 Ghost Dance ceremony. If Shakerism was the impetus for Wovoka's trances, either through the Prophet's travels or diffusion, then it is important to note that the religion he eventually founded was phrased differently from the one being developed by John and Mary Slocum and their disciple, Louis Yowalich, in Washington state. For there were no bells, books, or candles in the 1890 Ghost Dance, whose ceremonies were held out-of-doors; and its dance steps were completely different (cf. Lauben and Lauben 1976:52-71). Furthermore, there is no evidence that Numu Ghost Dancers ever "brushed off sin" or practiced those ritualized hand greetings characteristic of the Shakers. Until any evidence which is solid and verifiable can be put forward, this case for direct borrowing of Wovoka's trances from Shakerism must lie in abeyance, especially in light of the fact that trances were part and parcel of traditional Numu culture.

"Not all shamans can go into a trance," Park (Dangberg 1968:12) could state. "Only the best and strongest doctors have this power." Numu shamans would induce trance states to retrieve the wandering souls of comatose individuals, Park wrote. For example, the 1870 Ghost Dance Prophet, Wodziwob, was called from his home on the Walker River Reservation to Smith Valley to revive 7 or 8 year old Mamie Bob circa 1898 (Hittman 1973b). Park (Dangberg 1968:11) also wrote of a Reno man who "was sick about a year and nearly died. He went into trances and then his body was stiff as a board. He dreamed that he went to the place where the dead are ...." Wovoka's father was a medicine man, so trance states undoubtedly belonged to his shamanic kit. Since the ethnographic literature is replete with data concerning the inheritance of shamanic powers (e.g., trances) along family lines, "There seems to be a general feeling that at least one child of a shaman will inherit powers" (Park 1938:31). The 1890 Ghost Dance Prophet probably learned its practice from Numu-tibo'o. And, even if Wovoka's father had been taken prisoner when he was a small child, surely at some point in his early years we would expect the Prophet to have been exposed to what Mooney witnessed at the Walker River Reservation in 1891, a Numu shaman healing a patient. Let us return again to the Dyer Manuscript for elucidation on Wovoka's ecstatic seizures:

> Jack Wilson's trances were, at least to Indians, very impressive productions. I can speak only as a layman in such matters but it is my belief that they were truly self-induced hypnotic trances of a rather deep nature. He wasn't shamming. His body was as rigid as a board. His mouth could not be pried open and he showed no reaction to pain-inducing experiments. At first his friends, thinking he was dying, made repeated and futile efforts to wake him up by physical manipulation and the administration of stimulation by mouth. He revived in his own good time. How and where he learned to place himself in a state of suspended animation is any one's guess. Perhaps he did visit Heaven — in his dreams. The whole matter is one to which I still confess considerable puzzlement.

Dyer's brother, Bob, added that "some [members of the Prophet's audience] even committed suicide" during those social gatherings we call the 1890 Ghost Dance. He mentioned wild parsnip, or **haakenobbu**, as its instrument, the root consumed either by shamans to demonstrate their trance powers or by depressed individuals; i.e., those who had been jilted in love. Ed Dyer also took note of that misguided follower's death:

> I personally witnessed the demise of one deluded victim and can attest that it was a long drawn out and agonizing death. Eating of wild parsnip to commit suicide was not an uncommon method

among the Indians. In this case and several others, the victim not only was in a hurry to visit Heaven but also was assured that he could return again as Jack had done, to find earth a much improved place, for better days were coming for the red men.

A tragic death, Dyer commented, occurring because Wovoka had "painted such an enticing picture [of the afterlife]."

Whether or not the Prophet himself ever consumed wild parsnip in public to induce the trance state, and the extent, if any, to which Numus living in Smith and Mason valleys and on the Walker River Reservation ever imitated these dissociative states, unfortunately, is not known. Recall that Wovoka related to Chapman that ecstatic seizures by followers were not part of his religion, and Mrs. George Plummer's statement to Wier, namely, her insistence that his trances had no connection whatsoever with his "dance." Lakota, Arapaho, Cheyenne, and other visitors did, to be sure, "let go." But their trances were observed on home reservations, never in any Ghost Dance ceremony in the Walker River area of Nevada. Our safest conclusion can only be, then, that with the exception of that single poison-induced death, only the 1890 Ghost Dance Prophet himself ever experienced shamanic-like trances during ceremonies. Did Wovoka originally induce these in front of large numbers of Numus gathered to witness demonstrations of his weather-control powers, or were his ecstatic seizures designed to impress visiting delegations of Native Americans? Still another question might be asked: By the use of trances, did the 1890 Ghost Dance Prophet aspire to a broader authority than that of the traditional healer? For, as we shall see, not only hadn't Wovoka yet become a medicine man in the late 1880s, but his demonstrations of "soul flight" took place in broad daylight, or precisely when the orthodoxy required that shamanic trances occur only during the nightly cure.[5]

Yet a third power associated with 1890 Ghost Dance ceremonies was its Prophet's invulnerability.

INVULNERABILITY

"He announced well in advance that he couldn't be killed by a gun," or so Ed Dyer wrote:

> He simply was able to render his body impervious to lead. Moreover he could create powder and shot out of dust and sand. He then proceeded to back up his claims with a demonstration that left no doubt in the minds of a very large and interested audience.

Understandably the Indians were interested. If one of them could become bullet proof maybe the condition could be made to rub off on the rest of the tribe. The average Indian was becoming thoroughly fed up with the white man by this time and longed to shoot all of them out of hand but the white man was prone to shoot back with deadly accuracy and moreover he controlled the supply of powder and shot. It is difficult to wage a war when one is dependent on the enemy for supplies. But that business of making powder and shot out of sand — or even snow — now that opened enchanting possibilities.

The demonstration came off in grand style. Jack, wrapped in a heavy blanket robe, produced a muzzle loading shot gun for everyone's inspection. Then he reached down at his feet, got a pinch of dust which he dropped down the barrel. Powder he explained and reached for a handful of sand. That as far as any one could tell also went down the barrel in lieu of shot. A bit of paper wadding pushed down by the ramrod completed the charge and the gun was then handed to Jack's brother who was delegated as shooter.

Jack strode majestically to a spot previously selected, some distance from the rest of the crowd but well within gun range. He removed his blanket, placed it flat on the ground, took his stance in the center of the blanket, faced his brother standing in the midst of the crowd and ordered him to fire. The brother took careful aim at the man on the blanket and pulled the trigger. A very real and authentic shotgun blast rent the air. Jack was seen to shake himself vigorously and then heard to bid one and all to come forward to him. The Indians came up to see a man standing on a blanket, absolutely unhurt but wearing a shirt riddled with shot holes. On the blanket at his feet lay the shot. That did it. The evidence of their own senses convinced every Indian present. No self-appointed debunker, had there been one, could have obtained a hearing. Those of my readers who see readily through mills stones provided with holes and consequently think the Indians displayed a measure of stupidity are reminded that it is very human to believe that which we desire to believe.

"Mr. Wilson" told Dangberg that Wovoka "let himself be shot at with buckshot, therefore [he] seemed invulnerable." This same Wilson also reported how he "used to aggravate him [Wovoka] — [He would] Ask [him] to let him shoot at him. 'Ah, no,' said Jack,'" however, came the reply. And when Chapman queried the 1890 Ghost Dance Prophet about allegations of his invulnerability, Wovoka reportedly stated, "It was only a joke." Was Wovoka being politic? According to Lt. Nat Phister (1891:107), who conducted an independent investigation of the new religion in Mason Valley, "The prophet had said that he was invulnerable and if anyone tried to kill him, the soldier will be killed. If cut into pieces the soldier will be without bones and collapse." Mooney, unfortunately, never fully treated the subject. His discussion focused instead on the question of those notorious Ghost Dance shirts worn by Lakota. "Wovoka himself expressly disclaimed any responsibility for the ghost shirt, and whites and Indians alike agreed that it formed no part of the dance costume in Mason Valley," Mooney (1896:791) wrote. And again, "The Ghost shirt was not aboriginal" (Mooney 1896:790):

> The author is strongly inclined to the opinion that the idea of an invulnerable sacred garment is not original with the Indians, but like several other important points pertaining to the Ghost-dance doctrine, is a practical adaptation by the Indians of an idea derived from contact with some sectarian body among the whites.

After comparing the Lakota 1890 Ghost Dance shirts to ascension robes worn by Millerites in the 1840s, Mooney (1896:945) settled upon the Mormons as their source. Owing to their presence in what was then Utah Territory, Mormon "sacred undergarments," Mooney felt, were the ultimate inspiration for Plains Indian Ghost Dance shirts. Was Mooney right?

Garold Barney (1986), in an exhaustive study of Mormonism and the 1890 Ghost Dance Religion, sketched what certainly are remarkable similarities between the two theologies: (1) the belief in a Messianic deliverer; (2) Indians seen as the Chosen People; (3) the apocalyptic expectation that this earth would be transformed imminently; (4) the "tree of life" as a symbol; and (5) the belief that 1890 was to be the year of the Millennium.

"Both Mormonism and the Ghost Dance Religion began as a response of a prophet who saw and talked with God, who carried His message to earth, and whose message, once delivered, was modified with time and varying cultural awareness," Barney (1986:219) wrote. Because they settled Genoa, Nevada, in 1852, some 60 miles northwest of Smith and Mason valleys, Barney (1986:161) quoted Paul Bailey's position that Mormonized eastern Nevada Indians flocked to Wovoka's home "by the score." Indeed, the Prophet's own daughter and son-in-law became Mormons, though only late in life, after their son Harlyn had converted.

Regarding the question of the 1890 Ghost Dance Prophet's invulnerability and its relationship to Mormonism, Barney goes on to show how Joseph Smith's bodyguard was believed to have been bulletproof. Also, the Mormon founder's personal physician, Dr. Richards, was said to have escaped unhurt from assassin's bullets in June of 1844, which claimed the life of Joseph Smith and his brother, Hyrum, in that Carthage jail in Illinois (Barney 1986:15-18) because Dr. Richards was wearing an endowment robe. According to Barney (1986:16, 181), Joseph Smith introduced a decorated undergarment for the faithful to wear, which was believed to render a person invulnerable to everything from shipwreck to temptation by the Devil, in a ceremony on May 4, 1842: "'This garment protects from disease, and even death, for the bullet of an enemy will not penetrate it,'" Barney (1986:214) also quoted the historian Bancroft.

On the other hand, whereas Garold reminds us that Black Elk assumed credit for having introduced the Ghost Dance shirt to Lakotas (cf. Neihardt 1961:206-207), Mooney (1896:790) identified the Lakota, Kicking Bear, as its originator. Moreover, not only was Crazy Horse thought to have been bulletproof, so too was the Son of the Morning Star, General George Armstrong Custer. So, too, one might add, the 40th president of this nation. Barney also cautions us to remember that Mormons were called back to Utah in 1857, where they proselytized Utes and Southern Paiutes. To which I might add that even though Chief Waker and three other Utes were baptized in 1854, hence becoming eligible "as [Mormon] elders...to wear the magnificent temple garment, endowed as it was with the promises to ward off disease, deceit and even bullets" (Barney 1986:57), there is no hard evidence Mormons then converted a single Numu living in either Smith and Mason valleys or on the Walker River Reservation. In fact, a letter cited by Barney (1986:93), which he received from the Church History Department of the Church of Jesus Christ of Latter-day Saints, states: "The records of the Church do not show that Jack Wilson (Wovoka), circa 1880-1890, was accepted into the fellowship of the Mormon Church." The important point to note here, however, is that the case for Mormon attribution as the ultimate source of Wovoka's invulnerability has not yet been proven. In the judicious wording of Garold Barney (1986:155):

> Because of their geographical proximity to Nevada, and because
> of their unique doctrine and powerful evangelical outreach, it is
> perfectly understandable that the Mormon Millenialist may have
> contributed a great deal to the enthusiasm that centered in the
> teachings of the Paiute Ghost Dance Religion. Unfortunately,

there is little empirical evidence that would lead to the conclusion that the Mormons and Mormon doctrine were in fact the
forces that produced the Ghost Dance Religion. On the contrary,
there is equal speculative evidence that would cause the conclusion
to be reached that the Ghost Dance, was indeed, uniquely Indian
in its origin, concept and application. It is far easier to believe
that Mormonism simply fanned the fire of Indian revivalism
that had already begun to rage in the west.

Pending more than circumstantial evidence, a safer course would be to consider traditional Numu beliefs in invulnerability.

Major John Wesley Powell (Fowler and Fowler 1971:246, 287) reported
that Numus believed certain men were "arrowproof." "Shamans with the
strongest powers were thought to be invulnerable against arrows and later
bullets," Park (1938:109) wrote. And this power, Park (1938:26) stated, "is
sought on a mountain near Wabuska.... [It] protects a man against bullets. It
makes him a great warrior. When a man gets power at this place he must run
down the side of the mountain without breathing.... This place is called **tagwani-
p.**" We read in Cora Du Bois (1939:5) that Frank Spencer, or **Weneyuga**, the
1870 Ghost Dance Religion's Apostle Paul, "was supposed to be invulnerable
when fired upon with a gun." Omer Stewart (1941:414) reported its absence
as a cultural trait among the Toboose tukadu; nevertheless, Corbett Mack
discussed invulnerability in his accounting of the four heroes' participation in
the Pyramid Lake War of 1860:

> They [Tom Wakeen or **Taboosigetyu**, Young Winnemucca or
> **Winnemucca Natsi**, and Bbooggoo Mahanudu (Pooggoo
> Mahanudu), or Horseman, Corbett's maternal grandfather] got
> horses but the other guys [Numus] don't need horses. 'Cause
> they can go just as fast as a horse can go. Stay right with them.
> Winnemucca Natsi says: 'Their guns too slow. We can dive right
> in there. We got a hatchet. We can go left and right. They die.
> They gone like a bird. They don't get up no more.'

Smith Valley rancher Frank Simpson had this to say to Dangberg
about Wovoka's invulnerability:

> One time J [Jack Wilson] was stacking hay. He wore one of his
> badges of his honor — a big brass button on his breast. As the
> fork swung around on the stack one of the tines struck him in
> the breast on the button and threw him off the stack. Mr. Simpson
> rushed around to pick him up and as Jack was coming to he
> said, "Oh, me alright, Frank. Me bulletproof."[6]

Yet, on the whole, Tibo'o interviewed by Wier and Dangberg were as disputatious regarding the Prophet's invulnerability as they were toward his other powers and miracles. Yerington Paiutes again, though, took issue.

"Yeah, I'd say Wovoka was bulletproof. Some of them people [with bbooha] were like that you know," Andy Dick (b. 1887) stated. He recalled how, as a small boy, he saw Wovoka once designate a Numu to shoot him. However, the potential assassin's fingers froze on the trigger of his own shotgun, prompting the 1890 Ghost Dance Prophet to take hold of the weapon, Andy said, and freely fire it. Wovoka was also said to have been able to shoot jackrabbits with a pinch of alkali or sand in his shotgun instead of powder. He "could make powder and ammunition from dirt," Bob Dyer told Dangberg. While his brother Ed offered the most complete description of the power:

> Of the other alleged acts of wizardry I can only speak from hearsay but I was most solemnly assured by countless Indians that this or that was true. When out on a rabbit drive, they said Jack was in the habit of dropping a pinch of snow or sand into the muzzle of his gun and forthwith bringing down a jackrabbit. He didn't need orthodox power and shot. They knew this to be true as they had seen it with their own eyes.

Take note of the association of Wovoka's "bullet power" with the annual November rabbit drive. During one fall drive, held either at the Pittman or the Gallagher Ranch in Mason Valley, the Prophet was said to have been accidentally shot. Yet, according to Andy Dick, those shells merely "bounced off his head." And while the interpretation of a similar incident given by Frank Quinn (b. 1902) is interesting in itself, it is the context of the rabbit drive which I argue might hold another important key for our understanding of the 1890 Ghost Dance in Nevada:

> Jack used to go all over to the rabbit drives. I guess somebody didn't like him, and somebody just shot at him, intending to kill him. I saw this because I was with the gang. I was just a little boy, bringing the team of horses for them. Anyway, when he got shot he was hollering at everybody and moving his hands up. He was standing there and he said, "Boys, I've been shot." Another thing he asked for was a handkerchief. You know the old time blue and white kind men used to wear around their neck in those days. When he stood up, there was an ant hill. Black ants. So he stood up there and put the handkerchief on the ground. When he unbuckled his belt and pulled out his shirt, and his shirt was

full of holes. And then when he done that, he took off his shoes, laid them right there. He shook himself off. He shook off all the shells and he stood and he said, 'Boys, you see all these bullets were intended to kill me.' Then he picked up the bullets and wrapped them up and passed them around for the men to see. When he pulled off his shirt, you could see where the bullets hit. There were lots of red spots on his body. That's the kind of man he was (*Numu Ya Dua,* Volume III:28, 4 June 1982).

Another aspect of Wovoka's invulnerability is the claim by Numus that he frequently doctored men who had been shot at those fall communal rabbit drives. In one such cure, the Prophet lay down next to his younger brother, Pat Wilson, on a canvas purposefully spread on the ground and began tapping Pat lightly with his hand, whereupon the BBs miraculously fell out. Another time, on another rabbit drive, Pat Wilson must have accidentally shot a fellow Numu. "He [the victim] was running behind him and fell and Pat accidentally shot him in the head." Once again the 1890 Ghost Dance Prophet was said to have successfully doctored a fellow Numu.

Park (1934:107), in his discussion of shamanism, did report that "Jack Wilson was an excellent doctor for a gunshot wound." Since there is this strong association between Wovoka's invulnerability and his successful doctoring at the annual fall rabbit drive, the following hypothesis can be suggested: That in addition to being able to control the weather and enter ecstatic trance states at will, yet a third factor responsible for Wovoka's initial acceptance among Numus living in Smith and Mason valleys, and probably Walker River Numus as well. It was the rash of accidental shootings and subsequent healing which occurred following the introduction of shotguns and rifles to the communal rabbit drive, or when the wings of sagebrush beaters finally converged on the nets. Wovoka may well have inherited the shamanic gift of invulnerability from his father. But this ability of his to heal Numu men shot during the annual fall rabbit drive can also be seen as the Prophet employing an important social occasion in the Numu ecological calendar. The traditional dances provided the basis upon which to graft the 1890 Ghost Dance. "M. Wilson" stated that Wovoka demonstrated his invulnerability in front of visiting delegations of Native Americans, whose dramatic appearance in Smith and Mason valleys within days of the Great Revelation would have added yet another dimension to the religious phenomenon known as the 1890 Ghost Dance Religion. Following in chronological order are the delegations.

1. "The Ute of Utah sent delegates to the messiah soon after the first Ghost dance in January, 1889" (Mooney 1896:806).

2. Five Shoshones came in a delegation to Mason Valley in the summer of 1889 headed by Tabinshi and Nakash ("Sage"), Northern Arapahos (Mooney 1896:807).

3. A delegation in the November of 1889 included Porcupine — the Northern Cheyenne from Montana; Arapahos — Flat Iron, Yellow Breast, Sitting Bull, Friday, and Broken Arm; Lakotas — Short Bull and Kicking Bear; and Shoshones and Bannocks from Fort Hall (Mooney 1896:817, 818).

4. A second delegation of Lakota, which included Good Thunder, Cloud Horse, Yellow Knife, and Short Bull, arrived in 1890 (Mooney 1896: 819).

5. A visit was made by 12 Cheyennes and Arapahos in the summer of 1890 (Dangberg 1968:30).

6. Porcupine, Big Beaver, and Ridge Walker went to Walker Lake in the autumn of 1890 from the Tongue Reservation to visit Wovoka (Gatschet 1893:108).

7. "Several of the leading [Shoshone and Paiute] men have gone to Walker lake to confer with a man who calls himself Christ," Mooney (1896:806) reported this November of 1890 visit by Native Americans.

8. Bannocks visited Mason Valley on December 17, 1890 (Dangberg 1968:30).

9. Mohave delegates attended a Ghost Dance ceremony in 1890 (Mooney 1896:805, 814).

10. "Taisitsie [a Wind River Shoshoni] was so intrigued by the Ghost Dance movement in 1890 that he visited Jack Wilson in Nevada. He discovered that the dance was to cause the dead to come closer, they would come to life some day. The dancers would stop, shake their blankets, then pound their chest to eliminate illness. Wilson made no claim that the white people would blow away" (Shimkin 1942:457).

11. The skeptical Kiowa, Apiatan, who subsequently received a medal from President Harrison for telling his people to stop Ghost Dancing, visited Wovoka circa fall 1891 (Lesser 1933:57).

12. "Three Cheyenne and three Navaho from Ft. Reno, Oklahoma to see Dave [sic] Wilson, Paiute Prophet. One of them was a policeman and he wore his badge with great dignity" (*Lyon County Times* 8 August 1891).

13. "Indians from Indian Territory and other eastern agencies [have

been visiting Wovoka] for the past year" (*Lyon County Times* 9 January 1892).

14. Black Bear, Sitting Bull, and Washee, Arapahos, and the half-Cheyenne, Edward Geary, left Darlington, Oklahoma, in autumn 1892 to meet J. Wilson, "who claimed to be only the mouth-piece of the real Messiah...." (Gatschet 1893:108).

15. "Quite a number of Idaho Indians — Bannocks and Shoshones — are in the valley and will enter the [Jack Wilson dance] scheduled for Sunday" (*Mason Valley Tidings* 19 June 1893).

16. "Quite a number of Idaho Indians — Bannocks and Shoshones — are in the valley and will enter the...fandango that Wovoka will toss tomorrow [Sunday]," the *Lyon County Times* reported on June 17, 1893.

17. Kicking Bear visits Wovoka in 1902 (Dangberg 1968:34).

18. Three Arapaho visitors met the Prophet in 1904 (*Lyon County Times* 20 February 1904).

19. Lakota visitors Cloud Horse, Chasing Hawk, and Bear-Comes were said to have been "out from Rosebud" in 1906 to meet Wovoka (*Lyon County Times* 4 August 1906).

20. "Broken Arm, Elk Horn, Kicks Back decide not to return home immediately from Walker Lake but to visit the Pacific Northwest" (Utley 1963:71).

According to Mooney (1896:805), representatives from over 30 tribes traveled to meet the 1890 Ghost Dance Prophet, including a Nez Perce who personally told the government ethnologist that there had been additional delegates (Paiutes?) from Warm Springs, Oregon.[7] Wovoka, of course, spoke his own language, Northern Paiute, and passable English as well. Mooney indicated that the Prophet did not know sign language, hence Wovoka's communications with so many delegates speaking so many different languages would have been problematic. Because Plains Indians were required to stop at Fort Hall, Idaho, Mooney (1896:807) suggested they hired Bannocks at this railroad hub to accompany them the rest of their way to Smith and Mason valleys, the Bannock language being mutually comprehensible with Northern Paiute. Even so, one can only imagine the amount of distortion that inevitably would have arisen when the inspired words issuing from Wovoka's heart and mind were translated from the Numic-English patois spoken by men such as Charley Sheep and Captain Josephus into the many different languages represented at any particular ceremony. To appreciate this one has only to read Porcupine's physical description of Wovoka in Mooney's great work (Mooney 1896:793-96).[8]

Another question which must be considered: What were 1890 Ghost Dance ceremonies in Nevada like? Mooney (1896:802-803) did not personally witness any, still this comment of his is noteworthy:

> When I visited the Messiah in January, 1892, deep snow was on the ground, which had caused the temporary suspension of dancing, so that I had no opportunity of seeing the performance there for myself. I saw, however, the place cleared for the dance ground — the same spot where the large delegation from Oklahoma had attended the dance the preceding summer — at the upper end of Mason valley. A large circular space had been cleared of sagebrush and leveled over, and around the circumference were the remains of the low round structures of willow branches which had sheltered those in attendance. At one side, within the circle, was a large structure of branches, where the Messiah gave audience to the delegates from distant tribes, and according to their statements, showed them the glories of the spirit world through the medium of hypnotic trances.

Ake Hultkrantz (1981:266-276) described the 1890 Ghost Dance ceremony as follows:

> The dancers, men and women, formed a circle, with their fingers interlocked. They progressed by taking small steps to the left, in a kind of shuffling movement. The dancers were surrounded by round structures of willow branches. The dancing which went on for four consecutive nights and a morning was accompanied by singing.

"M. Wilson," as previously cited, recalled it in the Dangberg Notes:

> Messiahship — Big Dance — Indians from V. City, Bodie, Walker Lake — held in this S[outhern] end of Valley. On Wilson ranch. Biannual dances. All Indians lived in this end of Valley. Each Fall and Spring dances. Had a dance. Jack conceived idea of being prophet. Old fellows gathered in a circle and smoked a pipe. Talk a little. Meanwhile others merry-making. Jack gave a big talk to whole trip [sic]. Proclaimed himself. Addressed whole trip [sic]. Unusual proceedings. Prophesied some things which came true. This a spring dance.

"By Fall dance men came from Oklahoma," David Wilson's son also noted for Dangberg. "Didn't talk much. [The] Less said the better for him [Wovoka]. Big dance advertised for Fall. J. [Jack] going into trance for the occasion. Many delegations." Wilson emphasized that the 1890 Ghost Dance Prophet went into a "3 day dance" for the visiting delegation, after which, Wovoka "prophecies (sic) a big wind and storm for three days. Wind then storm [came]. Plus shirt stunt. Prophecied [sic] trance then 'came back' and told what he had seen."

Clearly these descriptions relate to ceremonies held for visiting delegations of Native Americans. Bob Dyer told Dangberg that "Indians from east come to learn dance, etc., stack money — in front of him and gifts," while his brother Ed gave an even fuller narration of one such occasion:

> I witnessed, sometimes in company with my brother, a number of those dances in which delegations of eastern Indians were present. They were generally proceeded [sic] by a solemn exchange of gifts. Jack Wilson would be seated on one side of a blanket and the chief visitors on the other. A gift would be placed upon the blanket with appropriate remarks in his own tongue by the visiting donor. A translation would follow, through one or more interpreters, with English resorted to as a language bridge in case of necessity. After a dignified acceptance by Wilson it was the next donor's turn. The blanket would be heaping with rich gifts before the end. The visitors usually received red ocher and other face paints together with magpie tail feathers in return.

The only Yerington Paiute who could provide a reasonably reliable account of an actual 1890 Ghost Dance ceremony was Corbett Mack. In 1895 or 1896 he was 4 or 5 years of age, and Corbett emphasized yet another aspect of these epigonic gatherings besides "gift-giving":

> Bannocks, you see, they got a bow and arrow. And them White fellows, they got to back up when we dance. 'Cause they [Bannocks] point at anybody with it. So white people, they afraid. Afraid they gonna turn that lose. But they don't do that. Just make believe. You know how they do it? Dodge around, lay down here. Just like that's a war. Yes, sir. That's what they doing. Showing these Indians here how they do it [dance] when they go to war.[9]

One additional description of an 1890 Ghost Dance ceremony in Nevada can be cited. Yeringtonian Alice Guild, in the 1950s, provided Robert Davidson (1952:16) with this following account:

> In the middle of the circle of dancers was a central bonfire which gave off a great deal of heat and light. Around the circle moved

the Indians hand in hand in a sort of shuffling side step. They kept chanting something to the beat of skin drums. Some members would fall out of the circle onto the ground in a trance-like state, and some, upon falling, kept wiggling.

Whatever 1890 Ghost Dance ceremonies were like originally, and how or whether or not they even differed from ceremonies Wovoka arranged for visiting delegations of Native Americans, these descriptions all make clear its formal similarity to the traditional dance of Numus, the Round Dance. Park (1941:184) called this "the most popular dance among the Paviotso [Numu]," the very "backbone of the [dance] complex." He also stated that "religious beliefs and activities are associated only with [it]." From his account of the Round Dance (Park 1941:184-87), its most essential features can be isolated:

1. The Round Dance was infrequently held, usually in late spring or in association with fish runs, and again in the early fall, during pine nut harvesting.

2. The Round Dance was pan-tribal. Numus traveled far and wide to participate in what was clearly an ecologically correlated ritual.

3. While the fisheries at Pyramid Lake and Walker Lake were two of the most popular locales for Round Dances, its residents did not necessarily host Round Dances, whose responsibility was defined as the joint enterprise of Numus electing to appear.

4. The Round Dance lasted five nights.

5. Temporary brush shelters were positioned around a cleared space reserved for dancing.

6. Fires were built on the outside of the dance circle.

7. A pole was erected within the center of the dance ground. It served as a point of orientation for the circle of dancers, or so Numus told Park, and had no symbolic or cosmological significance.

8. In preparation for these ceremonies, dancers painted their faces and parts of their body with simple bars and dots in red and white mineral pigments.

9. Men and women comprised the dance circles. Joining hands, their palms pressed together and their fingers interlaced, participants would circle the pole in a clockwise direction.

10. No instruments were used in the Round Dance, the only music was provided by the singer.

11. Singers stood on the inside of the circle, Round Dance leaders or headmen, who were in charge of the entire ceremony, positioned them-

selves on the outside.

12. Round Dance leaders were not necessarily shamans.

13. Round Dance leaders "talked" while the people danced.

Indeed, weather-control bbooha was "practiced at the social round dances," this ethnographer (Park 1938:60n18) stated. "While the dancers are moving in a circle a headman, not necessarily one with supernatural power, walks around praying for rain in order to insure abundant wild products." Again, "it is just like praying. He talks about the weather. He asks for rain so the people will have plenty of roots and seeds. He wishes for pine nuts and other foods for the coming year. He talks to some kind of spirit," Park (1941:186) wrote. And quoting an informant, Park (1941:184-185) additionally noted: "'It is the big dance; it is to pray for good crops and to ask for game. The dance is for a good time, for many seeds and pine nuts; it lasts five nights.'" Since the Round Dance had "the double function of bringing people together for a thorough going good time and for an appeal to vaguely conceived supernatural powers that are thought to control human health and supplies of wild seeds and game" (Park 1941:186), by substituting "1890 Ghost Dance," it becomes apparent at once just how similar the two ceremonial forms were. Thus, the 1890 Ghost Dance Prophet can be likened to the traditional Round Dance leader, who was not necessarily a shaman. Wovoka similarly "talked" or prayed — prophesied — for rain (cf. Park 1941:187), and like his Round Dance counterpart, the 1890 Ghost Dance Prophet also addressed prayers to some "vaguely conceived supernatural powers that are thought to control human health and supplies of wild seeds and game." Even the traditional Round Dance division of ceremonial labor between "talker" and singer appears to have been observed in what we call the 1890 Ghost Dance. This was revealed by the following anecdote told by a Yerington elder about Wovoka's having given his "bone" to Potato Sam, which allowed the assistant to "sing all night long" at a Walker River Reservation ceremony.[10]

Park's description of Round Dance ceremonial grounds compares favorably with what Chapman recorded for the 1890 Ghost Dance. Round Dances were "held on a flat cleared space 200 to 300 yards in diameter," Park (1941:184) wrote. Chapman, in December of 1890, reported seeing three of their dance grounds.

> They had been cleared of sagebrush and grass and made per-
> fectly level, around the outer edge of which the willow sticks
> were still standing, over which they spread their tenting for shelter
> during these ceremonies. The cleared ground must have been

from 200 to 300 feet in diameter, and only about four places left open to enter the grounds.

On the other hand, there were formal as well as functional differences between the ceremonies of the Round Dance and the 1890 Ghost Dance. No center pole or "cosmic pillar," as Ake Hultkrantz (1979:23) calls it, was used in the religious ritual inspired by Wovoka's Great Revelation. "Never saw a pole in the center," George Plummer told Dangberg. "Painted [themselves] but just to look pretty. This man [Wovoka?] sits on the ground in the center and talks; then another man." Also Angus McCloud (Dangberg Notes), who recalled a "Ghost dance near here [of] 1000 people," stated that he "never saw a pole in the center." Indeed, if anything upheld "the cosmic vault of heaven" (Hultkrantz 1979:23), it was not the sacred cedar, willow, or pine tree but the personality of "The (Wood) Cutter," Jack Wilson (Wovoka), whose demonstrations of weather-control power, trance states, and invulnerability were what initially attracted Numus, and Native Americans from around the country later on. For Wovoka's 1890 Ghost Dance ceremony was anything but an ecologically-related traditional event. It was the product of a charismatic "talker" who superimposed his own inner or revealed eschatological timetable upon a traditional dance form. Hultkrantz (1981:276) has called the latter a "Father Dance," but formal similarities aside, Wovoka's 1890 Ghost Dance clearly had nothing to do with pine nut harvests in the fall, rabbit drives in November, or spring fish runs. Defined by anthropologists as a nativistic movement (Linton 1943), a revitalization movement (Wallace 1956), and a transformative social movement (Aberle 1966), the 1890 Ghost Dance Religion, along with its predecessor, the 1870 Ghost Dance, has been the subject of a much lively debate.

In one camp, the Boasian scholar Leslie Spier (1935:7) explained these and other Native American religious movements, Shakerism, for example, as culturally determined reflexes of a time immemorial Basin-Plateau ceremonial complex. This Spier dubbed the "Prophet Dance."

> [The belief that] falling stars, earthquakes, and other strange happenings in nature portended the destruction of the world; certain prophets having communicated with God in their dreams, or having gone to the land of the dead and returned predicted doomsday when they would rejoin the dead, and preached a more righteous and God-fearing life; and these prophets led special dances and songs concerning the salvation of mankind.

Because Spier wrote in an era when Native American cultures were thought entirely comprehensible, without consideration of the impact of Euro-American civilizations, one can say that the "Prophet Dance" itself was culturally determined.[11] It was not until the late 1930s and early 1940s that an opposing view emerged.

This was the concept of "acculturation" (Linton 1943), which differed from the prevailing view of diffusion insofar as its emphasis was the qualitatively different impact one culture might have upon another, especially in situations involving imperialism. The idea of "deprivation" followed next. With its origins in A.L. Kroeber (1925), Alexander Lesser (1933:109), Philleo Nash (1937), and Bernard Barber (1941), the scholars David Aberle (1959, 1966), Deward Walker (1969), and Joseph Jorgensen (1986, 1987) have most recently argued that such Native American holocausts as loss of land and defeat in war to Euro-Americans can combine with their subjectively perceived feelings of diminished worth and behavior to more powerfully explain religious events like the Prophet Dance, Ghost Dance, etc.. Thus, the religions of Wodziwob and Wovoka are now defined as "religions of protest" (Kobben 1960) or "crisis cults" (La Barre 1970) among the "oppressed" (Lanternari 1965).

Of course the two approaches need not be antagonistic — as Christopher Miller (1985) successfully showed in his eclectic re-examination of the so-called Prophet Dance in the Plateau. It may even be said that scholars who continue to champion one approach at the expense of the other risk distortion comparable, say, to Plains Indians interpretations of Wovoka's Great Revelation.[12] The 1890 Ghost Dance Religion arose within the context of Tibo'o settlements in Smith and Mason valleys. Therefore, "relative deprivation" (Aberle 1959) faced by Numus in the late 1880s ought to merit equal consideration with traditional beliefs and rituals (the "Prophet Dance") before any understanding of Wovoka's religion is even remotely possible.

The Prophet himself would have been 13 or 14 years old at the time of Wodziwob's revelation. We can assume he was familiar with the theology and ritual practice of the 1870 Ghost Dance for the following reasons: (1) the proximity of Smith and Mason valleys to Walker Lake Valley, where Wodziwob's religion began; (2) the cultural and linguistic ties between Toboose tukadu and Agitukadu, or Walker River Reservation Numus; (3) inter-valley traffic which increased in the post-contact period because of the demand for Numu laborers on the ranches and farms in Smith and Mason valleys; (4) the fact that Wovoka held Ghost Dance ceremonies on the Walker River Reservation (Mooney 1896:802-803); and (5) because the 1890 Ghost Dance Prophet sought allotted land on the Walker River Reservation.

In one version of Wodziwob's prophecy (Du Bois 1939), the arrival of a train in the West carrying the dead was expected to trigger an apocalypse. Evil (=Euro-Americans) then would be destroyed, and Numus would revert to a life they had never known before. There would be food in miraculous abundance and they would dwell alongside the resurrected dead in a land or world free of sickness, aging, and death. The 1870 Ghost Dance Religion, which erupted on the Walker River Reservation by May of 1869, no doubt rested upon a Prophet Dance core — the apocalyptic belief in a flat earth on which evil more rapidly than goodness accumulates, causing it eventually to tip, whereupon the bad people fall off and good people enjoy an Eden-like existence, albeit temporarily (Hittman 1973b). However, the assortment of miseries from the decade 1860-1870 needs to be factored into any explanation of Wodziwob's religion. The loss of Numu lands and the disruption of their traditional food cycle; governmental promises of assistance made to transform them into self-sufficient farmers on the Walker River Reservation that could not be kept on account of the Civil War; the bitterly resented grazing of Fort Churchill horses on the reservation; depletion of their fishing resources at the mouth of Walker Lake because of year-round human overcrowding; and, finally, starvation and the epidemics of the late 1860s, which were said by Indian agents to have taken the lives of at least one member of every Walker River Reservation Numu household (Hittman 1973b).[13] If the 1870 Ghost Dance Religion needs to be examined in light of American Manifest Destiny, shouldn't this hold true for the 1890 Ghost Dance, which erupted more than thirty years later?

We have already seen how the traditional culture of Walker River area Numus helped to frame their initial acceptance of the Prophet, and unless one is prepared to simplistically argue that Numus rallied around Wovoka in the late 1880s because of the "environmental crisis" which this Prophet was believed able to solve, ethnohistorical evidence does not at all point to "deprivations" comparable to what members of Wodziwob's birth cohort faced at the time of the 1870 Ghost Dance. This finding relates to the question of Wovoka's original message.

The "great underlying principle of the Ghost dance doctrine...[was that the] time will come when the whole Indian race, living and dead, will be reunited upon a regenerated earth, to live a life of aboriginal happiness, forever free from death, disease, and misery," Mooney (1896:777) wrote. But hadn't the Prophet himself stated that the living will join with the dead in the world to come?[14] Mooney's Plains bias appears to have led him to recapitulate as the core of the 1890 Ghost Dance Religion what his beloved Kiowa, etc., told him, rather than what he heard from Wovoka and others in Nevada with his own ears, and also read in Chapman. Moreover, Mooney (ibid.) wrote: "The White race being alien and secondary and hardly real, has no part in this scheme of aboriginal regeneration, and will be left behind with the other things of earth that have served their temporary purpose, or else will cease entirely to exist." And again, "It seems un-questionable that this [doctrine of racial equality] is equally contrary to the doctrine as originally preached" (Mooney ibid.). Yet Chapman reported that the 1890 Ghost Dance Prophet had seen Numus, as well as non-Indians, in Heaven. If Chapman were correct, then not only did Mooney's Plains bias again lead him to err, but Wovoka's religion was all the more remarkable insofar as it projected a racially-integrated life to come.

Of course one solution might be that like other prophets, Handsome Lake, the Seneca, for example (Wallace 1970), Wovoka too had different revelations. The accounts he proffered to Chapman, Mooney, Porcupine, Kicking Bear, et al, would have then reflected doctrinal shifts with the passage of time and changed circumstances. Indeed, by December of 1890 Wovoka was already complaining to the Indian scout Chapman that "people were lying about what he had said." Overholt (1974:49), as a result, concluded that on account of Wounded Knee, Wovoka muted his threat of supernatural destruction of this world when he spoke with Mooney in 1892. But why would the same man who told Chapman two years earlier that he had no fear of soldiers for he possessed that power as well as the ability to make this world over again transform his original revelation so dramatically? Similarly, there are those who argue that the 1890 Ghost Dance Prophet wasn't jack rabbit hunting — or working for Tibo'o — in East Walker Valley when Mooney arrived. They say he was hiding out of fear lest the military arrest him as perpetrator behind the massacre in South Dakota. They need to explain this. Especially when, in contrast to the situation surrounding the 1870 Ghost Dance, there is no evidence that Wovoka or his followers experienced disillusionment with prophecies that failed (Hittman 1973a). On the contrary, Wovoka appears to have main-tained faith in his original revelation and supernatural powers to the very end.

One way of approaching the original ideology of the 1890 Ghost

Dance is to pose the following ethnohistorical question: Would Numus living in Smith and Mason valleys have been dancing for the end of this world and the return of the dead in the late 1880s? Here again, an examination of the local newspapers becomes instructive.

On September 10, 1890, the editor of the *Lyon County Times* wrote that "...something...[must] be done with the Indians in Mason and Smith Valleys. They are becoming impudent and treacherous, and we think it would be a good idea to confine them on the Reservations for a time." In the following year, on January 29, 1891, the *Walker Lake Bulletin* stated: "The Piutes [sic] in Mason Valley are all well armed and very saucy. They say pretty soon they will own the stores and ranches and houses." A few days later we read in the *Lyon County Times* (31 January 1891): "The Piutes [sic] in Smith Valley are reported to be very ugly. They say that the country all belonged to them once and that pretty soon they will own the farms and horses away from the white man." Similarly, Zadok Pierce of Wellington, Smith Valley, who was Mooney's host, probably authored the following statement to Chapman: "He could see that the Indians were a little more exacting every day. Only recently did one of them, with all his stock, move into a white man's field and would not go out when he was told to do so." Whether or not it was Pierce who personally threatened to throw the militant Numu off his land, Chapman reported what the latter defiantly said to the Tibo'o in question: "'You had better bring a big crowd if you attempt it.'" Finally, Ed Dyer could note that for all his years of association with Numus, the "small group" assembled on that "most solemn occasion" under a cottonwood tree awaiting the block of ice to fall from the sky seemed "distinctly not talkative to a white." With these indications of Numu militancy at the time of the 1890 Ghost Dance, don't they therefore once and for all prove that Wovoka's eschatology was originally militant, and that he perhaps had opportunistically shifted to pacifism? Local newspapers notwithstanding, I argue the contrary.

To begin with, Sally Zanjani (1988) reported, in a recent study of Nevada's political climate at the time of the 1890 Ghost Dance, how powerful individuals were busily attempting to exploit the national hysteria provoked by Wovoka's new religion. Their motivation was to solicit state funds for construction of a fort in the Hawthorne area, this historian wrote. Her conclusion, therefore, was that "Wovoka's teachings strongly opposed warfare with the whites...." (Zanjani 1988:121).[15] Mooney (1896:828) expressed himself identically: "Among the Piute [sic] where the doctrine originated and the messiah has his home, there was never the slightest

Greenfield Took Pride in Company "I" Formed To Discourage Indian Uprisings in Early Days

PLATE H. National Guard Unit, Lyon County, 1890. *Courtesy Mason Valley News*

trouble." Because Numus living in the Walker River area had "steadily resisted the vices of civilization," he wrote (Mooney 1896:1050), they "would be the last Indians in the world to preach a crusade of extermination against the whites, such as the messiah religion has been represented to be." Even Mooney's (1896:772) assessment of the opinion of Wovoka held by the local citizenry of Smith and Mason valleys led him to conclude that "only a few of the white men...were suspicious of Wilson's doctrine." Still another proof of Wovoka's pacific doctrine comes from Lt. Nat Phister. On the basis of his interviews with "many of the Nevada Indians on the subject," Phister (1891:107) wrote that the 1890 Ghost Dance was not anti-white: "The doctrine as preached by Kvittsow [Wovoka] is not at all in the nature of a crusade against the white people."

"Wilson was cooperative, neither cringing, bellicose nor evasive," Ed Dyer echoed this viewpoint. A "'hell-of-a-good Ingin!'" were the words of the otherwise jingoistic *Walker Lake Bulletin* (26 November 1890). "[Wovoka was] a Simon pure, yard wide, all wool Christ...who advised peace and performed miracles which made all people feel good." And years later, in 1917, when Special Inspector Lafayette Dorrington visited the Prophet's home in Mason, he could state that "from all accounts...[Wovoka] has always been friendly with the whites" (Stewart 1977:221-22). After a useful survey of the Nevada newspaper articles written about the 1890 Ghost Dance, Brad Logan (1980:278) observed: "But in western Nevada, during the four years of marked proselytism of the Ghost Dance, with delegations of Indians entering the area continuously, the tone of the official dispatches and most of the newspaper articles remains fairly calm."

Certainly, then, the burden of proof rests on those who feel Wovoka's original ideology was anything but pacific and otherworldly. For by 1890 it is entirely clear that the subsistence economy had collapsed. Numus were involved in wage labor, as shovels, pitchforks, hoes, derrick rakes, washboards, iron kettles, and dish pan took the place of winnowing baskets and **manos** and **metates**. A new generation had appeared, a birth cohort (1860-1884) reared entirely within the Euro-American orb. Though their working hours for Tibo'o were long and wages were marginal, Numus received more food, clothing, and material than ever before seen and possibly even dreamed. One might even speculate that the years immediately preceding the eruption of the 1890 Ghost Dance in the Walker River area were perceived by them as an unparalleled era of technological and alimentary well-being. To be sure, scarlet fever and other diseases took their toll on Numus in the late 1880s. But, nevertheless, one searches in vain for evidence of the kind of deprivation, say, which preceded the 1870 Ghost Dance on the Walker River Reservation. We do not even read of alcoholism as a social ill in Smith Valley or Mason Valley in the late 1880s — implied by the absence of a temperance plank within Wovoka's ideology.

The 1890 Ghost Dance in Nevada was a "get-along" religion. It was "accommodative," as Alice Kehoe (1964, 1989) has described it, and a "reformistic" or "redemptive" (Aberle 1966; Jorgensen 1986, 1987) social movement contrasting with the utterly radical and revolutionary "transformative" doctrine of Wodziwob's 1870 Ghost Dance. In spite of Wovoka's proclaimed supernatural powers to destroy this world, if the highly acculturated Numus living in the Walker River area thought to participate in a militant movement to eradicate Tibo'o,[16] they would have been easily dissuaded from acting this out. A special edition of the *Mason Valley News* (2 June 1961) suggests why. On that date, there is an 1890 photo of the Greenfield Guard's Company I of the National Guard unit to which Ed Dyer belonged (Plate H). Fully armed, these uniformed volunteers, drilling in the hot sun, would have intimidated ghost dancing Numus. "The use of firearms against Indians in this valley was never once displayed," we read in the July 18, 1975 issue, which reports a total of 125 recruits.

Furthermore, the *Lyon County Times,* on July 14, 1888, characterized Fourth of July doings in Greenfield (Yerington) in these words: "More Piutes [sic] [are] in town than for many weeks before.... Indian race of 1/4 mile was then run by a large number of Piutes [sic] and the wind up there was a string of bucks for 1/4 of a mile all in Indian file." And, if Numus of Smith and Mason valleys were indeed as "ugly" and hell-bent upon Tibo'o destruction as the editors of the *Walker Lake Bulletin* and the *Lyon County Times* seemed to suggest, their participation in such annual festivities would certainly be enigmatic. But far more difficult to explain was their reaction to the fire which broke out in Greenfield at 5:45 on a Monday morning in December of 1893, ultimately destroying 12 wooden buildings. Would Numus who were dancing to destroy every last Tibo'o in this world, and to bring back their dead, have come "flocking into town in droves shortly after daylight and worked well to save property (*Mason Valley Tidings* 30 December 1893)?

The 1890 Ghost Dance was relatively short-lived in its homeland. What began probably in late December of 1888 was effectively over by 1892. "Jack always says the White man got too much power and guns, Indians cannot kill them," Mrs. Chapin told Wier. Moses (1985:342-43) stated much the same: "When Wovoka learned about Wounded Knee, he understandably feared that he would be blamed. He counseled delegates who, with ardor, still sent them to Nevada seeking news of the millennium, that they should return to their respective tribes and stop the dances. The Indian resurrection had been postponed." And Mooney (1896:913) himself quoted the Prophet as having told a skeptical Kiowa delegate in 1891 "to quit the whole business." And again, in October of 1892, Wovoka reportedly told Sitting Bull that he was tired of visitors and wanted them to go home and stop dancing (Mooney 1896:901).

"Jack Wilson avoids people here," George Plummer (Wier Notes) more or less stated. "Never told [Plummer] anything about [his] religion." J. I. Wilson, reporting the alleged visit to Wovoka by the "head of Bureau of Indian Affairs," told Dangberg how this government official had driven "to see him in a rig [on the Wilson Ranch?] — [but] Jack shut up — Wouldn't speak. Wouldn't look at him. All information got from Mr. Wilson." And Bob Dyer (Dangberg Notes), too, related that Wovoka grew "quiet after Mooney interviewed him." Finally, Andy Vidovich (Tape 90:8) would recall how Wovoka "used to tell me, 'My boy, don't mention it to the white people.'"

How does one explain the Prophet's "reticence?" Because so much of the 1890 Ghost Dance appears to have been directly tied up with Wovoka's spectacular demonstration of supernatural powers, the least that can be said is that the religion he founded ended when he wearied of rumors and falsehoods attributed to him and retired into a kind of semi-seclusion.[17]

ENDNOTES

1. One wonders, too, whether or not systematic efforts then to sell or "open" the Walker River Reservation to prospectors and miners contributed to Wovoka's popularity among its Numus. Thus, on June 15, 1889, we read in the *Lyon County Times:* "This territory will never be of benefit to the Indian. He is too indolent to go prospecting, and too ignorant to develop a mine after it is found. The Piute [sic] would lose none of the prerogatives they now enjoy, by the abandonment of the Reservation, except that of preventing the Whites from doing that which they will not do themselves. They could work a little, steal a little, beg a little, borrow some and ask for more, and would in all respects be happier and more comfortable according to their ideas of happiness and comfort."

2. One is reminded here of the various portents experienced by related Nahuatl-speaking people in the Valley of Mexico at the time of the coming of the Spaniards in 1517 — 1519.

3. Even I was teased about having weather control bbooha following a torrential rainstorm in Pine Grove the day after I'd been taken there by my Numu family to photograph the mining camp where Wovoka lived.

4. Solberg, on the other hand, informs me that Ruby Conway, a Yerington Indian Colony resident,

told him in the early 1970s that Wovoka used to descry the usage of opiates among Numus.

5. Cf. "When shamans get power it always comes from the night. They are told to doctor only at night. This power has nothing to do with the moon or stars. I knew one woman who used the sun, moon, and stars for her power. I saw her fill her pipe and just as the sun came up she puffed and started to smoke. I saw her do this several times. I watched her closely but she did not use matches. Her power lighted her pipe" (Park 1938:17).

6. As Solberg suggests, we can also view this comment as self-deprecatory, an instance perhaps of the Prophet's sense of humor (Chapter Five).

7. Michael P. Carroll (1975:400) tabulated 37 tribes who accepted the 1890 Ghost Dance Religion, a figure which Gail Landsman reduced to 35. Alice Kehoe (1989), however, most recently challenged those numbers.

8. Some Plains delegates even testified that Wovoka could speak all languages.

9. Park (1941:187-88), incidentally, noted that Pyramid Lake Numus had borrowed a dance from the Bannocks which they incorporated into their Round Dance ceremonies.

10. Sven Liljeblad (1986:647), commenting upon similarities between Round Dance and 1890 Ghost Dance songs, wrote: "[They have]...one thing in common: unless a song refers directly to the dance as such, each song is an image in miniature of a scene from nature.... [They] express the delight in dancing and the beauty of nature, not its usefulness."

11. The rigidity of Spier's position is made evident by the following observation by Park (1941:198): "...important similarities between the cultures of the Plateau and the Great Basin are commonplace in ethnological literature but it is significant that there are almost no resemblances in the dance practices of the two areas."

12. In addition to these approaches, Michael Carroll (1975, 1979) and Joseph Jorgensen (1986) have attempted to correlate the presence or absence and "density" of such institutions as unilinear descent groups with acceptance or rejection of the 1890 Ghost Dance. Gail Landsman (1979) focused upon the General Allotment Act as its explanatory variable, while Russell Thornton (1986) recently suggested that demographics also can explain the rise both of the 1870 and 1890 Ghost Dance mnovements.

13. Elsewhere I have likened the 1870 Ghost Dance to "mourning" and "increase" ceremonies (Hittman 1973b) and discussed how Numus from the Walker River area might have rationalized the Fish Lake Valley prophet Wodziwob's prophecy of resurrection of the dead in light of their traditional "fear of the dead."

14. Dangberg (1968:10), on the other hand, argued that Numus danced the 1890 Ghost Dance with fervent conviction that their ancestors were coming back again to live on this earth, a doctrine she stated was "not Indian and may reasonably be ascribed to Christian and particularly Mormon influence."

Interestingly, too, Mooney (1896:703) quoted a letter from Franklin Campbell, an Indian Bureau employee on the Walker River Reservation who, on November 19, 1890 had this to say about the 1870 Ghost Dance Religion: "(The) 'Supreme Ruler...was then on his way with all the spirits of the departed dead to again reside upon this earth and change it into a paradise. Life was to be eternal and no distinction was to exist between races.'"

15. Zanjani (1988:121) also reported that "panic spread in Mason Valley when an Indian let it be known that his people planned to steal the arms in the armory and burn the town." Its source, however, is not indicated.

16. "The messiah himself has set several dates from time to time, as one prediction after another failed

to materialize, and in his message to the Cheyenne and Arapaho, in August of 1891, he leaves the whole matter an open question," wrote Mooney (1896:778). Unfortunately, I have no evidence either way concerning specific prophecies that Wovoka might have made regarding any final apocalypse and the start of the Millennium.

17. Cf. "The movement in western Nevada was bound up with the personality and power of its Prophet and when the Prophet retired into semi-seclusion after 1893 the movement fell apart" (Logan 1980:280).

CHAPTER 5

Wovoka, The Man

"The prophet is an individual who said No to his society" (Heschel 1962:xix).

Our earliest physical description of the 1890 Ghost Dance Prophet comes from Chapman. In a newspaper article entitled "Circle of the Shades," published soon after his December 1890 visit, the Indian scout offered this portrait of Wovoka to the *Spokane Review:*

> The only thing that I noticed is remarkable about his head was an unusually low forehead. The hair of his scalp grows within an inch of his eyebrows, and such eyebrows I never saw. They are the heaviest and shaggiest that ever grew on an Indian's head. His head is particularly prominent in the back and crown. His cheekbones are not prominent, but his lower jaw is massive, abnormally so. He does not have a hook nose. It is decidedly Greek. In fact, a finer cut nose I never saw [Ghost Dance File No. 188, Federal Archives, San Bruno, California].

Mooney's initial impression is also noteworthy. Snow was on the ground that New Year's Day in 1892 when he, Charley Sheep, and Ed Dyer went looking for Wovoka in East Walker country — a blizzard the government ethnologist was told had been caused by the Prophet's vaunted weather control powers. Mooney (1896:768-69) wrote:

> As he approached I saw that he was a young man, a dark full-blood, compactly built, and taller than the Paiute generally, being nearly 6 feet in height. He was well dressed in white man's clothes, with the broad-brimmed white felt hat common in the West, secured on his head by means of a beaded ribbon under the chin. This, with a blanket or a robe of rabbit skins, is now the ordinary Paiute dress. He wore a good pair of boots. His hair was cut off square on a line below the base of the ears, after the manner of his tribe.

The Numu's "countenance was open and expressive of firmness and decision but with no marked intellectuality," Mooney (ibid.) continues. "His features were broad and heavy, very different from the thin, clear-cut features of the prairie tribes." Ed Dyer, who had almost daily contact with Wovoka for several years, also left a memorable portrait of him.

> [Wovoka] was a tall, well proportioned man with piercing eyes, regular features, a deep voice and a calm and dignified mien. He stood straight as a ramrod, spoke slowly, and by sheer projection of personality commanded the attention of any listener. He visibly stood out among his fellow Indians like a thoroughbred among a bunch of mustangs.

Another invaluable description is found in Lafayette Dorrington's letter to the Commissioner of Indian Affairs. Written in 1917, this Special Indian Agent stated: "Jack Wilson is a very dignified and striking Indian. He is about sixty-five years of age and of good stature, weighing about 185 pounds (Stewart 1977:221-22).

Finally, Dr. George Richard Magee, United States government contract physician to Numus living in Smith and Mason valleys (his office was in Yerington), recalled the 1890 Ghost Dance Prophet in the years 1917-1918 in a letter to Gunard Solberg:

> Well, he seemed to be a kind person, well-liked. I don't ever remember in all the time I was down there that he ever got into any kind of altercation. He was very quiet, he never discussed [?] when we talked. In fact, he rarely discussed anything with me (Gunard Solberg — Personal Correspondence).

Photographs of Wovoka are also illuminating. For example, we observe at once, in the 1916 series taken by Samuel Barrett of the Milwaukee County Museum (Plate I.1 and I.2 and I.3), his large round craggy face. The Prophet's nose is isosceles shaped, he wears his hair short and parted in the middle, it covers both ears. Cheekbones are not high at all and a dimple hollows the left cheek. In his mid-fifties then, Wovoka's hair and facial whiskers were mostly white; and we notice, too, the deep furrows on his forehead, age lines radiating from the corners of his narrowly-slit eyes and beneath them. There is a stillness about his mien that one senses. As if the 1890 Ghost Dance Prophet, as Mooney (1896:764) suggested, was someone who "by nature...[was of] a solitary and contemplative disposition, one of those born to see visions and hear still voices." Handsome and photogenic, Wovoka's tightly-pursed lips are also striking about him in this series. They seem to express a grimness, or poignant sadness, which as we shall see was commented upon by someone who knew him well.

Plates I1, I2 & I3. Wovoka,
1914. Photo taken by Samuel
Barrett. *Courtesy Milwaukee
Public Museum*

The 1890 Ghost Dance Prophet's attire also merits discussion. S.S. Sears, Walker River Reservation superintendent, described the clothing style of Numu men from this time as follows: "From the habits and customs of savages, the warlike Pah-Utes [sic] have in twenty-five years advanced into the domain of civilization as far as cowhide shoes, duck-lined pants, red-flannel shirts, and shoddy felt hats would permit...." (Annual Report to the Commissioner of Indian Affairs, 29 August 1889, p. 249). Yet in Barrett's photographs, Wovoka wears a brand new collarless striped shirt and pin-striped denim breeches, or so-called "apron overalls" or "bib trousers." Since the latter item was not only popular in the 1890s but manufactured in Wisconsin (Worrell 1979), the suspicion here is that it (they) were purchased for the Prophet by Barrett for the purpose of the photography session. In all other photographs of him, however, suit pants and jackets, white shirts, neckerchiefs, gold watches, vests with fobs, long black coats and Stetson hats (Plates J and K) predominate. Yerington Paiute elder Howard Rogers was not alone in emphasizing these outfits worn by Wovoka:

> He stood straight. Hair's cut straight like that [above the ear]. Oh, and he wears regular shoes. Moccasins sometimes. Levi jeans, suit pants. But he always has on that black suit coat, though. And any kind of shirt. Yeah, and he also owns a hat that nobody else wears.

But lest we might imagine that this "cut above" dress code, which was certainly befitting his divinely ordained political status as "President of the West," was unique to Wovoka, other Numus also preferred dress suits to the working man's attire of denim and flannel. Numus in Smith and Mason valleys were quick to point out that Tom Mitchell, Walker River area medicine man extraordinaire, also wore dress suits rather than the working man's denim, as did Chief Winnemucca, Young Winnemucca, Gilbert Natches, Johnson Sides, and other Numu mediators and transla-tors ("Peace Chiefs") during those early years of contact.

In yet another incarnation, Wovoka's attire seems even more striking. This is the photograph on the cover of the book. In a penny picture postcard circa 1905, the Prophet poses in dress suit pants, vest, and Stetson hat from the Euro-American civilization, while wearing an (eagle?) feather in his hair, beaded gorget around his neck, beaded bandoleer across his chest and wound once around his waist, and beaded moccasins on his feet — the latter, no doubt, accoutrements collected during VIP travels to Native Americans living in Oklahoma and elsewhere. The buckskin gloves seen in

Plates L, M, and N were apparently the gift of one Navaho enthusiast who surprisingly (cf. Hill 1944) visited Wovoka in Mason Valley in October of 1914 (Appendix D). Plates L and M, incidentally, also belong to the penny picture postcard series, of which there were three in all. They depict Wovoka on either the Fourth of July or Nevada Day, standing in front of the Mason Valley Bank in Yerington, which happened to be owned by J. I. Wilson, the Prophet's childhood friend.

His fondness for neckerchiefs, eagle feathers, and five and ten gallon Stetson hats requires special attention. While describing Wovoka readying himself to be photographed in 1892, Mooney (1896:775) mentioned the "knotting [of] a handkerchief about his neck" (cf. Plates A.1 and A.2). According to one Yerington Paiute, anyway, the cotton cloth had magical significance. Frank Quinn narrated for Winona Holmes (Appendix K) Wovoka's request to borrow a handkerchief from a fellow Numu after he had been shot during a communal rabbit drive. "You know the old time blue and white kind," he related. "Men used to wear around their neck in those days." And why did Wovoka request the handkerchief? "When Jack stood up, there was an ant nest, so he stood up there [on it] and he put the handkerchief on the ground." According to Frank Quinn, the many shots riddling the 1890 Ghost Dance Prophet's body immediately then fell straight to the ground.

Wovoka's love of eagle feathers and Stetson hats are evidenced in the earliest photograph of him to date, circa 1875 (cf. Plate B), and Dangberg, interestingly enough, recorded this anecdote about the Prophet's youth. "M. Wilson remembers him first when he was crossing the river to go courting — Smith's Valley," she wrote. "Got his boat — and dressed up. Dumped [in the] river. [Stetson?] Hat floated off down the river. Finally rescued it. Still laughs about it." Mooney (1896:775) also wrote about this. While preparing for the historic photo session in 1892, the Prophet was said to have "fastened his eagle feather in his right shirt sleeve and placed his sombrero [white Stetson] on his knee" (cf. Plates A.1 and A.2).

We know that he sold eagle, magpie, and possibly crow feathers in the years that followed the 1890 Ghost Dance, and that the sale of his Stetsons were also a part of a brisk trade in thaumaturges conducted with Ed Dyer. "I afterward learned that the feather and sombrero were important parts of his spiritual stock in trade," wrote Mooney (1896:775). Wovoka's Philadelphia-manufactured Stetsons were either white (Plate A) or black (Plate P), round or stove-piped.

Moreover, the eagle feathers were said to have had magical properties.

PLATE J. Wovoka, studio posed. *Courtesy Nevada Historical Society*

"In talking with Tall Bull [the Cheyenne who visited Wovoka in 1889]," Mooney (ibid.) reported that:

> ...he said that before leaving they had asked Wovoka to give them some proof of his supernatural powers. Accordingly he had ranged them in front of him, seated on the ground, he sitting facing them, with his sombrero between and his eagle feathers in his hand. Then with a quick movement he had put his hand into the empty hat and had drawn out from it "something black."

Tall Bull, however, was not willing to admit "that anything more had happened," Mooney (ibid.) observed, contrasting his view of them with Black Coyote, who, being of a less skeptical nature, recast the same incident entirely in magical terms:

> Black Coyote told how they had seated themselves on the ground in front of Wovoka, as described by Tall Bull, and went on to tell how the messiah had waved his feathers over his hat, and then, when he withdrew his hand, Black Coyote looked into the hat and there "saw the whole world."

Or, as Mooney (1896:776) succinctly paraphrased the contrast, "Black Coyote saw the whole spirit world where Tall Bull saw only an empty hat." Asked to view the photograph on the cover of this book, Yerington Paiutes were evenly divided regarding what appears as something sewn inside the top lining of the Stetson Wovoka holds in his hand. Some felt it was his money, others saw the lining in magical terms, it contained their Prophet's medicine bundle or bbooha, they felt.

There are related questions to be asked: How did the 1890 Ghost Dance Prophet speak? Where did he live and how did he live? What foods did Wovoka eat?

"'It's just much yours like mine,'" said Andy Vidovich, quoting his father-in-law's reaction to the wagon he and Alice once presented as a gift. Earl Kerstein (Ms.) offers yet another comment attributed to Wovoka, this one in response to a week-long visit to Alice and Andy Vidovich's house in Sparks, Nevada: "'Me don't like the big town. Me and Mary go home.'" Dangberg (1957:285), finally, quoted Carrie Wilson nee Willis (1868-1925) on Wovoka's bafflement regarding certain requests for medicines that he received from loyalists: "Carrie, you tellum, I don't sabbe that kind."

If the Prophet, then, spoke the patois common among Numus his

Plate K. Wovoka in Yerington, circa 1915. *Courtesy Nevada Historical Society*

PLATE L. Wovoka in front of Lyon County Bank, circa 1907. Picture postcard. *Courtesy Nevada Historical Society*

PLATE M. Jack Wilson "Big Piute Chief" Wovoka wearing beaded gloves in front of Lyon County Bank, circa 1907. *Courtesy Nevada Historical Society*

Plate N. Wovoka, circa 1920.
Courtesy Nevada Historical Society

age and generation, who no doubt were influenced by roughened team-sters, miners, settlers, and the like, the impression also gained from accounts of Yerington Paiutes was that his speech was strikingly unprofane — a conclusion which has been independently confirmed by the 1938 letter of J. W. Wilson to Dangberg (1968:35). In it, David Wilson's oldest son wrote: "I spent considerable time with Jack from 1906 to 1916 and in all that time I don't think I ever heard him use the word 'damn,' or any other swear word."

He was "usually dependable — trust [him] as much as any Indian," J. W. Wilson's brother told Wier. Mrs. Plummer (Dangberg Notes) remarked similarly about the Prophet's character: "He was modest and unassuming to a degree about his power." Also, in a letter which Gunard Solberg generously has allowed me to quote from, Isabelle Creighton, Wovoka's neighbor in Mason in 1915, characterized the Prophet as follows: "Yes, Jack smiled, and could laugh, but I can also remember, that a great deal of the time, it was a sad and discouraged smile. A look of resignation, shall we say.... To us children, he was always kind and gentle, but boy if he told us to mind, we minded."

Yerington Paiutes paint the following composite portrait of their Prophet: Jack Wilson was a "nice, quiet old man" who lived in a "lumber house" and "talked good" and was "regular" in every way except one — "He never did a day's work!"

Regarding his domicile, Mooney (1896:770) wrote that he was still living in a traditional tule house in 1892:

> On entering through the low doorway we found ourselves in a circular lodge made of bundles of tule rushes laid over a framework of poles, after the fashion of the thatched roofs of Europe and very similar to the grass lodges of the Wichita. The lodge was only about 10 feet in diameter and about 8 feet in height, with sloping sides, and was almost entirely open above, like a cone with the top cut off, as in this part of the country rain or snow is of rare occurrence. In the center, built directly on the ground, was a blazing fire of sagebrush, upon which fresh stalks were thrown from time to time, sending up a shower of sparks into the open air…. The only articles in the nature of furniture were a few grass woven bowls and baskets of various sizes and patterns. There were no Indian beds or seats of the kind found in every prairie tipi [sic], no rawhide boxes, no toilet pouches, not even a hole dug in the ground for the fire. Although all wore white man's dress, there were not pots, pans or other articles of civilized manufacture, now used by even the most primitive prairie tribe, for, strangely, although these Paiute are practically farm laborers and tenants of the whites all around them, and earn good wages, they seem to covet nothing of the white man's, but spend their money for dress, small trinkets, and ammunition for hunting, and continue to subsist on seeds, pinion nuts, and small game, lying down at night on the dusty ground in their cramped wikiups [sic], destitute of even the most ordinary conveniences in use among other tribes. It is a curious instance of a people accepting the inevitable while yet resisting innovation.

Since Wovoka was hunting and camping in East Walker Valley — if not working on the Morgan Ranch and/or hiding from military authorities — when Mooney finally located him, the traditional tule house no doubt was only a temporary dwelling. For according to Corbett Mack, the 1890 Ghost Dance Prophet was also distinctive insofar as, while other Numus lived in tents around the turn of the century, Wovoka was the first Numu in Smith Valley ever to build or own a "lumber [frame] house." Wovoka was said to have sold it circa 1910 to Corbett's father, Big Mack Wheeler, because of his decision to move to Mason Valley; that is, the Prophet's

Plate O. View of dwellings at the Yerington Indian Colony, circa 1917. The Prophet's residence (1917-1932). *Courtesy Nevada Historical Society*

flimsy, one-room, wooden structure built on an earthen floor could not be relocated. Gunard Solberg (Personal Correspondence), on the other hand, learned that Wovoka lived in a tent at Nordyke from 1900-1913, and subsequently also in Mason. Probably the Prophet lived in a variety of dwellings before finally settling into his wooden house at the Yerington Paiute Colony in 1917 (Plate O). In this regard, then, Andy Vidovich's suggestion (Vidovich-Wheat Tape 100:4-6) that Wovoka had taken over Numu-tibo'o's frame house following the latter's death around 1914 or 1915 is noteworthy.

Vidovich stated how it was upon the advice of his Stewart-educated and "progressive" daughter, Alice, that the 1890 Ghost Dance Prophet dramatically broke with Numu tradition by not tearing down Numu-tibo'o's lumber house. "We'll clean, and mop up up [sic] the walls and clean up everything," Vidovich summarized his wife's argument to her father. "And then we'll clean up that stove, and we'll polish up that stove, and fix it all up nice, and change the windows to a different location." In relating how he personally repaired the roof, replaced the windows, and divided up the rooms, Andy Vidovich illustrates the types of profound changes occurring within Numu mourning culture, the physical alteration of private dwellings rather than setting them on fire following any deaths in the family.[1] Because Isabelle Creighton mentioned that Wovoka had objected to his stepdaughter's desire to own a dresser and bed, it is probably true he initially objected to Alice's newfangled idea about retaining Numu-tibo'o's

PLATE P. Wovoka in Mason, December 1916. Photo by L.A. Dorrington. *Courtesy Smithsonian Institution*

house as well. Quoting from that letter, anyway, Mrs. Creighton offers the following reminiscence of the 1890 Ghost Dance Prophet's life and domicile in Mason circa 1912-1915:

> We purchased the property in the summer of 1912, as I was six years old, and my grandparents moved down from the Mason Valley Mine, to put me in school. When we first moved they [Wovoka's family] were not there, as an old brick yard or the remains I should say, were on the south of us, where Jack lived. There was a big Indian camp on the north [of] us tho [sic]. Jack, must have come either the latter part of 1912, or early 1913, and when we burnt out in October 1915, they were still there. They got water from our well, as did all the Indians. In 1915 before we burnt out, Jack, came up complaining to grandmother, about Alice, wanting a bed, and dresser, and not willing to have a tent unless it had a floor in it. He couldn't see why she was not satisfied with the ground same as he had always been, but grandmother tried to make him see that if Alice, was to accept the white man's way she should have these things, and Jack gave in, and got them for her. Jack, was a bright man, and if he had had any chance for an education in the white man's language and ways would have gone far, and also might I say, he was a grand person and neighbor.

And Wovoka might well have still been living in his father's lumber house when L. A. Dorrington photographed him in Mason in 1917 (Plate P). Dorrington (Steward 1977:221) described the Prophet's house in these words:

> [Wovoka]...lives in purely Indian custom. He resides with four or five other Indian families, who are squatters on land in the vicinity of Mason. His house consists of rough boards divided into two rooms, the probable cost of which does not exceed $80.00. He owns or possesses a team, buggy and harness valued at about $250.00. He lives purely Indian customs with very little household effects. They sleep on the floor and from all appearances also use the floor as their table for eating.

But following the purchase of the 9.456 acre Yerington Indian Colony from Frank Bovard's estate in Mason Valley for $1,025.64 in that year, Jack and Mary Wilson permanently relocated onto what became known as the Yerington Indian Colony. They moved a short distance of three or so miles from Mason and resided in a small frame house built on an earthen floor that was situated at the northwest arm of the central road running through the center of the colony. After Mary Wilson's death in August 1932, the Prophet took up residence in a shack with his grandson, Dennis Bender, at the opposite corner of the federal reservation. The Prophet lived here until his own death one month later.[2]

Regarding his diet, Yerington Paiutes allowed that Wovoka ate no differently than they: jackrabbit, deer, pine nut soup, buckberries, etc., from the traditional cuisine; fried potatoes, boiled beef, white bread, coffee, and other staples from the dominant society. Earl Kerstein (Ms.), interestingly enough, learned that salmon and steak were among the Prophet's favorite foods. The allegation that Wovoka "never worked" has already been discussed, and will be taken up again in the next chapter. Here again we note only that he neither gambled, drank, nor used opiates. Noteworthy, too, is that in spite of the impression of grimness gained from photographs — Wovoka's tightly-pursed lips, the "look of resignation" previously commented upon by Mrs. Creighton — there is plenty of evidence that the 1890 Ghost Dance Prophet had a pithy sense of humor. Newcombe, for example, related Wovoka's reaction to the news that a Native American he attempted to cure through the mails had died:

> I was the telegrapher at Mason, Nevada, the place where Jack sent and received his messages from those that thought he was a great medicine man. One day Jack came into the office to mail one of his customary small packages of red ground-up rock to an Indian patient. Jack would send the packages, collect $15.00 and promise to make them well. This day I had a message for Jack so I read it to him. The message said, "Father Wovoka — you no make my wife well no more — she dead now" (Davidson 1952:47).

"Jack laughed and laughed and laughed," Newcombe related. "And he said, 'Well, we all have to die sometime.'" The Mason telegrapher then went on to suggest that the Prophet was "a sly ole boy; he was smart, no question about it. He could sure get a kick out of a good joke."

Grace Dangberg similarly wrote that when "Mrs. [David] W. [Wilson] once was scolding Mr. [David] W. [Wilson] for not shutting the screen door," the 1890 Ghost Dance Prophet sardonically commented: "'Oh, you gettin' all same Paiute. Paiute gettin' same [as] white man.'" When Mr. Wilson retorted, "'Paiute gettin' all same [as] white man?'" Wovoka's quick rejoinder was, "'Yes, P [Paiute], he gettin' all same white man.'"

And J. W. Wilson also commented upon the Prophet's cutting, if you will, sense of humor. In another letter to Dangberg, this one dated July 19, 1939 (Appendix E), the oldest of the three Wilson sons commented on the block of ice miracle: "Your article has emphasized the religious side of Jack, which I think is fine. There was one side of Jack I also remember, and that is that while he was good at heart and desired to do good he, at times, was roguish in his methods, rather a delightful rogue I would say."

"Jack learned to play [these] practical jokes by playing with the Wilson boys," Genevieve Chapin, who might have been commenting upon what was generally perceived to be a miracle by Numus and an entirely discreditable hoax so far as the Wilsons and other Tibo'o were concerned, the block of ice in the Walker River in the summer, observed in the Dangberg Notes. Her words, I would argue, belie a world of meaning. Recall the Prophet's response to Chapman's inquiry about that other spectacular demonstration of his supernatural power, Wovoka's invulnerability — "That was just a joke!" His defensiveness here is obvious enough, but can we not read more into this?

"Pis.a suwa_idi, sikwiapa sagwa._idi." "The one who laughs well is quick to anger," as Sven Liljeblad (1986:643) rendered the Numu proverb. If ethnic group humor, as Joseph Dorinson (1988) reminds us, can be the vented rage of despised and depressed categories of people and ethnic groups against social injustices, then Wovoka's "jokes" and "pranks" perhaps ought to be re-evaluated, especially in light of Liljeblad's insight into the Numic "mind."

"About 10 years after [?] [Wovoka] brought in some rich rock to Pine Grove mine," we read in the Dangberg Notes. Bill Wilson, the Prophet's boyhood friend had "paid him $30 to show him the place, [and] J. [Jack] set a time.... One day others followed Mr. B. [Billy] Wilson and Jack. [But when] Jack saw others following [he] ran away leaving [the] horse. [He] Never did show the real place." "A big rascal!" the 1890 Ghost Dance Prophet was therefore chastised in this source, the reason given, Jack Wilson "used to take prospectors out to show them rock. $20 apiece. He was showing them Pine Grove rock. [So] Billy Wilson ran him out."

With gold so ever-present a constant factor on the minds of many Tibo'o ranchers and farmers living in Smith and Mason valleys — "After discovering the mine, William Wilson's principle occupation was mining at Pine Grove gold," his brother, David, related to Weir — local Numus no doubt, with their knowledge of the surrounding mountainsides, were always placed at a premium as prospecting guides for them. In the instance cited above, however, Wovoka appears to have gone out of his way to purchase $20 worth of gold dust, which he then allegedly loaded into his shotgun and fired against the wall of a cave. The following is Ed Dyer's version of the "prank":

> I never heard of his attempting to put over anything on a white man except once. That incident occurred early in the game and may have been in the nature of a test case of his ability. Lack of results may have been discouraging. In any event he attempted to pick up a few dollars from one of the members of the Wilson family, who had an avid interest in mines, by offering to show him a gold mine. In those days that was a natural as the whites were always trying to pump Indians regarding the location of gold deposits which they were supposed to know of. In this case Jack thoughtfully and artistically salted a large boulder by means of a little gold dust loaded into a shot gun. A lack of knowledge of geology defeated him however, as he made the fatal error of picking a granite boulder. To any readers with a similar lack of geologic learning I might explain that the occurrence of gold in granite is about as rare as its occurrence in a hard boiled egg.

Bailey (1957:71-74), who must have picked up this story from Dyer, described it as the only instance in which Jack Wilson had ever attempted "to put over anything on a white man." And in J. W. Wilson's assessment, this was the "only time he [Jack Wilson] ever appeared to be dishonest."

If humor can be a mask for anger, this follow-up question then needs to be asked: Are there any evidences in which the 1890 Ghost Dance Prophet ever acted out this hypothesized anger? Although we must discount the infusion of rage attributed to Wovoka in Bailey's (1970) fictionalized biography, we do, however, have certain solid hints of the Prophet's wrath. In the first of these, Wovoka, as we have already seen, causes torrential downpours to flood Smith Valley following the death of his beloved son, around 1900. Also, one might see, in the Prophet's discontinuation of his own religion, Wovoka's fury with Plains Indians for their inversion of his Great Revelation. Finally, in a third example, the 1890 Ghost Dance Prophet quite plainly loses his temper with a Smith Valley Tibo'o.

Alex Miller reported to me a visit by Wovoka to the Colony District of Smith Valley to purchase watermelons from his mother-in-law, Mrs. Ben Dickinson, wife of one of the valley's original settlers. When Wovoka concluded that Mrs. Dickinson was overcharging, he became so incensed that, according to Miller, the Prophet not only refused to pay but threatened to cause the Walker River to rise and destroy her watermelon patch, flooding the entire valley as well.

1. This relates to the issue of the return of the dead in the 1870 Ghost Dance (cf. Hittman 1973b). Reflecting the dramatic Numu change in their stance toward the dead, headstones also began to appear, and graves were decorated with flowers on Memorial Day.

2. Hattori (1975:20-22) offers an excellent description of the evolution of post-contact Numu housing types.

CHAPTER 6

The Middle Years

"The life of an itinerant magician, like that of an actor on tour, is likely to be a picaresque novel without a plot — a string of incidents connected mainly by the central character" (Morton Smith 1978:109).

We can conveniently group what is known about Wovoka's life from the end of the 1890 Ghost Dance Religion to circa 1920 into these five headings: (1) travel; (2) correspondence and income from the sale of thaumaturges; (3) his shamanic practice; (4) various land disputes; and (5) exercise of the Prophet's divinely revealed political powers.

TRAVEL

According to J. I. Wilson (Dangberg Notes), the Wilson family had received "permission" to take Wovoka from Smith and Mason valleys to the World Columbia Exposition in Chicago in 1893.

> About [the] time of [the] Chicago Expo, Mr. Wilson wanted to take Jack back there. Could make a lot of money. [So he] got government permission to take him. But Jack went back on [the] agreement one month before they were to start. Finally he went into the hills in Smith Valley 2 months past [the] time to go.

Dangberg (1957:284) related the same aborted trip: "It was expected that Jack's fame would make him an attraction at the World's Fair and that the venture would be a profitable one for all concerned."

John Greenway (1969:47) repeated Mooney's assertion that last heard from, the 1890 Ghost Dance Prophet was "selling himself" as a sideshow attraction at the Midwinter Fair in San Francisco in 1904; however, there is no evidence to substantiate that Wovoka went there either. According to his son-in-law (Vidovich-Wheat Tape 100:12), the Prophet did travel to Indian reservations in Wyoming, Montana, and Kansas, as well as to the former Indian Territory of Oklahoma several times.

D. B. Shimkin (1942:457) reported one such visit made to Shoshones of the Wind River Reservation, Wyoming. "In 1910, the Ghost Dance

PLATE Q. Wovoka "On the Road" (with Andrew Vidovovich). *Credit: Unknown*

Messiah, Jack Wilson, visited the reservation, arriving just before the Sun Dance. They held a Ghost Dance in his honor." And Forrest R. Stone, superintendent of the Wind River Agency, stated in a letter to Dangberg (1957:284) that Wovoka traveled to Oklahoma in 1911 or 1912. On November 27, 1916, Special Indian Agent, C. H. Asbury, wrote the Commissioner of Indian Affairs that the Prophet had been to Oklahoma twice, for a "few months" early in the year, and later again in October. Asbury also stated that Wovoka had also visited the Wind River Reservation on July 1, 1916 (cf. Appendix E), while Ake Hultkrantz (1981:272) reports a 1917 visit there.

Commenting on Wovoka's travels in the years 1906 and 1916, Dangberg (1957:284) wrote: "On each of these [occasions] he was accompanied by a boy 18 to 20 years of age who, he said, was his nephew. This boy had attended Stewart Institute near Carson City, Nev., and was thus equipped to manage the details of rail travel." Plate Q shows the Prophet on the road. At his right, Wovoka's traveling companion has been identified as his son-in-law, Andrew Vidovich. Yerington Paiutes also suspected that another son-in-law, Pete Penrose, was a frequent traveling companion of the Prophet's, as well as Billy Sheep, the son of Mooney's Walker River Reservation host and a cousin-brother of the Prophet, and a Carson City Numu named Tommy Cyphers, who has been identified as the figure standing to Wovoka's left in Plate J.

Several anecdotes about the 1890 Ghost Dance Prophet's "foreign" travel exist. Dangberg (1957:284-85), for example, wrote: "Once Jack planned to take Mary, his wife, with him; in preparation for this event he painstakingly instructed her in the art of eating with a knife and fork. Mary, however, soon grew weary of this unaccustomed exertion and decided to remain at home." Unfortunately the year and destination of this out-of-state trip are not indicated. "Woman cut no figure back east," Wovoka was also quoted by Mrs. Webster (Dangberg Notes) as having once commented on why he did not allow Mary Wilson to accompany him. Wovoka's ability to quip, illustrative no doubt of his keen sense of humor, is evidenced in the Prophet's following exchange with J. I. Wilson. When his former playmate inquired whether he, Joe Wilson, could take Mary Wilson's place, Wovoka reportedly replied: "No, Joe, you talk too damn much."

Then there is Tim McCoy's fuller account of a visit by Wovoka to the set of "The Thundering Herd," a silent film shot in 1924 near Mulner Lake, California. After having been hired as technical director of the project,

PLATE R. Wovoka with Arapahoes, 1924. Mulner Lake, California. *Courtesy Smithsonian Institution*

McCoy, according to his son Ron (McCoy 1977:216), recalled:

> We were shooting scenes near Bishop in northern [sic] California and were about a day's automobile ride from Wovoka's old stomping grounds. While I felt I might very well be embarking upon a fool's errand, I decided to borrow a company car and drive toward the place to which Yellow Calf and Sage, Short Bull and Kicking Bear had journeyed more than a quarter of a century before. I was going to try and do as they had once done: find the messiah.

With his stated intention to impress the nine Arapahos whom he'd hired for the film, insofar as they were participants in Wovoka's religion (Plate R), the cowboy movie star Tim McCoy drove ninety miles or so north to the Yerington Indian Colony where the Prophet lived. After McCoy's initial request for an interview had been turned down by Wovoka's grandson (Dennis Bender), he eventually was successful in convincing the 1890 Ghost Prophet to visit the movie set. "Alright, I'll go," Wovoka was quoted by McCoy as having said. "You send a car for me tomorrow," remarking also that he had never traveled to Arapaho country. So on the very next day Tim McCoy "borrowed" the producer's limousine and sent a hired driver to bring the famous Numu onto the set of "The Thundering Herd."

> At about four-thirty the long black limousine, carrying the chauffeur, Wovoka, his grandson and what must have been about five hundred pounds of polished chrome decoration, drew up alongside me. As I directed the driver to keep on going until he reached the dance circle, I noticed that the car was followed by a convoy of five dilapidated jalopies, driven by and filled with Paiutes (McCoy 1977:219).

If McCoy's memory is accurate, the Arapahos joined the twenty or so Numus from the Yerington Indian Colony, who reportedly accompanied Wovoka in separate cars, in bowing their heads as soon as the revered Prophet stepped from his limousine. A sumptuous meal followed. "The Paiutes, including the messiah, gorged themselves, [while] the Arapahoes danced, showing off to what they called the 'root diggers,' but with only half their hearts" (McCoy 1977:220). After dinner, the knowledgeable McCoy doing the interpreting, the 1890 Ghost Dance Prophet, who was majestically seated in the director's chair, addressed his audience arrayed in a semicircle on the ground surrounding his feet.

The earth, he explained, is divided into three parts. There is the layer below the one in which we live; then there is the middle part on which we dwell; finally, there is the top place, heaven. And that's exactly what he called it, "hebbin," because if anybody ever got the Indian's beliefs of Medicine jumbled up with the white man's belief in Christianity and mixed them into a fine, confusing brew, it was Wovoka.

It was, he said, to that uppermost layer that New Year's Day, 1889, when both he and the sun died. He met with God, they talked and God told him he was the messiah. Tell my children, the Indians — God directed — always to do the right thing, tell no lies and live in peace with everyone. And that's what he told all the Arapahoes and Sioux who came to him. That and nothing more. But some of them, particularly the Sioux, got carried away and took back this idea about Ghost Shirts, because they wanted to fight the white man. God was not pleased with this and, Wovoka said sadly, the Sioux were killed and the Medicine turned bad. So God decided that the spirits of the dead Indians, and the elk, antelope and buffalo, would not return. At least not now (McCoy 1977:221).

"The idea, he maintained, was the same as it always had been," Tim McCoy (ibid.) recounted, "and all of his children must try to stick to God's law."

And just to keep everything in good order, he was going to give them some of the same batch of paint he had given to Yellow Calf and Sage, Short Bull and Kicking Bear. White paint to cure sickness and red paint to wear during their dances. What's more, he proclaimed, he was going to work a miracle so they would know he was not speaking out of the side of his mouth.

He asked if any of the Arapahoes had been sick. William Penn rose and stood in front of the awed crowd of Arapahoes and tapped his chest. He had tuberculosis and, as he explained, had not been able to dance for a long time. Wovoka directed him to lie down on the ground, painted William's face with white paint, and sang some songs over him and, bending down, sucked out what Goes In Lodge afterward swore was "the bad Medicine" out of his chest (McCoy 1977:221-22).

"But," Wovoka explained, "there was still more to come. He was going to teach them a dance to give them good Medicine. They were to take this dance back to Wind River and teach it to their fellow tribesmen." And, this, according to Tim McCoy (ibid.), was none other than an authentic 1890 Ghost Dance ceremony.

While ethnohistorical research remains to be done on the Prophet's visits to Oklahoma and elsewhere, the suggestion by Dangberg (1957:284) was that "on all of the journeys he was treated with great deference and entertained lavishly; he slept in feather beds in carpeted rooms and was served the choicest of food." A letter from J. W. Wilson might also very well capture something essential about Wovoka's out-of-state travels:

> I happened to be present at the time Jack returned from his eastern trip. Jack was very much elated and my memory of Jack telling of his meetings with the Indians was that there were immense crowds; he said, "Me stand up from sun up until sun down, me shakum hands all day. Me pretty tired. Five big Indian chiefs layum $20.00 [gold] in my hand. Me likum that way shakin' hands. Me think that a pretty good way shakin' hands" (Dangberg 1957:284-85).

Chester Smith, who lived near the Prophet at the Yerington Indian Colony, recalled one such return from out-of-state:

> Wovoka left with one suitcase and he returned with four. His suitcases were filled with all sorts of things: beads, beaded moccasins, buckskin clothes. And Jack'd lay it out to show us, you know. Spread out some canvas 'cause Indians those days don't use tables and chairs like nowadays. They even slept on the floor. I know Jack Wilson did. Same like me.

Ed Dyer's manuscript reveals much the same:

> His correspondents in Indian Territory began to write importuning him to visit them. At the outset he was somewhat leery, half suspecting a trick to get him where hands could be laid upon him in revenge for letting them down with those ineffectual ghost shirts. But eventually he was persuaded, partly by my assurances that law and order prevailed in Oklahoma and he made a trip back there. He was lionized and on his return was loaded with presents of money but mainly of items such as moccasins, vests, belts, gloves, buckskin breeches and other articles of finery dear to the Indian's heart. The loot would have made a collector of Indian hand work green with envy. Every-

PLATE S. The Prophet's root cellar. Wilson Ranch with Nordyke ranch house in background. *Courtesy Nevada Historical Society*

thing was of the finest quality, adorned with beads, porcupine quills, animal teeth and claws. Twenty years later he still wore some of those vests and moccasins. As time went on he was forgotten by some of his Eastern friends but the Pahutes never faltered or forgot their fealty.

Although the duration of any of these sojourns is unknown, Isabelle Creighton's letter to Gunard Solberg in the 1970s would suggest that some might have been quite lengthy:

Jack himself would go off and be gone for sometimes 6 months at a time, taking part of the [Mason] encampment with him, but the entire Indian camp would not leave. Sometimes Jack would only be gone for a period of 3 months. He always told us that he had to go to take part in a big pow-wow, religious like, at least that was our impression.

Interesting, too, in this regard is the following recollection of the Prophet by Mrs. Creighton:

> Each time Jack, went off in reply to one of the letters, all the guns and anything they had of value, reposed in one end of our big kitchen until they returned. We never knew actually where they went for the pow-wows, or why.... (Gunard Solberg, Personal Correspondence).

"Jack had an old time trunk, round on the top, which he used to store blankets, moccasins, beaded sashes, gorgets, buckskin gloves, the entire miscellany he received while traveling," Numu Chester Smith further recounted. The whereabouts of these handicrafts is, of course, pertinent for any biographer of the 1890 Ghost Dance Prophet. Since Numus traditionally buried all belongings of the deceased — "ghost sickness" (Whiting 1950) being a leading theory of sickness and death — we can safely assume that some were placed alongside Wovoka in his Walker River Reservation grave. Apparently none were discovered in Wovoka's root cellar at Nordyke, which since 1912 has incorrectly been identified as "Wovoka's home" (Plate S). There is also evidence that some of Wovoka's gifts ended up in storage at the Nevada State Museum. Judge Clark Guild, a former Yeringtonian, recounted the following to Mary Ellen Glass, principle researcher in the Oral History Project sponsored by the University of Nevada: "...my step-father-in-law, Bill Powers, learned to talk Paiute. And Jack had given him, in his life-time, his buckskin suit and several other very splendid articles of Indian make. Bill donated those to the museum." William Powers himself related as much to Dangberg in the 1920s:

> Fine collection of presents given to Jack. Bought them for a song and he sang for it: 4 pair beaded moccasins, Sioux war bonnet, two pairs of buckskin trousers, bonnet eagle feathers, buckskin, strip of deer fur, dyed horse hair ornamented or cemented on ends of feather.

Dr. Magee told Gunard Solberg that he accepted samples of Wovoka's collection as payment for treating the Prophet. Quoting from Solberg's correspondence with the former contract physician to Numus living in Smith and Mason valleys in the 1910s:

> Solberg: I suppose he had a great deal of respect for you as a doctor?

Magee:	He may have. He must of liked me because, I say, he gave me these gloves and moccasins, and a belt or something. I've still got them up at my Tahoe home, the things that he gave me. They were all lovely gifts, they weren't used or old or anything, they were all in excellent conditions.
Solberg:	How would he present them to you?
Magee:	He would just bring them in person and give them to me. He would tell me, he said, 'These weren't made by me and my friends, they were a gift to me. I'm giving them to you.' I'm sorry I don't know more about his life and all, as I say, he wasn't very communicative in our dealings.

Andy Vidovich stated that "one whole wall" of his home in Sparks and his home in Carson City was "covered with things Wavoka [sic] had given me...[a] lot of moccasins hanging on the wall...beaded vests, and oh, everything." These, the Prophet's son-in-law recalled, had gone to Dr. Magee as payment for treating Vidovich's family during the 1918 influenza epidemic, as noted later. And I would argue, too, that the occurrence of thefts during the opiate scourge in the Walker River area would account for the disappearance of some of Wovoka's prized collections. One additional circumstance can be suggested. Genevieve Chapin remarked to Wier that Wovoka had once sold a gold watch and case for $3.50. Nearly twenty years later, Lt. Dorrington (Stewart 1977:223) similarly noted that the former 1890 Ghost Dance Prophet was selling his "valuable Indian handiwork...for good sums."

CORRESPONDENCES AND INCOME FROM
THE SALE OF THAUMATURGES

"Then everybody lined up to shake hands with him, paying from $.05 to $20 for the privilege," Shimkin (1942:457) reported on Wovoka's visit to the Wind River Reservation in Wyoming in 1910. "He was supposed to read minds." Indeed, as early as 1894, a newspaper account from Elko, Nevada, which was reprinted in the *Reno State Journal,* revealed that a Pawnee Indian had "slipped" $5 into the Prophet's hand for that same privilege (Appendix D). We also read of this in the McCoy-McCoy transcripts:

And I had a room fixed there for him. And he brought an inter-

preter, his nephew or grandson, I think it was his nephew.... And I brought these Arapahoes out to meet him. I'll never forget this night. He sat there as tho he were Queen Victoria in a chair at the end of the room, and these Araphaoes came one by one, they had every bit of reverence they would have had it been the Pope giving an audience to them. They were so embarrassed, they were so awed, that they wouldn't even look up at him. They kept their heads down. But when they came up to him, and I introduced each of them by name, and you know that those guys were slipping $5 bills into his hand....

Although no Yerington Paiute could claim memory of any parents ever "slipping $5 bills into Wovoka's hands," it is significant to note that coins were said to have been placed into the hand of feared shaman Tom Mitchell in the streets of Yerington — so that he could eat, they rationalized. Since Wovoka, too, was a powerful shaman, can we also assume that the same held true for him?

One clear source of income derived from the sale of his photograph.[1] Mooney (1896:774-75) states:

I had my camera and was anxious to get Wovoka's picture. When the subject was mentioned, he replied that his picture had never been made; that a white man had offered him five dollars for permission to take his photograph, but that he had refused. However, as I had been sent from Washington especially to learn and tell the whites all about him and his doctrine, and as he was satisfied from my acquaintance with his friends in the other tribes that I must be a good man, he would allow me to take his picture. As usual in dealing with Indians, he wanted to make the most of his bargain, and demanded two dollars and a half for the privilege of taking his picture and a like sum for each one of his family. I was prepared for this, however, and refused to pay any such charges, but agreed to give him my regular price per day for his services as informant [$1.00/day] and to send him a copy of the picture when finished. After some demur he consented.

And 25 years later, in 1917, Lt. Dorrington reported much the same:

A recent picture of Jack, taken by myself, is attached. It cost me the sum of one dollar, that is, Jack made a "touch" for that amount after the picture had been taken, informing me that he was very much in need of a dollar that morning (Stewart 1977:221-22; cf. Plate P).

We would expect, too, that Wovoka was paid for some if not all of the other photographs taken of him; the series of penny picture post cards taken in front of the bank in Yerington, for example. Ed Johnson, director of the Stewart Indian Museum, recently pointed out to me what appears as paper money of unknown currency in the Prophet's right hand in Plate T, which was taken in front of the Baptist Mission at Stewart Institute by matron Lillie Corwin. Posing for photographs, however, could not have provided much income. The evidence for income, instead, pointing to the mail order business in thaumaturges that he and Ed Dyer conducted after the turn of the century.

"At this point I became a sort of confident of his and functioned as his secretary," Dyer recalled.

I shared these roles at times with the late J. I. Wilson of Yerington with whom I later held many talks on the enigma that was Jack Wilson. At that time I was operating a store and Jack dropped in often to get me to answer letters which he got in considerable numbers from Indians, particularly in Oklahoma.

Andy Vidovich (Tape 90:1) stated that his father-in-law maintained postal boxes in Mason, Nordyke, and Yerington, and that his wife Alice "always went for the mail for Wovoka when they were living in Mason." But to

Grace Dangberg (1957, 1968), though, goes credit for first reporting the cache of letters found in the Prophet's root cellar on the Wilson Ranch by J. I. Wilson's wife, Carrie Willis Wilson (Plate T.1.). This plate, incidentally, also nicely shows the Wilson family ranch house at Nordyke, where Wovoka was first exposed to Presbyterianism.

"The letters were found in a cellar on the J. I. Wilson ranch, near Nordyke," Dangberg (1957:285) wrote. "The cellar had been constructed by Jack for the purpose of storing vegetables and other supplies, with other things which he considered of no value." Reporting that there were 21 in all, many of them fragments, Dangberg wrote that these letters to Wovoka were penned from August of 1908 through December of 1911 by twelve different men and one woman. "They were almost invariably post-marked Darlington, Oklahoma and written by one, Grant Left-Hand, who appeared to function as scribe for most of the Indian Nations," Ed Dyer said. Apparently Dyer wasn't the Prophet's only amanuensis, for Dangberg (ibid.) also wrote that Mrs. Carrie Wilson, along with her son, J. W. Wilson, and daughter, Genevieve Chapin, used to "read Jack's letters to him and wrote the answers at his dictation."

Except for the so-called Messiah Letter (Appendix F), no letters dictated by the Prophet have turned up as yet.[2] Nevertheless, we do know the content of those addressed to him. "The letters to Jack were always asking Jack to make it rain more and to cure their people who were ill with imaginary diseases," J. W. Wilson explained to Dangberg (1957:285). "Therefore, when Jack wrote a letter to the patients he would always insist that his own letter close with the statement that, 'We have lots of rain here and my people are all very well and happy.'" Dangberg (ibid.) herself commented upon them as follows:

> Letters came asking not only for guidance in domestic crises such as the illness of children or wife, the necessity for limiting the number of children in a too rapidly increasing family, and other intimate concerns of family life. Occasionally, wearied with trying to solve such problems, the prophet, according to Mrs. Wilson, would say, "Carrie, you tellum, I don't sabbe that kind." Then Mrs. Wilson would prescribe Thomson's Eye Water for sore eyes, German Cough Syrup for a stubborn cough, and other suitable patent remedies; often for good measure she would counsel living in the open air and eschewing gambling and drinking.

Since Dorrington (Stewart 1977) wrote that monetary gifts received from Native Americans around the country seemed "to be his [Wovoka's] almost entire source of income," it is instructive to sample the letters written to the 1890 Ghost Dance Prophet in order to gain some sense of the earnings contained within.

(a) "...I was going to send you $6 dollars...." (August 10, 1908)

(b) "The people here have raised $37.00 and send [sic] them to you." (January 17, 1909)

(c) "P.S. There is $32.00 in altogether." (February 12, 1909)

(d) "...about that $10.00...." (April 6, 1909)

(e) "I send [sic] you five dollars...but the money order returned to me...and I sent you another five dollars Cash." (April 27, 1911)

(f) "I send [sic] you a dollar bill." (April 29, 1911)

At least once, Wovoka apparently had even suggested a fixed sum.

(g) "Well father you ask of me $25.00, but I send [sic] you $37.00 on Dec. 7." (March 17, 1909)

According to Ed Dyer, "most letters asked for something of Jack's in the way of a 'gift.' Magpie feathers, red ochre for paint, clothing that he had worn." And as for the Prophet's "exchange rate," Carrie Wilson nee Willis told Dangberg (1957:285), in the 1920s, that Wovoka received $.25 for crow feathers and $2.50 for eagle feathers. "Dyer said that eagle feathers brought Jack 2 1/2 dollars and magpie feathers, 1 dollar," Dangberg (ibid.) also wrote. "Magpie or crow feathers, twenty-five cents." And James L. Long wrote Dangberg (ibid.) from Oswego, Montana, to say that "Jack Wilson also sent eagle tail feathers for fifty cents each."

Informants told Wier that "Jack gets eagle feathers in Smith Valley," while according to Russell Dick, the Prophet would pay Numus $1.00 for every magpie, **kwedakogoe**, killed. Apart from its availability, the question of why this scavenging bird (which was considered ominous by Numus) entered service in Wovoka's thaumaturgical sales is perhaps hinted at by the following anecdote given by Russell Dick: "Magpies can do something good, you see. One time, a magpie came to the door of a friend of mine who was sick, and he got better afterwards."

On January 5, 1939, Indian agent Long wrote Dangberg (ibid.) about the "red paint" which Wovoka was also selling as a thaumaturge to Native Americans in Montana:

> Jack Wilson has also received money and goods for his red paint
> and roots and his medicine. The Fort Peck Leaders would solicit
> other neighbors and gather together money and goods and send
> it to Jack Wilson and he would send them paint and medicine

according to the amount of money and goods that he receives and when the goods came, the leaders called a "dance" and during the dance, they distribute the paint and medicine to those that paid.

Wier learned that the Prophet got his red ochre — **pesape** — "from Paint Mountain, [which is] not [the] same as Mount Grant in Sweetwater District." "I have ask [sic] you to send soft red paint, and white earth," a Native American reportedly wrote to him on April 6, 1909 (Dangberg 1968:42). While yet another faithful correspondent wrote: "I ask of you to gett [sic] you soft red paint & feathers again, hear me father I stand befor [sic] you to day, I will send you $2.50 a pices [sic] (10 April ?)."

"The shaman told her to put red paint on all her joints," Park (1938:42) described the typical use of this medicine in Numu cures. "She was to paint red and white bands around her joints." Not surprisingly, then, we read in the Vidovich-Wheat Tapes (100:26) that Wovoka "always used the red paint to stop the sickness from goin' on." He was "always getting his red paint up around Pine Grove," Andy Vidovich related. And Mooney (1896:778-79), who called pesape "the principal paint used by the Paiute in the Ghost dance," wrote that "small portions of it are given by the messiah to all the delegates and are carried back by them to their respective tribes...." Mooney (1896:797), who wrote how he had been given a small amount of the thaumaturge by Wovoka to distribute among Oklahoma followers, described the powerful medicine as follows:

> This is a bright-red ocher, about the color of brick dust, which the Paiute procure from the neighborhood of their sacred eminence, Mount Grant. It is ground, and by the help of water is made into elliptical cakes about 6 inches in length.[3]

While we know from Bob Dyer (Dangberg Notes) that Wovoka sold red paint for $20.00 a piece, the actual number of coffee tins containing these "balls of red ochre" unfortunately is unknown.

Regarding yet another source of the Prophet's income, Bob Dyer (Wier Notes) stated that "Jack's old clothes [were] in demand," particularly, his Stetson hats. "In time a great many requests were for hats, specifically for those which he had personally worn," we read in the Dyer Manuscript. Recall, if you will, Black Coyote's comment about Wovoka's Stetson and the view by some Yerington Paiutes that the Prophet carried his bbooha sewn within its top inside lining. Indeed, the Prophet's ten gallon black Stetson was called a "magic hat" by Dangberg (1968:17): "The magic hat in which Wovoka was usually photographed and which was never off his head except when he lay down to rest was a more important symbol of 'power' in that it was more intimately associated with his person."

In fact, these Stetsons were in such demand that Wovoka often would send his hats along to Native American petitioners, often straight from his own head. In the words of the Prophet's business partner, Ed Dyer:

> I was very often called upon to send them his hat which he would remove forthwith from his head on hearing the nature of the request in a letter. He expected, and got, $20 for such a "gift." Naturally he was under the necessity of purchasing another from me at a considerable reduced figure. Although I did a steady and somewhat profitable business on hats, I envied him his mark-up which exceeded mine to a larcenous degree. But somehow this very human trait made him all the more likable.

J. W. Wilson estimated that as a result of these combined enterprises, Wovoka "received about $35.00 per month in either money, Indian gloves, moccasins, or other presents." Lt. Dorrington (Stewart 1977:223) assessed his net worth in 1917 as "$400.00 in cash, besides valuable gifts from Indians and whites," which the Prophet had reportedly received during "a recent trip to Oklahoma."[4]

Although Dangberg (1968:16) felt compelled to state that "the Wilson family all say that Jack was no mercenary," the Wier Notes suggest the opposite. "Always tell them to send more money," we read in this source. The Wier Notes even quote a Wilson family member, George Plummer, who suggested that the Prophet was not only a "mercenary" but a religious fraud as well: "Jack Wilson told Mr. D. [David] Wilson one day, 'I know there's nothing in it, but keep still. I get money from Indians.'"

On the other hand, Ed Dyer stated that Wovoka's "list prices for magpie tail feathers and red ocher were also on a par with those asked for similar 'war-paint' and geegaws [sic] in our modern salons." Ignoring this obvious double standard applied to the 1890 Ghost Dance Prophet, Tibo'o cynicism ought at least to be tempered, if only because healers in Numu culture had to be paid lest they lose their power and possibly die (Park 1938, Whiting 1950). Moreover, Wovoka had a large extended family to support, and the evidence suggests that he effectively had ceased laboring for farmers and ranchers of the Walker River area after the 1890 Ghost Dance ended. This brings us to yet another source of income, the Prophet's shamanic practice.[5]

SHAMANIC PRACTICE

"He is also known as a 'medicine man' and practices some among his people, but most of the time is believed to be spent visiting the distant and more prosperous tribes and individuals from whom he procures large sums of money," Special Indian Agent Dorrington (Steward 1977:222) wrote in 1917. The 1890 Ghost Dance Prophet, then, was not unlike his immediate predecessor, Wodziwob, of 1870 Ghost Dance fame, who also became a **poohaguma** or shaman after the religious movement he founded also abruptly ended. And though Andy Vidovich (Tape 100:12) quoted his father-in-law as saying, "I cannot accept any pay for my work. If I do, I'll be punished," Yerington Paiutes were unanimous in their disagreement with that statement.

Vidovich, in Tape 90:10-11, recalled that "Tybo" (Numu-tibo'o) bequeathed his healing powers to his son Wovoka. According to what Park's informants told the ethnographer about the 1890 Ghost Dance Prophet's bbooha:

> One was a straight high cloud. This was for snow. The other cloud was dark and close to the ground. It was for rain. Wovoka could see a man's arm sticking out of the white cloud. One time the arm would be pointing north. Another time it would be pointing south, east or west (Park 1938:20).

Significantly, too, Park (1938:18) also learned that Wolf, **Esa**, the Northern Paiute demiurge and culture hero, was yet another source of Wovoka's power. While interesting in itself, this fact is especially so in light of Wovoka's self-projected attempt to revitalize Numus. What remains unclear, however, is both the sequence and relationship among the various powers Wovoka received from his biological and spiritual fathers: from Numu-tibo'o, or "Northern Paiute-White Man," from "God," and from the Wolf.

"Certain shamans, such as Wovoka, are credited with unusually strong powers for curing the injured and the wounded" (Park 1938:59). The 1890 Ghost Dance Prophet could doctor Numus who had been shot with rifles, as we already have seen. Wovoka, however, was said to have worked quite differently from traditional Numu healers in that he never "sucked" (the oral extraction of "poisons" magically sent by cannibalistic **jaab**, or witches, into the bodies of hapless victims). This was the most commonly heard attribute cited by Yerington Paiutes when they wished to contrast Wovoka's method of curing with the standard technique employed by shamans (Whiting 1950). Hazel Quinn commented upon one of Wovoka's cures.

> When Jack doctors you, he don't have to use his mouth. I know that 'cause he doctored my brother Henry Bob one time. [Wovoka] uses water, he sprinkles it on your body. He dips his hand in that basket and he sings and takes your illness away. Good doctor! Never sits down when he cures you either.

Numus maintained that Wovoka's degree, so to speak, was in the eagle feather. Andy Vidovich (Tape 90:7) said as much to Wheat:

> He had a feather about that long. And he would take his eagle feather and sing his little song and he would go over that sick person's body with that, over those legs, knees, everywhere, come on back over the head, everywhere. He don't miss a part. And then after he gets through you will see that eagle plume dip. That's a mystery, ain't it?

While it is true that other Numu shamans also employed eagle feathers as part of their shamanic kit (Stewart 1941:414), the 1890 Ghost Dance Prophet was said to have only to wave his eagle feather at patients, and bullets, for example, would magically alight. Howard Rogers once remarked that Wovoka's manner of doctoring with an eagle feather was so strong, it felt as if he were sucking out the poison. According to Vidovich, this power from the eagle was inherited by Wovoka from Numu-tibo'o in 1914 or 1915, or immediately around the time of his father's death.

Like other shamans, Wovoka also danced around his patients, presumably counterclockwise, the direction recorded by Park (1938:53) for the traditional healing rite. Even the dirt beneath his feet was said by informants to have magically scattered while Wovoka danced. Some controversy, though, exists with regard to the Prophet cum shaman's fee. Mrs. Quinn, on the one hand, stated that Wovoka was "cheap, he only charges you $5"; another Yerington Paiute, on the other hand, maintained that even though he routinely quit at midnight — which was cited by some as an additional proof that the Prophet was an extraordinary healer — Wovoka's price nevertheless remained high: $10 for half-a-night's work, $35 for two or more nights.[6]

Frieda Dick, a descendant of the Prophet, recalled his use of a deer gourd rattle in his right hand while doctoring, and how the eagle feather planted in the ground near a patient's head to signal the restoration of health would magically flutter during each and every successful cure. Stanley

McCloud in 1968 told me that when Wovoka attempted to cure his crippled leg at the Yerington Indian Colony, Stanley's mother, Annie McCloud, was the tuneggwukeadu or "designated-repeater," another standard feature of Numu cures. But over all, the 1890 Ghost Dance Prophet was still perceived by Yerington Paiutes as a qualitatively different kind of healer.

Whereas every member of that great confraternity ran the constant risk of being stoned to death as witches if too many patients died, I never heard a single accusation of sorcery leveled against Wovoka. "Jack Wilson was a good man," the consensus ran; i.e., he was not a witch. Following is a sample of Wovoka's cures.

Hazel Quinn reported that, around 1917, the Prophet had correctly diagnosed her daughter's pneumonia. By lightly moving his hand across her little girl's chest while he sang his fifth song, Wovoka caused the "bad (bewitched) blood" to come gushing out. In another cure, Nellie Emm (b. 1906) stated that he doctored her husband after a near-fatal car accident. Here again, Wovoka had but to wave his eagle feather over Brady Emm's face to cause the windshield glass pitting it to come flying free. For Winona Holmes, Mrs. Emm taped yet another of the Prophet's cures, this one involving her younger sister.

Louise Emm had been shot by Nellie's first husband in a drug-related incident, and the narrator related for Mrs. Holmes how the government contract physician in Yerington administered shots of morphine to both, as counteractive for their withdrawal symptoms as well as to alleviate the girl's painful gunshot wound. But when the pain persisted, Wovoka was summoned to cure her.

> And he [Wovoka] never used anything, just sang his Indian doctor song, I guess. He put the eagle feather near where the wound is, in here [under the arm]. You know how the feather is. You can see the blood was coming through there [the feather's quill]. That he was getting out his feather in the wound and the blood was drawn out. You could see the blood going through that feather. Blood went into Jack's mouth and he spit it out again. Later, after he had done this a number of times, Jack sat down. He said, "She has a chipped bone. Piece of bone from her rib." Said he was going to take it out. That piece of bone was about as big as a sliver. After Jack spit it out, he showed us. Then he put it in the palm of his hand and rubbed his hands together. Sang one of his medicine songs. When he opened his hands the sliver of bone had disappeared. My sister got well and in two weeks she was walking again.

"It was just like that!" Andy Vidovich (Tape 100:10) clapped his hands together for emphasis while discussing Wovoka's dramatic cures. "Not him!" Vidovich additionally related how his father-in-law did not require the standard all-night session. "Not all night long. He didn't have to!" In the first of these remarkable cures that he related to Peg Wheat, the 1890 Ghost Dance Prophet was said by his son-in-law to have successfully doctored Andy's entire family during the worldwide influenza epidemic of 1918 (Vidovich-Wheat Tape 100:10).

They were then living in Sparks, Nevada, where Vidovich worked in a car shop. When their infant son, Harlyn, took sick, a local Tibo'o doctor exasperated them by announcing that the boy would not live long. Alice Vidovich then caught the flu, so a second **mu dota'e** (or Tibo'o) doctor was brought in, Dr. Magee. According to Andy Vidovich, Dr. Magee accepted their offer to give him "everything [Wovoka's collection of handicrafts] off the wall if he cured her." But when Vidovich himself caught the flu and had his brother Jerry bring in a third physician, a Dr. Harper, who gave quinine to the members of his family and left, Wovoka suddenly appeared.

As he recalled the Prophet's dramatic entrance, a fog had begun to settle in and you could hear the Virginia-Truckee Railroad steaming into the Reno-Sparks area. Within a few moments the streetcar came rambling down Twentieth and G and there was a banging on the front door. Vidovich struggled to his feet to answer, the Prophet and his wife were standing outside. Wovoka inquired whether any family members had caught the dread sickness. He immediately got down on the rabbit skin blanket he'd manufactured for his grandson, and with the assistance of Mary Wilson, Wovoka extracted the "poison" from Harlyn Vidovich's body. "Here Mary, you take it," the Prophet said to his wife afterwards. Wovoka jokingly offered what was in his hands to the participants in the room after first singing and performing elusive hand movements over it to render the poison benign.

In the second text, Andy Vidovich alone was doctored by him (Vidovich-Wheat Tape 100:15-20). While employed in the Buckskin Mine in Mason Valley during the copper boom at the turn of the century, a large boulder had gotten caught in the jaws of a crusher one day. Vidovich described how a particle of rock struck him between the eyes, after he volunteered to shatter the obstacle with a sixteen pound sledge. Sent home to recuperate, he visited the company doctor the next day because of lingering headaches; but Dr. Edwards, who "opened" him up, could find nothing. Mary Wilson asked her daughter, Alice, whether or not she would object to Wovoka doctoring Andy Vidovich. The Prophet's daughter agreed and reportedly headed straight for her father's camp in Mason, where Wovoka was said to have been working on the Scierone Ranch close by, "stacking hay for six wagons." "He did the work of two or three boys!" stated the irrepressible Andy Vidovich, who could never resist boasting when it came to his illustrious father-in-law. In any event, upon receiving permission from his boss to miss the remainder of the work day, Wovoka told his daughter Alice, "Too hot now. I take care of him when sun gets over hill. Along about five o'clock."

That same evening, Wovoka cupped his hands together "about six inches over the top of my head" before removing from between the patient's eyes "the sharpest pointed rock you'd ever seen." Once again he teasingly offered possession of a dangerous object to attending family members, who wisely refused. "'Rock no more,'" the 1890 Ghost Dance Prophet was quoted as saying. "'He all right now. Andy get well, and maybe you can't [even] see 'em scar.'" Which led to this comment by Peg Wheat, "She [I] can't!" The Prophet's "mind" not only told him the exact moment of the accident, but according to Vidovich, Wovoka had also clairvoyantly seen him pause to examine a pretty cactus flower on the way to the mine that same morning, debating whether to pick it for his wife Alice before or after work.[7] Furthermore, in rendering Wovoka's explanation for his accident, the raconteur Vidovich recalled him saying, "And rock say, 'I punish you like you punish me.'" An attribution which reminds us of the Numu folktale about Flint, Coyote, and Rock, and how this world was made (Hittman 1984:1).

A third cure pits Wovoka against a rival shaman. Following the witching of a Numu woman named Shaw (from Bishop?), presumably because she won $78 at a card game in Death Valley from a sorceress, the Prophet, according to Andy Vidovich (Tape 100:23-25), left off watching men throw ring toss at a carnival in Yerington to grab hold of Mrs. Shaw's right wrist with his left hand and force open her hand. From her palm Wovoka then transferred into his own right hand a rattlesnake that the rival shaman would use to venomously shoot her victims. "A regular live rattlesnake," Vidovich remarked. "The most perfect thing you've ever seen in your life.... It must have been about a foot and a half long. I seen it." Andy Vidovich also quoted Wovoka's rebuke of the witch: "'Don't you use that again!'" "And I didn't see what she [the witch] done with it," he continued. "I walked away and he walked away. His job was done. He had given back the snake that she had put into that woman. She was using it to keep that woman sick. The curse was killing her. So he [Wovoka] intervened. He removed the snake."

The Vidovich-Wheat Tapes (100:14) also provide us with one other text revealing another magical battle between the 1890 Ghost Dance Prophet and a rival shaman. In it, Yerington Indian Colony resident Ernest Keats was said to have happened upon a shaman who was peeling a willow stick one day. Willow sticks, according to Park (1938:49, 55), were intrinsic to the Numu healer's paraphernalia. They were three or four feet long, were painted with red or white bands, had feathers attached to one end, and were planted in the ground beside the patient's head during cures. Although Keats fell under the sorcerer's control, Wovoka's intercession led to his freedom from the curse. Or, as Andy Vidovich tells it:

> Probably while he was peeling it, he [the rival shaman] was asking for more power and so he could identify it and all that, and go through the performance. He probably asked his oracle, as he was peeling it, to give him the power to do this and that, and ask for his power over Wilson's power to find it. And there were probably a lot of other things in there [too].

> So...he [the rival shaman] told the boy to go back of Brady [Emm]'s [house at the Yerington Indian Colony], and go on the other side of the river, and stick that willow into that water. And he said, "Wavoka [sic] will never find it. And then you go see Wavoka [sic] and tell Wavoka [sic] what I said."

> And so the boy hid the stick and went to Wavoka [sic]. So Wavoka [sic] smiled and after a little he said, "I tell you what you do. I can see your tracks where they go down to the water. You leave tracks where you come to that water. (Wavoka [sic] hadn't left home. He saw the tracks in his mind.) Your tracks are on the other side of the bridge, and they come into the water."

According to Vidovich, the Prophet then said:

> "You put 'em stick in deep water. Can't see 'em stick. Easy, I know. You go back and take 'em stick from that water, and you take 'em and put 'em on the left side in that willow. Push 'em down, clear down. And you cut another willow branch and you drag 'em over your track (so he won't leave any tracks). And

then you take that willow and throw it in the river. And then I'll blind him so he won't know it's you that took that willow. He'll think somebody else take 'em."

"Well he [Wovoka] blinded him so he wouldn't know Ernie had taken it," Andy Vidovich concluded. "Otherwise he'd be able to question Ernie."[8]

In addition to these, Tim McCoy was reported by Bailey (1957:207) as having accompanied the 1890 Ghost Dance Prophet to Pyramid Lake Reservation in order to treat a Numu who suffered with tuberculosis. Dr. Magee, interestingly enough, wrote Solberg (Personal Correspondence) describing Wovoka's effective technique of removing pterygiuum from a patient's eye with salt grass, referring all terminal cases of tuberculosis meningitis to him, however. One additional cure can be cited.

According to Andy Vidovich (Tape 90:11), a baby had died, and Wovoka "lay with his head to the north and feet to south [next to the baby] and said that he would go into a trance state for three days and people will think he's dead. Then when he awoke, the baby would be alive again." In the version of this I heard, it was the Prophet's own son whom he revived, Bill Wilson, who not only was said to have died but was already "buried in his best blankets." And in what might yet be another version of this miraculous cure, the patient was said to be Wovoka's grandson, Andrew Penrose. Indeed, but for a shift in gender, Dangberg (1968:27), too, could have been referring to it when she wrote: "Sometime during the 1880s the body of an Indian girl who had died was burned near Hawthorne. It is reported that 200 Indians saw Jack, as he had promised, raise the girl from the flames to the 'God's house'."[9]

LAND DISPUTES

In 1912, some 23 years after his Great Revelation, 24 years before a reservation was finally purchased to "rehabilitate" landless Numus living in Smith and Mason valleys, the 1890 Ghost Dance Prophet sought an allotment on the Walker River Reservation. Jack Forbes (1967:176) related the incident. Walker River Reservation Superintendent Samuel Pugh apparently thought to make use of the Prophet's reputation to implement the Indian Bureau's policy of deculturation. So, in 1912, three years after assuming his new post, Pugh wrote the Commissioner of Indian Affairs as follows: "If I can get him to work for me, which I am confident I can, I can make him a power for good. And if not, then I can demonstrate to his people that he has no power at all" (Appendix E). Ed Johnson (1975:197) described conditions on the Walker River Reservation during those tumultuous years: "The Superintendent moved to stop any dancing by the People on the Fourth of July, and apparently took action against some native doctors." Indeed, in 1915, one Numu would shoot and wound Pugh's successor, Dr. Hubert V. Hailman, for attempting to suppress shamanism (Johnson 1975:198). Wovoka, in any event, would have been living either at Nordyke or in Mason in 1912. His refusal to cooperate with that policy of forced cultural change so greatly infuriated Superintendent Pugh that he immediately withdrew what appears to have been an offer of 20 acres of alloted land on the reservation.

Nevertheless, we read again that, on February 1, 1912, the 1890 Ghost Dance Prophet appeared at the Walker River Reservation as the leader of a delegation of "30 Numus from Mason Valley" (Forbes 1967:176). Wovoka and company were there to examine rumored available allotments at the north end of the reservation, we learn. Or, as G. W. Ingalls (Davis, 1913:141, Vol. 1) reported:

> He [Wovoka] has made formal application to the officers of the Indian Department for 40 acres of land which he agrees to cultivate and make a permanent home. He will also erect a cabin and give up his wickie-up and tent and occupy the cabin as other civilized Indians are doing.[10]

But when Pugh told him and his fellow Toboose tukadu that the allotments in question were knotted in thorny heirship disputes, they apparently were incredulous. The superintendent lamented: "So you can see what simplemindedness I have to contend with...even Jack Wilson, with his superior intelligence, and very friendly feelings toward me" (Forbes 1967:177).

Four years later, in 1916, we learn from the Annual Report to the Commissioner of Indian Affairs that Wovoka "has been in the [Walker River Reservation] office upon two different occasions to complain that he is being deprived of the use of his land in Mason Valley, which was alloted to him about the time the [Copper Belt] railroad was built in that valley." At issue were "papers" for a tract of land on the Wilson Ranch that Wovoka claimed he had received from J. W. Wilson. David Wilson died in 1915, and his oldest son, interestingly enough, wrote to the Indian Bureau that the 1890 Ghost Dance Prophet had indeed received a deed to some of his father's land, but the deed had burned in a fire. While cross-cultural misunderstanding no doubt figures in this dispute, there may well be some credence to the Prophet's claim.

First of all, Yerington Paiutes speak of the "papers" and "treaty" which should have entitled Big Mack Wheeler and Blind Bob Roberts to large holdings within Mason Valley and Smith Valley. Valuable documents, which, unfortunately, were also said to have burned in separate fires. Secondly, a series of correspondences in the government record do seem to support Wovoka's claim to a share of the Wilson Ranch. The Prophet was said to have "made an outlay of $475 in cash" and done "considerable work" toward "improving the [Wilson Ranch] land" (Appendix E). Wovoka expressed pique upon finding his claimed land fenced in by the new manager of the Wilson Ranch, Archie Brown, who additionally infuriated him by offering to sell to the 1890 Ghost Dance Prophet its cultivated hay "for $10.00 per ton" for his horses.

The Walker River Reservation Indian agent wrote to Ed Dyer's brother, Bob, for clarification, in a letter dated May 4, 1916. The stationary is headed "R.C. Dyer/General Merchandise: Groceries, Meats, Vegetables, Hardware, Shoes, Clothing, Schurz, Nevada," the reply could only have fed Wovoka's distress:

> I never knew of him having any [land]. The Wilson Bros. at Nordyke, Nv gave him use of some land he claims. I never seen any papers of his land. this land was under there [sic] ditch and I think they took it up from the States (Appendix E).

POLITICAL POWERS

"You will doubtless be amazed at the letter you will have received from Jack Wilson the prophet," the Indian agent and farmer-in-charge of the Walker River Reservation, James O. Gregory, wrote to Superintendent S. S. Sears. As this was the letter Gregory told Mooney he refused to write for the 1890 Ghost Dance Prophet, someone else obviously authored it. More importantly, its contents reveal that for a "small regular stipend" Wovoka volunteered to take up immediate residency on the reservation and apprise Tibo'o of the latest news from Heaven, additionally furnishing them rain "whenever wanted" (Appendix E). Mrs. George Webster (Wier Notes) related that "J [Jack] said if all the Indians would give $2.50 apiece [he] would make feed for Indians' horses.... One old Indian said after to make it $1.50." Control over the weather, as I already have suggested, was not only the basis of his charismatic appeal to Walker River area Numus, the power also carried the potentiality for the Prophet to control the regional economy as well — meaning that every Tibo'o employer of Numu laborers would have theoretically fallen under the suzereinty of 1890 Ghost

PLATE U. Wovoka (behind flag at right) at a political rally for Warren G. Harding, Walker River Reservation. *Courtesy Agnes Sammaripa Collection*

Dance Prophet, Jack Wilson. The 1890 Ghost Dance Prophet also claimed, through his Great Revelation, a political as well as religious mission on earth — that God wanted him to reign as "President of the West." Effective January 1, 1889, America was to have become a triarchy, Wovoka declared: One nation under one God but with two chief executives, Benjamin Henry Harrison, the elected President of the United States, ruling only now in the East; and Jack Wilson (Wovoka), Numu, divinely-appointed "President of the West." Because scholars routinely emphasize the religious aspect of the 1890 Ghost Dance — Wovoka's "magic and the millennium," to borrow the felicitous title of Bryan Wilson's (1973) useful compendium of these movements — its political side has been altogether ignored. What the biblical scholar Norman K. Gottwald (1985:308) wrote about Hebrew prophets seems especially pertinent here:

> It is no longer permissible in biblical studies to neglect the immersion of prophets in sociopolitical conflict on the basis of arguments that we lack such information or that prophets were so totally "religious" that they had no determinable secular intentions, functions, or meanings.

But do we possess any hard evidence to prove that the 1890 Ghost Dance Prophet had attempted to exercise this divinely revealed political power? On March 9, 1916, the *Mason Valley News* stated that Wovoka was thinking of visiting President Wilson in order "to terminate the murderous war in Europe." The Prophet, according to Dr. Magee, had even correctly predicted Woodrow Wilson's election victory:

> I heard that he gave a talk to a very large number of people on Bridge Street in Yerington, right at the bridge, you know, where the Walker River comes down. He stood out in the water, and there were people lining the banks, white and Indian, and predicted — this was in 1916 — Wilson's election, and also said if the Germans did win the war he was going to freeze the Atlantic and send all of the Indians over there and equip them with ice. I don't know if they were going to be ice bombs or what they were going to be" (Gunard Solberg, Personal Correspondence).

Less than 10 years later, Wovoka once again expressed his willingness to undertake political action. Ed Dyer, who reported this, wrote that the Prophet wanted to intervene on behalf of Utah officials during some troublesome dealings with the western state's original inhabitants:

Uncle Sam had doled out some largess to the Utes in the form of cash. When public inebriation resulted, Wovoka, upon learning this, was immediately prompted to request that a telegram be sent to Mormon state authorities, advising that if they couldn't resolve the confrontation, he would, and "with a word."

Another incident from his middle years illustrates the kind of latent political power inherent within Wovoka's seemingly "religious" mission.

Once when Mr. Simpson was peddling beef at an Indian dance someone stole a piece of meat. Mr. Simpson told Jack, whereupon he went out in the crowd where he made a peculiar call. The thief came forward like a "whipped dog," had the stolen meat weighed and paid for it (Dangberg 1968:30).

The 1890 Ghost Dance Prophet's bbooha in this instance is reminiscent of the kind of social control exerted by Cargo Cult leaders in Papua during the so-called Vailala Madness, for example (Worsley 1957). For that matter, consider also the behavior of another "Big Man," Moses's successor, the divinely-inspired Benjaminite, Joshua ben Nun, who was able to identify Achan as the culprit whose greed for booty (when the Israelites were under the herem or ban) was said to have led to their first defeat during the conquest of Canaan (Joshua:6, 7).

And there are two other examples of political action on the part of the 1890 Ghost Dance Prophet. In Plate U we see Wovoka sharing the grandstand with Walker River Reservation Numus during a rally for Warren Harding's presidency. Circumstances surrounding the incident are unfortunately unknown. The second example dates from March 3, 1929, less than two years before his own death. On that day, the Prophet sent the radiogram, reproduced below, to newly-elected President Herbert Hoover's running mate, Charles Curtis: "We are glad that you are Vice President and we hope some day you will be President. Signed, Jack Wilson, Chief Pah Ute." Charles Curtis was a Sac-Fox from Kansas (Unrau 1985), and one interpretation of Wovoka's radiogram might be that the former 1890 Ghost Dance Prophet sensed in the election of this Native American that the Millennium was close at hand. Soon Curtis would assume the Presidency, whereupon he, Jack Wilson, would finally achieve his divinely appointed, comparable post as "President of the West," ushering in the Apocalypse, or era of equality between the races in the Hereafter. Notwithstanding Indian Agent Gregory's bemusement with this desire expressed by Wovoka "to be recognized by the government as a prophet and

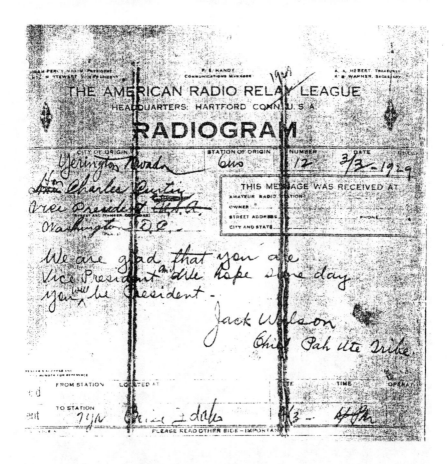

THE AMERICAN RADIO RELAY LEAGUE
HEADQUARTERS: HARTFORD CONN., U.S.A

RADIOGRAM

THIS MESSAGE WAS RECEIVED AT

We are glad that you are Vice President and we hope some day you will be President —

Jack Wilson
Chief Pah Ute Tribe.

spiritual leader of his people" (Moses 1979:298), the radiogram can also serve to reveal how Wovoka maintained belief in his divinely revealed political status until the very end of his life.

We have, in addition, these other glimpses of Wovoka from his "middle years." In one, Desert Creek rancher Frank Simpson (Dangberg Notes) reported the Prophet's reaction to the first telephone in Smith Valley:

> [The] first telephone [was] installed between two of the Simpson ranches. An Indian died on one ranch and they telephoned Jack on the other. Jack had heard of the operation of the telephone but when he heard it "talk" Paiute he was skeptical and immediately mounted a horse and set out as he said to see if he talk right.

In another, Superintendent Pugh, on Labor Day 1912, reported to his superiors in Washington, D.C., how he'd warned the "Messiah" that if any "war dances" were held in Mason or Yerington, its leaders would be arrested. War dances? Were these a revival of the 1890 Ghost Dance cer-

PLATE V. Wovoka with G. W. Ingalls, 1919. Baptist Church Temperance Society Meeting. Mason, Nevada. *Courtesy Smithsonian Institution.*

emony? Most likely they were not. Wovoka was probably being feted by visiting delegations of Native Americans with their traditional dances. The Acting Commissioner of Indian Affairs, in any event, wrote back to express his complete support for the Walker River Reservation superintendent, who, incidentally, went to great lengths to demonstrate in his letter that he had not interfered with traditional Numu celebrations such as the annual Fall Pine Nut Festival. The official reply read:

> Your telegram Twenty Sixth relative Indian War dance to be held Labor Day I disapprove Indians gathering for the purpose of Holding dances...[would] give their Ancient and Barbaries [sic] Customes [sic] especially where they are injurious to their Moral and Civil industrial welfare.... Make it plain to them that the office will not sanction any affair which will subject the Indians to criticism for conditions and the service for permitting barbaries and harmful pastimes (Appendix E).

Then there is the reference to Wovoka's attendance in 1919 at a meeting of the Baptist Temperance Society in Mason. Plate V shows the Prophet with Major George W. Ingalls, who in the summer and fall of 1873 had joined John Wesley Powell's expedition to investigate the "conditions and wants" of Numic-speaking tribes of the Great Basin (cf. Fowler and Fowler 1971). On the back of this photograph the following inscription is found:

> Major G. W. Ingalls in 1876 [sic] had this photo taken and his own after holding temperance meeting here in the Baptist Church and got this Ghost dance noted leader with nearly 100 other Pai Utes to sign the temperance pledge and agree to aid US officer arrest whiskey sellers.

The pair of mourning calls that the 1890 Ghost Dance Prophet paid to local Tibo'o in this period should be also mentioned. Dangberg (1968:35) reported Wovoka experiencing "deep grief," in 1913, over the death of Zenas Wilson (1894-1913), the second of five children born to J. I. and Carrie Willis Wilson. The Prophet's emotional ties to the Wilson family are probably revealed by the comment Mrs. Plummer made to Dangberg following the death of Zenas Wilson's younger brother, Donald (1906-1926): "J. [Jack] and Mary adored Donald Wilson. [They] Wanted to take him pine nutting." And once again in 1919, when George Plummer died, the Prophet was there to grieve. Quoting Mrs. Plummer, Dangberg (ibid.) reported that Wovoka visited the Plummer Ranch "to comfort the family,

Plate W. Wovoka "in chains," circa 1916. *Courtesy Smithsonian Institution*

remaining, in the latter case, with the widow for a long enough time to remark that 'Mr. Plummer was a good man.'"[11]

And one more item ought to be cited. In 1916, the Lyon County sheriff's Court Book carries the following entry: Arrest of "Jack Wilson, aged 50. Charge: Fishing out of season. Penalty received: The 10th of April, 1916, spent in County jail." Balance of the assessed fine was said to have been "paid in full."

Does this explain that most curious photograph of them all? Plate W, which depicts the Prophet on folded knees, kneeling outdoors on what appears to be a bedroll on the ground. Squinting, probably because he is staring at the sun, Wovoka wears striped tailored trousers and a white dress shirt that is buttoned high on his neck at the collar. The Prophet's pocket watch chain dangles loosely across a black vest and his black Stetson is tipped uncharacteristically way back on the Prophet's head, while in his hands, he seems to be holding a chain which might otherwise be used for shackling someone. A bushy moustached man stands off to Wovoka's right, or slightly behind him. Though his vest is unbuttoned, this individual too is wearing tailored trousers and a white dress shirt. His black banded white summer hat is drawn low across his forehead, or close to his eyes. And what appears to be a flask or a pistol protrudes from his front pants pocket, left side. The third person in the photograph is a woman, a Tibo'o. The car has been identified as a 1913 Essex.

When I asked Roy Wittacre of Yerington to identify the second male in the photograph he said after considerable deliberation, "Barney Reymers!" Barney Reymers (b. 1849), a German descendant and wealthy Mason Valley farmer (cf. Angel 1881:411) who eventually became state senator, was never a game warden, however, and would have been well into his seventies, if the 1916 dating of this photograph is correct. Ernie Conway, however, identified the figure as a fellow Numu. He was Jack Dalton of Fallon, Nevada, a shaman, a Campbell Ranch resident in Mason Valley in the 1930s, and also formerly the Yerington Indian Colony policeman, Ernie Conway declared. But when I inquired whether or not Wovoka might have been only playfully posing following this, his only arrest, Mr. Conway laughed and answered as follows: "Jack Dalton was never a game warden, and, anyway, Numus weren't arrested for fishing out of season in the old days!"

ENDNOTES

1. Gunard Solberg also reminds me that the famous Sitting Bull sold autographed photographs of himself while on tour with Buffalo Bill Cody's Wild West Show.

2. A flour sack that the Prophet used for sending medicines to James Roberts, Assiniboine, Fort Peck Reservation, Montana, carried these words printed on it: "J. W. Wilson & Bros. Flour Milling Co., Nordyke, Nevada" (Dangberg 1957:286).

3. After noting its use among Plains Indians — to ward off sickness, and as an aid in obtaining visions — Mooney (1896:779) poignantly described how that small cake of red paint he had been given by the Prophet to carry to Oklahoma friends of the 1890 Ghost Dance Religion was nearly erased as a result of their efforts to obtain its blessings by rubbing it.

4. Dorrington (Stewart 1977:223) also noted that Wovoka once had been sent $50 by a Native American in South Dakota for railroad fare to heal the correspondent's daughter. Wovoka's reply, however, was that "he was too busy to leave at that time but that he would use the money anyway, and that he did."

5. I note, too, in this regard, the following "Brief Item" in the *Lyon County Times.* Dated 15 August 1891, we read that Yerington grocery store owners Ed and Bob Dyer had recently earned "over a thousand dollars" as a result of those visiting delegations of Native Americans to 1890 Ghost Dance ceremonies in Mason Valley.

6. Cf. "Both the shaman and interpreter were paid by the sick person or his relatives. Nowadays the shaman receives about five dollars for each night and the interpreter two or three dollars. In the old days both were paid with skins, moccasins, or beads. The fee that a shaman asks is set by his power. If he asks more or less than his power instructs harm will come to him. He will sicken and no longer be able to doctor" (Park 1938:15).

7. "There must be a Heaven," my Numu mother, Ida Mae Valdez, once remarked. When I inquired why, Ida Mae answered that it was because she once had seen a "perfect" flower in the mountains. Interestingly, Park (1938:54) reported that if a shaman envisioned a flower during the trance state it meant the patient would recover. Most recently, too, Kenneth Ring (1984) reported numerous case studies of Near-Death Experiences involving visions of beautiful flowers.

8. Regarding sorcery, Moses (1979:344) quoted an 1894 newspaper account from Elko, Nevada, in which Wovoka allegedly had refused a gift of 40 silver dollars dumped at his feet by a Pawnee employee of the Indian Bureau. The money was said to have represented a collection taken up by Pawnees. "[Johnson] Sides," or so we read the reason for his behavior, "explained that Wovoka feared the money was tainted and that he might be killed through witchcraft."

9. Yet in her field notes, Dangberg recorded the "cure" as follows: "A girl died and the Prophet cremated her body."

10. Ingalls, however, related that the application for land was made in 1913 not 1912.

11. The year of George Plummer's death appears as 1921, however, in the David Wilson family tree that I was given by John "Frank" MacGowen of Yerington.

CHAPTER 7

Wovoka's Prophecies

*"The ultimate purpose of a prophet is not to be inspired,
but to inspire the people; not to be filled with a passion,
but to impassion the people with understanding of
God" (Heschel 1962:115).*

Wovoka prophesied that rain would fall in three days time, and the 1888-1889 drought came to an end. He prophesied a block of ice from Heaven in the summertime, and this miracle, too, according to believers, took place. But there were other prophecies, other miracles, attributed to him as well.

Andy Vidovich (Tape 96), for example, in characterizing the Prophet's clairvoyant perception of the exact moment of his grandson's birth, offered the following remarkable account. The year was 1919, and upon receiving news of the birth, Vidovich, a proud new father, promptly left his place of employment, the Thompson Smelter in Mason Valley, for Carson City, where he and Alice were then living. Meanwhile, unbeknownst to him, Wovoka and Mary Wilson simultaneously headed for the state capital. The grandparents rode the Tonapah-Goldfield and Southern Pacific Lines, arriving in Jerry Vidovich's house on Corbett Street, where Alice had apparently given birth, a city 60 miles away from Yerington that the Prophet reportedly had never once set foot in. Wovoka "came in and walked down the hall cut over near to the lavatory and went left, like he'd been there a thousand times," Vidovich recalled for Peg Wheat. The Prophet and Mary Wilson remained in Carson City for four days, according to Vidovich. Right before they left, however, Wovoka ordered water to be boiled:

> So he told Alice, "Tomorrow morning, the fourth day, we'll take
> the little baby and go over to that hill, right there on the other
> side of Corbett Street...." Oh, and he made a big fire and he cut
> brush and everything and made a nice fire.... This was before the
> sun came up. You know I thought it was kind of cold even if it

was July the 2nd. But Wavoka [sic] said, "The baby won't get sick. We have to do this."

Vidovich recounted the Prophet's baptismal blessing over his new grandson next: "'Give him a good body, a good mind, and so that the mind will act in unison with the body, and keep his spirit good and keep it clean.'"

Whereupon the following prophecy was delivered by the 1890 Ghost Dance Prophet:

> "This little fellow will go to school. He won't go to the Indian school, where you and his papa go, but he'll go with his White brothers and sisters. And he's not going to be back in his lessons at school. And he's going to grow up and be a clean fellow. He'll be a credit to his people." And he says to Alice, "This little fellow will use a pocket knife of his father's and his father uses a sharp knife...." [Wheat describes the narrator as having produced a knife at this point, about which she commented, "He always keeps it sharpened."] And Wavoka [sic] said, "You can let him use it. He won't cut his hands. He'll make his own toys."

And without ever cutting himself, Harlyn Vidovich was indeed able to preternaturally carve model airplanes with his father's pocket knife, or so Andy Vidovich declared. A skill, one might say, which reminds us of the Prophet's most commonly recorded name, "The (Wood) Cutter." Returning to Wovoka's prophecy, however, Andy Vidovich completed it as follows:

> And then Wavoka [sic] said, "He'll be flying in the skies." There weren't many airplanes them days. "And then he's going to join

Plate X. Harlyn Vidovich, "Flying Tiger." The Prophet's grandson, circa 1942. *Courtesy Inex Jim*

the United States Flying...Outfit." He didn't come out and say The Air Corps. "And then he'll be flying in the skies. He'll have a good mind, good body, sharp eyes, everything. And he will lead the white men in the skies. He will become a great captain."

Born in Carson City and raised in Sparks, Nevada, the life of Harlyn Vidovich (Plate X) can be viewed as the realization of his famous grandfather's prophecy. For, after attending junior college in Arizona where his father was employed in Sacaton as a cabinet maker and carpenter for the Bureau of Indian Affairs, the Prophet's grandson attended Western Airlines Flying School, earned his gold wings from the Civil Aeronautic Society of America and flew briefly as a commercial pilot. "That prophecy really went through," Andy Vidovich proudly told me in 1970. And in displaying Harlyn Vidovich's posthumously awarded Distinguished Flying Cross, he related much the same story — heard by Bailey, Kerstein, Solberg, and many others no doubt — about how his son became a Flying Tiger pilot under General Claire Chennault and lost his life when his plane was shot down over China in 1944, and of the burial with military honors in Reno, Nevada. The prophecy (or miracle) of the white horse is considered next.

Hazel Quinn narrated it for Winona Holmes in the 1970s, and its text was reproduced in Volume III:28 (4 June 1982) of *Numu Ya Dua*, "Northern Paiute Speaks," the tribal newspaper of the Yerington Paiute Tribe (ed. by Michael Hittman). "Thousands and thousands" of Numus had assembled below a mountain near Nordyke, the post office and flour mill on the Wilson Ranch, Mrs. Quinn began.

> In five days, Wovoka said a horse will appear on top of the mountain. And sure enough a beautiful white horse appeared on top of the mountain. And that horse was so beautiful, it was the color of snow. My mother Maggie Bob [b. 1870?] told me this, she saw it happen. It was before my time. And Jack, he kept talking to the people same time, motioning the horse to come down. So slowly it came, once in a while it would stop. Slowly it came, taking its time. And it would nay once in a while, too. It was so beautiful. And when it was coming, it looked like its hooves weren't even touching the ground. My mother thought to herself — What kind of animal would understand him? [i.e., What kind of powerful man was the 1890 Ghost Dance Prophet?]

According to her, Jack Wilson had to beckon the recalcitrant horse to approach. In the meantime, curious Numus, who were assembled at the foot of that mountain, began sprinkling water on the exact spot where the magical animal was to stop, as per their instructions from Wovoka. "To meet his children," Mrs. Quinn explained. "Watch the heavy cloud," Wovoka then said. "Watch it closely," he told the crowd. "And a heavy cloud started to move towards them, coming closer and closer. It came right on top of the horse." Hazel Quinn's interpretation of the "heavy cloud" was that it "was for bringing rain for the people to drink — for all the people to drink from the cup." She also suggested, "This White Horse has pity on you. He wishes you all abundance. Then it left."

Shortly before she died in 1987, the Yerington Paiute elder retold this prophecy or miracle of the white horse. It was translated for me by Hazel Quinn's daughter, Mary Lee Stevens, with supplemental details provided by Mrs. Quinn's nephew and niece, Russell Dick and Ida Mae Valdez:

> Jack Wilson gathered his people together at Nordyke. Why? 'Cause they wanted to hear him talk. So after they ate, he tells all: "Wash your faces." Says, "Up in the mountains you'll see a horse coming. It's coming fast."
>
> Well, here comes that horse. It's white as snow. It turns around. Also neighs up there. And that horse comes to the [designated] place and whirls around. Dust can surely fly!
>
> The [Numu] People have got something big on the ground [canvas?]. The horse keeps turning around. Jack, he's talking to that horse. He [horse] neighs five times, that was his welcome. White Horse then turns around a few times more, then he leaves same way he came. Trots off.
>
> And Jacks says, "Go get a bucket. The water will come from this horse." And it sure did!
>
> Yeah, that was no lie. That horse was real. It had a body. Jack hollered at it real loud after it went away but the horse kept on trotting up the hill. Indians then drank from that big bucket. Lots of water was dripping off that horse. So that' what he gave them — the horse, water. Jack said goodbye to the horse. And the ground shook after the horse left.

The number five, as already indicated, was sacred to Numus. The significance of the horse's color will be discussed in Part II.

Yet a third prophecy attributed to Wovoka might be entitled "The Prophecy of Two Sisters." As recounted for Peg Wheat by Andy Vidovich (Tape 100:20): "There are twin mountain peaks near Rawhide, Nevada, and so one day, Wavoka [sic] says: 'One of those sharp peaks will sink into the ground before I go.'"

Warren Emm of the Walker River Reservation, who also heard this prophecy from Mae Jim, his mother, said that she identified Pilot Peak as the mountain. Its meaning? "When the smaller of those two peaks is worn down, this world will come to an end," Mr. Emm, a Seventh Day Adventist, explained.

Another prophecy concerns peyote. At least twice in their recent history, efforts were made by others to introduce the hallucinogen to Numus of Smith and Mason valleys. Omer Stewart (1944) documented how Leo Okio, Raymond Lone Bear, and Johnny Wright were responsible for initial desultory efforts. However, it was not until 1936, when the Washo-Paiute named Ben Lancaster, or Chief Grey Horse, returned from Oklahoma with peyote that the Native American Church took firmer root in the valleys. Of course, by 1936 Wovoka was already dead, and despite hysterically-bred government suspicions (cf. Appendix E), there is no evidence that Wovoka ever attended a ceremony, let alone proselytized peyote (Stewart 1971). Indeed, the 1890 Ghost Dance Prophet's condemnation of the "diabolical root" can be seen as prophetic, for it paralleled those very negative descriptions I obtained in the late 1960s and early 1970s (Hittman 1972) regarding the behaviors of Numu devotees of Ben Lancaster's cult at Campbell Ranch.

Andy Vidovich (Tape 100:21-2) quoted Wovoka as having said: "'If you keep on using it you will walk on your hands and feet like a dog. Don't use it [peyote]. [Because] I don't like that.'"

Gertrude Webster and Earl Kerstein contribute these additional vignettes to Wovoka's legacy as prophet and miracle-worker.

"For five years, [Wovoka] never missed a prophecy concerning weather and sun dogs (1886-1890)," the East Walker River settler told Professor Wier in 1910. And the cultural geographer Kerstein, in the late 1960s, wrote, "Sometimes, in the morning, he would predict who would be coming in the afternoon and at what time they would arrive."

This last entry concerns alcohol, a substance Numu peyotists were specifically enjoined to forsake. While Wovoka's words might not technically constitute a "prophecy," they sound reasonably enough close to one to belong in this section.

In Chapter Six we saw that the 1890 Ghost Dance Prophet had

signed a Temperance Society pledge in the Baptist Church in Mason town in 1919, to aid Treasury Department agents with their suppression of the illegal sale of alcohol to Numus (cf. Plate V). Contrary to the insistence of Yerington Paiutes that Wovoka never publicly preached — "talked" — against the evils of drinking (or opiates), Andy Vidovich (Tape 100:21) nevertheless has stated that during a Pine Nut Festival held in Wellington Hills, west of Smith Valley, the 1890 Ghost Dance Prophet once rose to rebuke drunks who were threatening to disrupt the sacred event:

> "Before I open up the sacred prayer, the sacred ceremony, for the benefit of next year's pine nut crop, then the drunks are not allowed here, because this is sacred.... If you attempt to come here and create trouble, the place is not here. Go up there on the mountains. Go up there if you want to get drunk, up there where nobody can see you."

And the Prophet's words, according to Vidovich, were sufficient to cause the prompt — "miraculous," one might suggest — departure of those drunk. Wovoka, acting the role of the traditional Pine Nut Festival Leader, sang all night lone, never singing "the same song over twice."

I reserve until Chapter Eight the inclusion of one final prophecy.

CHAPTER 8

The Final Years

"There is reward for your labor, declares the Lord. They shall return from the enemy's land. And there is hope for your future, declares the Lord. Your children shall return to their country" (Jeremiah 31:16-17).

Toward the end of his life, Wovoka's sight and hearing had begun to fail him. The contrast between the Prophet's health in the years 1915 and 1920 couldn't be any more dramatic. Dr. Magee, who treated him around 1915, spoke of "mostly bronchitis and then some intestinal upsets which weren't getting serious. Nothing real serious. He was always well-nourished and looked still like a powerful man, even when he was old. I don't recall if he had any eye complaints. I don't think I ever examined to see if he had trachoma...." (Gunard Solberg, Personal Correspondence). By 1920, however, Mrs. George Plummer could tell Dangberg that "Jack was getting blind and deaf and has cataracts."

There are only a few mentions of the 1890 Ghost Dance Prophet during this last decade of his life. Grace Dangberg (1968:17), who attempted an interview in 1920, reported her meeting as follows:

> It was a sunny Sunday morning and Wovoka was lying outside, in the shade, on the north side of his cabin at the Yerington Indian colony. When we approached he sat up in evident embarrassment which I attributed to the fact that he was without his shirt but which I subsequently realized should have been attributed to the fact that he was being seen without his wide-brimmed black sombrero. His usual poise and dignity were restored as soon as he had reached for the hat and placed it on his head still sans top shirt!

Tim McCoy was successful (Plate Y). Notwithstanding Mrs. Plummer's observation about Wovoka's ill-health, McCoy in 1924 noted that he "seemed robust and at least twenty years younger" (Bailey 1957:207). And as for their conversation:

[Wovoka] talked readily of the ghost dance religion, and of the great visits he once had with the tribal leaders from the east. He still talked of the coming millennium, in which the Indians would be given a new earth to dwell upon. He still emphatically declared that he visited God, and had talked to Him...and still talked of the coming millennium (Bailey ibid).

While in his autobiography (McC oy 1977:222), the famous movie star and showman recalled that meeting as follows:

The last words Wovoka said to me were the first he had uttered in English. As he climbed into the limosene [sic] and settled into his seat for the long ride back to Yerington, he looked out the window at me. Then he rolled the window down, stuck his unscarred hand out into the air, dropped a cake of red paint into my coat pocket and whispered, "I will never die."

"Is that so?" McCoy reported asking him. Wovoka nodded vigorously in reply. "Never?" McCoy asked. "No, never," Wovoka replied firmly.

Andy Vidovich (Tape 100:2) emphatically denied that his father-in-law had ever declared he would live forever. "What he said was, 'When my body is placed in the ground, my body goes back to the earth, where it belongs. And my spirit lives on forever with the Great Messiah.'"

In 1931, Genevieve Chapin reported how she went to the Indian village to see him. Wovoka "was so happy to see me!" Mrs. Chapin told Dangberg (1968:37). Upon discovering "that he needed more food," Mrs. Chapin told that she "took him eggs and bread a number of times." One year later the 1890 Ghost Dance Prophet was dead.

"Death at 74," the Lyon County coroner wrote of the Prophet's passing on the Standard Death Certificate. "The (Wood) Cutter" died in his cabin at the southeast end of the Yerington Indian Colony on September 29, 1932, after having been attended to since September 13 by an Indian agency physician, who noted on the Standard Death Certificate Wovoka's "enlarged prostate cystitis." The Prophet's death occurred at 1:00 a.m.; nephritis was given as the cause. Mr. and Mrs. Hall, owners of a grocery store at the edge of the Yerington Indian Colony, recalled that "they [Numus] put Jack's body inside a coffin. The coffin was under a willow shelter. It was warm weather, so finally the authorities had to come in and tell them to bury Jack's body. He wasn't embalmed either." Freida Dick, one of Wovoka's many descendants, recalled in 1989 that the Prophet's granddaughter, Ina Sharp, provided a comforter to bury him in. The casket

PLATE Y. Wovoka with Tim McCoy, 1924. *Courtesy Nevada Historical Society*

itself was provided by the Indian Bureau. On September 29, 1932, Wovoka was laid to rest alongside his wife of 50 years, Mary Wilson, by Ina and Dave Sharp. He was buried in the Sharp family plot on the Walker River Reservation, following a brief service conducted by Methodist Pastor E. E. Ewing. Joseph McDonald, of the *Reno Evening Gazette,* would devote a three-column obituary (Appendix J) to Wovoka's passing, which was not even mentioned in the local Yerington newspaper.

"How can he die? He's such a smart man!" Nellie Emm, in 1968, could still recall her mother's shock and disbelief. And since natural death was essentially alien to the traditional Numu way of thought (Whiting 1950), contrary rumors to the medical report and suspicions inevitably arose.[1] Because Wovoka was perceived to have been in relatively good health at the end — "still good," Yerington elders recalled — there were those who felt he had been witched by **Songoe'e,** or "Hummingbird," the only remaining shaman in Smith and Mason valleys, who, at his own death at age 97 in 1945, was probably the longest practicing Numu healer. A second opinion has the Prophet dying of venereal disease (syphilis) caught from a Fallon woman. This was even though Wovoka's great granddaughter Inez Jim, a retired United States Public Health Service nurse who both saw the body and attended the funeral, reported his swollen legs were indicative of kidney shutdown. Yet a third view was propounded by Russell Dick in 1988. The Prophet died because his instructions to a fellow Numu had been disregarded, this Yerington elder explained. "Fouled him up," explained Mr. Dick, a view that is entirely consistent with Numu guidelines regarding the practice of shamanism (cf. Park 1938).

A plain wooden marker stood at the head of the Prophet's grave until 1980 (Plate Z). It read: "Jack Wilson, died 29 September 1932, aged 74." Tribal Enterprises of the Walker River Tribe, however, ordered a head stone to be carved by Tad Boone Memorials of Sonoma, California, in that year. "Wovoka, 1858-1932," are the words authored by Walter Cox, former publisher of the *Mason Valley News,* "Founder of the Ghost Dance. His teachings of hope, good will, and promise of life after death will live as long as man inhabits this earth."

Yerington Paiutes also sought to honor their illustrious Prophet. With funds made available by the state of Nevada, their Tribal Council passed a resolution on December 17, 1975 calling upon Boone Memorials to cut a memorial stone to be erected at the Yerington Indian Colony, site of Wovoka's final 15 years of life. But when Pastor Gladys Rushing of the Assembly of God Church, which leased land at the Yerington Indian Colony,

STATE OF NEVADA

DEPARTMENT OF HUMAN RESOURCES
DIVISION OF HEALTH
VITAL STATISTICS

Nevada State Board of Health
BUREAU OF VITAL STATISTICS

State Index No. **2208.**

I. PLACE OF DEATH

STANDARD DEATH CERTIFICATE

Local Registered No. **32-000996**

County **Lyon**   State **Nevada**

Registration District _____   Village _____

City **Yerington**   No. ____ St. ____ Ward

Length of residence in city or town where death occurred ____ yrs. ____ mos. ____ ds. How long in U. S. if of foreign birth? ____ yrs. ____ mos. ____ ds.

2. FULL NAME **Jack Wilson**

(a) Residence: No. ____ (Usual place of abode) **Yerington** St. ____ Ward ____ (If nonresident give city or town and State)

PERSONAL AND STATISTICAL PARTICULARS	MEDICAL CERTIFICATE OF DEATH

3. SEX **M**   4. COLOR OR RACE **4/4Paiute**   5. SINGLE, MARRIED, WIDOWED, OR DIVORCED (write the word) **Single**

21. DATE OF DEATH (month, day, and year) **Sept 29** 19 **32**

5a. If married, widowed, or divorced HUSBAND of (or) WIFE of **Mary Wilson**

22. I HEREBY CERTIFY, That I attended deceased from **Sept 13** 19 **32** to **Sept 28/32** 19 ____

I last saw h1m alive on **Sept 28** 19 **32**, death is said to have occurred on the date stated above, at. **1 am**.

6. DATE OF BIRTH (month, day, and year) **1858**

7 AGE Years **74** Months ____ Days ____ If LESS than 1 day, ____ hrs. or ____ min.

The principal cause of death and related causes of importance in order of onset were as follows:

Nephritis

8. Trade, profession, or particular kind of work done, as spinner, sawyer, bookkeeper, etc. **Indian Medicine Man**

9. Industry or business in which work was done, as silk mill, saw mill, bank, etc.

10. Date deceased last worked at this occupation (month and year) ____ 11. Total time (years) spent in this occupation ____

Contributory causes of importance not related to principal cause:

Enlg.Prostate

Cystitis

12. BIRTHPLACE (city or town) **Mason Valley** (State or country) **Nevada**

13. NAME **Unknown**

14. BIRTHPLACE (city or town) **Unknown** (State or country)

Name of operation _____ Date of _____

What test confirmed diagnosis? _____ Was there an autopsy? _____

15. MAIDEN NAME **Unknown**

23. If death was due to external causes (violence) fill in also the following:

Accident, suicide, or homicide? _____ Date of injury ____ 19 ____

16. BIRTHPLACE (city or town) **Unknown** (State or country)

Where did injury occur? _____ (Specify city or town, county, and State)

Specify whether injury occured in industry, in home, or in public place.

17. INFORMANT _____ (Address)

Manner of injury _____

18. BURIAL, CREMATION, OR REMOVAL Place **Schurz** Date **Sept. 29 32**

Nature of injury _____

19. UNDERTAKER _____ (Address)

24. Was disease or injury in any way related to occupation of deceased? If so, specify _____

20. FILED **Jan 6 33** _____ Registrar.

(Signed) _____ M.D.

(Address) **Agency Physician**

This is to certify that the above is a true and correct copy of the certificate on file in this office.

Date Issued: **AUG 25 1989**

By: _____ Deputy Registrar

objected to the proximity of the Wovoka Memorial to her building — she claimed it would serve as a conduit for "Devil Power" — the Yerington Paiute Tribal Council politely demurred. On April 9, 1975, the commemorative was instead located on a vacant lot on the east-central side of this federal reservation. When Pastor Ruhing resigned, and her position remained unfilled, the church building was converted into the **Toboose Tukadu Nobe**, the "Home of the Taboosi-Eaters," an elder center, and the Wovoka Memorial was then relocated to its originally proposed site. There it stands today, close to the Prophet's first house at the Yerington Indian Colony.

"This historical marker was erected by the Yerington Paiute Tribe in honor of Wovoka or Jack Wilson, a spiritual leader whose influence was so great that many considered him a great prophet of God," are the words I wrote in 1975 in conjunction with a special committee appointed by the Tribal Council:

> Wovoka was born in Smith Valley in 1856, the son of a medicine man named Numu-Taibo [Numu-tibo'o] or 'White Indian.' Later, he moved to Yerington where he lived the last twenty years of his life.

> After a mystical revelation, he was given power by our Great Father to control the natural elements. There were several instances when Wovoka demonstrated his power, one of which occurred at a place called Circle in Smith Valley. Several men pitching hay for a local rancher saw him coming and began yelling — "There goes the Rainmaker." Wovoka made the rain fall only on the spot where the men were haying. It rained so hard that no one could travel through. He also caused it to rain during droughts.

> Wovoka was further instructed by Our Great Father, to stress brotherhood among all Indian peoples, and between the Indian and the White man. Representatives from more than thirty tribes came to visit him in Mason Valley in order to hear his words and see him demonstrate his powers. We know of this as the 1890 Ghost Dance religion. This religion spread throughout a large part of the United States and even into Canada.

But the Prophet's death was dramatic in yet another way. Some time before he died, Wovoka was said to have prophesied that he would shake this earth if he ever reached Heaven again. Three months to the day, earthquakes did indeed rock Mason Valley. "The most severe earthquakes felt by the majority of Mason Valley residents in their lives," was how the *Mason Valley News* reported the event on December 23, 1932:

> The most severe earthquakes felt by the majority of Mason Val-
> ley residents in their lives occurred at ten thirty Tuesday night
> and was followed by ten or more less severe ones occurring
> round eleven thirty which nearly started a second stampede shook
> virtualy [sic] the entire Western United States and was felt as far
> north as Canada and as far south as the Mexican border. The
> first quake, a prolonged tremor, occurred at 10:10 p.m., while a
> second quake much later was felt at 11:45 p.m. Other minor
> shocks were felt in Yerington later.

Nor were Yerington Paiutes alone in crediting their Prophet with having caused that earthquake. Claude Keema, a former Lyon County sheriff, and son of a Mason Valley rancher for whom Wovoka worked as a young man, told me in 1968: "Son-of-a-gun, Jack! Said he was gonna shake this world if he made it [to Heaven], and, by God, he did!"

Wovoka's final prophecy contrasts with his immediate predecessor, Wodziwob, whose grave, like his religion in history, stands directly behind the 1890 Ghost Dance Prophet's at the Walker River Reservation (cf. Plate Z). According to what this Fish Lake Valley denizen told Corbett Mack near the end of his life (Hittman 1973a), Wodziwob "no longer believed in his dream." By then a powerful shaman, the Shoshone or Shoshone-Paiute had reportedly decided to travel back to the place seen in his great revelation one last time. So Wodziwob sent his "mind" (soonamme-ggwitu) to the Land of Dead, only to discover a world of shadows: no flowers, there was no paradisiacal land of perpetual bounty, no dead ancestors whose youth had been restored. Out of desperation he called out to the shadows. Only Owl responded. **Moohoo'oo**, that harbinger of death, blinked his blank stare at Wodziwob and ignored him. Du Bois (1939:5) suggested disillusionment as the cause of the demise of the 1870 Ghost Dance Religion — Wodziwob having been caught planting dynamite in the ground in an apparent effort to hasten the apocalyptic arrival of a train from the east, which he prophesied would be carrying the Indian dead. However, Wodziwob's alleged case of "disillusionment" reads very much like Numu oral literature, in particular, the tale of "Hummingbird in the Land of the Dead."

Isabel T. Kelly (1932:436) recorded it among the Surprise Lake Paiute

PLATE Z. Gravesite of the Prophet, Walker River Reservation. *Courtesy Village Voice*

of California. She wrote that Hummingbird decided one day to travel beyond the Sun, or to the Land of the Dead. So he filled his pants pockets with what he thought was an adequate supply of **atsa**, an edible red seed, and up, up, straight upwards into the radiance of the heavens Hummingbird then flew. Only to have to prematurely return again to earth, Kelly wrote, because he ran out of food. Whether or not Wodziwob's personal disillusionment was a cultural response built into those apocalyptic-type beliefs in the Plateau and Basin areas that Spier termed the "Prophet Dance," it is significant to note here that Wovoka's prophecy at the end was also consistent with Numu traditions.

Park (1938:69), for example, wrote of the belief that when Numu shamans die "clouds gather in the sky, rain falls, or other changes in the weather take place." Park (ibid.) also stated: "Another [informant] asserted that earthquakes mark a shaman's death." Furthermore, there is a Toboose tukadu folktale which also echoes the final prophecy of the 1890 Ghost Dance Prophet, and that is their creation story.

In it, Wolf (Esa) returns home from hunting one day only to find his beautiful wife crying. This **ur-Numu** Woman, whom his younger brother Coyote feminized, laments that she can no longer tolerate the constant bickering of their four children. So Wolf violently reacts. First he boots his children off their island paradise, one brother and one sister landing in the Walker River area to become the Numu, the other pair of siblings landing in northern California to become the **Sai-i**, traditional enemies of the Northern Paiute. Wolf himself then announces that he, too, is leaving. He is leaving this world, Wolf says, and is headed for the "Land Beyond The Clouds." "But don't cry for me," the demiurge and culture hero says to his wife, "For you shall see me again when you die." And in a variant of this tale that I collected, Wolf declares that if he does reach the "other side," he will signal his achievement to her by "shaking the earth."

Wovoka's earthquake prophecy, then, biography or myth? That line is difficult enough to maintain for ordinary human beings, but from the point of view of Yerington Paiutes, anyway, this question with regard to Wovoka is not relevant. For them it was and remains his stirring message that counts. In founding one of the major religions in the history of the world, the 1890 Ghost Dance Prophet continues to serve as an inspiration today, in large part because of the way in which he was able to synthesize elements from those different worlds to which he, as well their other ancestors, were exposed. From the traditional culture, Wovoka took the notion that an individual's thoughts and actions carry ecological and social consequences; from the dominant culture, a moral order and the Judeo-Christian belief which reinforced their own that a moral life will reap untold harvests in the next life. Like the prophet of the 1870 Ghost Dance before him, Wovoka, too, constructed an weltanschauung. But whereas Wodziwob's was xenophobic and unrealistic, Wovoka proffered a vision which was universalistic and pragmatic. Despite its End of Time, or eschatological core, the 1890 Ghost Dance Religion, with its belief in a reunion with the dead in Heaven, the Land of Dead Land, or "beyond the clouds," did not urge escape into a remembered past, which is both romantic and impossible to achieve. The eternity Wovoka saw in his Great Revelation of January 1, 1889 was accessible not only to Numus but to Native Americans as well, and, in fact, to us all.

"'I don't know whether there's anybody in my family who can take my place, and it will probably be forgotten when I pass away,'" the Prophet, when close to death, reportedly told Andy Vidovich (Tape 100:7). Because none of Wovoka's children aspired to his bbooha, we say with Andy Vidovich that the 1890 Ghost Dance Prophet's "feather was put down...in his grave." However, we also say that the message of the 1890 Ghost Dance Religion founded by Wovoka (Jack Wilson) did not die; that one century later, the Great Revelation seems more timely than even before:

HONESTY

THE IMPORTANCE OF HARD WORK

THE NECESSITY OF NONVIOLENCE

and,

THE IMPERATIVE OF INTER-RACIAL HARMONY.

ENDNOTES

1. There are even conflicting reports regarding the Prophet's final resting place. While the majority insist that Wovoka was buried in Yerington rather than in Schurz, others said the Indian cemetery near Mason. Significantly, too, one Yerington Paiute reported that he had been told by a Walker River Reservation elder the 1890 Ghost Dance Prophet was buried on Mount Grant!

Part II

CHAPTER 9

Author's Conclusion. . . The Red and the White: Color Symbolism

"Where there is no vision, the people perish"
(Book of Proverbs 29:18).

Sun — eclipse — drought — cloud — rain — water — red paint — fire — invulnerability — the rattlesnake — curing — eagle feather — a white horse — white paint, these were major elements of the prophecies and miracles of Wovoka, 1890 Ghost Dance Prophet.

Park (1938:17) observed that "sun, moon, and stars were power-endowing entities in Northern Paiute shamanism." Among these, however, Sun (**taba**), according to Fowler and Liljeblad (1986:453), was the "most powerful and respected." In the words of Hultkrantz (1986:632): "Sun may be a manifestation of the supreme being." Fowler and Liljeblad (1986:453-454) further observed that, in the daily lives of Numus, "many people addressed morning prayers to...Sun...asking that it have a good journey through the sky and that it take their troubles with it as it entered the 'big water' to the West" (cf. Park 1938:24). Prayers to the moon (**muha**), on the other hand, were "less frequently addressed" (Fowler and Liljeblad 1986:453-54).

So central was the Sun to Numu religion that it even carried a second or sacral name (Liljeblad 1986:641-42), though Numus generally called it "Our Father, Tamme Naa'a, and Wolf in post-contact times" (Hultkrantz 1979:25-26). Hultkrantz (ibid.) further noted that Sun (or Tamme Naa'a or Wolf) paradoxically was and was not proximate, was and was not invisible, and was and was not mythologized.

And this primary deity was not only manifested by its "ruinous blaze" but by "bursts of thunder and in flashes of lightning" (Hultkrantz 1979:44) as well. Thunder (**nuunuawunu**), or so Fowler and Liljeblad (1986:453-54) also argue, was conceptualized in the kin-oriented, familial culture of Numus as younger brother to the Sun. "In Northern Paiute beliefs Thunder or 'rain chief' lived on the clouds. He was a kind of badger who, when lifting his head to the sky, made the rain come" wrote Hultkrantz (1986:632), who, like Mooney, felt that Numus "believed that an eclipse...was the sun dying":

> Just as in other places around the world, a solar or lunar eclipse causes great alarm among American Indians.... [They thought of these as] heavenly bodies...devoured by a monster. By howling and screaming, beating on drums, boards...[they made] attempts...to scare off the beasts (Hultkrantz 1979:48).

But which "monster" did Numus conceptualize as potentially devouring Thunder's all-powerful **pabe'e** or "older brother?" "The Northern Paiute believed that an eclipse of the sun was the sun dying, or the sun being eaten by a snake," Hultkrantz (1986:632) wrote (cf. Kelly 1932:200, Fowler and Fowler 1971:243). He also argued that Numus, like other Native Americans, believed the Sun's abode to have been the "Land of the Dead" (Hultkrantz 1979:49). Numus populated their afterlife with "gods and spirits but also...human beings, animals, plants, and the everyday world" (Hultkrantz 1979:14), and that the afterlife's "pervading characteristic" was that of being a "true copy of the living" (Hultkrantz 1979:134). Or, in the view of the linguist Sven Liljeblad (1986:652), Numu Heaven, the Land of the Dead, was a "legendary underworld [which] was no Hades, but a delightful place, a populated, beautiful valley with plenty of game, green grass, and streams flowing from the mountains lined with willows and cottonwood, an idealized copy of human life on earth." "**Me nawha numu muddha**, 'It is told that under there are people, too.'"

Yet another salient characteristic of the Numu traditional religion was "ghost fright" or "fear of the dead." A summary of mortuary customs given by Hultkrantz (1979:636-37) suggests the following: corpses were taken to the mountains and covered with stones; possessions belonging to the deceased were destroyed; their houses were also burned and their personal names were avoided; and Numic settlements were relocated. Numus would even attempt to repress dreams of their lost loved ones by tossing dirt onto the grave site and uttering this standardized prayer — "Don't come back and bother me again. You're going to a better place!" Any violations of these taboos could result in the return of haunting dead souls (**moogwa**) via dreams at night, or in their presence as whirlwinds during the daytime, or both. (Dead souls might also return simply because they desired the company of the living.)

Despite this, Numus told ghost stories, Liljeblad (1986:656) observed, and "more frequently than any other kind of fiction." Numu Heaven (the Land of the Dead) was a place in which "night was day, but otherwise life was [as] on Earth," Fowler and Liljeblad (1986:453) wrote. Perhaps it is not surprising then, that a Pyramid Lake informant would draw the following distinction between two types of night for Park (1938:23): the first, or observable night, and the "second night," during which Park (1938:17) was told "only the shaman can see."

In fact, healing could only take place during this "second night" — "the only time when dead people come together," or so Liljeblad (1986:656) wrote. Not only did shamans then sing, dance, induce trances within themselves, and otherwise work to cure their patients, but Pine Nut Festivals, as well as other public ceremonies such as those held during the November rabbit drive and spring and summer fish runs, were only permissible at night. "To dance at night," Jay Miller (1983:73) persuasively argued, was vital "for controlling power." Miller's (ibid.) conclusion was that the Circle, or Round Dance, was the "primary vehicle" for the attraction of bbooha, a "Holy Wind" with associations to darkness (night), caves, water, and mountain peaks that Miller (1983:69) further likens to energy.

Miller (1983:70) also wrote that power, which "was strongly attracted to water," was the "keystone of Basin religion," a linguistically proven fact, he felt, by the close relationship between the Shoshone words puha ("power"), pa-a ("water"), and po-ai ("path"). "Power," in any event, was obtained by individuals in a variety of ways. It could be inherited from parents, deliberately sought in the vision quest, or granted "in dreams and visions" (Hultkrantz 1986:635). "In addition to securing power from these sources, shamans also derive supernatural aid from ghosts of the dead," Park (1938:15) wrote. But according to Miller (1983:76), when power was obtained from grave sites, more often than not it led to suspicions of sorcery. Thus, Park (1938:25) reported the case of a Numu who had been sick for one year with recurring dreams of the dead:

> He almost died. When he was sick he went into trances and his body was stiff as a board. He dreamed that he went to the land of the dead. He dreamed that way all the time when he was sick. He said that ghosts of dead people came and tried to steal his soul. His father was a shaman. The man almost died, but his father finally cured him.

The acquisition of power (bbooha) ordinarily led one to become a poohaguma or shaman in Numu society. And power had its specialties. While some individuals might possess love magic, others might possess gambling magic, or success as a warrior, or even the power of invulnerability from arrows. Moreover "power could be used for ecological and social reasons" Hultkrantz (1986:635) wrote. For example, Numus who acquired Thunder as their personal guardian spirit could "bring rain or stop it," Fowler and Liljeblad (1986:453) have noted.

To conclude this brief overview of Numu theology, a final observation by Liljeblad (1986:656-57) is in order, for it, too, calls to mind the syncretic religion founded by the 1890 Ghost Dance Prophet. Numus, this linguist wrote, were generally less concerned with how the world began than "cosmological order and how it might end," creating a "gap" in their conceptions of "Heaven" which was "barely filled by post-contact borrowing from biblical motifs."

Bedridden with high fever, after probably having had previous revelations, Wovoka spontaneously recovered from a Near-Death Experience on January 1, 1889 to announce that he had been to "Heaven," The Land of the Dead. "Probably the Paviotso [Northern Paiute] regard dreams as the chief cause of all illness," Park (1938:39) wrote. And, if I. M. Lewis (1971) is correct about affliction carrying the seeds of its apotheosis, then Wovoka's restored personal health, coupled with his startling announcement that he saw the dead in "Heaven," could automatically have created the suspicion among Walker River area Numus that he received bbooha from "ghosts of the dead." Nevertheless, the groundwork for perceiving him as a shaman was already laid, especially since Wovoka's father was a medicine man, and Numus no doubt already shared some pre-existing belief that he might some day inherit Numu-tibo'o's powers of invulnerability. If we assume a formal if not functional correspondence between "God" = Sun, then since the locus of Wovoka's weather control power was said to be "one or two clouds," we can also say God = Sun = Cloud. And since Thunder was reportedly a close kinsman of this primary Numu deity (Sun's younger brother), then God = Sun = Cloud = Thunder, becomes an association of elements whose ethnohistorical context is clear.

First, those unusual earth tremors, etc., and climatological incidents such as heavy fog, etc., in Smith and Mason valleys in the late 1880s, and second, the severe regional drought of 1889-1890. I have argued that Wovoka's initial acceptance by Numus living in Smith and Mason valleys had to do with their belief that the 1890 Ghost Dance Prophet restored environmental normalcy to the Walker River area. While his specific prophecy that rains would fall in three days time not only meant an end to that regional drought, it allowed Walker River Reservation Numus to continue farming their own lands. In fact, the two would have been mutually reinforcing, as can be seen, for example, when Numus from Walker River Reservation joined their congeners in Smith and Mason valleys in attempting to secure employment on the ranches and farms that dominated the regional economy. This wage labor relationship, in fact, controlled their lives. The 1890 Ghost Dance Prophet, in effect, claimed to control this condition with his supernatural weather control power.

Since Wovoka's Great Revelation coincided with the January 1, 1889 eclipse and night was the optimal time for obtaining and demonstrating bbooha, Numus additionally could conclude that his power had enabled him to save the Sun. In other words, the 1890 Ghost Dance Prophet had personally delayed the Apocalypse, which Liljeblad (1986:659) was told would take place in 2000 A.D. Along the way he demonstrated those powers he received from "God" at social gatherings: (1) the miracle or prophecy of ice dropping from Heaven in the summertime, yet another successful demonstration of his supernatural weather control bbooha; (2) the demonstration of having inherited his father's invulnerability at communal rabbit drives, during which Wovoka, in broad daylight, also doctored Numus who had been accidentally shot with rifles belonging to the new technology; and (3) the Prophet's trances, which, dangerously, he also demonstrated in broad daylight. As a result of these demonstrations, Wovoka thereby dramatically revealed that he was no ordinary shaman. He had extraordinary powers. And with local newspapers dubbing him the "Great Weather-Prophet" and "The Rain Maker," when visiting delegations of out-of-state Native Americans arrived to greet their native son with messianic awe, Walker River area Numus no doubt would have been additionally impressed.

As for the religious movement he founded, Wovoka's 1890 Ghost Dance was a direct reflection of its prophet's mixed background. From traditional religion, Wovoka took concepts such as shamanic bbooha, supernatural weather control, belief in dreams and visions, invulnerability, trance states, and the Round or "Father" Dance; from David Wilson's Presbyterianism came a modified decalogue, belief in the resurrection of the dead in Heaven, and the role of the charismatic evangelist — "saddle bag preachers" — leading revivalistic camp meetings. Because the Numus of Smith and Mason valleys were not yet Christians in the late 1880s, they danced the traditional Round Dance per instructions from the Prophet, even though it had nothing at all to do with their traditional subsistence cycle and ceremonial calendar. Did they anticipate a relief from the daily grind of ranch and farm labor implied by Wovoka's apocalyptic assurance that a better life awaited them in the future? Perhaps. But in the meanwhile, here on Earth, Numus were to adhere to a few simple Biblical commandments in addition to their traditional ritual form. Numus were smug, no doubt, with the belief that, until this world finally come to an end, everyone in the western part of the United States, Tibo'o included, were to take marching orders from the 1890 Ghost Dance Prophet, whom they respectfully addressed by their name for the Sun, Tamme Naa'a, or "Our Father," their own Northern Paiute kinsman, Jack Wilson, President of the West and Co-President with Benjamin Harrison of America.

I would like to argue that color symbolism can aid our understanding of those seemingly disparate elements listed at the head of this chapter — particularly, the colors red and white.[1]

On a most cursory level, red and white can represent the thousand-year-old Numu desert culture and its Euro-American conquerors. If the color red, therefore, specifically stands for Wovoka's food-named "band," the Toboose tukadu (Stewart 1939), then white represents the Tibo'o settlers of Smith and Mason valleys — in particular, the family headed up by David and Abigail Wilson, on whose ranch and to whose family Wovoka became so strongly attached. That feelings of ambivalence would necessarily figure in any psychological study of him. But red and white were also the colors of sacred "paints," or primary medicines, used by Numu shamans (cf. Hultkrantz 1979:82). Park (1938:58) noted that:

> The use of two native paints, red (**pesape**) and white (**ebe**), is very common in curing practices. Both of these paints are secured from natural deposits of earth. The uses to which the paints are put are manifold: the bodies and faces of both shamans and spectators are painted, the patient is sprinkled with the dry powder, and the feathers and the wand used in curing are painted. There are no fixed patterns that determine the way in which the paint is to be used, nor is one color preferred to the other. Either red or white paint, and often both, appears in every phase of the shaman's practice. The use of these paints, however, is by no means confined to curing rites. In daily life these paints are employed for utilitarian as well as ritual purposes and bodily decoration with these paints is also common on social occasions.

Nevertheless, the paints are thought to be very potent in aiding the recovery of the sick.

Menstruating women at cures could be detected by the shaman, who "then demands that the guilty woman come forward, and she is required to decorate herself with red paint and to sprinkle some of it around the fire," Park (1938:52) also wrote. Miller (1983:68) suggested that the color red symbolized "joy" for Numus, and Andy Vidovich made clear that his father-in-law went for pesape to the Pine Grove Mountains, where he had also received his Great Revelation. We saw, too, in the Wier Notes, that participants of 1890 Ghost Dance ceremonies were preliminarily required to paint their faces red as well as white. Furthermore, the Prophet asked Mooney to deliver a sample of his red paint to those Oklahoma Native Americans who'd visited him in Nevada. We also saw that Wovoka sent the sacred medicine through the United States mail as part of his relatively lucrative business in thaumaturges, conducted with the help of Yerington store owner Ed Dyer. And from the Vidovich-Wheat Tapes (100:26) we learn that with pesape, or red paint, he once encircled the swollen leg of a man from Bishop, California, while healing him of a shotgun wound acquired perhaps during a local rabbit drive:

> Like that fellow down in Bishop was shot and they brought him up there and his leg was turning bad. And he put that paint around him and Wavoka [sic] said the swelling won't go past that. And he took the buckshot out of him. He didn't have to cut to get them out, either.

But there were other traditional uses of red paint or ocher. For example, Yerington Paiutes would demarcate a designated pine nut gathering area in the mountains by sprinkling pesape on the ground in a circle to render the space inviolate from rattlesnakes. Snake, as we have just seen, figured prominently in the Numu explanation of solar eclipses; and Yerington Paiutes warn that if you kill a rattlesnake (**togoggwa**), be certain to dispose of the corpse in a shady area, lest its spirit cause excessive (solar) heat. In Chapter Six we examined a text which involved the defeat of a rival shaman by the 1890 Ghost Dance Prophet, who extruded a "regular live rattlesnake" from the hand of a bewitched woman. Thus, if red = Sun = eclipse = rattlesnake = the power to cure, can this color also be linked with rain? In other words, can this primary color in Numu taxonomy also symbolize the Prophet's divinely revealed weather control power?

Like other Numu shamans, Wovoka was able to light his pipe from the sun and form icicles in his hand. Irene Thompson related how he could place a glowing charcoal on his bare arms without burning himself, and then employ it to tame rainstorms. Since the linguistically-related Papagos of Arizona used to annually induce rain from the Sun by painting the soles of their feet and hands red while lying on top of their ramadas in the summer, is it legitimate to inquire whether or not comparable practices existed among Numus? Although these are unreported for the traditional religion, an Indian agency employee in Montana wrote the following in a letter to Grace Dangberg (1957:286): "Jack Wilson sent his correspondents red paint with which to decorate themselves before a rain and instructed them to stand out in the rain and let the drops wash it off." Interestingly, too, the color white, which Miller (1983:68) felt was sacred to Numus, not only relates symbolically to Wovoka's shamanic curing power, but to the Sun, Rain, Thunder, and Clouds as well.

Hultkrantz (1979:25-26), while remarking about Sun's "white radiance," also characterized Thunder as its voice. And ebe — white paint — was used by shamans much the same as pesape or red paint: they would color patients' faces with the pigment during cures. Andy Vidovich (Tape 100:26) stated that Wovoka would "chew it [white paint] up, but he didn't eat it. And while he was doctoring his patients he would use that for his purification. He'd blow it on his patients.... He'd put it over the sick, over the part where the sickness was."

Ebe was obtained in the Wabuska Hills, perhaps in the very same caves used by Numus who aspired to invulnerability and other shamanic powers (cf. Park 1938:26), and the 1890 Ghost Dance Prophet was said to have gone there for his supplies of white paint as well as to obtain eagle feathers. These were white eagle feathers that enabled Wovoka to end forest fires with his weather control power, as well as to successfully heal patients.

If he wasn't wearing one as a teenager (cf. Plate B), then certainly when he posed for Mooney 17 years later the Prophet took the time to affix an eagle feather to his right sleeve (cf. Plates A.1 and A.2).[2] And, of course, we also see Wovoka wearing a feather on the cover of this book. Andy Vidovich (Tape 90:9) made explicit the association between Wovoka's eagle feather and his ability to bring rain:

> I says to him, "How did you get that [eagle feather], how did you
> do that?"
>
> He says, "I'll tell you, my boy. You can do it. Anybody can do

it. But you'll have to have love, special love. Big love for the Great Messiah. And if you love the Great Messiah with all your mind, your body and your spirit, he will show you many things of the mystery of the earth. And if you believe in him with all of your spirit, when the land dries up, if you believe that there is a Great Messiah, when the water dries up and there will be no water, He will give you the power, when you enter the dry mountains will come." Now that's faith ain't it?

Thus, the color white = ebe = Thunder = rain = eagle feather = curing. Coupling this sequence with Nellie Emm's reminiscence, we now can tie in another of those seemingly disparate elements associated with Wovoka's remarkable career, the prophecy of the white horse.

According to Mrs. Emm (Appendix K), Wovoka was told by his father one day to seek "white dirt" in the caves of the Wabuska Hills. In preparation for this, the Prophet was supposed to tie an eagle feather around the neck of a "horse that has never been ridden," and one on each of his arms at the elbow. "He [Wovoka] was to ride that horse to the Wabuska Hills and remain for three days and nights," narrated Mrs. Emm. And afterwards, Numu-tibo'o reportedly said to him: "'You get on that horse and you can fly off the mountains!'" This Wovoka did. "He flew down over the big bushes and big rocks, landed on the high peak in Wilson Canyon [separating Mason Valley from Smith Valley]."

Of course, horses — like guns — would have been a readily available symbol of Tibo'o. Mustangs were acquired early enough in their acculturation to allow Numus to transform their foraging desert culture way of life into equestrian predatory bands, which raided Tibo'o encroachments upon their lands for nearly a decade (1850-1860), after which they began to hire out as ranch and farm hands in the regional economy, and as pakeada'a, or cowboys. Indeed, Numus were racing horses during Fourth of July celebrations in Dayton and Pizen Switch (Yerington) as early as the 1870s, and the Yerington Paiute Tribe today has had its share of national rodeo champions. The 1890 Ghost Dance Prophet himself owned horses.

"He did drive a wagon with two beautiful horses," Mrs. Isabelle Creighton wrote Solberg. "Their horses got better care than they [Carson Indian school children] did, and were always well fed." But what color, or colors, were Wovoka's horses? Dr. Magee in 1973 told Solberg: "I knew he had a couple of white horses...." Also Lee Little, a Yerington resident, recalled much the same for him: "He had two white horses, in 1915 or 1916, and a Baines wagon. Used to call 'em 'Paiute wagon.' It was a little bit bigger than a buckboard." Mrs. Creighton felt that "the horses were not entirely white, but more dappled" (Gunard Solberg, Personal Correspondence).

Horses became a primary means of transportation for Numus and remained so until the advent of the automobile. Still, the question that needs to be asked is: Why did the color white figure in this prophecy of a horse attributed to the 1890 Ghost Dance Prophet? Is it possible that Wovoka was influenced by popular American culture of the late 1880s? Buffalo Bill, for example, appeared on a white steed when his Wild West Show played the Virginia City opera house on April 24, 1879 (Hattori 1975:23), and the Wild West Show was close enough to Smith and Mason valleys for Wovoka to have heard about the event. Since we already have seen that the Prophet went to the Yerington Movie Theatre at least once in his life, why not imagine that he'd deliberately selected a white horse for his Baines wagon as the result of the influence of Hoot Gibson, Ken Maynard or Tom Mix, or that fourth silent film cowboy movie star, Tim McCoy, who not only rode a white horse across the silver screen but also dressed in black? No matter what its ultimate derivation, though, the fact remains that in one of the major prophecies or miracles attributed to the 1890 Ghost Dance Prophet, Wovoka gathered Numus together at the base of a mountain on his employer's ranch to witness the appearance of a magical white horse. "In dreams after that I saw a horse coming from the East," Park (1938:24) quoted an informant. "When I first heard him, he was on the other side of the mountain. Then I saw him come over the ridge. He came toward me and when he got close, he made a big circle around me. Then he went back. That horse had nothing to do with my power." William Paddy of Fort McDermitt also narrated how a white horse had become the source of an individual's shamanic power:

> After the new doctor would dream about it, he'd go get the horse. It would have to be pure white. Then he'd pray to it, get sagebrush, put it in water, and give the horse a shower bath with it. He'd stroke always down, all over the horse's body. He would use the roots and all of the sagebrush. Then when he doctored, he'd tie the horse up outside. The horse would get the power, too; he'd feel real good. He wouldn't be able to stand still. When the doctor sang, he'd go around and round, neigh and holler. I was five when I saw this one time in Owyhee (Olofson 1979:16).

Since white horses then also introduced into the Numu shamanic vocabulary, species and color were obviously important enough to Numus living in Smith and Mason valleys to have been reworked into the mythopoeia surrounding the 1890 Ghost Dance Prophet. I would even argue that the color white also has bearing upon a long-standing question about Wovoka, namely, his putative identity as the Messiah or the Christ. Before tackling this, however, we must first examine a popular Yerington Paiute folktale, "The Tale of the Rainmaker."

Yerington elder Ida Mae Valdez (b. 1921) spontaneously related this to me on my way to Reno Cannon International Airport in 1986, after a week spent conducting ethnohistorical investigations into the life of the 1890 Ghost Dance Prophet:

> We had a Messiah long ago. White people don't believe these stories handed down to us, but Mother [Mamie Dick nee Bob] used to tell me them. Her father [Blind Bob Roberts] called them **tunedweppa**, "Coyote stories."
>
> Mother said there was once an Indian man who rode down from Nixon on a white horse. They called him the Rainmaker. He took a squaw and he went up to Heaven with her.[3]

Upon subsequent inquiry, I learned these details about The Rainmaker. He was a "stranger," a Numu with a "long white beard" and a hat, who appeared either from the north or the south, riding a white horse that was "bigger than ours." "Just like a ghost," another Yerington elder commented. And like the mythical he-goat in Daniel's second apocalypse, the Rainmaker's white horse was also capable of traveling with its hooves barely touching the ground. "How does he know all the water holes?" yet another Yerington Paiute elder reflected. This, after having characterized the legendary figure's trip from the Walker River Reservation to Fallon, Nevada, a journey during which Rainmaker was said to have deliberately stopped to drink water from mountain springs inhabited by **pa-oha'a** or "water-babies," those hideous-looking and dangerous dwarf-women that Miller (1983:75-76) wrote were also an important source of power for shamans.

Because he enjoys women as much as gambling, Rainmaker first seeks out groups of Numus who are engaged in a favorite pastime, Hand Game, then invites the best-looking girls in the community for "rides" on his magical white horse. He demands something from his hosts next which is not forthcoming — meat, in one version, and lard in another. Angered, the Rainmaker promptly lowers his head, whereupon clouds form overhead and a rain storm follows, which subsides only when he raises his head again. The Rainmaker is angered again, after a second misinterpreted request, and he departs from this world with the most beautiful Numu girl in the community on the back of his white horse, which miraculously ascends toward the stars, storm clouds and torrential rains immediately occurring.

Liljeblad (1986:642-43) defined the "Stranger" or "Wandering Man" tale among Numus, arguing that "personification...[was] the productive principle when appealing to nature for aid in everyday affairs." The Rainmaker, too, might also be seen as a manifestation of the male counterpart to the perfect woman in the Numu Creation Story (Chapter Eight).[4] And that Wovoka shared much in common with Rainmaker is obvious enough. The 1890 Ghost Dance Prophet could not only cause but stop his own rain storms; Wovoka, too, wore a hat and was said to have owned a white horse; and, as we saw in Chapter Seven, he also was associated with a mythical or magical white horse. True, Wovoka did not ride skyward off the mountainside at Nordyke with the most beautiful Numu girl in Mason or Smith valleys, but there is that vision quest-type story told by Nellie Emm regarding the Prophet's magical flight on the back of the heretofore unridden white horse.

Ignoring the question of anachronism for the moment, we can easily now expand the previous formulation as follows: The color white = "white radiance" (of the Sun) = Thunder = cloud = rain = eagle feather = curing = the Prophet's white horse = the magical White Horse = water (i.e., the Inexhaustible Cruse motif) = "Tale of the Rainmaker" = Wovoka, the Rainmaker. Yet when I asked Mrs. Valdez whether or not Wovoka therefore was The Rainmaker = The Messiah, or the Christ, she answered, "Most assuredly not!"

Yet Chapman alluded to him as the "new Messiah," and in Mooney's great work, we read that it was the overwhelming belief of Plains Indians that the 1890 Ghost Dance Prophet was, indeed, the **waneika**, the Son of God = the Christ, who had returned to Earth to benefit Native Americans and to punish whites on a second sacrificial go-around. "I am the only living Jesus there is. Signed, Jack Wilson." This is the inscription which appears on back of the 1917 photograph of Wovoka taken by Special Inspector Lafayette A. Dorrington (Plate P).[5] Could a perception of Wovoka as The Rainmaker = Messiah = Christ, which belonged to that generation of Numus who actively participated in his religion, either have been forgotten or repressed by younger Yerington Paiutes, who, in the main, are

Christians today? Did Wovoka think of himself in those terms?

To begin with, formal instruction in Christology did not begin in Smith and Mason valleys in any systematic way until Carson Institute opened its doors in 1890. Numus, then, who were old enough to have participated in the 1890 Ghost Dance lacked its prophet's kind and degree of exposure to Christianity, so argument which holds that they perceived him as The Christ seems dubious. "Messiah" and "Rainmaker," as will be seen, are separate, perhaps even thornier matters. And then, too, neither Chapman, Mooney, or Dyer specifically mentioned that Wovoka ever called himself the Christ. Nor is there any evidence for this revealed in the local newspapers, the Wier Notes, or in Dangberg's Composition Notebook, where Wilson family members expressed strong enough feelings about the Prophet to have slurred him as a "hoax," a "fraud," and a "mercenary." If Wovoka imagined himself to be the resurrected hero of the Gospels, then surely this is one of the best kept secrets in the history of world religions.

Moreover, there isn't a shred of evidence to suggest that any disillusionment occurred in Nevada with the religious movement he founded. No "prophecies that failed," as was true with its immediate predecessor, the 1870 Ghost Dance (Du Bois 1939). Other than the controversial "Messiah Letter," the 1890 Ghost Dance Prophet, unlike Wodziwob, made no specific prophecies of the kind that could spell eventual disillusionment. Yet another important contrast between these two historically related and successive revitalization movements can be made. Wovoka believed in his powers until the very end, whereas Wodziwob had apparently lost faith in his original revelation (Chapter Eight). And judging from the reminiscences of Yerington Paiutes who knew Wovoka (Appendix K), these descendants of 1890 Ghost Dance enthusiasts certainly seem to hold him in high esteem today.

Returning to "The Tale of the Rainmaker," if we assume it was told by Numus living in Smith and Mason valleys in the late 1880s, the legendary figure's white horse — if not his hat also — is obviously an anachronism. Since Wovoka owned five songs to control the weather and successfully demonstrated that power, one might even say that a functional equivalence between the legendary or mythical Rainmaker and the historic figure, Wovoka, Northern Paiute, would be expected. And what might have begun as a private speculation, once it became aired the prophecy of the white horse probably followed easily enough.

But Numus, as we also saw, called Wovoka Tamme Naa'a, "Our Father," and the Prophet = Rainmaker was said not only to have derived his bbooha from "God" but from Wolf as well. Wolf, Esa, as Hultkrantz previously showed, was identified in the traditional Numu religion with "Our Father," or the Sun. Because Wolf = "Our Father" = Sun = God was thought to be all-wise and all-good (albeit pompous and humorless, as Miller (1983:71) rightfully has pointed out), Christianized Numus today often equate the demiurge with Jesus, completing this formulation by identifying Wolf's younger brother, the Trickster Coyote, as the Devil. More importantly, however, if we argue that Wovoka = Rainmaker = Wolf = Our Father = Sun = God, it can be said that there is, indeed, something messianic about Esa, the great Northern Paiute creator and culture hero.

Hultkrantz (1979:34) wrote that Native Americans shared a belief in someone who "has withdrawn, but will return at some future time," and although Wolf certainly doesn't speak about returning to earth again in the Numu Creation Story, he does tell his beautiful Numu wife before deserting her not to cry because she will have a reunion with him again in Heaven, the "Land Beyond The Clouds" (Chapter Eight). And reunion with the dead is also something characteristic about Wovoka's Great Revelation.

Therefore, Wovoka = Rainmaker = "Messiah." But not the Judeo-Christian Son of Man, Wovoka = Rainmaker = Wolf = Messiah. And if we also say that Wovoka = Rainmaker = Wolf = Messiah = God = Our Father = Sun, given that Thunder was believed to be Sun's younger brother and that the 1890 Ghost Dance Prophet's weather-control power derived specifically from "one or two clouds," we can easily enough expand this formulation to include: Wovoka = Rainmaker = Messiah = Wolf = Our Father = God = Sun = Thunder = Clouds = Rain. Which, I would further argue, leads us back again to color symbolism and to the prophecy of the white horse.

Among the four preconditions listed by Alice Fletcher (1891:58) for Lakota acceptance of Wovoka's new religion, she included the "belief in a deliverer who is known as the 'Son of God' and [who] is lighter in color than most Indians." Mooney's own explanation for the widespread belief among Plains Indians that Wovoka was white or light-skinned rested upon the blending by Native Americans of stellar mythology such as Star = Sunrise with Judeo-Christian messianic beliefs in the "Son of Man," or Christ, which took place during acculturation. Of course Mooney effectively demolished the notion that Wovoka was Caucasian or even mixed: "The impression that he is a half-blood may have arisen from the fact that his father's name was 'White Man' and that he has a white man's name" (Mooney 1896:771).[6] Simply stated, then, the argument here is that

Wovoka's prophecy of a white horse entered the Numu vocabulary of Wovoka lore for reasons similar to those which led to the Prophet's transformation into a "white God" by Plains Indians. They were: (1) the importance of the horse in Numu adaptations to their changing environment; (2) the symbolic load that the color white already carried in their traditional color taxonomy and belief system; and (3) because it was the color of Euro-American conquerors.

Recalling Don Handleman (1967), who argued for the creativity of Native American shamans especially during stressful periods of acculturation, I argue that the color white enabled creative Numus to draw the following functional equivalencies: white = Tibo'o = Wovoka's white horse = the prophecy of a white horse = Messiah = Wolf = Our Father = God = Sun = Thunder = (white) cloud = rain = The Rainmaker = eagle feather = curing = ebe, the sacred white paint.

But there is another association with the color white that can be suggested, the Prophet's invulnerability. Corbett Mack, as we have seen, described how four brave Numu soldiers dodged bullets while riding on their horses in the Pyramid Lake War of 1860. Nor did bullets faze him, or so the 1890 Ghost Dance Prophet had himself declared. He was invulnerable, and he matter-of-factly told Chapman that he possessed the power from "God" to destroy this world and to make it over again. Even 27 years after his Great Revelation, Wovoka could still think to visit President Woodrow Wilson in 1916 and offer to personally "terminate the murderous war in Europe."

My own view is that the "loud noise" Wovoka heard in Pine Grove, and that Chapman wrote was responsible for the onset of the 1890 Ghost Dance Prophet's Great Revelation, symbolically allows us to link up Tibo'o with his invulnerability. For, if a thunderclap was instrumental in triggering Wovoka's Near-Death Experience and resultant Altered State of Consciousness, what more obvious equation than loud noise = thunderclap = rifle shot = Tibo'o? And if we join the potential that Wovoka's weather control bbooha gave to him to totally control the Walker River regional economy with his invulnerability, then even the cavalries, cannons, and Hotchkiss guns belonging to the vastly superior military arsenal of the conquering Tibo'o would be reduced to a trifle by this supernatural gift. This gift was a power Wovoka successfully demonstrated more than once by inviting his brother and others to take shots at him, and by doctoring Numus who had been shot with rifles as well.

Thus, the color white = thunderclap = rifles = Tibo'o = the Prophet's invulnerability = Wovoka's ability to doctor gunshot wounds = the white horse = the prophecy of the white horse = the Messiah = Wolf = God = Our Father = Sun = Thunder = clouds = rain = The Rainmaker = water = eagle feather = shamanic curing = ebe (white paint). And with the equivalencies previously suggested for the complementary color red (= pesape or red paint = Sun = eclipse = rattlesnake = curing = rain = Thunder, etc.) can we then not also say, white = red? A balanced equation which the 1890 Ghost Dance Prophet himself surely would have positively endorsed.[7]

ENDNOTES

1. According to Jay Miller (1983:68), the Numu classification involved five primary colors: yellow, blue-green-gray, black, white, and red, though only the last three carried "heavy symbolic loads." Miller also suggested that there might even have been an association between colors and cardinal directions. Black, for example, with center. Although black (toohoo-ggweddaddu-nabo'o) and yellow (oha-ggweddadu) paints were used by healers, any Numu could sprinkle these onto his or her forehead to prevent recurrent dreams. Wovoka, of course, ordinarily dressed in a full length black overcoat and is usually envisaged wearing a black ten gallon Stetson. Indeed, one of the nine Numu Ghost Dance songs Mooney (1896:1053) recorded contains the following lines: "The black rock/the rock is broken" (Appendix G).

2. From Wovoka, Arapahos apparently acquired the custom of tying eagle feathers "on the shoulders and on the sleeves," in turn, teaching this to the Lakota (Mooney 1896:798).

3. The tale is reminiscent of Plateau stories involving the demiurge Coyote, who "demands a 'wife' at each village, and if his request is granted he makes that place a good fishing [salmon] spot" (Ricketts 1987:168).

4. Numus also pray to **tamme pea**, or "Our Mother," but pointed out to me that their prayers more frequently were directed to the Sun.

5. Beth Ellis, on the other hand, told Solberg that Wovoka could write "Father Jack" (Gunard Solberg, Personal Correspondence).

6. B. C. Hedrick (1971) has argued that it was the dominance of Euro-American cultures which led to the belief that the Toltec-Aztec culture hero Quetzalcoatl was a "white" or light-skinned deity. This has not only been exploited by Mormons and Bahais but finds recent expression in such films by Werner Herzog as "Fitzcarraldo" and "Aquirre, The Wrath of God."

7. A symbolic interpretation of numbers, too, might reveal much about Wovoka's religion. Thus, the Prophet had been given 5 songs by God and was instructed to tell his people to perform the nanigukwa or Round Dance for 5 nights in succession, or so Mooney wrote (5 being a sacred Numu number). Also, the white horse neighs 5 times, swishes his tail 5 times, and turns about 5 times. Captain Josephus, on the other hand, told Chapman that Wovoka had prophesied rain in 3 days time. In Josephus's account, Wovoka had been directed from On High to instruct Numus that they must "dance five nights in succession and then stop for three months." Unless Hultkrantz is correct that three was a traditional number, one therefore gleans how the blending or syncretism between Numu and Judeo-Christian traditions took place in the evolution of the 1890 Ghost Dance Religion.

CHAPTER 10

More about Wovoka

"By any standard, Wovoka, the Ghost Dance Prophet, was one of the most significant holy men ever to emerge among the Indians of North America" (L. G. Moses 1985:348).

"He wasn't a fighting Indian; he was one of these preaching Indians, " (Judge Clark Guild 1967:276).

"Jack's just the same as any preacher. Talks to God" (Andy Dick, Yerington Numu Appendix K).

Scholarly research and popular interest in the 1890 Ghost Dance religion have continued apace these past seven years (cf. Josephy, Thomas & Eder 1990; Osterreich 1991; Vander 1997), yet the questions raised in the first edition of this book remain:

Exactly when did Wovoka begin having visions, and how many did he actually have?

What did the 1890 Ghost Dance prophet originally see, and what were his instructions, and to whom were they intended?

Were there changes over time in these, and, if so, in what way(s) were they reflections of national events such as the Wounded Knee massacre?

Did Wovoka speak of or prophesy the resurrection of Indian dead and a nativistic-type restoration of aboriginal life, that is, the "Prophet Dance" (Spier 1935)?

What was the extent of the impact of mid-nineteenth-century frontier Presbyterianism and Wovoka's knowledge of Judeo-Christian millennialism, gained in the Mason Valley home of David Wilson, upon his vision of an otherworldly future (Heaven)?

Was Heaven only for faithful Numus? For all Native Americans? Or, were **taivos**[1] (whites) also included?

What were Wovoka's initial Round Dance cum "ghost dance" ceremonies in Smith and Mason valleys and on the Walker River Reservation like?

How, if at all, did the so-called 1890 Ghost Dance change in response to the steady stream of Native Americans who began arriving from around the country soon after his Great Revelation?

The Four Primary Sources

In lieu of texts stating exactly what this prophet said, our knowledge of this end-time religious movement must continue to rely primarily on the published, translated accounts of what four Numus, including the Prophet himself, told two taivos: the Indian scout, Arthur I. Chapman, and the ethnologist, James Mooney, who interviewed Wovoka some thirteen months later, on 1 January 1892.

ARTHUR I. CHAPMAN

No Ghost Dance scholar, present company included, has given proper emphasis to Chapman's recounting of *three separate and distinct visions* experienced by Wovoka, all in the same night, and each with divers content (Appendix A). It will be recalled that the first vision consisted of a visit to heaven, the second the revealing by God of the fundamental precepts of the religion, and the third, a return to heaven, the acquisition of weather-control powers by Wovoka, and instructions from God to "say to his people that they must meet often and dance five nights in succession and then stop for three months." Information about Wovoka's three revelations was given to Chapman by James Josephus, a Numu and "Captain" of the reservation police force.

The significance of the Christian number *three* in these instances is obvious enough in this account—as mentioned in Chapter One, Josephus had recently converted to the Ghost Dance religion and had become a follower of "the new Christ" following a fulfilled prophecy of rain from Wovoka. No mention of these three separate visions, however, was made by Wovoka when interviewed by Chapman (and reported in the dialogical form [cf. Tedlock 1979] it presumably took).[2] Interestingly, Wovoka's interpreter, Ben Ab-he-gan of the reservation police, was present throughout Josephus's (English) recounting of the Great Revelation(s) and reportedly "corroborated every word he spoke" (Appendix A).

JAMES MOONEY

I turn next to what can be supplemented to the account obtained by the "Indian Man," James Mooney (1861-1921), who interviewed Wovoka in January 1892 (Appendix B). We have already seen how Mooney, too, gained an initial understanding of the 1890 Ghost Dance through a Walker River Reservation Numu: Charley Sheep.[3] Mooney reported at that time that he had stayed a week with Wovoka's uncle (without disclosing how he met Sheep or learned of his kinship with the Prophet) and that Sheep "spoke tolerable—or rather intolerable—English, so that we were able to get along together without an interpreter, a fact which brought us into closer sympathy, as an interpreter is generally at best only a necessary evil" (op. cit.).

Many years later, however, in an 18 January 1910 speech to the Nebraska Historical Society, Mooney (1911:179-80; reproduced as Appendix B.1) recalled his encounter with Sheep differently. Stating that he had "stopped about two weeks with his uncle," Mooney went on to claim that "the old man [Sheep] could not speak English at all." This statement not surprisingly prompted Mooney's biographer to ask "How would Charly [sic] Sheep translate Mooney's interests to Wovoka when he spoke no English?" (Moses 1987:139).[4] Did Chapman's Walker River Reservation interpreters, the Indian Police Captains Josephus and Ben, assist Mooney with the various songs, myths, and games that he cagily collected as pretext to gaining Sheep's "confidence"? Moses's query raises questions about what actually took place between Mooney, Wovoka, Charley Sheep, and E. A. Dyer (a Yerington grocer who would also be recruited, along with a teamster, for the famous expedition because he spoke Numu and "seemed to be on intimate terms" with Wovoka).

Mooney's lecture reminds us once more of how the quartet traveled twelve miles south from Yerington to Wovoka's camp on the East Walker River, on a bitter cold, final day in December 1891, through snow which Charley Sheep explained was the direct result of his nephew's weather-control **booha** or "power." Having written in his official study that he learned from Sheep that the Prophet "found the visits increasingly annoying, particularly after the government branded the religion dangerous and inimical to order and progress," Mooney (1911) would again recall in his lecture that Wovoka "was very suspicious." Even after so many years, James Mooney felt it important to restate Wovoka's agreement to be interviewed, in the evening after he'd finished hunting jackrabbit.

Mooney's remarks in his lecture about the peaceful intent of the 1890 Ghost Dance religion echoes what he originally wrote and ought to put to rest any thoughts that its prophet might have mutated an original revelation from militancy to pacifism: "He taught that the whole human race was of one kindred, and particularly that the Indians of the several tribes were all brothers and must give up tribal warfare and all thought of warfare with the whites" (Mooney 1911:180).[5]

EDWARD A. DYER

Two newspaper articles and a taped interview (Appendix C.1) by Margaret (Peg) Wheat with Edward A. Dyer supplement his 1965 memoir about Wovoka, entitled "Wizardry" (Appendix C).

In a 29 January 1960 article in the *Fallon Eagle Standard* entitled "Ed Dyer, Nevada Pioneer Observes 89th Birthday" (Box 4:30 "Wilson, Jack," Margaret M. Wheat Papers, #83-24," Special Collections, University of Nevada–Reno Library), we learn that he was born in Vallejo, California, on 20 January 1871. After moving to Virginia City with Ed's mother in 1874, the Dyers relocated to Mason Valley six years later (1880), following his parents' divorce. His remarried mother purchased a ranch several miles south of Yerington, and Dyer recalls opening his first grocery store at the age of seventeen. In a follow-up 21 August 1959 story in the same newspaper, Dyer recalls that he continued as a "merchant" for twenty-five years, eventually owning a "chain store" with branches in Schurz (Walker River Reservation), Rawhide, as well as in the tiny railroad hamlet of Wabuska on the Carson and Colorado, in northern Mason Valley. These newspaper articles also mention Dyer's marriage to Nettie Mae Hayes, in 1902, in the Riverside Hotel in Reno, their departure for California during the Depression and return to Fallon, Nevada, in 1937, and the establishment of the Dyer Brothers' Ranch in Schedkler District with their sons, Ed Jr., Leete, and Chandler.

Margaret Wheat's interview with Dyer (Appendix C.1; Tape 17, Wheat Papers) provides more significant supplemental information. Dyer claims that Mooney interviewed Wovoka not in the Prophet's wickiup, but in the house of a Maine compatriot of Dyer's parents:

> So, we all went over to [George] Plummer's ranch. He's a friend of mine, a man my folks knew back East, back in Maine. I asked him if he had some place in the house we could go? Had a table in the house we could write [on]? He welcomed us all in. Took us into a room there. So, Mr. Mooney opened his briefcase and got out his writing materials and everything. So, we was there several hours, interviewing Jack Wilson. Mooney wrote up a lot about him: Myths and songs and stories, you know. Lots of things.

Indeed, how could Mooney have been able to see well enough in the dark **qanee** or tule house belonging to the 1890 Ghost Dance prophet even to transcribe a single one of his many reported names! And if he didn't interview Wovoka that night in his house—Mooney in his lecture years later (1911; Appendix B.1) differently recalled that the interview did not occur until the following day—what was discussed inside Wovoka's home that night? The famous photograph of Wovoka seated in a chair alongside Charley Sheep (Plates A.1 and A.2), then, must have been taken by Mooney on the Plummer Ranch.

Even if Dyer's memory was inaccurate in these regards—he had had a stroke—his written statement (Appendix C) that "Wilson was known to have a good working knowledge of English but not quite up to explaining obscure points of Indian theology," coupled with his professed role as key translator, begs the question of Charley Sheep's contribution to the interview.[6] As Dyer recalled for Wheat (Appendix C.1): "I furnished the material, he [Mooney] done the writing. He [then] changed it. It wasn't in the exact language that I gave, but he changed it to suit himself." This comment concurs with Dyer's claim in his written memoir about his role during the interview: "Mr. Mooney went into tribal lore and religious beliefs. I translated legends, stories, songs and dance chants, all of which were duly recorded in Mr. Mooney's notebook" (Appendix C).

Yet another contribution of the Dyer Tape to our knowledge and understanding of the 1890 Ghost Dance Prophet is the disclosure that Wovoka purchased from Dyer's general store and sold to followers not only tall "Texas Plaza hats" but also "calico [ghost] shirts." The sale of these items joined the sale of eagle and magpie tail feathers and red paint as part of the income he derived from thaumaturges.

PAUL BAILEY

Further critical consideration of Paul Bailey's biography of Wovoka, which was considered a fourth "primary source," is necessitated by an interview conducted in February 1966 with Alice Wilson Vidovich, Wovoka's youngest daughter, and her husband (Appendix L; Tape 74, Wheat Papers).

Alice Wilson Vidovich in the interview enumerates five specific "hurts" or objections to Bailey's biography (Appendix L). Revealing a bitter sense of betrayal,[7] her complaints included: (1) Bailey's ridicule of her famous father's "rifle power" or claim of being invulnerable; (2) his contention that Wovoka had "seeded" a goldmine with fool's gold as revenge against slights from his white "blood brother"; (3) Bailey's argument that the 1890 Ghost Dance prophet traveled to the Pacific Northwest, where he borrowed various "tricks," such as trance, from the Indian Shaker Church and used them at home to dupe Indians; (4) the related allegation that Mormonism was also essential to the new religion founded by Wovoka; and (5) Mrs. Vidovich's belief that Bailey attributed her only son's death during World War II to divine retribution for her father's supposed role in the Wounded Knee massacre. These objections will be examined in turn.

Bailey (1957:124-27) does not take seriously Wovoka's demonstration of his booha; he was a "fake" who put a pinch of sand or snow in his gun, yet somehow brought down a jackrabbit with this shot in front of "gullible Paiutes." This "trick," originally "staged" before three hundred visiting Indians, was repeated by the 1890 Ghost Dance prophet, who hung his "ghost shirt" on a clothesline and told assembled Indians to shoot, their bullets against the free-swinging cloth falling harmlessly onto the ground (Bailey 1957:123).[8] Bailey (1957:154) goes on to claim that Wovoka's "fakery of inviolability in the face of gunfire became the basis for the 'ghost shirts.'" Having learned from visiting "Mormonized Indians" that their sacred garments were protection against disease and death, Wovoka, according to Bailey, adopted this belief, painting the garment with "magic red ochre" and assorted "symbols."

The **nomogweta**, or the "stolen," Alice Wilson Vidovich presumably had some traditional cultural knowledge of Numu shamans' invulnerability. Defending her stepfather, she declared: "[Bailey said] he went out and had people shoot at him. And he wore a bulletproof vest. Well, how does an Indian know that? Indian don't know anything about that!"[9]

A second characterization of Wovoka equally troubled her. Bailey (1957:72) reports that Wovoka's alleged "blood brother," J. I. Wilson, had "laughingly asked" the Prophet to employ his "gift of divination in the location of a worthwhile claim." After Wovoka to no avail prayed and meditated, "Bill shamelessly laughed the Paiute prophet into derision among the white people of the valley."[10] In retaliation—and a major theme of Bailey's biography is Wovoka's desire to overcome his second-class citizenship and low income from farm labor by becoming a prophet/messiah in the face of his three white Wilson brothers' success in the regional economy—the Prophet deceitfully "seeded" a cave by cashing in twenty borrowed dollars for a handful of gold dust, which he then shot against a cave wall (Bailey 1957:73-74). Billy Wilson "never quite forgave Wovoka for the thing that he had done," Bailey concluded (1957:74). The biographer then tags onto this discussion the insensitive suggestion that the three babies in a row subsequently born dead to Jack and Mary Wilson were "almost as punishment," whereas Bill Wilson's children in contradistinction lived (ibid).

Alice Wilson Vidovich's rejoinder was regrettably brief: "And then salting the mine with gold—Where would he get the gold to salt the mine with? Well, gosh, that's unreasonable!"[11]

Her third objection to Bailey was really twofold. First, his contention

(1957:68) that Wovoka not only procured Numu laborers, but, for personal gain, led them over the Sierra Nevadas for employment in the California and Oregon hop fields. Second, once there, the Prophet borrowed from the Indian Shakers the idea of trance and was even tutored by them (Bailey 1957:50). Ignoring the fact that trances are part and parcel of Numu shamanic culture, Bailey argued that "like the Shakers," Wovoka "faked a trance" (Bailey 957:62).

Alice Wilson Vidovich's reply is to the point:

> And then it says that Dad took these people to Sacramento and up and Oregon, to give them work. And then he collected tithes from them. And Dad never done that! The only person who done that was Johnson Sides! He's the one take them to Sacramento and Oregon. And he [Bailey] said that he joined the Quakers, the Shakers, or something... And, Dad, he never believe—Well, he believed there was a supreme being, but he never went toward this church or that church. Or any other church! He had his own belief.[12]

Alice Wilson Vidovich also objected to Bailey's discussion of the influence of Mormonism upon her father. Bailey describes (1957:75-76) the arrival of "Mormonized Indians" that supposedly followed the visit to her father by "Slocum's Indians." The former allegedly showed Wovoka their sacred garment and explained their "idea of being white and delightsome"; much as Wovoka was intrigued with these, "he summarily rejected Mormonism" (Bailey 1957:76).

Aside from scoffing at Bailey's remarks, neither Alice Wilson Vidovich nor her husband, Andy, offered specific evidence to refute a connection between Mormonism and Wovoka. Admittedly, there are longstanding Mormon connections to the Wilson family. At some point Alice and Andy Vidovich did become members of the Church of Latter Day Saints; it is also known that their son Harlyn joined in the 1930s, while in his teens. On the other hand, the impressive scholarship of Garold Barney (1986) clearly demonstrates that frontier Mormonism, although certainly influential, can be assumed to have had no *direct* impact upon Wovoka and his new religion.[13] Overwhelming ethnographic evidence indicates that apocalyptism as well as both trance and invulnerability were culturally consistent with traditional Numu beliefs (cf. Chapter 4).

Alice Wilson Vidovich's fifth and most emotional objection was her belief that Bailey interpreted her only son's death in World War II as retribution for the 1890 massacre at Wounded Knee, which was indirectly caused by Wovoka's religion. She sobbed to Wheat, "And that's what Paul Bailey said: That my boy paid for that!" (Appendix L). Perusal of his biography, however, fails to reveal any such statement. Such an interpretation does appear in Dyer's memoir, though stated less provocatively: "But the debt [for Wounded Knee], if any there was, can now be marked 'paid in full' for his grandson gave his life for his country" (Appendix C).[14]

Not surprisingly, Alice Wilson Vidovich's contempt for Bailey extended far beyond her five particular objections[15]:

But I think Paul Bailey, I think is the lowest type of white man to run down a poor old—Oh, of course, he just think that it's just, oh, they're just Indians, and that's all. Nothing! You see, that's the way some people think. And they act it, too!... But, I say, we're just human beings, just like anybody else...To me, his book is just—out of whack, that's all. Of course, it makes it real bad, you know, for us. Maybe the government will take his word more than others? Maybe they might say that Jack Wilson was a bad man? (Appendix L)

Family

Having supplemented and further interrogated the four primary sources, what do the new data add to our understanding of the life of Wovoka and the religion he founded?

PARENTS

I have long questioned (Hittman 1973a, Chapter Two this volume) Mooney's assertion that the Prophet's father died when Wovoka was in his early teens. Wovoka's son-in-law, Andy Vidovich, independently supported this assumption in a late 1960s interview with Baha'i enthusiasts. A summary of the interview reports: "Mooney's sources say that Taivo [**Numeraivo**] died in 1870 when Wovoka was about 14 years old, but Andy says differently. Taivo died somewhere long about [the] middle of June in 1914... Wovoka was long about 60 or 65 years old at the time" (Baha'i Mss. p. 6).[16] Andy Vidovich also recalled that the 1890 Ghost Dance prophet and his father were both six feet tall (ibid).

Eileen Kane's field report "On Wovoka" (Appendix M) provides some additional information about his father. In addition to the names of Numuraivo and Buckskin, Kane records yet another—**Pana**. Contrary to the portrait of him in the first edition, she also reports that Wovoka's father worked for whites.

THE PROPHET'S WIFE

In a 1966 interview with Margaret Wheat (Appendix L), Alice Wilson Vidovich fills in considerably our knowledge of the character and life of her mother, Mary Wilson. Many interesting details are recalled—whom Mary Wilson worked for, her continual domestic responsibilities, her relationship with her children. Several years later, Andy Vidovich also offered a fond recollection of his mother-in-law:

> Mary was a wonderful woman, an adaptable woman. She was a hard working woman. She was a plain woman. Mary was like Wovoka—she never used liquor in any form. Mary live a clean life. Mary done many things for the family. Them days, living among the Indian people was very, very hard—getting substance to eat. Mary always was willing to get out and pull weeds for the family and pick potatoes and onions for the ranchers, too, and then do ironing and washing for the white people. Mary was one of the most wondersome women I've ever known (Baha'i Mss. p. 25).

Some information has also emerged about Mary Wilson's sister, whose name is unfortunately not known. Nettie Dyer, the wife of Edward S. Dyer, had moved to Mason Valley in 1892, where Wovoka and his wife and sister-in-law had also resettled. When interviewed by Margaret Wheat, Nettie Dyer remembered that Wovoka's sister-in-law did not have any children but did help Mary Wilson take care of Wovoka's children (Tape 17, "Edward S. Dyer Interview," Box 16, Wheat Papers). It is not known whether or not Wovoka had sexual privileges with his sister-in-law (Park 1937; Stewart 1939), or, in the fashion of shamans and other outstanding Numu individual males, if he were more conventionally married to her. Nettie Dyer admitted, "Now, whether she was his wife too, I don't know." Both Mary Wilson and her sister, as will be seen, are reported in Indian Census returns.

CHILDREN

There are new facts regarding the children of Wovoka and Mary Wilson. Nellie Emm (b. 1906) described the children to Margaret Wheat on 23 May 1969 (Tape 110, Box 13, Transcript pp. 1-2, Wheat Papers):

> The oldest child was named Rose. Rose Penrose was her name, she was married to Archie Penrose's father. [Wovoka's second daughter was] Ida Sharp—when she died her name was Sharp, Ina James' mother. Rose, Ida, and Alice Vidovich, that's all my mother ever spoke of... But I know that my mother said that Rose was his favorite. And he used to do anything for her. And when she died, he had a lot of feathers. He believed that helped him along with his power. And he put a lot of those feathers with her in the grave. And then that's when he started to lose his power.[17]

Newly discovered information brings into sharper focus the relationship between Wovoka and Mary Wilson's youngest daughter, Alice Wilson Vidovich. A taped conversation between Numu Edna Jones and Peg Wheat in December 1957 (Box 4:29, Wheat Papers) supports the story of Alice's seeming estrangement from her stepfather as originally suggested in the first edition of this book:

> When Alice was born to Jack Wilson's wife she was very light-skinned. Jack Wilson was convinced that she was the child of one of the white men on the ranch where they worked. He therefore didn't want her and decided to kill her. Two old women who didn't have any children and who were distantly related to Alice's mother took her and raised her for the first few years of her life. They were fond of the child and dressed her in long dresses like an old Indian lady with a scarf around her head.[18]

Recalling that "she sure looked cute," Edna Jones then related to Wheat how later, when Alice was older ("old enough so that she could remember"), "She went back to live with her mother. Then Jack Wilson liked her."

Alice Wilson Vidovich herself would recall (Appendix L) being "cuffed" by the 1890 Ghost Dance prophet, though she maintains that she received punishment only when deserved:

[And he] Never was cross with us kids. Never! Only when we were naughty, he'd switch us on our legs. But we deserve it, 'cause, we all have to have that... I would [can] still feel it on the leg [laughs]. He never hit us on our head, or body, only on our leg with the switch. And he didn't do that very often. Just once in a great while.

While reviewing those circumstances surrounding her temporary adoption or extended family care placement, she further told Wheat:

And then Aunt—Ana Wasson—took me away from my mother when I was 15 months old. She raised me right up here... No, I didn't stay with my mother, I stayed with my aunt. Right up here by the [Schurz] graveyard; beyond the graveyard. And then she used to take me down here, and Bob Dyer [Ed Dyer's younger brother] used to hold me and carry me around. And tell everybody that I was his daughter! [But] He just said that, you know. And there used to be a big platform there in front of his store—was facing the [railroad] track. And Indians'd sit along this, and people would go down when the train stop; people get out and walk around.[19]

"I was a little teensy weensy girl," Alice Wilson Vidovich continued. "I don't remember very much of it, but they used to give me nickels; they'd give me their lunch. Like that. I guess I looked so pitiful, that they give me their lunch." After Wheat had suggested how cute she must have looked when both aunts dressed her like a "little old lady," Alice mused, "Well, could be, you know? I didn't know how I was dressed, only that my aunt, **Tuzeeqama**, that she used to make clothes for me. And more likely she did dress me like a little old lady!"

Wheat's interview with Alice Wilson Vidovich also reveals interesting circumstances surrounding the premature birth of Wovoka's step-daughter in 1902:

"I was born at Day's Ranch, Smith Valley; near Colony [District]. Biggest ranch they had was Day's Ranch. That's where I was born. That's where all those happenings [Ghost Dance ceremonies?] were, where my mother raised all these kids....

See, it was the third of July, and she was expecting a big company: People coming from San Francisco. And she [Mary Wilson] moved some bedsteads from downstairs upstairs, then she'd bring the others downstairs. And she overdid herself. [So] On Fourth of July morning, two o'clock, well, I was born. Mother couldn't show up to work, to help her, so she [employer's wife] sent down a man: To see if my mother was alright. Then Mother told her we had a little baby girl, and we don't know if she's gonna live or not. She's only a seven month baby. Of course, she came down and took me over—over to her house. And I stayed with her, my mother, for a long time. And they raised me on cow's milk. And now I just hate cow's milk!

[So] That's how it happened. I was only a 7 month baby. Well, I guess if it was 8 months, I guess I'd have been dead!

Alice Wilson Vidovich also shed alternative light on her name, which might have been mistakenly given as "Patchquilt" in the first edition of this book.

And they always call me, **Pozina**. Means 'rabbit kidney.' [Because] If they were eating rabbit, I'd crawl all over everybody and ask for it. That was my specialty! They just let me do anything, I guess, because there were so many of us. They'd be eating, and I was the littlest. My brother and I was the smallest in the family. So, whatever we asked [for], we got.

Two written documents about Alice Wilson Vidovich have turned up in the federal archives as well. In a 9 October 1917 inquiry regarding her school truancy, superintendent of the Walker River Agency and School Robert E. Burris would write: "As to Alice Wilson, mentioned in yours of October 3, I have to state that she is married so I will not consider her in my round up." In the second letter written several days later, James B. Royce, superintendent of the Carson Indian School on 15 October 1917, stated:

In regard to Alice Wilson, I understand that she is married to Andrew Vidovich. I am just in receipt of a letter from his sister in which she is very much concerned about Andrew. She states that she understands they were married Indian fashion and not legally married. She also states that Andrew is only nineteen years of age and has a legal guardian, and for that reason he cannot secure a license. She desires that Andrew be sent back to school and compelled to remain at school until he is twenty one. If you are at Yerington any way soon, I wish you would investigate the matter. While at school, Andrew was one of the best boys we had. He is a good worker and a first class carpenter, and if he could be induced to attend school longer he could prepare himself for a good position (RG 75, Box 248A, Carson Indian School Correspondence, Walker River, 1902-1906, Federal Archives, San Bruno, California).

Mooney, it will be recalled, mentioned that the Prophet had a four-year-old son, commenting on the overt affection expressed by Wovoka toward the boy during their New Year's Day meeting on 1892. Bob Dyer spoke of six deceased sons born to Wovoka and Mary Wilson; their Yerington relations, however, seemed to agree only that one son was killed in a runaway wagon accident, causing storms to be unleashed by his angry father.[20] This incident is supported by an unidentified informant, who told the ethnographer, Willard Z. Park (Field Notes III:21. In possession of Catherine S. Fowler, p. 98):

When a doctor or member of his family dies it affects the weather. A hard wind comes up. When Jack Wilson's son died a very hard wind came up nobody could stand up against it. Nobody could make food so everyone had to go without food. The wind lasted all day and stopped about sunset when Jack told everybody to dance.[21]

Walker River Reservation Numu historian, Ed Johnson, records the event similarly (1975:54):

> The People on the reservation lost some respect for the prophet when he was unable to prevent his infant son's death after a wagon accident between Mason Valley and Schurz... It is said though that Wovoka became very angry and caused a wind storm to come up. The people's tents and summer shades were blown away while the prophet's brush shade barely moved in the wind because he had placed an eagle feather at each corner.[22]

More information about the incident is supplied by Fallon Numu Wuzzie George, the primary informant for Wheat's *Survival Art of the Primitive Paiutes* (1967), as well as star of incomparable ethnographic footage demonstrating these crafts (Video Tapes 1-4, Wheat Papers). In an interview by Margaret Wheat (Tape Transcription p. 2, Box 4:31, Wheat Papers), Mrs. George remembered:

> Jack Wilson have boy wagon run over. We stay home, but my father and aunt, mother's sister, come over to Schurz to dance. That time was when wagon run over (boy), Jack Wilson doctored him. He (boy) throw up the blood: Break a rib. After that [the] boy was dead [?]. He [Wovoka] tried to clean him on the inside. He suck blood. Indian doctor do that. He suck him, any place, when sick. He put white paint on. Paint goes through the skin.[23]

This knowledgeable Fallon Numu unfortunately did not say whether or not Wovoka saved his own son's life.

When asked directly in 1966 about her brother's death in this alleged incident, Alice Wilson Vidovich (Appendix L) would supplement our genealogical knowledge of her famous family by recalling:

> I don't remember [an older brother], I don't know. They never said. But my little brother, him and I are the two different [i.e., full-blood] kind. And he died—he was about 6 years old when he died, my little brother.

"No, he just took sick and he died, that was all!" she responded to Wheat's follow-up suggestion that her younger brother might have died in the wagon accident. "Nice little boy, he looked something like [nephew] Harley: brown hair. He was younger than me." When pressed further by Wheat about the possibility of an older brother's death, she admitted, "Could have happened, I don't know anything about it. You see, I don't know, I was so young at the time I don't know very much."

The Baha'i Manuscript now allows us to name one of these boys, perhaps the four-year-old son of the 1890 Ghost Dance prophet seen by Mooney. "Andy [Vidovich] recalls, also, that Wovoka had three daughters and a son," we read in a section entitled "Impressions of Wovoka" (p. 25). "The oldest girl's name he has forgotten, but the second was Ida and the youngest was Alice. His son, Timothy, was killed at about seven or eight years of age, when a team of run-away horses threw him out of the wagon, and the wheels ran over him."

Additional information can also be presented about Wovoka's grandson, Harlyn S. Vidovich, made famous in his own right as a World War II hero, and the subject of a prophecy discussed in Chapter Seven. Harlyn Vidovich was the only child of Alice and Andy Vidovich. Born on 3 July 1920 in Carson City, he went through grade school in the state's capital, becoming a Mormon when his parents moved to Reno's twin city of Sparks. Margaret Wheat notes that Harlyn Vidovich "was always active in church work, and [that] before entering the [armed] service he served with Bishop Hicks of the Papago Ward at Scottsdale, as First Councilor," after moving to Saceton, Arizona, where his father found employment as an Indian Bureau carpenter (Box 4:29, Wheat Papers). Harlyn graduated from Casa Grande High School, earning the first of his many remarkable distinctions by attending Phoenix Junior College and graduating from Tempe State Teachers' College as a mathematician. Next, he went to the Civil Aeronautic School in Sky Harbor, Phoenix, where he enlisted in the Air Corps. And with training at Kelly Arledge, Randolph and Foster Fields, but especially as a single-engine fighter pilot in Lake Charles, Louisiana, and in Texas, Harlyn Vidovich received his commission on 2 July 1942, at Foster Field. Sent overseas 28 July 1942, he served in Africa and India, and was credited with downing three Japanese planes in air, and two probable hits. On 9 March 1944, his parents were notified that their son had crashed into a mountain in Eastern China while returning home to base in routine flight and was found dead amidst the wreckage of his plane.[24] His funeral service was held at the LDS Church in Sparks, under Bishop M. A. Piggott. There was a graveside military service in the Mountain View Cemetery (Reno Post No. 407, VFW), and memorial services were also observed on Sunday 19 March 1944 at the LDS Church in Salt River.

Wheat (ibid) also observes that Harlyn's death apparently escalated an already simmering tension between his mother and Edna Jones.

> Edna and Alice were not on speaking terms. Edna doesn't know just why Alice was mad at her. A friend told Edna that Alice was mad because Edna had told all around town that Alice's son had been killed, a fact which Alice never acknowledged... It seems that when the telegram arrived from the War Dept., Ina took it over to Edna's house. Alice was away at the time. Ina and Edna cried over the fact that Alice had lost her only boy. Edna said that it was the War Dept. that had spread the news. She asked Ina, "Why does my 'sister' treat me this way?"

The Early Years

No new information has been found about Wovoka's childhood. Ake Hultkrantz has charged that, in the first edition of this book, I failed to consider the impact of the 1870 Ghost Dance upon the young (ca. twenty-three-year-old), future 1890 Ghost Dance prophet. My response is to acknowledge that Wovoka must have known about Wodziwob's religion (cf. Hittman 1973a, 1992), but there is no known proof that he attended those ceremonies that began around May of 1869 at the adjacent Walker River Reservation, some twenty miles away.

As for the questions previously raised about this prophet's early years, we still need to know the following: How old was Wovoka when his seeming life-turning relationship with the Wilsons took place? Which Biblical stories were read by the woman of this frontier house during meals? How much English did the young Numu possess at the time, and how much of what he learned about Judeo-Christianity did he understand? Resolving such questions will help us better comprehend Wovoka's syncretic theocracy, a blend characterized by Mooney (op. cit.) as "confused" and by Tim McCoy (op. cit.) as "jumbled." The Baha'i Manuscript (p. 5) might be the only place where this issue, albeit mystified, is clearly addressed:

> It has been assumed by many that, because of this experience that he merely took what he had learned of the Bible from the Wilsons, rephrased it and took credit for a new revelation. This would be near impossible since he knew no English at this point and picked up only a very few words later. It is also quite reasonable to assume that neither Mr. nor Mrs. Wilson read the Bible in Paiute. What little English Wovoka learned was the skanty [sic] amount needed between him and his playmates, the Wilson boys, which was certainly unrelated to the archaic English of a King James Bible.

The 1890 Ghost Dance Religion

Additional sources help supplement the reconstruction of the 1890 Ghost Dance religion in Nevada, attempted in Chapter Four. Two sources challenge the characterization of the Ghost Dance religion given by Mooney (1896) and echoed later by Moses (1985:340). Mooney, it will be recalled, claimed that "The great underlying principle of the Ghost Dance doctrine is that the time will come when the whole Indian race, living and dead, will be reunited upon a regenerated earth, to live a life of aboriginal happiness, forever free from death, disease, and misery" (1896:777). This view was expressed again years later in the influential *Handbook of American Indians North of Mexico*, where Mooney (Appendix B.1) argued that the Indians would be "restored to their inheritance and reunited with their departed friends." In his subsequent public address (Appendix B.2), Mooney once more sums up the core belief of Wovoka's religion as "the new Indian world would come and they would be put upon it." In the first edition of this volume, and elsewhere (Hittman 1992), I have contested Mooney's characterization of the 1890 Ghost Dance religion, attributing his view of the movement to a "Plains bias."

Nellie Emm describes the beliefs of Wovoka's religion differently than Mooney (Tape 110, Transcript p. 2, Wheat Papers):

> My mother was there all the time. Everybody was there. Because, she claims, that everybody should be there. Some people have just lost their loved ones. They've just died, and he [Wovoka] said, "Don't feel bad. Because when you die you're going to meet them up in heaven."

And you know, when you read your Bible now, you believe what he told me.

Because Ms. Emm was a devout Christian, her view of the 1890 Ghost Dance might be regarded as somewhat slanted or even anachronistic. Yet, her characterization remains consistent with our knowledge of the Prophet's exposure to Christianity; his amity with local taivos; and the high degree of acculturation and corresponding relative absence of "deprivation" evidenced in Smith and Mason Valleys in those last decades of the twentieth century. Interestingly, Eileen Kane arrived at the same conclusion about Wovoka's religion during her fieldwork in Yerington in 1964 (cf. Appendix M):

> Wilson, however, according to locals, did not preach this [return of dead]: he promised that the dead were happy in heaven and that the living would one day join them there.

Kane (p. 196) went on to argue cogently:

> If the present attitude regarding burial customs and the treatment of the dead is any indication of the attitudes of the mid-nineteenth century toward the same, there would be real fear attached to the return of the dead: a present Paiute burial custom involves a ritual beseeching the dead NOT to come back.[26]

New sources also address another "Plains bias," the alleged militancy of the original message of the 1890 Ghost Dance religion. Corbett Mack, who was born in Smith Valley in 1892, recalled seeing as a four- or five-year-old "Ghost Dance" ceremonies with seemingly hostile intent (Hittman 1996a: 182-84); these ceremonies, however, were performed by visiting Bannocks. The *White Pine News* on 27 December 1890 mentions a "Bannock's Ghost Dance" in Mason Valley, while on 10 January 1891, the local paper, the *Lyon County Times*, also reported recent troubles involving these same Native Americans, though at Fort Hall. It nonetheless concluded that it was "improbable" that the natives would "think of fighting this winter." On this same date, the *White Pine News*, under the headline "Indian Troublemakers at McDermitt," noted that "the actions of the Indians are anything heretofore seen." Two weeks later, the following eerie comment in the *White Pine News* (24 January 1891) makes it abundantly clear that these activities were, indeed, "Ghost Dancing" in its classic, or at least Plains tableaux: "haunted [Indian] houses, unearthly sounds, the suggestion of ghosts in streets, murmurs," followed by the statement that Indians had just left "Death Mountain" to dance at Battle Mountain, home of Western Shoshones.[27] The *Walker Lake Bulletin* (Appendix D) reported on 31 January 1891 that "Hawthorne Paiutes," that is, Walker River Reservation Numus, were attempting to get up a similar ghost dance; in response, local citizens met for protection and called for arms. Rumors circulated that the Indians were "fortifying themselves on Pancake Mountain, between Eureka and Hamilton." Two weeks later (14 February 1891), when responding to this "local scare," the sheriff discovered only a netted enclosure constructed for jackrabbits! This newspaper admitted that "all stories of trouble with the Nevada Indians is simply nonsense." The research of historian Sally Zanjani (1988; cf. Chapter Four) suggests that we must read these newspaper reports as consistent with a new type of jingoistic journalism that was probably born with Wounded Knee (cf. Watson 1943; Jenson et al. 1991).

Edward Dyer did recall "one time when the Indians were in a rather ugly mood" (21 August 1959, *Fallon Eagle-Standard*):

> They were threatening to clean out all the whites in Mason Valley. Indians from surrounding areas gathered at the camp and for several days they chanted and danced and uttered ominous threats. The whites in the valley became quite alarmed and notice was sent to Virginia City concerning the serious situation. It was thought that the local Company I might need some assistance in dealing with an attack. The militia company and the Emmet Guards at Virginia City gave assurance that they were on the alert and would come at a moments notice should they be needed. A train was put at their disposal ready to roll. Chief Wasson and Captain Ben were the Indian leaders at the time and as I could speak the Piute language fluently I was delegated to go to the camp and talk with them in an attempt to persuade them to simmer down.

> Accompanied by several other whites I went to the camp where we held a PowWow. After a somewhat lengthy discussion during which it seemed we were getting nowhere someone suggested that Chief Wasson and Captain Ben be asked to visit the Armory and take a good look at the rifles and ammunition which were ready to use if we deemed it necessary. This the Indian leaders agreed to do. After sizing up the layout at the Armory they seemed duly impressed and decided that the white man's "Medicine" was considerably more potent than that which they possessed. They beat a hasty retreat to their camp where the rest of the tribe was informed of what they had seen. All was peaceful and quiet the next morning so evidently they had decided it was not a propitious time for an assult [sic] on the whites.

One would assume that if Wovoka, the Numu business associate and friend of Dyer, had played any role in this supposed incident, he would have been mentioned in this account.

Was there local militancy associated with Wovoka's teachings? Whatever else the 1890 Ghost Dance became when it diffused throughout the Plains and elsewhere, in Smith and Mason Valleys, Nevada, it seemed "little more" than the attempt by one extraordinary thirty-year-old to communicate, if not impose, the sum and the substance of at least three separate and distinct visions initially upon close kinsmen via shamanic-like displays of weather-control booha and invulnerability. Utilizing the traditional Round Dance, the charismatic Wovoka might well have even intended to fuse the Numu time-honored status of "weather doctor" with that of frontier Presbyterian "saddle bag preacher," exhorting kinsmen and other local Numus to hasten the end of the world by dancing and to inaugurate a millennium characterized by resurrection, perpetual youth and prosperity, and immortality in a prophesied next life, one in which even their taivo employers were to be included. In the meantime, they were to perform wage-labor and "get along" with them (cf. Kehoe 1989) in a regional economy, over which God granted him implicit control through weather-control powers: One biracial/bicultural/bilingual nation under God, with two presidents, a Numu and non-Numu![28]

Wovoka, the Man

To the portrait of Wovoka given in Chapter Five can be added observations by others, including his daughter and son-in-law, Alice Wilson Vidovich and her husband Andy, and a taped comment about the watermelon incident which Alex Miller previously discussed with this author (Appendix H):

> "Oh, he's always kind to everyone," Alice Wilson Vidovich told Margaret Wheat. "My Dad was kind! And if you come to his house, he would say, 'We don't have much, but if you want to eat what we've got, you're welcome!' That's what he always says... I've never seen that man mad. Or say a unkind word to anybody. He's always kind to everybody. And then people from all over would come and talk to him ask for advice."

Andy Vidovich (Baha'i Mss., 24) in the late 1960s recalled his father-in-law as follows:

> Wovoka was a big man, fine, superb looking man, straight as an arrow, powerfully built, and had acquired the physique of his father Taibo ... He was long, over six feet in height, and he weighed all the way past two hundred pounds. His name Wovoka signified "the man with an axe," and he was a mighty man with an axe (Appendix L).

In this interview, Andy Vidovich also related two new facts about the 1890 Ghost Dance prophet. First, at the Indian game of football, Wovoka "had no superior." Second, the Prophet had also been a well-known participant in the "Rock Contest," which resembled holiday flour-sack carrying contests among taivos:

> From the line where it sat originally, it was packed by Indians from different tribes in resemblance of strength to see who could pack the rock the farthest distance, and also representing the tribe he belongs to. And I been told many, many times by Indians of old, there's a feat done by Wovoka whenever asked if he would pack that rock and see how far he could pack it. I wish to tell you that Wovoka buried himself under his shirt, his underwear, when he picked up that great big rock and made a mark with his feet where the rock was, and then he packed that rock many, many steps. It was beyond the distance of many other men. And instead of leaving the rock down where he packed it, he made another mark with his feet, and then marched on back with the same rock and set it back where he first picked it up off the ground. And that feat was never equaled ever since. For it showed

that Wovoka was also a powerful man, beside being a spiritual man" (Baha'i Mss., 48-49).

"Oh yes!" Nellie Emm told Margaret Wheat (Tape 110, Transcription, p. 2, Box 13, Wheat Papers). "Everybody liked him because he was a good man. He was always laughing and joking." When asked why Wovoka appears so solemn in photos, she demurred: "No. To me he was never too serious about anything. He always laugh and make jokes about everything. He lived there in Yerington and to me, when I seen him, and we did see him, we were around him, he was always laughing and joking. He was a real enjoyable man to be around, I think."

Laura Miller, who was the daughter of a Smith Valley pioneer, and source of an early photograph of Wovoka (Plate B), offers a slightly more amplified, though no more enlightening, version of Wovoka's dispute with her mother, Mrs. Dickinson, over the price of watermelons (Tape 157, "Mrs. Alex Miller," Wheat Papers):

> I was nine when Jack came to our place—shortly after my brother died. And my father had always raised a big Indian garden. Garden was ready with watermelons and all. Jack, I can remember, Jack wanted to buy. He had Indians with him. He wanted to buy watermelons. He asked mother how much watermelons would be? She said $.50. And he attempted to Jew her down. And mother said, NO! She said it would be $.50. He said, "I'm going away." He said, "I'm gonna send a big rain and wash all your watermelons away!" "Alright, Jack," she said. "That will be alright!" And the rain never came.

Margaret Wheat asked Miller "Did whites like him?" "They took him to be a smarty," she replied. When asked about Ghost Dance ceremonies, however, Mrs. Miller suggests more chicanery on Wovoka's part: "I don't know anything about that. But I do know in Pine Grove, outside Indians come in. And they believe it. Some say, well, things he done in town: He told some Indians around here he had peacock feathers, and he told them they were eagle feathers."

The Middle Years

We can begin by noting Wovoka's enumeration in two Indian Census tracts during April and May of 1910 (Microfilm Roll #859, 1909-1925 and 1930, Federal Archives, San Bruno, California). The Prophet's name, age, place of birth, and occupation appear in the Smith Valley Precinct: "Jack Wilson. Age 52. b. California. Laborer (odd jobs)." His father and mother are noted to have been born in California. Mentioned as well in the Census tract were Wovoka's "wife Mary. Age 45. b. Nevada," whose parents were recorded as being born in Nevada. Mary Wilson is listed as a "washerwoman and farms." Completing the Wilson family entry, we read of "Ida, age 25 [Mary Wilson's sister?]: Washerwoman & farms; Alice, age 9; Annie, age 8; Billie, age 12; Joe, age 13;" and "granddaughter Annie, age 6." If Alice was his stepdaughter, who was the younger girl? A sister no one previously reported? And were the enumerated boys brothers? Adopted children? Nephews? The name "Pat Wilson (age 30)," which also appears there, no doubt, was Wovoka's younger or middle sibling.

One decade later, the 1920 Nevada Census (No. 1004 T. 625. Micro-film Roll #859, 1909-1925 and 1930. Federal Archives, San Bruno, California) would report the following information: "Jack Wilson age 63. No work. Married to Mattie Wilson, age 63." Both were recorded as living at the Yerington Indian Colony. And these returns also list "Pat Wilson, age 46. Married to Annie, age 41: kids Emma, age 19; Sadie, age 17; May, age 14; Woodrow, age 8; James, age 3"; as well as a "three-month-old baby."

The maladies that the Indian contract-physician George Magee reported Wovoka suffering from in 1920 had, in fact, plagued the Prophet for the better part of a year near the end of the century. In Volume 1 of the bound "Health and Sanitary Records," dated 1897-1910 (RG 75. #68427. Federal Archives, San Bruno, California), we read about his repeated treatment at the Walker River Reservation hospital primarily for:

Bronchitis—March 2 & 25, 1898;
Bronchitis—April 3 & May 6, 1898;
Malarial Fever—September 29, 1898 & October ? 1898;
Bronchitis—In September of 1898;
Bronchitis—July of 1898.

Both Wovoka's wife and mother are recorded as having received medical treatment for grippe in January 1898, enabling us to determine that Wovoka's mother was, indeed, alive *after* the Great Revelation. Consequently, Chapman's received translation of the Great Revelation from Captain Josephus, in which the Prophet sees his dead mother in Heaven, is either an error or suggests some hitherto unrecognized subtle theological point about the 1890 Ghost Dance.

The above source also reports the receipt of the following issued items by Wovoka: New shoes on 1 October 1901, which were repaired on 21 November 1901, then again on 2 January 1902. A second pair of shoes were received by Wovoka on 5 January 1902.

More data of this sort are contained in a separate "Issue Book" (Book 1, p. 88, RG 75. Carson Industrial School, 1898-1902. Box 1 of 3. Federal Archives, San Bruno, California). He reportedly received these issuances in the following years:

1897:
    Dec 1: mittens
    Dec 12: pants
    Dec 13: overalls
    Dec 14: shoes
1898:
    Jan 8: gloves
    Feb 6: hat
    Feb 13: shoes and pants
    Feb 23: uniform suit
    March 7: cassimere [sic] suit
    May 1: shoes

Jun 26: straw hat, coat, pants, jeans
July 2: shoes
July 23: suspenders
Sept 18: coat
Sept 25: boots
Nov 20: overalls, cap
Nov 21: boots
Nov 24: mittens
Dec 18: gloves
Dec 23: suit school
1899:
Jan 5: overthrows
Feb 28: shoes
Nov 21: suit, suspenders?
1900:
Jan 25: shoes

Is it possible that as a result of his advocacy of education, the famed Wovoka was fully clothed by the boarding school established in Carson City after the Great Revelation?

The question of Wovoka's performance of manual labor after the 1890 Ghost Dance was raised by a reviewer of the first edition.[29] It can now be asserted with confidence that contrary to what many Smith and Mason Valley informants also claimed, Wovoka did, indeed, "work" after the Great Revelation, if only intermittently. "I remember he had to go and get his own wood and he'd go to haul it in," Andy Vidovich told Margaret Wheat (Appendix L). "And work to buy food for his family. Pitch hay, believe me. He was supposed to be one of the top men, old as he was making four dollars—." His wife recalled differently, claiming that the Prophet made "four dollars a day for stackers, and dollar a day for the putting it on the wagon." In the context of describing their house on the David Wilson Ranch, Alice Wilson Vidovich added this remarkable new fact about Wovoka's labor for money during this time:

Dad worked in the mill... [M]y Dad would sack the flour, and the barley. Not barley. the grain. Then he used to count all the wheat that come in. He knew everybody in the valley, then he'd say: "So-and-so bring 14 sack or 15 sack of wheat." And he'd have it in his mind. And then he would tell Billy Wilson. Then he'd [Wilson] put it down on the paper. And then he [Wovoka] would say: "Well, so-and-so brought so much wheat," and then Billy would put it down. And just how many sacks of flour he [Wovoka?] had sacked that day. And he had it in his mind. He never had a day of school, but he knew how to count.[30]

SHAMANIC PRACTICE

New information regarding Wovoka's career as a **poohagooma** or shaman during these years (ca. 1910-1930) is also available. Pyramid Lake shaman, Joe Green, who originally told Park about the two clouds which were the source of Wovoka's supernatural power, also gave a specific example of Wovoka's healing ability (Park's Field Notebook III:48, 49. In possession of Catherine S. Fowler, p. 88):

> I saw Jack Wilson doctor a man who broke his ribs when a team ran away. He bled inside and Jack sucked the blood out. He knew how to suck out the blood. He spat the blood out and everybody could see it.

Rosie Plummer fills in more details about Wovoka's role as a shaman. She told Park, "Jack Wilson was a doctor who could bring back people who had died. He would 'die' himself for a while and when he came back he would tell the people how it looked where he had been." Plummer confided to Park that "not all doctors can do that," and then quoted Wovoka as saying "Just the good doctors who have more powers than others can do that." (Park's Field Notebook III:28. In possession of Fowler, p. 91).

In a similar vein, Billy Roberts commented favorably about Wovoka's healing abilities to Park (Park's Field Notebook IV:16, 17. In possession of Fowler, p. 125):

> Jack Wilson was a good shaman for curing gunshot wounds. He sucked out the bullets. Jack Wilson could bring rain or a heavy wind when ever he wanted to. There were few cases of any kind of sickness that he could not cure. He was the last good shaman among the Paiutes.

Missing from the first edition of this book was the following published report of a remarkable cure of a Washo by the 1890 Ghost Dance prophet. Tom Snooks (Washo) experienced bodily pains which other doctors failed to alleviate, so he then visited Wovoka, who apparently a good friend. Snooks's brother George later described the healing to Edgar Siskin (1983:209 n.22), who dates the cure to 1912-1913:

> Jack doctored him only a short while one night and removed a fishing tackle with copper wire, swivels, rings, spoon, leader, and hook. He removed it with his cupped hands without sucking. Shortly before he started doctoring, he placed in the ground in front of him an eagle feather about a foot long.

George Snooks continued:

> As soon as he put it in, it sank down about half way. After he took out the tackle he told Tom he became sick with it because a couple of years or so before in a fit of anger he had handled the tackle roughly, tearing up the wire and everything and throwing it away. Tom then remembered he had done this. Jack told him exactly what he had done.

Wovoka's cure of Nellie Emm's sister, described in Appendix K, is also given in the Margaret M. Wheat Papers (Tape 110, Transcription pp. 3-4.):

> To be frank about it, I had him for my sister. When my first husband shot my sister, I didn't want no Indian doctor, because I don't believe in that. My husband's name was Bill [Miller]. My husband shot her with a .44 pistol, right under her arm. And it came out right above the kidney. And she didn't have no doctor, just him. We had Dr. Reese

[sic]. But he didn't do anything for her because she didn't want him. You know Indians never did believe in white doctors. He, the doctor, said, "I'll take her down to my office, and wash that wound out." But she said, "No, I feel alright." And I prayed for my sister, real loud. I believe in prayers. And I prayed for my sister that night, that she would be saved, because there was no cause why she should be shot. She wasn't to blame for anything. I don't know what he did it for. He was just shooting around like that. And he shot her. Just right. And I prayed that night and she wasn't too sick. She overcame her sickness.

"And then he [Bill] went and got Jack Wilson the next day," Mrs. Emm remembered:

And he doctored her, maybe an hour, an hour and a half. He never used anything, just sing Indian doctor song, I guess. And he put the eagle feather near where the wound is, in her. You know how the feather is. You can see [the blood being sucked up through the quill?], the blood was coming there, that he was getting out. He said that the bullet had chipped part of her rib, in there. Not too much. That's what he told me. And then he said that she had double pneumonia, which I know that she had. At the same time. But she overcame that.

"[So] I feel that prayers is answered," Nellie Emm then concluded:

I don't know whether she was cured by prayers or by that doctor. Who knows? But he Indian-doctored her. And he told me she was going to be all right. And in two weeks she was up and around. A short time for anyone who was shot at that distance.

Finally, ethnomusicological aspects of Wovoka's shamanic practice were discussed by either Birdie Dave or Helen Williams:

Yes [Wovoka was a good doctor]. He was very gifted. He was a very smart doctor. He did a lot of miracle work. He go up in the air after a person dies. He sits there and waits for the spirit to rise up. He will sing and call the spirit back and then the dead person comes to life again. The song Jack Wilson sang was Natches' brother's song (Tape 103:1, Wheat Papers).

Stories of rivalries between shamans, of course, abound in the literature. Such friction and envy figures prominently in an account of a trip taken by Wovoka during his middle years to Oklahoma. The story was told by the Numu Harry Sampson to Park (Field Notebook I:93, 94. In possession of Fowler, p. 107):

Jack Wilson was an especially strong and good doctor. He had very strong power. Tommy Cypher who now lives near Yerington was Jack's interpreter. They made several trips to Oklahoma together. On one trip a medicine man in Oklahoma met them at the station. He was jealous of Jack's power. This man concealed in his hand a crescent shaped stone. When he shook hands with Jack Wilson the stone went up through Jack's arm and shoulder and down in his heart. When Jack left Oklahoma to come home the man told Jack that he would not live long, that Jack was already sick, and that he had stronger power than Jack. On the way home Jack was terribly sick. When he got to Yerington he called many people around him and squatted down and started to doctor himself. He sang his songs, then he told Tommy Cypher to hold out his hands and to drop what he put in them. Then Jack drew that stone from his arm and put it in Tommy's hand. It was very hot. They buried the stone. Jack Wilson's power was stronger than that of the other shaman's.

Another example of shamanic rivalry from this time was recalled by Nellie Emm to Margaret Wheat (Tape 110, Transcription pp. 4-5, Wheat Papers):

And to make everything short, she said another time, too, people came from the East, to visit when they were having big dance there, in the main place. And they come there, and they were supposed to be powerful men. Just like him, they thought they were powerful; smarter than him in their beliefs. They were three of them, it seems like, maybe four. But there was a group and one was supposed to be smarter [i.e. more booha] than him. They were dancing and having a good time. And they went away, the next day or so. They had visited him and there on that little knoll. And they took off East. And he said, "Do you know, we've been tricked?" He says, "I feel like there's something wrong here." So he starts to pray, and, whatever his power was, it told him that they [assembled crowd] were all supposed to die in a little short while. The man had left his own power to kill them. He says, "Whatever it is [the visiting shaman's medicine bundle], would lay in my hand." And a flint arrow-head landed in his hand. He said, "There it is," and went around and showed it to the people. "This is supposed to kill us all off, when he's gone a day or two. Maybe we all get sick and die." And so he said, "Now, who wants to chase him?" Some volunteers went, warriors, he called them. So they chased him East, and I don't think they got too far, maybe they were going over into Schurz, because that's a short cut right behind there, that trail.

Mrs. Emm continued:

And they were going to cut across there on horseback. And they caught up with him. "Wavoka [sic] want to see you." So they came on back. And this man know why he was called back. And he began shaking all over. The power reversed on him, and he started shaking. He says, "I didn't think you were going to find out right away." And they told him, "Yes. You did wrong. You're not going to get very far yourself, when you do that." So they started back. So he died on the road going back.[31]

SALE OF THAUMATURGES

That the Prophet during his middle years had become a personage of local, regional, as well as national renown, is well documented. Wovoka traveled to Oklahoma, the former Indian Territory, several times, as well as to Wyoming and Montana. More frequently, however, visitors (usually Native Americans) made their way to his various homes in Smith and Mason Valleys. Since the first edition of this book, we still have no accurate estimate of the number of gifts and amount of money given to the "Rain Maker"; certainly enough gifts arrived to warrant a separate display case in the Nevada State Museum, Carson City.

RELATIONSHIP TO INDIAN BUREAU

Wovoka during the 1910s once again came under Indian Bureau scrutiny, particularly by Walker River Reservation agents, whose indirect responsibility was the forced acculturation of Smith and Mason Valley Numus. This campaign focused on "dances" that the retired Prophet was in some way associated with; Wovoka's claim of land, both on and off the reservation, as well as the unfounded rumor that he was also then proselytizing peyote figured in their investigation as well. A series of letters discovered in the federal archives allows us to appreciate better the tensions between Wovoka and the Indian Bureau.

As pointed out in the first edition, native dances of any sort became a bone of contention between the government and the retired Prophet. On 19 December 1911, S. W. Pugh, the superintendent of the Walker River Agency, wrote to Wovoka, warning him against dancing:

> I have been told by some of the Indians here [Schurz] that you were talking about having a dance there soon. I think they have made a mistake, but I thought best to write you and tell you that there will be no dance there now and if you have made that arrangement you will please tell the Indians there will be no dance there. I wrote you before that all that country was now under my charge and any time you want to do anything of that kind you must first talk about it. (Appendix E.1)

Pugh was quite unpopular, having also opposed Christmas dancing at Schurz as "debilitating" (cf. RG 75, Walker River Indian Agency Correspondences, Box 316, fy 1909-1916, "Official and Unofficial Correspondences," Federal Archives, San Bruno, California).

Several months later, on 4 June 1912, Pugh wrote with alarm about an anticipated fall dance and an associated fair also supposedly to be sponsored by Wovoka. In a letter dated 20 August 1912 to "Jack Wilson and Jack Bovard, Indians, Yerington, Nevada," he warned of "instructions from Washington to allow no war dances [sic]" and demanded to know if "the plans [are] for Monday and who are the white people getting it up. [Because] I will not permit it unless I know all about it, and then I think we will arrange to have it down here" (Appendix E.).

This celebration, as we have seen, appears to have been the efforts of a taivo Labor Day Committee, which had approached Wovoka for Numu cooperation. The financial rewards reaped by these local businessmen is suggested by a 21 August 1912 letter from Pugh to "H. Pilkington of Yerington," which, in fact, mentions a previous "dance" (July 4?) which appears to have taken place despite his disapproval:

Indians inform me that you white people are planning to give them a big feed and prizes for races &c., and they expect to have a dance in connection with them &c., and it seems that you are one of the prime movers in the affair... From all accounts, the dance held last year at Mason by the Indians was the rottenest affair of the kind in the history of Indian dances. You have admitted the inability of the community to control the constant drunkenness and debauchery among the Indians there and yet you will encourage such gathering among them. You may be working for the financial interest of your town but it is my duty to protect these Indians, so I thought it advisable to notify you that I will not permit those Indians to participate in the proposed games there. I wish your town and community unlimited prosperity but I am informing the Indians that they can not participate in those games. We will have them later down here. (Appendix E.1)

One day later, Superintendent Pugh sternly reminded Wovoka and Jack Bovard, a Yerington Indian Colony Numu whose exact tie to the Prophet is unknown, not to attend the dance:

I guess you got my letter that I wrote to you a few days ago. I find that the intention is to have a dance there so I wirite [sic] again to tell you that there will NOT BE ANY DANCE THERE AND I EXPECT YOU AND JACK BOVARD TO [word? word? word?] they do not let them try. If they do there will be some of the leaders arrested. I expect to be there myself. I have promised the Indians a dance and good time here this fall but have told you before that there will none there because they get too much whiskey. I have my instructions from Washington and intend to carry them out. You can tell these Indians not to dance. (Appendix E.1)

Pugh's concern about intemperance was not unfounded: Wovoka during this time was living in Mason, where opium addiction had joined alcohol in wrecking the lives of one entire birth cohort of Numu men and women (Hittman 1973a; 1996).

An important letter from Pugh to Wovoka, dated 28 August 1912, provides insights into the Prophet's rage against the Bureau, presumably for interfering with Numu culture as well as for failing to satisfy ownership claims he had made for land on and off the Walker River Reservation (Chapter 6):

Beg to advise that I received a telegram from Washington this morning disapproving of your dance on Labor Day. So you will see that they do [sic] not have it. The rest of the program is alright.

I understand *that you told the Indians last Sunday that the Indians were the same as in jail* and that you would do as you please up there. I wrote you before that you Indians had been placed under the charge of this Agency, and you know that the Indians there are drinking and using opium and doing things that are wrong and I am trying to help you stop such things but if you want to work against me I will have to take the matter up with you. I expect you to work with me. *You wanted land here and I thought it would be a good thing* as we could [sic] the work together, and help each other, *I have been holding land for you and wrote you long time ago to come over, but if you do not come pretty soon I will give it to some one else.*

You know yourself that last year your people got into lots of trouble at a dance at Mason. So I don't want any more such things there. We can have them here and have no trouble. (Emphasis added. Appendix E.1)

Government officials' distrust of Wovoka was also due to his alleged involvement in the proselytization of peyote. This hallucinogen, as already shown (Letter 38, Appendix E) did not take firm root in Smith and Mason Valleys until the return of the Washo Ben Lancaster in the middle 1930s, after Wovoka's death. The Prophet was apparently suspected of facilitating the earlier efforts of the Lakota Sam Roan Bear ("Leo Okio") to introduce peyote into the region (Stewart 1987). The following letter, accessed 11 December 1916, from Assistant Indian Commissioner Merritt to J. D. Oliver, Superintendent of Stewart Institute, reveals the extent of the government's suspicions about Wovoka in this matter:

There is inclosed herewith a copy of a letter from Special Agent Asbury relative to the proposed visit of Jack Wilson, The Messiah, to your reservation and the possibility of his introducing among your Indians the use of an article known as peyote, and which the Office is making every effort to suppress.

You should give careful consideration to this matter and be on the look-out for Wilson, and if he visits your reservation observe his actions and endeavor to offset his influence if he attempts to get the Indians to use peyote. (Appendix E.1)

Andy Vidovich mentions his father-in-law's opposition to peyote (Appendix L), while Kane (p. 38) reported what I also heard, namely that "both Tom Mitchell and Jack Wilson lost theirs in later life, and became senile or insane as a result of this [peyote]."

Wovoka's Prophecies

What new information is available about the miracles and additional prophecies attributed to the 1890 Ghost Dance prophet? A number of additional examples of Wovoka's weather-control powers have surfaced. An unidentified informant told Park (Field Notebook III:9. In possession of Fowler, p. 95) that "Jack Wilson could make it rain or snow." This power was also possessed by another Numu, Arthur Patten from Bishop, who, Park learned, "was... like Jack Wilson... [also] a good doctor" (ibid.). Although Tim Hooper of Tonapah considered Wovoka "a lot of wind" and a "funny man," he readily admitted that the Prophet "can make it rain whenever he want. Snow too. He can make the wind blow too. Everybody know that" (Box 4:29-30, Wheat Papers). Hopper also described to Margaret Wheat two instances of Wovoka using his powers for revenge:

One time he want to buy some hay from a man. That man not sell him any. That nite that man make that whole stack blow away—every bit of it. All Indian know that. Paiute and Shoshone too...

One time they put him in jail and it start to snow and it get deep. One man, maybe Italian, he go there and tell them to let him loose. Two-three hours later the snow stopped. (Box 4:29-30, Wheat Papers).

Nellie Emm explicitly connected the Prophet's weather-control powers to the famous solar eclipse on New Year's afternoon of 1889:

And about the eclipse: He told them [of it] way before time. And he told everybody to get together over there [at a knoll] and we're going to get ready. And get food and blankets and wood, especially. He said, "Pile lots of wood. It'll be windy, and when the sun don't come up in the morning, we'll be ready." She [her mother] said the sun came up just real red. Maybe about nine o'clock it started to fade, and by noontime it got pitch dark. Until evening, almost sundown, it started to lighten up again... My mother never did say if it was summer or fall or winter or spring, or what" (Tape 110, Transcription p. 6, Box 13, Wheat Papers).

"[And] He just prayed," Mrs. Emm further related what her mother told her:

He talked in Paiute. He says, "Fatha." And that big snow fell on his hands. My mother called it that... And in that book [Bailey], which they have in the library over at Yerington, it was icebergs that were rolling down the river. But it really wasn't. Which it wasn't. Un un! [Because] To me he was a gifted regular Messiah (ibid., p.1).

The sole new reference to Wovoka's power of invulnerability is from Rosie Plummer of the Walker River Reservation:

One time Jack told his brother Pat to take a shot at him before witnesses. It had no other effect then [except] to make marks on his red shirt. He kept that shirt for special occasions. Warrior chiefs got power from bears. People could shoot at them but could not kill them. Jack Wilson was this way. (Park's Field Notebook III: 28. In possession of Fowler, p. 91)

Wovoka's visions and prophecies are mentioned by a few new sources. His visions of heaven while in a trance-like state were noted by Nellie Emm (Tape 110, Transcription p. 2, Wheat Papers):

He [Wovoka] knew a lot of things even if he never read the Bible. He knew a lot of things, like of what was coming. And he even said he'd seen the heavens. He said down here it stinks. And nothing is good. But up there, you walk through the streets. He said you can't describe it. Flowers that's just purty [sic]. So good. He said down here we have a stinky place. Yeh! When he went to sleep, he was gone for about half a day. And then he'd tell the Indians, "When it's time for me to wake up, you sing songs, a certain kind of song, and that will revive me again." So they did sing those songs and when he came back from

Heaven he told them about this. About this beautiful place he'd been to.

In contrast to the specificity of Wodziwob's prophecy of the train and the apparent disillusionment that followed (cf. DuBois 1939; Hittman 1973b), Wovoka delivered no particular millenarian "prophecies that failed" (cf. Festinger et al. 1956). This is not to say that his prophecies always satisfied the expectations of other Numus. For example, Helen Williams tells of her mother and grandmother's disappointment that Wovoka did not raise the dead during a ghost dance at Lovelock. The Prophet had apparently promised that "all the dead people would come down and dance with them." That ceremony apparently began with Wovoka building a "big, round corral."

> And it had one opening—Well, my grandmother told me this. And that she said they sat all around the edge, while the one man was singing. I presume it was Jack Wilson, singing at the head of the opening. He was singing this song, [32] and all the other Indians sang with him while he was singing this song. And the song is,
>
> "Ghost come back, you know, through the mugua." (Means your spirit comes back down through that trail and back down here through this opening.)
>
> "And come down here and see us."
>
> See, that's what he wanted to do, was to bring the spirits from the dead, so they can come and talk with people; I mean, their own relatives.
>
> So, my grandmother at the time was sitting in one of the— well, I don't know where she was sitting, but around in the cage, uh, the big corral built with the one opening here. So, she sat somewhere, and she wondered:
>
> "What am I going to say to my mother while the song is going on?"
>
> She just thought and she thought, you know, what she would say when they start to come to that gate. 'Cause everybody said, well, he was going to bring them back. They believed him! So, she sat and wondered, "What am I going to say? What shall I say to them? What do I do?" And, so, while she was sitting there, I think she told us this before, that her nose, there was a thump to her nose, like this—she called it in Indian. I forget what she said. A hollow sound to the nose, that tells you, you're not going to see anything like that. Nothing's gonna come. And that was true. She sat there, and said her nose told her that nobody was coming. Nobody [no matter] how long they sang; no matter how many days and nights they sat there and sang, she knew it meant nothing like this would ever happen. Nothing would come of it.
>
> So, I guess they went to their own homes after they sang this one. This took place right here in Lovelock! [33] (Tape 90, Transcription in Box 13:12, 26 February 1969, Wheat Papers).

According to Tim McCoy, the last words spoken to him by the aged 1890 Ghost Dance prophet in 1924 (op. cit.) were that he (Wovoka) would never die. Nellie Emm disclosed the great shock her mother experienced upon learning of Wovoka's death (Appendix K). I was told by other informants of their suspicion or surprise (or their parents' surprise) at that news.

Final Considerations

One can only hope that in the anticipated second century of Ghost Dance research, Native American scholars, and particularly Numus, will develop alternative understandings of the life, times, and religion of Wovoka (cf. Thornton 1986; Vizenor 1990; Glancy 1993). Future ethnographic interviews with the Prophet's descendants appear unlikely.[34] Additional letters may yet be revealed which were dictated by Wovoka and sent to the parents of Plains natives educated in boarding schools.[35] The following historical avenues of research might also provide new clues about the founder of the 1890 Ghost Dance.

Daniel Dorchester was a Methodist minister and Superintendent of Indian Education. According to Moses (1987:146 n.23), Dorchester "had been present for a few days at Walker River reservation in June, 1890, at the very time that Acting [Indian] Commissioner Robert V. Belt sent out circulars to agents asking them for information about the Ghost Dance, [and] had been assigned by the Indian Commissioner Morgan to investigate the Ghost Dance in spring of 1891. A number of visiting delegations of plains Indian were then present at Walker River." Since Dorchester reported his findings in the Annual Reports to the Commissioner of Indian Affairs for those years, any notes, diaries, or other personal papers of his might reveal additional information about Wovoka.

The same can be said for the papers of Lt. Hugh Lenox Scott. He was the young calvary officer who, in February and March of 1891, was among the very first government officials to identify correctly the 1890 Ghost Dance prophet. He wrote, "That this dance is intended as a worship of the white man's God there can be no doubt in the mind of any intelligent person who hears what they have to say on the subject" (in Moses 1979:306). Since Scott alluded to his residence either at or close to the Walker River Reservation (Moses 1979:305), one can only hope he left behind materials containing pertinent new information.

"Wovoka, however, never said he was the messiah, claiming only to be a prophet of God," wrote John Mayhugh, the former Western Shoshone Reservation agent and allotment officer of the Nevada tribes. Mayhugh, in this important letter to the Indian Commissioner, dated 24 November 1890, identified Wovoka as the Prophet, according to Moses (1979: 302; Special Case 188. Reel 1, frames 25, 33, 653. Federal Archives, San Bruno, California), and even requested that he be allowed to visit the nation's capital and meet with Indian Commissioner Morgan. Mayhugh went on in this letter to record the following fascinating observation about Wovoka's beliefs:

He [Wovoka] tells them he has been to heaven and that the Messiah is coming to earth again and will put the Indians in possession of the country—that he has seen in heaven a heap of Indians some of which are dressed in white man's clothes—he counsels the Indians not to disturb the White Folks saying that the blanket—or Rabbit skin that was put over the moon by the Indians long ago will soon fall off and then the moon which is now on fire will destroy the whites.

Mayhugh's skill as an observer suggests that his other papers might shed valuable light on Wovoka.

By the same token, the notes, diaries, or other personal papers belonging to Lt. Nat Phister, Franklin Campbell, and, of course, Arthur Chapman, could possibly help solve very many Ghost Dance puzzles. Like Chapman, Phister (1891:105) conducted interviews about Wovoka with Numu followers in Mason Valley:

> The writer, having recently been placed in a position which has offered singular facilities for an investigation of this matter, has gone very fully into the details of it; *has questioned many of the Nevada Indians on the subject,* and is now able to give a very correct account of the tenets of the faith. (Emphasis added.)

Campbell, who became resident-farmer at Nespelem Mills on the Colville Reservation (Washington state) after serving for a decade (1862-1872) as agent-farmer at the Walker River Reservation, penned a vital account of the earlier 1870 Ghost Dance which originated there (Mooney 1896:702-703). In September of 1891, he contributed to Indian Commissioner Morgan's final report some information about the Walker River Reservation origins of the later Ghost Dance movement (Moses 1985:308-309). Also, any notebooks or diaries belonging to Chapman would be interesting, particularly if they contain the exact words used by Captains James Josephus and Ben Ab-he-gan when describing Wovoka's religion.

A final possible source of new information on Wovoka would be, of course, additional notes made by James Mooney. "I expect that those notes he took probably are still extant," Edward Dyer Jr., or his brother, Chandler, commented at the end of his father's tape for Wheat, and speculates:

> Quite a number of things Dad mentions I haven't found in Mooney's book. Especially some of the Indian stories and myths and legends and so on. I wonder if he'd written them in other publications, or were they... Well, they probably are in his notes, and I should wonder what the Smithsonian, or Mooney's heirs would have those notes? They might be published elsewhere, but it struck me in reading Mooney's book that there was a chance for some research there—to get authentic dope on Indian stories.

One can only wonder what other hidden treasures about Wovoka and the 1890 Ghost Dance might yet remain in Mooney's papers![36]

1. Corrections to the first edition: Tibo'o should be **taivo** throughout the book. It was incorrect to state that Wovoka was orphaned. Also the statement that his mother, if not father, had no local kin ties ought to be amended, insofar as it now appears that she had family on the Walker River Reservation, at least after her youngest daughter's birth. In Chapter Three, it was foolish to write that cedar, in contrast to the pinion-pine, was not sacred, an egregious error and embarrassing misunderstanding of Numu religion (cf. "In this performance a cedar pole about two feet high was planted in the center of the circle. Two feathers, one a tail-feather painted red, the other a soft white feather taken from under the tail of an eagle, were suspended by a string from the top of the pole," Park 1938:135 on Round Dances; also cf. Miller 1983). Similarly, the scuffed trousers worn by the young prophet need not evidence early wage-labor. Wovoka could have received them second hand, or easily scuffed them at play.

In Chapter Four, the name **Natseekweedee** erroneously appears as "Natsiwidi," while the "Inexhaustible Cruse" is misspelled as "Inexhaustible Cruise." On page 90, items 15 and 16 both document a single arrival of Idaho Indians to Ghost Dance ceremonies in Smith and Mason Valleys. It doesn't make sense in this chapter to characterize the apocalypse associated with 1870 Ghost Dance prophet Wodziwob as a promised *reversion* to a life they had never known! The figure from Landsman in Endnote 7 is from 1979, and Endnote 13 is unclear. A better way to state it would be to say that starvation and epidemics created a crisis of such proportions that Walker River Reservation Numus might then have been willing to rational-ize or overturn their "traditional fear of the dead" in order to accept Wodziwob's prophesied resurrection of the *recent* dead. "Tavibo" should appear as "Taivo" in Appendix I.

2. Gunard Solberg informs me that the requisite forms he filled out with the United States Army (Order for Copies of Veterans Records) for information about Arthur I. Chapman, Indian Scout, led to naught.

3. According to Moses (1987:146 n.23), Mooney during his subsequent Walker River Reservation visit also met with the Democrat Gregory, who had been replaced the previous summer as its farmer-in-charge by Nelson Hammond, Republican, during a change in the national administration.

4. A minor quibble with this historian's otherwise highly commendable research: E. A. Dyer is mistakenly given as F. E. Dyer by Moses (1987:139), who also records Mooney as travel-ling twenty miles northwest from the Walker River Reservation by train to interview the 1890 Ghost Dance prophet, then twelve miles again southeast, which of course would very nearly return the ethnologist to where he started.

5. Yet Omer Stewart (1980:179) would take Mooney to task for two "mistaken and unfortu-nate" beliefs: (1) Mooney's assumption of the "universality of messianic movements"; and (2) his insistence upon the generally militant characteristic of all revitalization move-ments. Stewart in particular disagrees with Mooney's "implied belief that violence is a natural, almost universal consequence of crisis cults and that the Sioux Ghost Dancers should be held responsible for the war against the Sioux and the massacre at Wounded Knee" (Stewart 1980:81).

6. Wovoka, according to Mooney (Appendix B), spoke "only a little English," and C. C. Warner on 2 October 1891 (Letter 11, Appendix E) would characterize the Prophet as follows: "He speaks English well, but is not educated." J. W. Wilson in 1938, the oldest of the three Wilson brothers, recalled for Grace Dangberg (Letter 45, Appendix E) that although Wovoka trav-elled with another Numa to Indian Territory, he "understood English quite well," while *Lyon County Times* owner Walter Cox (Appendix H) told me in 1988: "He spoke very good English, you know. Don't talk 'hogadai,' 'I'm hungry.' Or 'Pahmu,' 'Give me a smoke!'"

7. A young anthropology graduate student from the University of Pittsburgh, Eileen Kane, noted in 1964, "The only problem which I encountered in this line was the public reaction among Indians to Paul Bailey's book, *Wovoka: The Indian Messiah*. There were gross distortions and betrayals of trust in this misinformed book: the attitude which I assumed with reluctant informants was that I was attempting to get the true story, to redeem Wovoka" (Kane 1964:61).

8. Barring an error in translation, Wovoka's response to Chapman, when directly questioned about this ("Did you tell them that you were bullet-proof, and to prove it...") remains one of the lasting enigmas about the 1890 Ghost Dance prophet: "That was a joke" (Appendix A).

9. One interesting sidelight to this discussion is found in a comment made by Fallon Numu Wuzzie George (Tape Transcription p.2, Box 4:31, Wheat Papers):

> When my boys go to war he (JG [husband?]) took all boys over there (Job's Peak), talk to mountain. Say, "You gonna help me boy." So bullet can't hurt my boy. That night he come back he dream. I guess that mountain told him to put white paint on face, on top of head, all over. In the morning all of 'em do that. Do that five days every morning. They say when bullet come, gonna miss you everytime. If he (bullet) come fast, gonna go over head. If come slow, gonna drop in front. White paint best, red one too. Red is as good. Put red on when chapped [face], mix with grease. Chap go away. Not white. Use red for baby powder (for baby's bottom).

Kane (1964) also reports that "Horseman, Winnemucca, and Jack Wilson, all had such [bulletproof] shirts, and the first two were wearing them in the battle of Fort Churchill, in the early 1860s."

10. See Chapter Five on this gold mine "hoax."

11. On the other hand, the Yerington Elder, Nellie Emm, who was also my informant, related a story to Wheat (Tape 116, Wheat Papers) which, unfortunately, further clouds this question:

> Jack Wilson found gold here [Pine Grove] and sold the site to the Wilson Brothers for $35.00 and one pony. He took the horse. He took off on the horse and never wait for his money. They didn't try to cheat him out of the money. They had the horse and the money to pay him. They said "Here's your horse." Well, he didn't wait for the money, he just took off. They may have given it to him later, but that's how they got that mine.

12. Recall that Chapman was told Wovoka never left "the valley," while Mooney heard the same. Dyer, on the other hand, wrote that "as a young man," the Prophet "did considerable wandering about this state and neighboring California." His assumption, however, is inferred from the fact that Walker River area Numus frequently performed this type of cash-work (cf. Appendices A, B, C).

Johnson Sides worked as a government interpreter and was Wovoka's bitter rival. Indeed, Wovoka appeared to have been more distressed by rumors of this fellow Numu's hatred of him (and Captain Sam, as well) than concerned about the U.S. military.

13. Note that the alleged Numu creation story narrated in Bailey (1957:28-31) is, in fact, nothing more than veiled Mormon racism, that is, the denigration of "dark" skin as punishment Native Americans received for allegedly killing the Second Coming of Christ in

America. Kroeber's (1948:368) eclipsed idea of "stimulus diffusion"—a "situation in culture history that is interesting because diffusion and invention enter into it equally"—ought not to be excluded as a possible explanation for similarities between Mormon and 1890 Ghost Dance apocalyptism.

14. Dyer, not without significance, regarded Bailey's book as "probably one of the best portrayals of an indigene of good will."

15. There is a generally insulting and degrading tone throughout the biography: "In his heart Wovoka senses shame for the quackery and trickery he had used to gain standing" (Bailey 1957:71); the Prophet was "inclined toward the lazy way of life" (36). Alice Wilson Vidovich must also have been offended by its many errors: The claims that her father was an only son (23); Wovoka had been orphaned early in life (25); he changed his wife's name to his taivo benefactor's wife's name, which happened to be Abigail Wilson (67); his own biological father was not a medicine man, because this profession was "too dangerous," but rather a prophet, "since he already was the son of one" (60); she, Alice Wilson Vidovich, was the only daughter to survive to "full adulthood" (206). How Moses (1985:346), then, could write the following is perplexing: "Like Mooney's study, Bailey's book is sympathetic to Wovoka but intimates that the Prophet trifled with fate and reaped the whirlwind." By the same token, Utley found the biography to be "competent" (1963:164, fn.5). Ironic is Bailey's (1957:13-14) expression of gratitude in his Acknowledgments to "Alice Wilson Vidovich, daughter of Jack Wilson (Wovoka), of Schurz, Nevada, who was most kind to men, *even in the face of the unkind things many writers have said about her father*" (emphasis added).

16. Unpublished manuscript in the author's possession. Andy Vidovich incredulously also relates in it a meeting by Wovoka's father with the "Great Messiah" ("on the east side of the Great Walker Lake"), and one that resulted in a revelation that not only was pacific, but contained the Ten Commandments as well (pp. 5-6). A stroke and beginning senility must be factored into what were always the honey-coated, hyperbolic recollections about Wovoka by this kind, sweet, charming Death Valley Shoshone raconteur.

17. Loss of power is a commonly reported happenstance for Numu shamans (cf. Park 1934, 1938; Olafson 1979).

18. Edna Jones's mother's mother was said to have been the sibling of Wovoka's wife's maternal father (Box 4:29-30, Wheat Papers).

19. According to Wuzzie George (Tape Transcription p.2, Box 4:31, Wheat Papers), Mary Wasson McMasters and Sally Wasson McMasters were the Walker River Reservation Numu sisters who raised Alice Wilson. Captain Wasson was, according to Dyer, a "dance chief" (cf. Appendix C.2).

20. Another reported incident of Wovoka sending rain in anger was told by the Northern Cheyenne to Grinnell (1891:67). When General Miles and his troops ignored their advice and went to arrest Wovoka, "the Christ made it rain for seven days and seven nights, and the result was that all the soldiers were drowned, General Miles alone escaping alive to tell the tale of the disaster."

21. Marlin Thompson was kind enough to allow me to read these pages, which remain in the possession of Catherine S. Fowler, whom I also thank for permission to cite. Her second edition of Park's Fieldnotes will be yet another of her vital contributions to Great Basin studies, and is eagerly awaited by us all.

22. In the Baha'i Mss., Andy Vidovich states that shortly after his marriage, Wovoka raised up from the dead the little boy of another Numu during a three-day trance (pp. 9-10).

23. Ake Hulktrantz (1993) correctly criticized this author for reporting that Wovoka's shamanic career was unique insofar as he used an eagle feather, that is, he did not remove intruded objects by sucking (cf. Chapter Six, "Shamanic Practice"; Chapter Seven; Appendix K). Published sources and informants provide contradictory accounts of Wovoka as a shaman. Because his career began through extraordinary circumstances as a prophet, his unique social status led contemporaries to represent Wovoka's booha in different ways.

24. In other words, Harlyn Vidovich's plane wasn't shot down in combat as stated in Chapter Seven.

25. Compiled from newspaper clippings ("Phoenix Skyways," "Vidovich Ends Boot Training," "Two Arizona Airmen Score against Japanese in China," "Indian Captain Missing in China," "Captain Vidovich, Sacaton Air Corps Officer Missing on Routine Flight in China," "Vidovich Is Found in his Fallen Ship"), as well as the funeral and special memorial service programs: "Vidovich Funeral Held in Sparks," "Memorial Services," and "Captain Harlyn Vidovich Meets Death in China: Memorial Service" (Box 4:31, Wheat Papers).

26. On this theme of "death and resurrection" in Numa mythology, cf. Powell (1971: 91-92), Lowie (1924a:229-31), Steward (1936:420-21; 1943a:229-31; 1943b:287-90), and Smith (1939:167).

27. Phil Earle was kind enough to direct me to these and other early newspaper items in the Nevada Historical Society.

28. By describing my characterization of Wovoka as the very "cosmic pillar" of Round Dance qua Ghost Dance ceremonies as "nonsense," Hulktrantz (1993:529) trashes a century of fruitful scholarship inspired by the German sociologist Max Weber's idea of rapid sociocultural change through charismatic leadership. Judith Vander (1997) has convincingly shown this Round Dance/weather-control aspect of **Naraya** or Ghost Dance songs for related Wind River Reservation Shoshones, demonstrating their remarkable persistence to the present.

Finally, Marxists should note that this pacifistic, apocalyptic revolutionary told the Army scout Arthur Chapman that taivos should pay him for rain "according to their means"!

29. Hulktrantz (1993:529).

30. Letter 45: "J.W. Wilson to Dangberg," Appendix E.

31. Needless to say, it is likely that accounts of this incident, and others like it, would have been inflated over time. Moses (1979:344) refers to "Johnson Sides, a Paiute who liked to call himself the 'peace maker' and who was for years Wovoka's enemy," who reported "that the Prophet refused a gift of forty silver dollars dumped at his feet by a Pawnee delegate who happened to be in the service of the Indian Bureau. The money," Moses wrote, "represented a collection taken by the tribe for the Prophet. Sides explained that Wovoka feared the money was tainted and that he might be killed through witchcraft." In the original citations (Appendix D) from these 1894 Reno and Elko, Nevada, newspapers, the amount was five dollars.

32. Birdie Dave sings a Ghost Dance song in spring of 1968 (Tape 77:1, Wheat Papers), then again on 8 May 1969 (Box 21, Wheat Papers). Mooney, of course, reproduced nine ghost dance songs (Appendix G), and I am indebted to Professor Alan Koeningsburg for the article by Smart (1980) about this collection cited at the conclusion of this chapter. Herzog (1935) wrote an ethnomusicological analysis of other Ghost Dance songs, and now, Judith Vander (1997) has written a masterful study of Wind River Shoshones' Naraya or Ghost Dance songs.

33. Robert Lowie (1909:226) reported that the soul at death becomes fog or cloud, and that half-way up to Creator Wolf's house, they are met by a "spirit descending on horseback, who then escorts them to their proper place. The **mu'gua** then becomes a **dzo'ap**, ghost." And Vander (1997) also reminds us that since ghosts in the Basin were believed to become wet clouds which bring moisture, mourners would throw dry dirt at "wet ghosts" to frighten them away. Ghost dancing, she then interestingly observes, could be seen as the attempt by Numus and other Basin peoples to bring back "wet ghosts" and end that terrible Western regional drought of the late 1880s.

34. In 1964, Eileen Kane (p. 33) had already experienced this problem: "Since many of his descendants are still present in the Mason Valley area, the potential for obtaining first-hand information concerning him was great: several, however, have made vows never to discuss Wilson, and the attendant difficulties in this type of situation have left my material with conflicting attitude studies, and some patently false information."

35. In Cody, Wyoming, for example, I was told at a bar in town by a (quite inebriated) Native American from Lander that these very letters could be found in the home of a certain individual in Etienne, Wyoming.

36. New insights into Mooney's fieldwork continue to appear. James R. Smart (1980:431) argues that the recordings of nine Ghost Dance songs Mooney collected were done by James and his brother, Charles Mooney. Smart contends that the weight of a gramophone would have made it difficult to bring one in the field and that thus "Mooney himself [probably] performed those chants in the [Emile] Berliner studio, and that the zincs were then given to [John Philip] Sousa and [F.W.V.] Gaisberg for transcribing after which they were mastered for publication." This set of zinc masters dated July and August 1894 in the Library of Congress collections bears the names of both James and Charles Mooney.

Part III

Part II

APPENDICES
APPENDIX A

The Chapman Interview

Report of the Secretary of War, 1891, Vol.1:191-194, reprinted in Logan 1980:284-288:

The supposed Messiah is a Pah Ute Indian named Quoitze Ow—commonly Jack Wilson, belonging to the Walker Lake Reservation in Nevada. An account of the doings of this Indian, beginning in 1887, is given in a report made in December, 1890, to the commanding general, Division of the Pacific, by Mr. A. I. Chapman, who was sent to investigate the matter, and is hereto attached, marked B. The pretensions of the Indian Jack Wilson were a continuation of those of a former Pah Ute prophet, and his association with the whites and religious instruction received by reservation Indians accounts for his teachings that the Indian ancestors would reappear, that he could cause rain to come, the destruction of the wicketed [sic] and opposers by water, etc.

Exhibit B

San Francisco, Cal.,
December 6, 1890

Gen. John Gibbon,
Commanding the Division of the Pacific,
San Francisco, Cal:

Sir: In accordance with your instructions of the 28th ultimo to proceed to Walker Lake Indian Reservation, Nev., and elsewhere in that vicinity, and gather certain and all information regarding the Indian who personated Christ at that place a year ago, I have the honor to report that I left this city at 7 o'clock p.m. on the day of receiving my instructions, and arrived at the Walker Lake Indian Reservation on the 30th following at 3 p.m. Here I found quite a number of Indians, including women and children, in groups here and there, sitting on the ground and playing cards. I made myself known to Mr. J.O. Gregory (Indian farmer), who was in charge of the agency, and inquired of him if he knew anything of an Indian in that part of the country by the name of John Johnson. His answer was that he did not, but there was a very old Indian living near the agency they called old Johnson, and another they called Squire Johnson. I then asked him if either of these Indians claimed to be a prophet or preached to the Indians at any time. He said they did not, but that there was an Indian in the country by the name of Jack Wilson, who claimed to be the new Messiah, and had been preaching for the last two or three years, and of late these ceremonies were becoming more frequent, and had a much larger attendance; that there were a great many strange Indians who attended these dances who he understood had come from a great way off; that these dances were held at intervals of about three months, first at one place and then at another; that this Indian, Jack Wilson, was mostly raised by a white man who lived in Mason Valley, 50 miles from the agency, and that he understood from the white people in that portion of the country that this new Messiah (Jack Wilson) had a good name for being an honest, hardworking Indian. Mr. Gregory remembers very distinctly the big dance which occurred near the agency, when the Cheyennes, Sioux, Bannocks and other strange Indians were present, that this meeting took place some time in last March. At this time the Indians were gathering around in considerable numbers and Mr. Gregory introduced the captain of the Indian police, Josephus, who he said could tell me more about the new Messiah (Jack Wilson) than he could:

Capt. Josephus, of the Indian police said: "I am ——— , a Piute Indian, was born at Carson Sink (sinking of the Carson River). I am now about 48 years old. I am captain of the police and also interpreter for the Government. I am well acquainted with Jack Wilson—this man who preaches; he is a Piute; his Indian name is Quoitze Ow; he was born here at this place of a poor family, and when quite a large boy he went to live and work for Dave Wilson, a white man, who lives in Mason Valley. When this Jack Wilson grew to be about 20 years old he got married and still lived with Mr. Dave Wilson (the white man) and worked on the farm. About three years ago Jack Wilson took his family and went into the mountains to cut wood for Mr. Dave Wilson. One day while at work he heard a great noise which appeared to be above him on the mountain. He laid down his ax and started to go in the direction of the noise, when he fell down dead; and that God came and took him to heaven and showed him everything there; that it was the most beautiful country you could imagine; that he saw both Indians and whites, who were all young; that God told him that when the people died here on this earth, if they were good, they come to heaven, and he made them young again and they never grew to be old afterwards; that the people up there were dancing, gambling, playing ball and having all kinds of sports; that the country was nice and level and green all the time; that there were no rocks or mountains there, but all kinds of game and fish; that God brought him back and laid him down where he had taken him from. He woke up and went to camp and went to bed. God came to him again that night and told him to tell all the people that they must not fight, there must be peace all over the world; that the people must not steal from one another, but be good to each other, for they were all brothers, and when he had finished this work God would come after him again. God came and took him to heaven again, and he saw all the Indians and white people who had died heretofore, that they were all young, and having a good time, dancing, etc.; that he saw his own mother; that God had given him great power and authority to do many things; that he could cause it to rain or snow at will, and many other things; that they would learn hereafter that God directed him on his return to say to his people that they must meet often and dance five nights in succession and then stop for three months."

Josephus (captain of the police) said: "At this time I did not believe in the new Messiah and thought I would try his power over the elements, as the country was very much in need of rain; that unless they got rain they would have no crops of any kinds, and it looked as though there was going to be great suffering amongst the people."

So Josephus concluded that he would visit the new Messiah and ask him to give them rain, or otherwise they would suffer. He took his horse and rode to the new Messiah's home, arriving there later in the evening, and explained to him the great importance of his mission. He said that Jack Wilson sat with his head bowed but never spoke a word during all this time, but he went off to bed and was up early in the morning. When he came in where Josephus was he said to him: "You can go home and on the morning of the third day you and all the people will have plenty of war [sic]." Josephus said that he went home and told not only his people but the white people too, and shortly afterwards it commenced to rain, and on the morning of the third day he got up at daylight to find Walker River out of its banks and all the lowlands overflown. "Now," said Josephus, "I am a strong believer in the unnatural powers of the new Christ."

Ben Ab-he-gan, of the Indian police, was present during all the time that Josephus was making this statement, and corroborated every word he spoke. I will state here that Mr. J.O. Gregory and Mr. Peas, employees of the agency, were both present during this interview with Josephus, and corroborated his statement in regard to the water. In fact, all the white people I talked with about the agency, and in Mason and Smith valleys, admitted that the rain did come, but they cannot convince the Indians that Jack Wilson had nothing [sic] to do with its coming. Some of the Indians of his own tribe and those of the adjoining tribes were inclined to look upon the new Messiah (Jack Wilson) as an imposter, and he sent them word to come and see him and hear him talk and he would convince them. The invitation has been the cause of many Indians visiting the Piutes and taking part in their dances. Among the tribes that have been represented there, so I was informed by Josephus and Ben Ab-he-gan (both of the police force at Walker Lake) are as follows: Cheyennes, Sioux, Arapahoes, Utes, Navahoes, Shoshones, Bannocks and a tribe to the south of them they called the Umapaws. I was told the Indians numbered about 1,600 at the big dance near Walker Lake, and were fed on pine nuts and fish principally during the meeting. Learning that the new Messiah was at his home at the head of Mason Valley, I took the train and came back on the road as far as Wabuska, where I took the stage for Mason, arriving there at 5 o'clock in the evening. I had not been in the place long before I learned through Ben, the Indian policeman, who had come with me from Walker Lake, that Jack Wilson had gone two days before to Desert Creek Valley, distant 60 miles, and across one range of mountains. I made arrangements for a team the next morning, and taking Indian Ben with me, started at 6 o'clock for Desert Creek Valley. After traveling 30 miles on the Desert Creek road we met some Indians on this road coming up from Bodie, Cal. They told us that they had camped at Wellington, on the west fork of the Walker River. We changed our course for Wellington, arriving there late in the evening. I sent for Jack Wilson to come down to Mr. Pierce's house, as the weather was not suitable for holding outdoor meetings, it raining and snowing alternately. He put in his appearance and I was introduced to him by Captain Ben, the Indian policeman. We shook hands, Jack Wilson remarking that he was glad to see me. I responded, saying that I surely was glad to meet one of such notoriety, and that I had heard a good deal of him through the newspapers, and would like to ask him a few questions, which I hoped he would answer freely.

Q. What is your name?

A. Jack Wilson.

Q. What is your Indian name?

A. Quoitze Ow.

Q. What tribe of Indians do you belong to?

A. Piutes.

Q. How old are you?

A. About 30 years old.

Q. Is your father living?

A. Yes.

Q. How many brothers have you?

A. Three; all younger than myself.

Q. Have you ever been away from your own country?

A. No.

Q. Are you a chief?

A. Yes: I am chief of all the Indians who sent representative to me.

Q. What do you mean by chief of all the Indians? Do you mean that you are head chief?

A. No; I mean that I am council chief.

Q. How many Indians are there in your tribe?

A. I do not know.

Q. When did you commence to preach to the Indians?

A. About three years ago.

Q. What do you preach to the Indians?

He then stated in substance about the same as Josephus, captain of the Indian police at Walker Lake had told me about going to heaven and seeing all the people who had died here on this earth, and what a nice place it was, the dancing and other sports, etc.; that God had visited him many times since and told him what to do; that he must send out word to all the Indians to come and hear him, and he would convince them that he was preaching the truth; that he must tell the Indians that they must work all the time and not lie down in idleness; that they must not fight the white people or one another; that we were all brothers and must remain in peace;

that God gave him the power to cause it to rain or snow at his will; that God told him or gave him the power to destroy this world and all the people in it and to have it made over again; and the people who had been good heretofore were to be made over again and all remain young; that God told him that they must have their dances more often, and dance five nights in succession and then stop. *** That their dancing would commence again next Saturday. Said he:

"This country was all dry early last spring; there was nothing growing, and the prospects for the future were very discouraging to both the Indians and the whites, and they came to me and asked for rain to make their crops grow. I caused a small cloud to appear in the heavens, which gave rain for all, and they were satisfied. I think that all white men should pay me for things of this kind, some two dollars, others five, ten, twenty-five, and fifty, according to their means. I told all the headmen who came to see me (meaning the representatives of other tribes) that when they went home to say to their people that they must keep the peace; that if they went to fighting that he would help the soldiers to make them stop. That the people (whites) of this country do not treat him and his people right; that they do not give them anything to eat unless they pay for it. If the whites would treat him well he would have it rain in the valley and snow on the mountains during the winter, so that the farmers would have good crops."

Captain Sam and Johnson Sides, two Piute Indians who did not believe in his doctrine, he said, are telling all over the country that the soldiers are coming to take him and put him in a big iron box, and take him out to sea on a big ship and sink him in the ocean; that he wanted them to stop talking to the people in this way and not be afraid but come and talk to him; that he hired out to white men to work all the time; that he liked to work.

Mr. Wilson, I want to ask you one or two more questions and that will be all.

Q.   Did you tell the Indians if they got into trouble with the whites that they must not be afraid, that you would protect them against being hurt.

A.   That was my dream; it has not come to pass yet.

Q.   Did you tell them that you were bullet-proof, and to prove it you spread a blanket on the ground and stood upon it, with nothing on you except a calico shirt, and had your brother shoot at you a distance of 10 feet, and the ball struck your breast and dropped to the blanket?

A.   That was a joke.

He said: "I heard that soldiers were coming after me. I do not care about that; I would like to see them. That is all I care to talk now. We are going to have a dance next Saturday."

In conclusion, I would say that I saw three of their dance grounds. They had been cleared of sagebrush and grass and made perfectly level, around the outer edge of which the willow sticks were still standing, over which they spread their tenting for shelter during these ceremonies. The cleared ground must have been from 200 to 300 feet in diameter, and only about four places left open to enter the grounds. The Piute Indians, men and women, dress like the white people, and equally as good as the average white man of that country. The men part their hair in the middle and have it cut square off even with the lower part of the ear. The women have their's banged and are exceedingly well dressed for Indian women.

The white people generally throughout the country spoke well of the Piutes as an industrious and hard-working people but preferred to work for the white people than for themselves. Only a few of the white men, Mr. Pierce, of Wellington, particularly, was suspicious of Wilson's doctrine, as it was giving him too much influence, and he feared trouble in the end; that he could see that the Indians were a little more exacting every day. Only recently did one of them, with his stock, move into a white man's field and would not go out when he was told to do so. When the white threatened to come down with his wagon and haul him out if he did not go out himself the Indian said: "You had better bring a big crowd if you attempt it." The Piutes are a very numerous and healthy tribe and are increasing very rapidly (so the whites tell me who have been living there for the last thirty or forty years.)

After gathering all the information I thought of interest I started on my return, arriving at Reno on the 4th instant, where I had a short interview with Johnson Sides, who appeared to be very much opposed to the doctrine preached by Jack Wilson; that he believed it all to be lies, and that it was only exciting the Indians and was liable to lead to trouble in the end.

In regard to the Cheyenne Indian, Porcupine, who gave an account of his visit to the Piute camp at Walker Lake, I will say that it is wonderfully correct, as far as I am able to learn; that on his visit he first met with the Piutes at Winnemucca, and then at Wadsworth, on the Central Pacific Railroad, where he fell in with Capt. Dave, of the Piutes, who took him and his comrades in a wagon and hauled them to Pyramid Lake Agency, where they remained several days when Capt. Dave's son took them in wagons and hauled them to Wabuska, where they took the cars for Walker Lake. This was told me by Capt. Ben, one of the Indian police at Walker Lake, and from other information I believe it to be true.

Very respectfully, your obedient servant,
A. I. Chapman

APPENDIX B

Mooney's Visit with Wovoka

Fourteenth Annual Report (Part 2) of the Bureau of American Ethnology to the Smithsonian Institution, 1892-1893, pp. 764-776:

When Tavibo, the prophet of Mason Valley, died, about 1870, he left a son named Wovoka, "The Cutter," about 14 years of age. The prophetic claims and teachings of the father, the reverence with which he was regarded by the people, and the mysterious ceremonies which were doubtless of frequent performance in the little tule wikiup at home must have made an early and deep impression on the mind of boy, who seems to have been by nature of a solitary and contemplative disposition, one of those born to see visions and hear still voices.

The physical environment was favorable to the development of such a character. His native valley, from which he has never wandered, is a narrow strip of level sage prairie some 30 miles in length, walled in by the giant sierras, their sides torn and gashed by volcanic convulsions and dark with gloomy forests of pine, their towering summits white with everlasting snows, and roofed over by a cloudless sky whose blue infinitude the mind instinctively seeks to penetrate to far-off worlds beyond. Away to the south the view is closed in by the sacred mountain of the Paiute, where their Father gave them the first fire and taught them their few simple arts before leaving for his home in the upper regions of the Sun-land. Like the valley of Rasselas, it seems set apart from the great world to be the home of a dreamer.

The greater portion of Nevada is an arid desert of rugged mountains and alkali plains, the little available land being confined to narrow mountain valleys and the borders of a few large lakes. These tracks are occupied by scattered ranchmen engaged in stock raising, and as the white population is sparse, Indian labor is largely utilized, the Paiute being very good workers. The causes which in other parts of the country have conspired to sweep the Indians from the path of the white man seem inoperative here, where the aboriginal proprietors are regarded rather as peons under the protection of the dominant race, and are allowed to set up their small camps of tule lodges in convenient out-of-the-way places, where they spend the autumn and winter in hunting, fishing, and gathering seeds and pinion nuts, working at fair wages on ranches through spring and summer. In this way young Wovoka became attached to the family of a ranchman in Mason valley, named David Wilson, who took an interest in him and bestowed on him the name of Jack Wilson, by which he is commonly known among the whites. From his association with this family he gained some knowledge of English, together with a confused idea of the white man's theology. On growing up he married and still continued to work for Mr. Wilson, earning a reputation for industry and reliability, but attracting no special notice until nearly 30 years of age, when he announced the revelation that has made him famous among the tribes of the west.

Following are the various forms of his name which I have noticed: Wo'voka, or Wu'voka, which I have provisionally rendered "Cutter," derived from a verb signifying "to cut;" Wevokar, Wopokahte, Kwohitsauq, Cowejo, Koit-tsow, Kvit-Tsow, Quoitze Ow, Jack Wilson, Jackson Wilson, Jack Winson, John Johnson. He has also been confounded with Bannock Jim, a Mormon Bannock of Fort Hall Reservation, Idaho, and with Johnson Sides, a Paiute living near Reno, Nevada, and bitterly opposed to Wovoka. His father's name, Tavibo, has been given also as Waughzeewaughber. It is not quite certain that the Paiute prophet of 1870 was the father of Wovoka. This is stated to have been the case by one of Captain Lee's informants and by Lieutenant Phister. Wovoka says that his father did not preach, but was a "dreamer" with supernatural powers. Certain it is that a similar doctrine was taught by an Indian living in the same valley in Wovoka's boyhood. Possibly the discrepancy might be explained by an unwillingness on the part of the messiah to share his spiritual honors.

In proportion as Wovoka and his doctrines have become subjects of widespread curiosity, so have they become subjects of ignorant misrepresentation and deliberate falsification. Different writers have made him a Paiute, a half-breed and a Mormon white man. Numberless stories have been told of the origin and character of his mission and the day predicted for its final accomplishment. The most mischievous and persistent of these stories has been that which represents him as preaching a bloody campaign against the whites, whereas his doctrine is one of peace, and he himself is a mild-tempered member of weak and unwarlike tribe. His own good name has been filched from him and he has been made to appear under a dozen different cognomens, including that of his bitterest enemy, Johnson Sides. He has been denounced as an imposter, ridiculed as a lunatic, and laughed at as a pretended Christ, while by the Indians he is revered as a messenger from the Other World, and among many of the remote tribes he is believed to be omniscient, to speak all languages, and to be invisible to a white man. We shall give his own story as told by himself, with such additional information as seems to come from authentic sources.

Notwithstanding all that had been said and written by newspaper correspondents about the messiah, not one of them had undertaken to find the man himself and to learn from his own lips what he really taught. It is almost equally certain that none of them had even seen a ghost dance at close quarter—certainly none of them understood its meaning. The messiah was regarded almost as a myth, something intangible, to be talked about but not to be seen.

After having spent seven months in the field, investigating the new religion among the prairie tribes, particularly the Arapaho, and after (ENCLOSED) having examined all the documents bearing on the subject in the files of the Indian Office and War Department, the author left Washington in November, 1891, to find and talk with the messiah and to gather additional material concerning the Ghost dance. Before starting, I had written to the agent in charge of the reservation to which he was attached for information in regard to the messiah (Jack Wilson) and the dance, and learned in reply, with some surprise, that the agent had never seen him. The surprise grew into wonder when I was further informed that there were "neither Ghost songs, dances, nor ceremonials" among the Paiute. This was discouraging, but not entirely convincing, and I set out once more for the west. After a few days with the Omaha and Winnebago in Nebraska, and a longer stay with the Sioux at Pine Ridge, where traces of the recent conflict were fresh on every hand, I crossed over the mountains and finally arrived at Walker Lake reservation in Nevada.

On inquiry I learned that the messiah lived, not on the reservation, but in Mason valley, about 40 miles to the northwest. His uncle, Charley Sheep, lived near the agency, however, so I sought him out and made his acquaintance. He spoke tolerable — or rather intolerable — English, so that we were able to get along together without an interpreter, a fact which brought us into closer sympathy, as an interpreter is generally at best only a necessary evil. As usual, he was very suspicious at first, and inquired minutely as to my purpose. I explained to him that I was sent out by the government to the various tribes to study their customs and learn their stories and songs; that I had obtained a good deal from the other tribes and now wanted to learn some songs and stories of the Paiute, in order to write them down so that the white people could read them. In a casual way I then offered to show him the pictures of some of my Indian friends across the mountains, and brought out the photos of several Arapaho and Cheyenne who I knew had recently come as delegates to the messiah. This convinced him that I was alright, and he became communicative. The result was that we spent about a week together in the wikiups (lodges of tule rushes), surrounded always by a crowd of interested Paiute, discussing the old stories and games, singing Paiute songs, and sampling the seed mush and roasted pinon nuts. On one of these occasions, at night, a medicine man was performing his incantations over a sick child on one side of the fire while we were talking on the other. When the ice was well thawed, I cautiously approached the subject of the ghost songs and dance, and, as confidence was now established, I found no difficulty in obtaining a number of the songs, with a description of the ceremonial. I then told Charley that, as I had taken part in the dance, I was anxious to see the messiah and get from him some medicine-paint to bring back to his friends among the eastern tribes. He readily agreed to go with me and use his efforts with his nephew to obtain what was wanted.

It is 20 miles northward by railroad from Walker River agency to Wabuska, and 12 miles more in a southwesterly direction from there to the Mason valley settlement. There we met a young white man named Dyer, who was well acquainted with Jack Wilson, and who also spoke the Paiute language, and learned from him that the messiah was about 12 miles farther up the valley, near a place called Pine Grove. Enlisting his services, with a team and driver, making four in all, we started up toward the mountain. It was New Year's day of 1892, and there was deep snow on the ground, a very unusual thing in this part of the country, and due in this instance, as Charley assured us, to the direct agency of Jack Wilson. It is hard to imagine anything more monotonously unattractive than a sage prairie under ordinary circumstances unless it be the same prairie when covered by a heavy fall of snow, under which the smaller clumps of sagebrush look like prairie-dog mounds, while the larger ones can hardly be distinguished at a short distance from wikiups. However, the mountains were bright in front of us, the sky was blue overhead, and the road was good under foot.

Soon after leaving the settlement we passed the dance ground with the brush shelters still standing. We met but few Indians on the way. After several miles we noticed a man at some distance from the road with a gun across his shoulder. Dyer looked a moment and then exclaimed, "I believe that's Jack now!" The Indian thought so, too, and pulling up our horses he shouted some words in the Paiute langauge. The man replied, and sure enough it was the messiah, hunting jack rabbits. At his uncle's call he soon came over.

As he approached I saw that he was a young man, a dark full-blood, compactly built, and taller than the Paiute generally, being nearly 6 feet in height. He was well dressed in white man's clothes, with the broad-brimmed white felt hat common in the west, secured on his head by means of a beaded ribbon under the chin. This, with a blanket or a robe of rabbit skins, is now the ordinary Paiute dress. He wore a good pair of boots. His hair was cut off square on a line below the base of the ears, after the manner of his tribe. His countenance was open and expressive of firmness and decision, but with no marked intellectuality. The features were broad and heavy, very different from the thin, clear-cut features of the prairie tribes.

As he came up he took my hand with a strong, hearty grasp, and inquired what was wanted. His uncle explained matters, adding that I was well acquainted with some of his Indian friends who had visited him a short time before, and was going back to the same people. After some deliberation he said that the whites had lied about him and he did not like to talk to them; some of the Indians had disobeyed his instructions and trouble had come of it, but as I was sent by Washington and was a friend of his friends, he would talk with me. He was hunting now, but if we would come to his camp that night he would tell about his mission.

With another hand-shake he left us, and we drove on to the nearest ranch, arriving about dark.

To be lost on a sage plain on a freezing night in January is not a pleasant experience. There was no road, and no house but the one we had left some miles behind, and it would be almost impossible to find our way back to that through the darkness. Excepting for a lantern there was no light but what came from the glare of the snow and a few stars in the frosty sky overhead. To add to our difficulty, the snow was cut in every direction by cattle trails, which seemed to be Indian trails, and kept us doubling and circling to no purpose, while in the uncertain gloom every large clump of sagebrush took on the appearance of a wikiup, only to disappoint us on a nearer approach. With it all, the night was bitterly cold and we were half frozen. After vainly following a dozen false trails and shouting repeatedly in hope of hearing an answering cry, we hit on the expedient of leaving the Indian with the wagon, he being the oldest man of the party, while the rest of us each took a different direction from the central point, following the cattle tracks in the snow and calling to each other at short intervals, in order that we might not become lost from one another. After going far enough to know that none of us had yet struck the right trail, the wagon was moved up a short distance and the same performance was repeated. At last a shout from our driver brought us all together. He declared that he had heard sounds in front, and after listening a few minutes in painful suspense we saw a shower of sparks go up into the darkness and knew that we had struck the camp. Going back to the wagon, we got in and drove straight across to the spot, where we found three or four little wikiups, in one of which we were told the messiah was awaiting our arrival.

On entering through the low doorway we found ourselves in a circular lodge made of bundles of tule rushes laid over a framework of poles, after the fashion of the thatched roofs of Europe and very similar to the grass lodges of the Wichita. The lodge was only about 10 feet in diameter and about 8 feet in height, with sloping sides, and was almost entirely open above, like a cone with the top cut off, as in this part of the country rain or snow is of rare occurrence. As already remarked the deep snow at the time was something unusual. In the center, built directly on the ground, was a blazing fire of sagebrush, upon which fresh stalks were thrown from time to time, sending up a shower of sparks into the open air. It was by this means that we had been guided to the camp. Sitting or lying around the fire were a half a dozen Paiute, including the Messiah and his family, consisting of his young wife, a boy about 4 years of age, of whom he seemed very fond, and an infant. It was plain that he was a kind husband and father, which is keeping wiu his reputation among the whites for industry and reliability. The only articles in the nature of furniture were a few grass woven bowls and baskets of various sizes and patterns. There were no Indian beds or seats of the kind found in every prairie tipi, no rawhide boxes, no toilet pouches, not even a hole dug in the ground for the fire. Although all wore white man's dress, there were not pots, pans or other articles of civilized manufacture, now used by even the most primitive prairie tribe, for, strangely, although these Paiute are practically farm laborers and tenants of the whites all around them, and earn good wages, they seem to covet nothing of the white man's, but spend their money for dress, small trinkets, and ammunition for hunting, and continue to subsist on seeds, pinon nuts, and small game, lying down at night on the dusty ground in their cramped wikiups, destitute of even the most ordinary conveniences in use among other tribes. It is a curious instance of a people accepting the inevitable while yet resisting innovation.

Wovoka received us cordially and then inquired more particularly as to my purpose in seeking an interview. His uncle entered into a detailed explanation, which stretched out to a preposterous length, owing to a peculiar conversational method of the Paiute. Each statement by the older man is repeated at its close, word for word and sentence by sentence, by the other, with the same monotonous inflection. This done, the first speaker signified by a grunt of approval that it had been correctly repeated, and then proceeded with the next statement, which was duly repeated in like manner. The first time I had heard two old men conversing together in this fashion on the reservation I had supposed they were reciting some sort of Indian litany, and it required several such experiences and some degree of patience to become used to it.

At last he signified that he understood and was satisfied, and then in answer to my questions gave an account of himself and his doctrine, a great part of the interpretation being by Dyer, with whom he seemed to be on intimate terms. He said that he was about 35 years of age, fixing the date from a noted battle between the Paiute and the whites near Pyramid lake, in 1860, at which time he said he was but the size of his little boy, who appeared to be of about 4 years. His father, Tavibo, "white man," was not a preacher, but a capita (from the Spanish capitan) or petty chief, and was a dreamer and invulnerable. His own proper name from boyhood was Wovoka or Wuvoka, "The Cutter," but a few years ago he had assumed the name of his paternal grandfather, Kwohitsauq, or "Big Rumbling Belly." After the death of his father he had been taken into the family of a white farmer, David Wilson, who had given him the name of Jack Wilson, by which he is commonly known among the whites. He thus has three distinct names, Wovoka, Kwohitsauq, and Jack Wilson. He stated positively that he was a full-blood, a statement born out by his appearance. The impression that he is a half-blood may have arisen from the fact that his father's name was "White Man" and that he has a white man's name. His followers, both in his own and in all other tribes, commonly refer to him as "our father." He has never been away from Mason Valley and speaks only his own Paiute language, with some little knowledge of English. He is not acquainted with the sign language, which is hardly known west of the mountains.

When about 20 years of age, he married, and continued to work for Mr. Wilson. He had given the dance to his people about four years before, but had received his great revelation about two years previously. On this occasion "the sun died" (was eclipsed) and he fell asleep in the daytime and was taken up to the other world. Here he saw God, with all the people who had died long ago engaged in their oldtime sport and occupations, all happy and forever young. It was a pleasant land and full of game. After showing him all, God told him he must go back and tell his people they must be good and love one another, have no quarreling, and live in peace with the whites; that they must work, and not lie or steal; that they must put away all the old practices that savored of war; that if they faithfully obeyed his instructions they would at last be reunited with their friends in this other world, where there would be no more death or sickness or old age. He was then given the dance which he was commanded to bring back to his people. By performing this dance at intervals, for five consecutive days each time, they would secure this happiness to themselves and hasten the event. Finally God gave him control over the elements so that he could make it rain or snow or be dry at will, and appointed him his deputy to take charge of affairs in the west, while "Governor Harrison" would attend to matters in the east, and he, God, would look after the world above. He then returned to earth and began to preach as he was directed, convincing the people by exercising the wonderful powers that had been given him.

■ ■ ■

In our conversations he said nothing about a mysterious noise, and stated that it was about two years since he had visited heaven and received his great revelation, but that it was about four years since he had first taught the dance to his people. The fact that he has different revelations from time to time would account for the discrepancy of statement.

He disclaimed all responsibility for the ghost shirt which formed so important a part of the dance costume among the Sioux; said that there were no trances in the dance as performed among his people—a statement confirmed by eyewitnesses among the neighboring ranchmen—and earnestly repudiated any idea of hostility toward the whites, asserting that his religion was one of universal peace. When questioned directly, he said he believed it was better for the Indians to follow the white man's road and to adopt the habits of civilization. If appearances are in evidence he is sincere in this, for he was dressed in a good suit of white man's clothing, and works regularly on a ranch, although living in a wikiup. While he repudiated almost everything for which he had been held responsible in the east, he asserted positively that he had been to the spirit world and had been given a revelation and message from God himself, with full control over the elements. From his uncle I learned that Wovoka has five songs for making it rain, the first of which brings on a mist or cloud, the second a snowfall, the third a shower, and the fourth a hard rain or storm, while when he sings the fifth song the weather again becomes clear.

I knew that he was holding something in reserve, as no Indian would unbosom himself on religious matters to a white man with whom he had not had a long and intimate acquaintance. Especially as this was true in view of the warlike turn affairs had taken across the mountains. Consequently I accepted his statement with several grains of salt, but on the whole he seemed to be honest in his belief and his supernatural claims, although like others of the priestly function, he occasionally resorts to cheap trickery to keep up the impression as to his miraculous powers. From some of the reports he is evidently an expert sleight-of-hand performer. He makes no claim to be Christ, the Son of God, as has been so often asserted in print. He does claim to be a prophet who has received a divine revelation. I could not help feeling that he was sincere in his repudiation of a number of the wonderful things attributed to him, for the reason that he insisted so strongly on other things fully as trying to the faith of a white man. He made no argument and advanced no proof, but said simply that he had been with God, as though the statement no more admitted of controversy than the proposition that 2 and 2 are four. From Mr. J. O. Gregory, formerly employed at the agency, and well acquainted with the prophet, I learned that Wovoka had once requested him to draw up and forward to the President a statement of his supernatural claims, with a proposition that if he could receive a small regular stipend he would take up his residence on the reservation and agree to keep Nevada people informed of all the latest news from heaven and to furnish rain whenever wanted. The letter was never forwarded.

From a neighboring ranchman, who knew Wovoka well and sometimes employed him in the working season, I obtained a statement which seems to explain the whole matter. It appears that a short time before the prophet began to preach he was stricken down by a severe fever, during which illness the ranchman frequently visited and ministered to him. While he was still sick there occurred an eclipse of the sun, a phenomena which always excites great alarm among primitive peoples. In their system the sun is a living being, of great power and beneficence, and the temporary darkness is caused by an attack on him by some supernatural monster which endeavors to devour him, and will succeed, and thus plunge the world into eternal night unless driven off by incantations and loud noises. On this occasion the Paiute were frantic with excitement and the air was filled with the noise of shouts and wailings and the firing of guns, for the purpose of frightening off the monster that threatened the life of their god. It was now, as Wovoka stated, "when the sun died," that he went to sleep in the daytime and was taken up to heaven. This means simply that the excitement and alarm produced by the eclipse, acting on a mind and body already enfeebled by sickness, resulted in delirium, in which he imaged himself to enter the portals of the spirit world. Constant dwelling on the subject I thought by day and in dreams by night would effect and perpetuate the exalted mental condition in which visions of the imagination would have all the seeming reality of actual occurrences. To those acquainted with the spiritual nature of Indians and their implicit faith in dreams all that is perfectly intelligible. His frequent trances would indicate also that, like so many other religious ecstatics, he is subject to cataleptic attacks.

I have not been able to settle satisfactorily the date of this eclipse. From inquiry at the Nautical Almanac office…. The total eclipse of January 1, 1889, agrees best with his statement to me on New Year's night, 1892, that it was about two years since he had gone up to heaven when the sun died….

In subsequent conversations he added a few minor details in regard to his vision and his doctrine. He asked many questions in regard to the eastern tribes whose delegates had visited him, and was pleased to learn that the delegates from several of these tribes were my friends. He spoke particularly of the large delegation—about twelve in number—from the Cheyenne and Arapaho, who had visited him the preceding summer and taken part in the dance with his people. Nearly all the members of this party were personally known to me, and the leader, Black Coyote, whose picture I had with me and showed to him, had been my principal instructor in the Ghost dance among the Arapaho. While this fact put me on a more confidential footing with Wovoka, it also proved of great assistance in my further investigation on my return to the prairie tribes, as, when they were satisfied from my statements and the specimens which I had brought back that I had indeed seen and talked with the messiah, they were convinced that I was earnestly desirous of understanding their religion alright, and from that they spoke freely and without reserve.

I had my camera and was anxious to get Wovoka's picture. When the subject was mentioned, he replied that his picture had never been made; that a white man had offered him five dollars for permission to take his photograph, but that he had refused. However, as I had been sent from Washington especially to learn and tell the whites all about him and his doctrine, and as he was satisfied from my acquaintance with his friends in the other tribes that I must be a good man, he would allow me to take his picture. As usual in dealing with Indians, he wanted to make the most of his bargain, and demanded two dollars and a half for the privilege of taking his picture and a like sum for each one of his family. I was prepared for this, however, and refused to pay any such charges, but agreed to give him my regular price per day for his services as informant and to send him a copy of the picture when finished. After some demur he consented and got ready for the operation by knotting a handkerchief about his neck, fastening an eagle feather at his right elbow, and taking a wide brim sombrero upon his knee. I afterward learned that the feather and sombrero were important parts of his spiritual stock in trade. After taking his picture I obtained from him, as souvenirs to bring back and show to my Indian friends in Indian Territory, a blanket of rabbit skins, some pinion nuts, some tail feathers of the magpie, highly prized by the Paiute for ornamentation, and some of the sacred red paint, endowed with most miraculous powers, which plays so important a part in the ritual of the Ghost-dance religion. Then, with mutual expressions of good will, we parted, his uncle going back to the reservation, while I took the train for Indian Territory.

APPENDIX B.1

Mooney, "Ghost Dance" (1907:491-92):

A ceremonial religious dance connected with the messiah doctrine, which originated among the Paviotso in Nevada about 1888, and spread rapidly among other tribes until it numbered among its adherents nearly all the Indians of the interior basin, from Missouri River to or beyond the Rockies. The prophet of the religion was a young Paiute Indian, at that time not yet 35 years of age, known among his own people as Wovoka ("Cutter"), and commonly called by the whites Jack Wilson, from having worked in the family of a ranchman named Wilson. Wovoka seems already to have established his reputation as a medicine-man when, about the close of 1888, he was attacked by a dangerous fever. When he was ill an eclipse spread excitement among the Indians, with the result that Wovoka became delirious and imagined that he had been taken into the spirit world, and there received a direct revelation from the God of the Indians. Briefly stated, the revelation was to the effect that a dispensation was close at hand by which the Indians would be restored to their inheritance and reunited with their departed friends, and that they must prepare for the event by practicing the songs and dance ceremonies which the prophet gave them. Within a very short time the dance spread to the tribes east of the mountains, where it became known commonly as the Spirit or Ghost dance. The dancers, men and women together, held hands, and moved slowly around in a circle, facing toward the center, keeping time to songs that were sung without any instrumental accompaniment. Hypnotic trances were a common feature of the dance. Among the Sioux in Dakota the excitement, aggravated by local grievances, led to an outbreak in the winter of 1890-91. The principal events in this connection were the killing of Sitting Bull, Dec. 15, 1890, and the massacre at Wounded Knee, Dec. 29. The doctrine has now faded out, and the dance exists only as an occasional social function. In the Crow dance of the Cheyenne and Arapaho, a later development from the Ghost dance proper, the drum is used, and many of the ordinary tribal dances have incorporated Ghost-dance features, including even the hypnotic trances.

The belief in the coming of the messiah, or deliverer, who shall restore his people to a condition of primitive simplicity and happiness, is probably as universal as the human race, and takes on special emphasis among people that have been long subjected to alien domination. In some cases the idea seems to have originated from a myth, but in general it may safely be assumed that it springs from a natural human longing. Both the Quichua of Peru and the Aztec of Mexico, as well as more cultured races, had elaborate messiah traditions, of which the first Spanish invaders were quick to take advantage, representing themselves as the long-expected restorers of ancient happiness. Within the United States nearly every great tribal movement originated in the teaching of some messianic prophet. This is notably true of the Pontiac conspiracy in 1763-64, and of the combination organized by Tecumseh and his brother, the prophet Tenskwatawa shortly before the War of 1812. Of similar nature in more recent times is the doctrine formulated on Columbia River by Smohalla.

APPENDIX B.2

Mooney (1911:179-80):

Later, in the middle of the winter, I went out to the Piute in Nevada to see the messiah who had started the ghost dance. I first stopped about two weeks with his uncle [Charley Sheep], an old Piute, at Walker River reservation. After this man thought he knew me pretty well he was willing to go with me out to Mason Valley, where his nephew lived, and get him to tell me the whole story. He said his nephew was a very great wonder-worker; that he had a repertoire of songs by which he could make it rain or snow or stop raining or snowing. There was a young white man [Ed Dyer] up that way who knew a good deal of the Piute language and Jack Wilson, the Messiah, and he volunteered to go as interpreter. The old man [Sheep] could not speak English at all. We had considerable difficulty in getting out to the camp, which was close to the base of the Sierras. Not to go into details, it was one of the coldest nights I ever experienced, New Year's Eve, with a deep snow on the ground and clumps of sage brush scattered about as high as a small house. The old Indian's eyes were bad. He lost his way in the dark, and it looked for a while as if he had lost the rest of us, but after floundering around in the sage brush and snow for several hours we at last struck the camp, and by good luck found the messiah himself. After some explanation from his uncle, because he was very suspicious, he said if I would come around the next day he would talk with me.

I went out the next morning and talked with him about the dance and the religion, and then made his picture, the only one ever made. From what he told me I decided that he was about forty years of age. He said his father had been a prophet before him, that a few years before the sun had died in the daytime (meaning that there had been an eclipse), that he had gone to sleep and in his sleep he went up to heaven and saw the father and all the dead Indians. He talked with God and God told him all those things that he was now telling to the other Indians. He told them to get all the Indians together and teach them this dance and that after a while the new Indian world would come and they would be put upon it. He believed that he had a direct revelation from God and had been able to convince a large part of his tribe and delegates from other tribes who had come hundreds of miles across the mountains during the past summer and winter to sit at his feet and learn about the dance and then take the story of it back to their own people.

* * * * *

I shall now explain the meaning of it all as preached by the messiah, a young Piute, who lived in Nevada. He taught that the whole human race was of one kindred, and particularly that the Indians of the several tribes were all brothers and must give up tribal warfare and all thought of warfare with the whites. You can imagine what it meant to tell an Indian that he must quit thinking about war. It is all right for missionaries to tell him that, but when an Indian preached to Indians that they must quit fighting, that they must not kill one another, that they must not touch a white man, you can imagine what an entire change of the point of view of life that involved. It meant that they must forego the war dance and the carrying of weapons in the ghost dance and, instead, cultivate a peaceful attitude of mind. The prophet taught that if they did these things, if they returned to the Indian dress and manner of life, if they wore the sacred feathers and danced this dance and sang these songs and performed all the other requirements, after a while this old world would be done away with and instead of it there would be a new world which was being prepared for them, with their dead children, their fathers, mothers, and companions who had gone before, with the buffalo and other game, and the old Indian life in its entirety. The new world was already advancing from the west, and when it came it would push the white people before it to their own proper country across the ocean, and leave this country to the Indians, the original owners. When it arrived the feathers that the dancers wore on their heads would turn into wings by which they would mount up to the new earth. All this was to come without fight, or any effort upon their part; they should only watch and pray in anticipation of it; and by doing as instructed, dancing and singing the songs, they would be enabled to see visions of what was to come, and to meet in advance and talk with the friends who had gone before. Consequently, they were all anxious to see the visions which appeared through the medium of hypnotism.

The Dyer Manuscript

Special Collections, University Archives, University of Nevada Libraries, Reno.

Fallon
May 16, 1965

Ruthie Friedhoff
Reno, Nevada

Dear Miss Friedhoff:

I am very happy to acquiesce in your desire to use material on Jack Wilson contained in my father's monograph and to reproduce it for the Universities (sic) files.

Much has been written about Jack Wilson, much of it as a result of little understanding and desire to cash in on the current public appetite for all things Western! Any attempt to preserve factual material I find extremely laudable. Despite the narrow opinion of some of Jack's white contemporaries in Mason Valley I submit that he was a very great man who without help, tools, or understanding tried to better the lot of his people who were hit by a cataclysm with which they were unable to cope. I regard Paul Bailey's book, Wovoka, the Indian Messiah as probably one of the best portrayals of an indigene of good will struggling with the inexerable [sic] advance of a much superior but alien civilization.

Sincerely with good wishes

Edward A. Dyer

Wizardry

by E. A. Dyer Sr.

The project, as recently reported in the press, to probe the minds of Nevada's Old Timers in search of historical facts and stories does give rise to a bit of reminiscence. Old people do tend to think of the past and long life generally supplies plenty of material. In my own case many names came to mind but particularly I thought of a man I deemed my friend once long ago. He was a full blood Pahute Indian whom the Whites called Jack Wilson. He made history and thereby hands a tale that should be told. Others have tried to tell it but few of them were ever in possession of the full facts. Some possessed a considerable fund of misinformation which they passed by word of mouth to writers from the East who were looking for something sensational, either to bolster their preconceived notions about the romantic lives of the noble redmen or the opposite picture of the fiendish, bloodthirsty savage. The results often left much to be desired.

At the outset, I should perhaps, present my own qualifications for claiming to be an authority. I am living in the 86th year of a life nearly all of which has been spent in Nevada. My parents brought me to the Comstock in 1875 and subsequently removed to Mason Valley in 1880. There I reached manhood and lived for a major part of my life. As a child and adult I mingled with the Pahute Indians and learned to speak their language fluently. At 18 years of age I joined the Nevada State Militia, formed to deal with Indian uprising and am the last surviving member of Company I of that organization. I held a commission as Lieutenant signed by Governor Colcord. I knew Yerington when it was simply Mason Valley Post Office, facetiously called Pizen Switch and later when it was officially Greenfield.

I first knew Jack Wilson as a grown man somewhat older than I, when in my teens I started a store in Yerington. Regarding his early life I am indebted partially to my wife who was born and raised in the mining camp of Pinegrove where Jack Wilson also spent some time and partly to the late J.I. Wilson, one time banker of Yerington, whose father and uncle were Pine Grove and Mason Valley pioneers. The Wilson family had a partial hand in the raising of the Indian lad and furnished him with his American name. The pioneer Wilson family had mining interests in Pine Grove and extensive ranching properties in the south end of Mason valley near Wilson Canyon which was named for them. It was at this ranch, where some of his relatives were employed that the Indian Wilson spent much of his youth. The early day members of the Wilson family, like many pioneers were of a devout turn of mind. The young Indian, accepted into the house, was thus exposed to some religious teaching through family Bible readings, evening prayers, grace before meat and similar family devotions. Indeed, some particular effort was made by the lady of the house to read to the boy some of the better known Bible stories. What he heard he may not have thoroughly understood but he was vastly interested and impressed. More to the point he learned that the white men had certain leaders, wisemen and prophets whom they revered and by whose laws and precepts they endeavored to live. Just as today's boy might day dream of becoming a space pilot, yesterday's young Indian might envision himself as some sort of an Indian version of an Old Testament prophet. Later events lend a certain credibility to the supposition.

After his teenage years were passed Jack Wilson drops out of sight for a time. Not much is known of his activities as a young man, except that he did considerable wandering about this state and neighboring California. Regarding his travels he was never loquacious. The Walker River Pahutes were in the habit about that time, of making seasonal trips en masse, perched atop the railroad's handy boxcars to northern California for the purpose of picking hops. As hop money could purchase fruit and particulary watermelons, few able bodied Indians passed up the seasonal excursion. Likely enough young Jack Wilson also travelled to the California hop fields.

About the time I got to know him he had made a start in his endeavours [sic] to make of himself a personage among the Indians and shortly thereafter those of the whites who held converse with the Indians, became aware of him as something more than just another Indian. He didn't aspire to be a chief. Chiefs among the Pahutes had few royal prerogatives. The role of medicine man was not for him either. He never attempted any healing. A wise decision in view of the well known limit on professional mistakes. But he did claim to have some facility in the matter of prophesy; he could perform certain feats beyond the abilities of most mortals; he could describe the delights of the Happy Hunting Grounds from personal observation— he'd gone there on short trips.

About this time he sought little more than recognition as a personage among his fellow men. We all like to bolster our ego. But among the whites his claims got a grin and a shrug, though some of the Indians were ready to believe him. That was not altogether strange as nature had given him a presence which made faith easy. Jack Wilson was a tall, well-proportioned man with piercing eyes, regular features, a deep voice and a calm and dignified mien. He stood straight as a ramrod, spoke slowly and by sheer projection of personality commanded the attention of any listener. He visibly stood out among his fellow Indians like a thoroughbred among a bunch of mustangs.

Like all who claim unusual abilities he had his skeptics and eventually he had to demonstrate or shut up. And demonstrate he did. He caused ice to come down from the sky. Not too difficult a feat if one possesses some ingenuity and a supply of ice. He went into trances in which he remained for as long as two days and when he awakened, announced that he had been to the Indian Heaven and was able to give a thorough-going description. He painted such an enticing picture that a few of his most faithful believers decided to hurry things up by eating wild parsnip root (water hemlock). I personally witnessed the demise of one deluded victim and can attest that it was a long drawn out and agonizing death. Eating of wild parsnip to commit suicide was not an uncommon method among the Indians. In this case and several others, the victim not only was in a hurry to visit Heaven but also was assured that he could return again as Jack had done, to find earth a much improved place, for better days were coming for the red men. Jack Wilson's trances were, at least to Indians, very impressive productions. I can speak only as a layman in such matters but it is my belief that they were truly self induced hypnotic trances of a rather deep nature. He wasn't shamming. His body was as rigid as a board. His mouth could not be pried open and he showed no reaction to pain inducing experiments. At first his friends, thinking he was dying, made repeated and futile efforts to wake him up by physical manipulation and the administration of stimulants by mouth. He revived in his own good time. How and where he learned to place himself in a state of suspended animation is any one's guess. Perhaps he did visit Heaven—in his dreams. The whole matter is one to which I still confess considerable puzzlement.

Regarding the ice episode, I can also speak as an eye witness. My brother, Bob Dyer, who was also completely bilingual in Pahute and I, became aware that some activity was going to take place which somehow concerned Jack Wilson. Upon learning the time and place we unobtrusively showed up to see what was afoot. The meeting took place along the river bank on a hot July day. A hundred or more Indians were present but there was no great excitement among them. Wilson was holding a sort of informal court at the side of a blanket spread upon the ground under a large cottonwood tree. Groups of Indians came up to talk to him and move away. Other small groups just milled around. We talked to some. They were distinctly not talkative to a white but we gathered that they expected Wilson to perform some miracle. Doo-mur-eye (accented on second syllable) they called it which means an act of wizardry. Suddenly a great outcry came from the group around Wilson. Every one rushed over to see what had happened. There in the center of the blanket lay a big block of ice some 25 or 30 pounds in weight. Wilson had caused it to come from the sky and the Indians explained to those who had their eyes turned the wrong way to see it for themselves.

I was willing to believe it had fallen alright, but from no greater height than the top of that cottonwood tree, whose dense foliage would serve to hide the object until it sufficiently had melted to release it from whatever ingenious fastening Jack had fashioned to hold it for a time. That explained why the type of miracle was unspecified in advance. No Indian was likely to look up into the tree as he might if he were expecting ice from Heaven. It also explained the blanket. No Indian would stand on Jack's blanket and perhaps receive a pre-miracle icy drip, or worse, be beaned by the chunk itself. The Indians, not being of my suspicious nature accepted the miracle in full faith. A wash tub was provided from somewhere, the ice placed in the tub, the tub on the blanket and as the ice melted the ice water was ceremoniously drunk. It might have been sacramental wine judging from the solemnity. Shortly thereafter, at Jack's order, the whole bunch stripped and plunged into the river. It wasn't until years after that I realized that I had witnessed an aboriginal distortion of communion and baptism inspired by Biblical tales imperfectly understood. A number of years later I heard of a feat in which the ice was made to come floating down the river. Whether that was a distortion of what I witnessed or a separate affair I can't state.

Of the other alleged acts of wizardry I can only speak from hearsay but I was most solemnly assured by countless Indians that this or that was true. When out on a rabbit drive, they said Jack was in the habit of dropping a pinch of snow or sand into the muzzle of his gun and forthwith bringing down a jackrabbit. He didn't need orthodox power and shot. They knew this to be true as they had seen it with their own eyes. This business with substitute ammunition led naturally to another act of which I pieced together a complete picture from descriptions of many of those who had also seen "with their own eyes." This feat, which brought Jack universal acceptance among the Indians and led eventually to considerable trouble for Uncle Sam, was a well staged major production. He announced well in advance that he couldn't be killed by a gun. He simply was able to render his body impervious to lead. Moreover he could create powder and shot out of dust and sand. He then proceeded to back up his claims with a demonstration that left no doubt in the minds of a very large and interested audience.

Understandably the Indians were interested. If one of them could become bullet proof maybe the condition could be made to rub off on the rest of the tribe. The average Indians was becoming thoroughly fed up with the white man by this time and longed to shoot all of them out of hand but the white man was prone to shoot back with deadly accuracy and moreover he controlled the supply of powder and shot. It is difficult to wage a war when one is dependent on the enemy for supplies. But that business of making powder and shot out of sand—or even snow—now that opened enchanting possibilities.

The demonstration came off in grand style. Jack, wrapped in a heavy blanket robe, produced a muzzle loading shot gun for everyone's inspection. Then he reached down at his feet, got a pinch of dust which he dropped down the barrel. Powder he explained and reached for a handful of sand. That as far as any one could tell also went down the barrel in lieu of shot. A bit of paper wadding pushed down by the ramrod completed the charge and the gun was then handed to Jack's brother who was delegated as shooter.

Jack strode majestically to a spot previously selected, some distance from the rest of the crowd but well within gun range. He removed his blanket, placed it flat on the ground, took his stance in the center of the blanket, faced his brother standing in the midst of the crowd and ordered him to fire. The brother took careful aim at the man on the blanket and pulled the trigger. A very real and authentic shot gunblast rend the air. Jack was seen to shake himself vigorously and then heard to bid one and all to come forward to him. The Indians came up to see a man standing on a blanket, absolutely unhurt but wearing a shirt riddled with shot holes. On the blanket at his feet lay the shot. That did it. The evidence of their own senses convinced every Indian present. No self-appointed debunker, had there been one, could have obtained a hearing. Those of my readers who see readily through mills stones provided with holes and consequently think the Indians displayed a measure of stupidity are reminded that it is very human to believe that which we desire to believe.

Now the Indians began to refer to Wilson as Numa-naha which means Pahute Father. Previously they called him by his given Indian name, Coo-ee-jo (accent of third syllable). At that time they seldom used his white name. Undoubtedly other tribes later gave him other appellations. I have seen some in published references to him but have no personal recollection of them.

Naturally news of such a phenomenon as a bullet proof Indian with its possible application by other and more disgruntled Indians soon spread by word of mouth beyond the immediate tribal area and in the course of time reached the Plains Indians and those in Oklahoma Territory. Various tribes at various times sent delegations out to Mason Valley to check upon the validity of the story. The Pahutes were vociferous in their claims for Wilson's power. Perhaps further demonstrations were held. At any rate many dances were held: a sort of religious fervor was generated. Fuel was added to the fire by the Prophet's declaration that better and happier times for Indians were coming soon. He didn't elaborate but then he didn't have to. I witnessed, sometimes in company with my brother, a number of those dances in which delegations of Eastern Indians were present. They were generally proceeded [sic] by a solemn exchange of gifts. Jack Wilson would be seated on one side of the blanket and the chief visitors on the other. A gift would be placed upon the blanket with appropriate remark in his own tongue by the visiting one. A translation would follow, through one or more interpreters, with English resorted to as a language bridge in case of necessity. After a dignified acceptance by Wilson it was the next donor's turn. The blanket would be heeping with rich gifts before the end. The visitors usually received red ocher and other face paints together with magpie tail feathers in return.

Parenthetically I might explain that my brother and I had been in the habit, together or singly [sic], of attending many Indian dances and other activities. We were never invited. As self invited guests we were tolerated but seldom welcomed except by an occasional individual. We were accounted friends by the Indians but would have been held to be presuming on that friendship if we did much more than silently observe. We were very circumspect as a mob of Indians under excitement of tribal ritual, a bit of firewater and ingrown dislike of white men were as unstable as nitroglycerine.

Gradually the belief built up that the Indian peoples had something at long last. They came to regard Jack Wilson as a veritable Messiah come to punish the Indian's enemies. There is no concrete evidence to show that Jack deliberately cultivated such a belief. He was content merely to bask in the adulation and veneration of his fellow Indians. But his fellow Indians having ideas of his own, ran off with the ball. They asked for Wilson's garments, particularly shirts. They began, by extension to attribute miraculous powers to shirts he had worn, owned, touched, looked upon or simply just thought about.

At this point I became a sort of confidant of his and functioned as his secretary. I shared these roles at times with the late J.I. Wilson of Yerington with whom I later held many talks on the enigma that was Jack Wilson. At that time I was operating a store and Jack dropped in often to get me to answer letters which he got in considerable numbers from Indians, particularly in Oklahoma. They were almost invariably post-marked Darlington, Oklahoma and written by one, Grant Left-Hand who appeared to function as scribe for most of the Indian Nations. Most letters asked for something of Jack's in the way of a "gift:" magpie feathers, red ochre for paint, clothing that he had worn. In time a great many requests were for hats, specifically for those which he he'd personally worn. I was very often called upon to send them his hat which he would remove forthwith from his head on hearing the nature of the request in a letter. He expected, and got, $20 for such a "gift." Naturally he was under the necessity of purchasing another from me at a considerable reduced figure. Although I did a steady and somewhat profitable business on hats, I envied him his mark-up which exceeded mine to a larcenous degree. But somehow this very human trait make him all the more likable. His list prices for magpie tail feathers and red ocher were also on a par with those asked for similar "war-paint" and geegaws [sic] in our modern salons.

I never heard of his attempting to put over anything on a white man except once. That incident occurred early in the game and may have been in the nature of a test case of his ability. Lack of results may have been discouraging. In any event he attempted to pick up a few dollars from one of the members of the Wilson family, who had an avid interest in mines, by offering to show him a gold mine. In those days that was a natural as the whites were always trying to pump Indians regarding the location of gold deposits which they were supposed to know of. In this case Jack thoughtfully and artistically salted a large boulder by means of a little gold dust loaded into a shot gun. A lack of knowledge of geology defeated him however, as he made the fatal error of picking a granite boulder. To any readers with a similar lack of geologic learning I might explain that the occurrence of gold in granite is about as rare as its occurrence in hard boiled eggs.

But his build up among the Indians everywhere went on unabated and they began to get restless. Hotheads among them clamored for some action. It remained for the Sioux, perhaps the most warlike of the plains Indians, to precipitate trouble. By this time governmental authorities had become aware of trouble brewing. To cool things off a bit it was decided to take into custody as a sort of hostage for good behavior, the nominal head of the Sioux, Sitting Bull. His followers objected strenuously, some sort of a hassle developed and in the melee Sitting Bull was killed. That dropped the fat practically into the fire but before a general war could be started a parlay was arranged with the Indians. It took place Dec. 29, 1890 near Pine Ridge in southern South Dakota. Neither side trusted the other. In consequence as arrangements shaped up, troops armed with the new Gatling gun (a forerunner of the modern machine gun) occupied the heights overlooking the conference area. Within the area were hundreds of blanketed Indians who were supposed to be unarmed as were the government spokesmen who were to confer with them.

Just what happened next has never been satisfactorily determined. Indians claimed overt acts and bad faith on the part of the whites. They in turn claimed the same of the Indians. It was said that Indians began to drop blankets, expose (sic) rifles and prepare to use them. Again, the first shot was attributed to a jittery soldier. It is futile to speculate at this late date but it is known that a shot rang out, several more followed and then the Gatling guns were turned loose. The result was little short of a massacre. Some 300 Indians lay dead with many more wounded. The surviving Indians were stunned and apparently the Army was somewhat astounded by this first bloody demonstration of the effectiveness of mechanized carnage. It took its place in history as the battle of Wounded Knee. To the victors of the Little Big Horn it was final and bitter defeat. No other tribe was prepared to face a similar debacle. Other isolated skirmishes among various tribes occurred well into the 20th century and several were accounted "the last Indian battle"

but Wounded Knee for all practical purposed marked the end of the Indian wars. A bloody period had been placed at the end of the last chapter of the annals of an era.

Inquiries among the surviving insurgents turned up many references to "ghost shirts" and the belief that their wearers were safe from bullets. Further probing revealed the name of Jack Wilson. Governmental authorities followed the case no further. But the Smithsonian Institute was still interested in details, not only as a matter of history, but as an insight into Indian psychology and lore. So the Institute dispatched an investigator, a Mr. Mooney to contact Jack Wilson and interview him. Mr. Mooney arrived in Yerington and contacted the writer for the purpose of discovering the whereabouts of the Indian Prophet and securing the services of an interpreter. Wilson was known to have a good working knowledge of English but not quite up to explaining obscure points of Indian theology.

However, finding him was another matter. Understandably he was no more than a little apprehensive as to what lay in store for him. His fellow Pahutes were not interested in disclosing his whereabouts either, but I finally cajoled them into telling. Wilson was not exactly hiding nor had he run away. Prudently he had removed his camp to the south end of the valley and located it in brush big enough to hide it from the casual observer.

Mr. Mooney and I drove to the camp in my buggy and found Wilson "at home." After introductions and assurances that nothing disagreeable was in store he was persuaded to talk. Thus began the first of many all day sessions of questions and answers. The catechism was thorough and when the subject of the ghost shirts and the prophet's connection thereto was exhausted, Mr. Mooney went into tribal lore and religious beliefs. I translated legends, stories, songs and dance chants, all of which were duly recorded in Mr. Mooney's notebook. Wilson was cooperative, neither cringing, bellicose nor evasive. At the end he posed, upon the promise of a print, for a formal photograph which Mooney took with professional skill. I was thoroughly convinced that Jack Wilson had at no time attempted deliberately to stir up trouble. He never advocated violence. Violence was contrary to his very nature. Others seized upon his prophecies and "stunts" and made more out of them than he intended. On the other hand it should be said that there is no evidence to show that he tried to restrain over zealous followers. in a way, once started, he was riding a tiger. It was difficult to dismount. And at the end, he evinced a very real regard at what had happened. There were no more demonstrations of wizardry.

Interested readers will find a report of those interviews and my part in them in the Year Books published by the Smithsonian.

And now, strangely enough, Jack Wilson acquired that which he sought all along, namely a quiet veneration by Indians everywhere. No Indian blamed him for the debacle at Wounded Knee, a point on which he had at first some misgivings. I continued to act occasionally as corresponding secretary. His correspondents in Indian Territory began to write importuning him to visit them. At the outset he was somewhat leery, half suspecting a trick to get him where hands could be laid upon him in revenge for letting them down with those ineffectual ghost shirts. But eventually he was persuaded, partly by my assurances that law and order prevailed in Oklahoma and he made a trip back there. He was lionized and on his return was loaded with presents of money but mainly of items such as mocassins [sic], vests, belts, gloves, buckskin breeches and other articles of finery dear to the Indian's heart. The loot would have made a collector of Indian hand work green with envy. Everything was of the finest quality, adorned with beads, porcupine quills, animal teeth and claws. Twenty years later he still wore some of those vests and mocassins. As time went on he was forgotten by some of his Eastern friends but the Pahutes never faltered or forgot their fealty. On a rabbit drive Jack rode in a wagon like the personage he was. He had no need to carry a gun. Every Indian contributed generously of his skill to swell Jack's share in the communal effort. Even my young sons fell victim to his personal charm and royal prerogatives. When they occasionally killed and sold jackrabbits to the Indians at the camp, Jack demanded and got a discount. To them it seemed only right and proper for you had only to look at him to see that he was something special.

His prestige lasted to the end. Once in the early 1920's I saw him in town and called his attention to a news item. It related to an incident which happened in Utah among the Utes. Uncle Sam had doled out some largess to the Utes in the form of cash. Some of the recipients had forthwith converted the cash to a more potable commodity and the resulting binge had caused the local constabulary considerable effort to control. The news item speculated about further violence. Jack asked me to send a telegram to the authorities informing them that if necessary he would and could stop any further trouble. Having considerable faith that the Utah authorities could cope with the situation I didn't send the telegram. But if they couldn't have handled it there is no doubt that Jack would have stopped it with a word.

Jack Wilson, perhaps inadvertently, nevertheless caused Uncle Sam considerable trouble. At the end he stood regretful and ready to atone but there was just no way. And now he was an old man. But the debt, if any there was, can now be marked "paid in full" for his grandson gave his life for his country. He was shot down in action while serving with Chennault's Flying Tigers in the China-Burma theater during

World War II. After the war his body was recovered, returned to his homeland and buried with full military honors.

In three generations the Indian of Nevada has come a long way over an incredibly rocky road. He was seldom led gently by the hand. More often he was impatiently and unnecessarily booted from the rear. Is it any wonder that he sometime stumbled? That he survived at all is the true Indian miracle. They had a name for it, doo-mur-eye, wizardry.

The Dyer Tape

Tape 17: Ed Dyer Sr., Margaret M. Wheat Papers #83-24. Special Collections, University of Nevada–Reno Library. Transcribed by Michael Hittman.

Your speaker's name is Edward A. Dyer. Born in Vallejo, California, in 1871; the 23rd of January. Came to Nevada at the age of 5 years: to Virginia City; and from Virginia City to Mason Valley. When I was 9 years of age, I went to Mason Valley; in 1880. My mother was divorced from father, and she remarried a man in Mason Valley. At that time [the settlement was] called Pizen Switch; later it was renamed Greenfield; and then a few years afterwards, Yerington. I enjoyed the ranch life very much—except the part of herding cows. I tired of that job in a few years—two or three years—and I got a couple of Indian boys about my age: one they named Louie Bennett, the other's Indian name was **Pahanokee**. Or, we called him for short "Tom." From them I learned a few words of Indian. [Though] Not enough to carry on a conversation. [For example,] The name of cows and dogs and things like that.

When I was 17 years of age, in the spring of 1888, I started in business for myself—on a shoestring; in the town of Greenfield. From the beginning, I had quite a number of Indians as customers. And they were good customers, too. In those days, they worked in the hayfields and acquired a lot of money. And [they were] very profitable. And [were] interesting customers.

One day, one of these Indians—we'd call him Frank, that was his name; all the name he had—I never learned it [Indian name]. We were out, sitting in front of the store, and he looked kind of disconsolate. And [so] I said, "Frank: What's the matter with you?" "Oh," he said, "Ed, I feel pretty bad." I said, "You look alright!" "Oh, yeah, [but] I feel pretty bad." I said, "What's the matter?" He said, "I got no name!" "They call you Frank, don't they?" "Yes, I ought to have another name. White men got two names, I only got one. I need another name!" "Well, don't feel bad about it," I said. "Don't let that worry you. You can have my name." "Yeah?" he said. I said, "Sure," I said. "Now you're Frank Dyer! That's your name." "Oh, that's good," he said. "What're you gonna do?" he said. "Well, I don't lose my name. We both have the same name: Dyer. I'm Ed, and you're Frank." "Oh, that's fine," he said. "I don't have much use for that name."

And, so, I said:

"I gave you my name, now you gotta do something for me." He said, "What can I do?" I said, "You can teach me to speak Indian!" "Do you think I can?" I said, "Sure you can! What you do is, just give me the names of things, I'll repeat them, and you teach me that way." So, he said "Alright!" So, I pointed to his head: "**Tsopeegee**." I repeated it. He said, "That's fine." "Hair: **gwa**." "Good," I said, "I'm learning fast!" Eyes: **bui**. Nose: **movee**. Mouth: **tamma**. I said, "That's pretty good." Hand: **mai'ee**. Foot: **kidi**. I said, "Well, that's lots. Maybe I got enough?" "No!" he said. "Little bit more." [And so] He said, "Shirt: **kwasi**. Pants: **qosa**. Shoes: **moqo**. Ears: **naqa**." And I said, "I guess that's enough for now." So, that ended that conversation. And from then on, when the customers came into the store—and most of my trade was Indian trade—they'd point to something on the shelves. [For example,] The squaws would come in, Indian women, and say **kwasi**: calico. And [if] the Indian boys wanted a hat, they'd say: **tsoteer**. And [so] everything like that in the store, I learned the name pretty quick. So, when they came in, instead of asking me in English what they wanted, they gave the Indian name for it. And it was no time before I learned the name of everything in the store. And after that they began to evince small conversations with them, and I began to learn slowly, and I could speak pretty good.

About a year or two after I opened the store, that business, Jack Wilson came. Of course I'd seen him before: He'd been in the store and bought stuff. He had a letter and he said, "Do you read 'em?" "Yes," I said, "I read 'em." "I like you to read 'em for me." "Alright! Here?" "Oh, no. Too many ears. Too many Indians. We go behind." [Well] I had a couple of rooms in back. We—my brother and I—kept house. [So] We took him back there and read the letter. And it happened to be from this Grant Left Hand. Some Cheyenne or Arapaho. And they called him "Father." And this one of them said he'd like to come and see him. And he hoped he'd answer the letter. Well, I answered his letter; invited him to come. And in a short time, about a half dozen of them Cheyenne and Arapaho showed up—Not in the store, but Jack Wilson's camp. [And] At that time, I don't know exactly [where the camp was]. Can't recall it right at present.

So, I answered his letter. More letters come every little while. They called him "Father," and they wanted him to send them some paint and magpie feathers. So, he brought in a bunch of paint; and it was in a ball—a ball of red paint. Jack Wilson, by the way, had a paint mine in Pine Grove: about a mile or two away from [its] town. My wife's seen the paint mine, she's been to it. Billy Wilson, a white man, who had a mine up in Pine Grove, he painted a house with this paint. I think it was iron stain. And he mixed some of the paint from this paint mine and painted his house with it. He [Jack Wilson] mixed it with some kind of oil or grease or something. When I saw it, he had it mixed in balls about the size of a baseball. Or larger? It was hard like clay, but didn't rub off in your hands. And that paint, and a bundle of magpie feathers—whether they didn't have any magpie feathers in Arapaho country, I imagine perhaps they didn't, because they were crazy about those magpie feathers [we sent] to Darlington, Oklahoma; to that Grant Left Hand. And he used to work in a store there, and he'd give them to the proper [?]. One of the [other] Indians was Standing Cow, an Indian name.

[Well, so] Letters began to come and ask for other things: They asked for a shirt, and he bought a shirt from me out of the store and sent it to them. And they said they didn't want new shirts, but something he had worn; [like] the shirt he'd worn himself. A shirt or even a hat. And, so, he sold them his shirts! And I done a landoffice business in hats and shirts after that! Jack Wilson bought another shirt and put on a hat. [And] As it happened, as luck would have it, I already laid in a stock of what they called at that time "Texas Plaza Hats." They were high-crowned and wide-brimmed. They wasn't a regular cowboy hat—the Indians, they wore a stiff-brim; cowboys wore a narrow brim hat, but not a stiff-brim. And those stiff-brimmed hats were called by the whites "Mexican hats." Perhaps they wore them in Mexico, those Mexicans? I don't know, perhaps they did? So, he sent them a shirt and a hat, and it wasn't long before letters come, and two or three more wanted hats. So, I'd order a dozen of those hats. And Jack Wilson bought two or three of those hats and sent them to them. Income came, and he was the guy doing the landover business. So, I sold him another hat. [And] He sent them the hat he'd been wearing, so, pretty soon a dozen hats were exhausted. And they wanted more shirts.

Then about that time some more Arapaho and Cheyenne arrived, and asked about Jack Wilson. Could [they] go to his camp? It seems, sometimes, he contrived to have a dance. [And] On two or three occasions he did. Chief Wasson, he was the dance chief; he'd start all their dance songs. (That's when the Cheyenne began to look on him as a messiah.) I don't know at these meetings what occurred, [with] Cheyennes and Arapahos; I wasn't there. But he got into the habit of performing different tricks, as you already know. And [so they] looked at him as a supernatural being. And they sent him money, and these shirts. The history of the ghost shirts I think came from that. Pretty soon it got so that the Sioux Indians got the belief that the shirts protected him from harm.

By that time I learned to carry on conversations with the Indian. My brother began to pick up a little bit of it, from being in the store. But I could speak it like any Indian at that time, and he was getting to learn it. But later he learned more of the language than I did.

In their war dance, they wanted a white man type shirt. (The war dances are different from their rain dances: They mixed the magpie feathers with the other types of feathers, I think.) Well, they had begun to send, as I said, money, and, finally, they began to send moccasins: beaded moccasins; you know. Beautiful patterns! And one of the things they sent him [was] a vest. And this vest was interwoven with porcupine quills. It was a buckskin vest. And gloves—buckskin gloves—and shirts. And pants. And all kind of Indian finery. And they'd send him some headdresses with eagle feathers, too. The Bannocks had those, they intermingled with them.

And by the way, I'm going to tell you something very few white people know: The Bannock Indians, from Idaho, speak the same language as the Paiutes! It varies a little, there are a few words in there. For instance, they call a dog **sadoo**, and Paiutes call one **w^zeeboog**. And they call the Bannock **k^ts^d^k^d^** [Buffalo eaters]. And one time, several of those Bannocks, they come down and were talking to the Paiutes. And they said, "**Sadoo pidza nuud^kado**. Dog is good to eat!" And the Paiutes, they were horrified, eating dog. They never eat anything like that. Kind of dumbfounded, but pretty soon, they begin to laugh and make a kind of a joke. And when they were among each other, I heard them saying, "**Sadoo pidza nuud^kado**." Like a joke...

I don't know much more...Oh, Mooney?

...

I don't remember any children around there. Mr. Mooney inquired in Yerington if anybody could help him find Jack Wilson. Nobody seemed to know. But they [townspeople] said: "If you want to know anything about Jack Wilson, or the Indians, you see Ed Dyer! He can tell you all about it. Where Jack Wilson lives." So, they came and asked me. I said, "Yes, I know where he lives." He asked if he could find it? I said, "I doubt it. It's up in East Walker." And he said, "Maybe it's asking too much? Would you go up there with me? Someone told me you speak Paiute." "Yes, to some extent." "Would you go with me?" he said. "Interpret for me? And help me find Jack Wilson. I want to interview him." I said, "I think I can get away." So, I managed to get away.

So we went up there. We found Jack Wilson's camp—It was, oh, maybe 3 or 4 miles above the forks of the Walker River: the East and West Walker River; about a mile above the bridge, the oldest, the earliest bridge, the Hillman Bridge. The Hillman Ranch, on the East Walker River, about a mile above that. It was on the righthand side of the river, going up. So, we crossed the bridge and struck on up the river, until we come to the Wilson Ranch. The one that married the Wilson girl—the oldest boy, [?] Plummer.

So, we all went over to [George] Plummer's ranch. He's a friend of mine, a man my folks knew back East, back in Maine. I asked him if he had some place in the house we could go? Had a table in the house we could write [on]? He welcomed us all in. Took us into a room there. So, Mr. Mooney opened his briefcase and got out his writing materials and everything. So, we was there several hours, interviewing Jack Wilson. Mooney wrote up a lot about him: Myths and songs and stories, you know. Lots of things.

And [then] we left there, and Jack Wilson went back to his camp, and Mooney and I went back to town. [And] In writing up about his visit there, he spoke about me—in one of his books; and said I was quite a help to him. He was representing the Smithsonian Institute at the time.

I furnished the material, he done the writing. He changed it. It wasn't in the exact language that I gave, but he changed it to suit himself. So, I was entitled to the compliment.

APPENDIX D

Newspaper Accounts

1888

The Mason Valley Piutes are having big dances every evening now (*Lyon County Times* 12/22/88).

1889

...a prophet has risen among the Indians at Walker Lake and is creating some excitement among the ignorant and more credulous Piutes. He says the spirits of all the Piute warriors who have died in the last five hundred years are to return to earth and resume their old forms. They have condemned the whites and the Indians who write or speak their language or adopt their customs, and will exterminate them from the earth." (Statement of Sarah Winnemucca, *Walker Lake Bulletin* 3/20/89, In Johnson 1975:46-47).

RAIN DANCE — The Piutes of Mason Valley had a big rain dance last week. Their big man who formerly brought rain when they desired it, died last summer, and therefore they have taken it upon themselves to pray for rain in their peculiar manner. If rain does not come soon there will be another big dance at the Walker Lake Reservation on which occasion the Piutes from all over the country will be notified to be present (*Lyon County Times* 4/20/89).

BIG PIUTE DANCE — The Piutes are having the biggest dance ever held in Mason Valley. Representatives of Big Indians are there from Montana, Idaho, Utah, and California. Nearly all of the foreigners are larger and better looking than the Piutes of this state. The great weather prophet is said to be a fine looking man, much resembling the late Henry Ward Beecher (*Lyon County Times* 8/3/89).

1890

TOO MUCH OF A GOOD THING — There is great talk among the Piutes at the reservation tonight. Some months ago, fearing another dry season, the Indians had a rain or wet talk. At that meeting one Jakey Wilson, the modern Moses of the Piutes, was deputized to go up in the mountains and "see Jesus," and ask for moisture. He went. The Indians all solemnly aver that Jakey saw Jesus, who promised that water should fall. The most skeptical cannot deny that the water fell. Now, however, Mr. Indian says he is too wet and cold and he can't steal wood enough to keep warm. Accordingly the Piutes will assemble tonight, and Jakey Wilson will again be sent up the mountain with a numerously signed petition that the flood gates be closed for a little while. Let us hope that Jakey will be successful in his mission (*Walker Lake Bulletin* 1/22/90, In Logan 1980:268).

This so-called Messiah first gained notoriety at the Walker Lake Reservation early last winter. The Indians wanted rain, and they assembled in conclave, and the

Messiah appeared, and they asked for water—not fire-water. The result was that the most severe storms of that stormy winter followed. After about a month of incessant rain and snow the Indians had enough, and again they sought the Messiah and asked him to let up. And lo and behold, the clouds rolled by, and soon the papers began blowing about the fine climate. And then the little daughter of a Piute brave died, and there was much grief, and the brave went up into the mountains and the Messiah appeared to him, and told him to sorrow no more—that in three days his little girl would return to life.

All of which, according to the solemn assurance of several "good" Indians, came to pass.

But we are a little skeptical as to this Northern Messiah (re: The Pine Ridge Reservation, M.H.), we believe he's a bilk. He incites his local people to unlawful acts and bids them prepare for war, while our local Messiah (who is no doubt the Simon pure, yard wide, all wool Christ) advised peace and performed miracles which make all people feel good. As Capt. Nobe remarks: "Him hell-of-a-good Ingin!" (*Walker Lake Bulletin* 11/12/90, In Logan 1980:268-69).

Capt. Josephus, who has been on a pilgrimage to all the Indian settlements in this county and western Nye, returned to the reservation last Friday. He says the Piutes will have a grand talk next week at which Piutes and Shoshones from all parts of the State will be present (*Walker Lake Bulletin* 11/20/90, In Logan 1980:269).

There are said to be about 800 male Indians in attendance at the dance now being held at Walker Lake Reservation. They are sulky and impudent and in case of an uprising they could perform all their deviltry before assistance could reach us. A military post at Hawthorne would be more effective as a scarecrow than a whole army would be after some mischief had been done (*Walker Lake Bulletin* 12/3/90, In Logan 1980:269).

NEVADA INDIAN AFFAIRS — Captain Sam, Chief of the Piute Indians, arrived in Carson Thursday from Mason Valley, where the Indians have gathered for a ghost dance. He says a stranger is in their midst proclaiming the coming of the Messiah. Sam has notified Johnson Sides to go among all Nevada Indians and explain the advantages of co-operating with the whites in case of war (*Lyon County Times* 12/20/90).

1891

VISITING INDIANS — A delegation of Indians representing the Kiowas, Arapahoes, Bannocks and Sioux has arrived in Nevada to see the Messiah. The chiefs were entertained regally by Agent Warner at the Pyramid Agency and furnished with a conveyance to Walker Lake, the home of the Prophet, who is an inferior Indian and known to the whites by the unpretentious name of "Jack Wilson." When the chiefs interview Jack they will not have such an exalted opinion of the prophet (*Reno Journal* 1/8/91, In Dangberg 1968:31)

THE INDIAN SITUATION — There is no reason to fear that the Piutes in this part of the State mean to fight. The report that several hundred of them had congregated at Pinenut, was without foundation, as there has not been an Indian in that vicinity for months (*Lyon County Times* 1/17/91).

The Piutes in and about Hawthorne have been growing impudent this week and the Government has sent the citizens arms so that in case the Red Man becomes too demonstrative, he can be effectually sat down upon (*Lyon County Times* 1/24/91).

PREPARING FOR WAR! CITIZENS FEARFUL OF AN INDIAN OUTBREAK. A PROTECTION COMMITTEE ORGANIZED AND ARMS ASKED FOR. ADDITIONAL GUARDS EMPLOYED TO PATROL THE TOWN. AN URGENT REQUEST FOR A MILITARY POST. RESULT OF A MEETING OF LEADING CITIZENS—There is considerable uneasiness felt among our citizens concerning the Indians in this vicinity. While there has as yet been no real uprising, still there has been no doubt that the Indian are in league with their brethren of adjacent settlements for some unusual purpose and whether their "intents are wicked or charitable" none can tell as yet.

The air is full of rumors of warlike preparations all around us. In Rhodes Marsh, the Indians are restless and impertinent. They work a few days and then refuse to work, when others are employed. They in turn earn a few dollars and then mysteriously leave.

Supt. Fleming of the soda works says that strange Indians have been among the workers later, and they have had dances and talks, with the above result.

The Piutes in Mason Valley are all well-armed and very saucy. They say pretty soon they will own the stores and ranches and houses.

The Indians of Owens Valley are spoiling for a fight. Nye country has recently been supplied with arms and the result is that people of Hawthorne are very nervous.

We are in the very heart of Indian country. Within the radius of 40 miles there are over 1000 able-bodied bucks, well-armed. If the Indians took a notion, fifty men could obliterate Hawthorne and its inhabitants from the face of the earth in one hours time. The application of a match on a windy night could destroy the town and then the people could be killed like rats in a hole (*Walker Lake Bulletin* 1/29/91, In Logan 1980:270).

INDIAN SCARE — For years the numbers of Indians in and about Dayton has not been so small as it has during the last six months. Since they went to gather pinenuts last Fall but few of them have returned, and at present there are not over a dozen bucks and their mahalas about town, while formerly there would be forty or fifty around at this season. The few that are here seem to know very little about any ghost dances, and say that the Piutes don't want to fight. They are very inquisitive, however, and want to know what the papers say about the. It is very probable that the Indians that used to be around here are now down about the Reservation and Hawthorne (*Lyon County Times* 1/31/91).

The Piutes in Smith Valley are reported to be very ugly. They say that county all belonged to them once and that pretty soon they will take the farms and horses away from the white man (*Lyon County Times* 1/31/91).

The Indians [at the Walker River Reservation] are very saucy and all say that pretty soon 'heep fight' (*Lyon County Times* 1/31/91).

A great many Piutes have been passing through town this week. Some were on their way to Walker Lake and others were returning. What their business was could not be found out *Lyon County Times* 2/14/91).

Captain C. C. Warner, Indian Agent at the Pyramid Reservation, and who has been on a business trip to Walker Lake Reservation, passed through on Wednesday's train on his way home. He reports all quiet among the Piutes (*Lyon County Times* 2/14/91).

Six Indians from near Fort Reno, in the Oklahoma country, were passengers on last Sunday's train bound for Mason Valley. Three of the Indians were Cheyennes and three Navajoes, and they were going to the Valley to see Dave [sic] Wilson, the Piute Prophet. Two of the Navahos talk pretty good English and write very well. One of them was a policeman and he wore his badge with great dignity. In conversing with the Piutes they talk English and then they have an interpreter to explain to them. They are a fine lot of looking Indians, far superior in intelligence to Piutes and Washoes and they carried grip sacks and trunks with them the same as white people (*Lyon County Times* 8/8/91).

During August, Spotted Tail, Black Crow, Big Man and Fill Up, war chiefs of the Cheyenne tribes, were at the Reservation at Walker Lake. When they arrived at Wabuska the other day, they walked into the dining room to eat, and were ordered into the kitchen, all same Piute? They told the landlord "not much" and seated themselves at a first-class table, devoured everything that was placed before them, remarking that it was pretty good meal for the money, although they would rather pay six bits more and get something real good (*Walker Lake Bulletin* 8/12/91, In Johnson 1975:53).

It is estimated by businessmen of Mason Valley that the Indians spent a thousand dollars in and about the Switch during their last big dance. They consumed about three thousand pounds of beef alone (*Lyon County Times* 8/15/91).

1892

THE INDIAN PROPHET — Indians from Indian Territory and other eastern agencies have for the past year been visitIng Jack Wilson, the Walker River Piute prophet, and on their return told some wonderful stories about his sayings. A white man from Fort Reno interviewed Jack a few days ago, and he denied some of the statements he was credited with. He did not deny, however, that he told the visiting Indions [sic] that God would look after things above, President Harrison would attend to affairs in the East, while he [Jack] would regulate Western affairs. He is getting the big head and will probably soon ignore his partners and go it alone (*Lyon County Times* 1/9/92).

NO USE FOR THE MESSIAH — A dispatch from Boise City, Idaho, says that the Indian Messiah at Walker Lake, this state, has sent emissaries among the Idaho tribes urging them to inaugurate ghost dances and prepare for war this spring. The rumors have been coldly received, the Idaho tribes being satisfied with their lot and afraid to dance as they did in 1890. Sargeant [sic] Jim, a leader of the once terrible Bannocks now living on the Fort Hall Reservation neare [sic)] Pocatello, declares that the Messiah will be assassinated if he does not cease his attempts to stir up trouble. Jim declares that the red men of the far West want no more trouble with whites, and the Bannocks will certainly take steps to have the false prophet killed if he sends any more runners in Idaho (Silver State) (*Walker Lake Bulletin* 11/9/92, In Logan 1980:277).

1893

Our neighboring county on the south, Esmeralda, may furnish an ethnological exhibit to the world's columbian exposition that will rank as one of the chief exhibits of the big show. Efforts are now being made by persons of a speculative turn living in San Francisco, to include Jack Wilson, known as the Indian "Messiah" to leave his wikiup near Pine Grove, and with his family to journey to the mighty city by the lake side, there to place themselves upon exhibition.

He is a strange creature this Jack Wilson, and every Piute in this portion of the country believes implicitly in him. Wise and dignified old chiefs from the Indian territory, from the Dakotas in the northeast and Idaho in the northwest have visited him in the past two years. All apparently went away satisfied, impressed with his wisdom, his meekness and his miracle-working powers.

White men admit that he is clever, but are unable to determine whether he is a prophet or a trickster. The Piutes point to two acts of the Messiah's in support of his claim to work miracles. First—they believe he has faced guns loaded with shot, and without a tremor given the signal to discharge their contents directly at him— the shot perforating his shirt yet not making a single scar upon his body. Honest men among the Piutes bear testimony to this shooting episode and if they are not mistaken who shall say that he is not a miracle worker?

Again three years ago he inaugurated a series of rain dances in the unpropitious month of August. He assured his immediate followers to have faith and he would cause water to fall from the skies. After two dances had passed and no rain had fallen the nonbelievers—and at that time they were largely in the majority—laughed his followers to scorn. The third rain dance was inaugurated in the presence of a vast gathering. The sky overhead was clear and old Sol's rays fairly burned the ground. The little band of believers were closely pressed by the jeering throng. All were intent upon watching the dance, so they did not glance overhead. The dancers were now well warmed up: the scene was wild and wierd. Jack Wilson came into the center of his people, muttered an incantation, threw up his arms, and lo! a brisk shower commenced to fall. Every Piute present at once became a believer.

Many white men bear testimony to the fact that showers fell that August day. Was it a miracle? We cannot say (*Mason Valley Tidings* 6/18/93).

1894

END OF THE WORLD — The Piute Indian prophet of Walker Lake, who caused a furor among his people several years ago by announcing the coming of the Indian Messiah and originating the ghost dance, is at his old business again with new tricks. He announces the end of the world to take place soon by a mighty rush of water that will tear down the mountains and make a plain of the earth. Every living thing will be destroyed, and a white grass will be left growing when the waters subside to basins created for them. Countless antelope, deer, buffalo, and other game which delight the Red Man, will grow fat and fast upon the white grass, and then only the Indians will return to enjoy the hunting grounds and monopolize the earth.

Captains Dave, Numana, Sam, Johnson Sides and other wise men call the prophet a liar and say his tongue is forked, and powwows will be held at prominent points in the State to speak the true words to the guileless buck and keep him in the narrow path (*The Elko Independent,* In Dangberg 1968:33).

WEE-VOO-KAH IN DISGRACE — Johnson Sides, the great Indian peace maker, says that on the 15th instant a Pawnee Indian in the service of the Indian Bureau, arrived here on his way to Walker lake to see Jack Wilson, the Messiah, whose Indian name is Wee-Voo-Kah, though sometimes called Co-Hee-Jow. Johnson Sides accompanied the Pawnee to Mason valley where they met Wee-Voo-Kah. Johnson said to Wee-Voo-Kah: 'This Indian come heap long way to see you. He like to shake hands with you.' Wee-Voo-Kah would not speak, neither would he shake hands with nor look at the stranger. The Pawnee put five silver dollars on Wee-Voo-Kah's hand, still he would not speak. Then he put five more silver dollars in his hand, but Wee-Voo-Kah kept silent. The Pawnee put the money on the ground, took out his peace pipe and passed it around. All smoked except Wee-Voo-Kah, who said, 'You Indians come from far away to kill me by witchcraft.' He then mounted his pony and galloped away toward Pine Grove. The other Indians took the money and gave it back to the Pawnee, who said Wee-Voh-Kah was no good and not worth noticing, though it made him feel bad to be treated so by him. Johnson then told the Indians that they were not to blame for what Wee-Voh-Kah did and that they must treat their Pawnee friend with consideration. He advised them to pay no attention to Wee-Voo-Kah who had been tormenting them for eight years, as he gives them no protection and they should not bother with him more.

The Pawnee told the whites that the Indians east of the Rocky Mountains had heard much of Wee-Voo-Kah. They thought he was a great man endowed with the spirit of prophecy, and at the request of the Indians the Government had commissioned him to visit Wee-Voo-Kah. He was now satisfied that he was a false prophet and did not amount to anything, and he so would tell his people when he returned home (*The Reno Journal,* reprinted *The Elko Independent* 8/22/94, In Dangberg 1968:33-34).

1904

The first of this week three prominent Arapahoe Indian arrived here from Oklahoma and continued on up to Pinegrove to consult Jack Wilson, the Piute Messiah, in regard to the supposed close approach of resurrection day, when all the departed members of the various Indian tribes are expected to return from the Happy Hunting Grounds. Just when the red brothers have arranged to have this event take place the paleface reporter wotteth not and the visitors were very reticent about the matter (*Lyon County Times* 2/20/04).

The Piutes have been having a big fandango at the camp below town this week. Many of the white people have attended during the evenings (*Lyon County Times* 6/11/04).

1906

SIOUX VISITORS — Three quite noted Sioux Indians paid Mason Valley a visit the first of this week. Their names were Cloud Horse, Chasing Hawk and Bear-Comes-Out, all from the Rosebud Agency in South Dakota, and their object here was to see Jack Wilson, the Indian prophet, on some important business. Captain Dave accompanied the three Sioux from Reno. They are large, good looking Indians, seemingly intelligent, but stoical and reserved. They held a pow-wow at the Indian camp above Bovard's Sunday night, talked with Jack Wilson and smoked the pipe of peace all round. They made Wilson a present of a beautifully carved stone pipe, and, having accomplished their end, just what, was not made clear to us, left for their homes Monday morning (*Lyon County Times* 8/04/06).

1912

LABOR DAY — The committee in charge for Labor Day has made arrangements with Jack Wilson, the Indian Messiah, for a War Dance on the evening of the day. A number of athletic young braves bare-limbed and painted with yellow and white and other rainbow hues arranged in feathers will give the grand kow-tow (*Yerington Times* 8/24/12).

1914

INDIAN BRAVES TO VISIT CHIEF — OCTOGENARIAN ARAPAHO WARRIORS IN RENO EN ROUTE TO SALUTE "MESSIAH" — RECALL EXCITING DAYS — JACK WILSON, "WAVOKA" OF HISTORY, STILL LIVING IN MASON VALLEY —

Indian memory of the days of the "Messiah" has not yet been banished from the reservations of the middle west. This was made picturesquely apparent in Reno yesterday by the arrival of Chief Heap of Crows, and Medicine Man Woods Old Bear, of the Arapahoes, from their reservation in Oklahoma on a pilgramabe [sic] to Mason Valley for a conference there with Wavoka, known to the whites as Jack Wilson, but remembered by Indians the country over as their "Messiah" of 1889.

Heap of Crows and oWods [sic] Old Bear, who are accompanied by an interpreter, both show the marks of eighty years and countless ghost dances — the wierd ceremony with which the revelations of the Phophet [sic] Messiah were celebrated when the excitement was at his height. Both are still the blanket Indians of the plains, and both the chief and the medicine man traveled the trail to Mason valley once before—in 1890—coming at that time to secure for their tribes the blessing of the "Messenger of the Red Men's God" preparatory to the participation of the Cheyenne and Arapahoes in the Indian wars that culminated in the massacre of Wounded Knee and the capture of Sitting Bull.

This time the mission of the ancient Indians is of a more peaceable nature. With an interpreter, Rudolph Left Hand, a graduate of the Indian school at Haksell, they are on their way merely to say a reminiscent "how" to the Messiah of other days, to talk over with him their memories of the stirring events that his prophecies and his ghost dance caused—events in which Heap of Crows and Woods Old Bear, according to the Indian records at Washington took full part in the enthusiasms of their youth when the doctrine of the Messiah was young.

The travelers came into Reno yesterday with the proverbial "quietness" of the trekking Red Man. Their former pilgrimage across the trail was made on horseback, in blankets, and with pigments handy for a hasty assumption of the war paint should emergency demand. This time they came in a tourist sleeper, in white man's clothes, and a roll of hundred dollar bills in place of the war paint pigments. For with the passing of the "Messiah" the Arapahoes turned to cultivation of the land given them by the government, and today the elder members of the tribe have achieved the best and distinction that comes with being landed proprietors who can lease their fertile acres to the despised "whites" and accumulate their quarterly income of rent.

The interpreter with the party, more used to city streets than his companions, found his way to the office of the Indian agent, C. H. Asbury, but it took considerable permission for the old chiefs to agree to pay a visit to the "white chief" in response to the latter's invitation. They finally consented, however, and commissioned Agent Asbury to send a "how" from them to the Indian agent at the Cheyenne reservation, with a report of their well being and the progress of their pilgrimage.

Until the coming of this party of Oklahoma to pay a visit to Jack Wilson—whom the old chiefs want to see once more before they died—the very existence of the "Messiah" had been forgotten, even at Washington, where there is a bloody record of deeds on the plains inspired by his sudden announcement, in 1888, that he "had gone to heaven when the sun died' and brought down for his people a message from God that soon there would be no more whites on earth and that all the land would blossom only for "good" Indians. But among the tribes which took such stirring part in the activities of Short Bull, Turning Hawk, Kicking Bear and Sitting Bull, Wavoka, the prophet still is revered and news of his welfare frequently passed about in council. In the meantime, Jack Wilson, "Wavoka," in the flesh, but little burdened with his years and the knowledge of the deviltry he caused, is making hay and plowing the ground on the same ranches in Mason Valley from which he stepped overnight into fame as the saviour of the red man. He mingles freely with his brothers but he charges several photographers who remember his existence and appear with a camera, three dollars for a sitting, and those who would hear a talk or two of his early experiences must pay the wily Lo at least five of the white man's dollars before he will grow the least reminiscent.

One of the mementoes of the Messiah days, and a remembrance of their first pilgrimage, bought by Heap Old Crows and Woods Old Bear, is a frayed, blood stained shirt, which was given them with a blessing by the Messiah, upon the occasion of their former visit. The shirt is similar to those carried away by all other chiefs who came out in 1889 and 1900 for the prophet's blessing and is supposed to be—or was—impervious to the bullets of the white man. That the blessing of the Messiah sometimes failed to stop a determined missile of lead, is made manifest by more than one powder stained hole in the relic brought by the Arapahoe chiefs.

The visitors, one of whom, Woods Old Bear, is almost blind, left last night for Wabuska, where they will change cars for the last stage of their journey to Mason

Valley. They will remain with Jack Wilson but a few days as both are due on their reservation September 15th, when the Arapahoes will celebrate their great sun dance. At this celebration Chief Heap of Crows will deliver whatever message Wavoka deigns to send the tribe, and will tell of their experiences on the trips into the west (*Nevada State Journal* 9/1/14).

1916

Jack Wilson to visit the East to see President Wilson to terminate the murderous war in Europe. He was once sent $200 by Oklahoma Indians to visit (*Mason Valley News* 3/9/16).

1926

Jack Wilson, the venerable Indian chief of the Piute tribe, is planning on getting the Indians together over the Fourth when there will be a large number in Yerington, and holding a dance, Saturday evening. Word has been sent out to the members of the tribe and unless plans go astray the dance will be held at the cottonwoods at the same time the white folks are attending the Legion dance at the Rink. If the dance is staged it will be quite an attraction to the regular Fourth program should provide an interesting sight to spectators (*Mason Valley News* 7/3/26).

Additional Newspaper Accounts

1890

A delegation of Cheyenne Indians from Oklahoma came to interview Jack Wilson, the Paiute prophet. One of them is a school teacher, and well informed (*White Pine News* 12/20/90).

1892

A letter from Henry Prescher to Whites, telling them that the (Shoshone?) Indians "do not believe in the Ghost Dance" (*Elko Independent* 3/5/92).

An Indian ghost dance, under the direction of Jack Wilson, the Messiah, is being indulged in at Pine Grove this week. Delegations of warriors from tribes east of the great divide are present (*White Pine News* 11/3/92).

1912

INDIAN BRAVES TO VISIT CHIEF

This man [Wovoka, according to J. T. Reid], as well as some chiefs had been in Lovelock to see Sarah Winnemucca Hopkins and Natches, her brother, in the 80s. "I recall seeing them talk on the railroad platform, also smoking 'Pipe of Peace'" (*Nevada State Journal* 9/1/14).

Appendix E

Government Letters and Reports

(1) 18 February 1890, J. O. Gregory, Farmer-In-Charge of the Walker River Reservation to S. S. Sears, U.S. Indian Agent at Wadsworth (Federal Archives, San Bruno, California):

...you will doubtless be amazed at the letter you will have received from Jack Wilson the prophet when this reaches you he has got the indians all wild at his wonderful command of the elements he claims that he alone is responsible for the storms of this season and they all firmly believe it. The letter he has written as he supposes to Washington is for the purpose of finding out if the government believes in him as a prophet. There was at least 200 Indians to say nothing of the squaws and papooses turned out yesterday in the face of a driving snow storm to see and hear him they took up quite a collection for his benefit fully $25 and they talk of nothing but Jack Wilson and the miracles he performs he would like to be allowed to come onto the Reservation to farm and guarantees the Indians that if the Government gives him permission to come he will cause lots of rain to fall and they will never lose a crop again. They are expecting a reply to his letter and if you see fit to answer as in your judgement would be proper (In Johnson 1975:48).

(2) 17 November 1890, Agent S. S. Sears of Pyramid Agency to Hon. T. J. Morgan, Commissioner of Indian Affairs, Washington, D.C. Letters Received, GD# 36400, RG 75 (Federal Archives, San Bruno, California):

Sir.

Office letter #32876, Nov 7, 1890, enclosing copy of letter from Hon. Secretary of War instructs me to warn Pan-a-mite and all other Pah-Ute Indians who engage in Medicine dances or other senseless and evil practices to descate [sic] and if possible, to enforce obedience.

According to Wallapai Charley of Kingman, Arizona, Pan-a-mite is a Piute of St. George, Utah of whom I never heard and who is many miles beyond the boundary of my official jurisdiction. A peaceable, industrious, but lunatic Pah-Ute aged about 40 years who lives in Mason Valley, this state, and works for the ranchers there, has attracted many Indians from abroad, the fame of his preachings expanding in the ratio of distance from point of delivery. He proclaimed himself an aboriginal Jesus who was to redeem the Red Man, also a prophet and worker of miracles, but so far as I could learn, neither his preaching or prophecies were of an incendiary nature, being held in this section to be as harmless as foolish—some of his utterances may have excited the superstitious of some the wilder tribes, but their effect upon the Indians of this Agency, is not noticeable. I have talked with Agency Indians a number of times about this man, assuring them that he is crazy and I think they now believe that statement to be true, as none of his prophecies have materialized though many of them long since matured.

The fact is the Indians of Nevada have generally profited by the advent of the whites and they are sufficiently advanced to recognize that fact. They also appreciate the power of the government and their own comparative helplessness, so that the danger of any general uprising among them is reduced to a minimum. Of the various wild alarms which have spread abroad in consequence of alleged outrages and depredations of Nevada Indians during the past thirty years, I can recall but one instance in which the principle (and generally the only element) was not mere "sound and fury," and that was in 1861; a battle being fought close to the ground now occupied by these headquarters; the whites being the assailants and the Indians the victors, though many were killed and wounded on either side.

Should I discover any action on the part of Agency Indians calculated to disturb the friendly relations between Indians and whites, or between tribes, the full extent of my official authority will be reached, if necessary, in the effort to suppress the same.

(3) 24 November 1890, John Mayhugh, ex-BIA official to Hon. T. J. Morgan, Comm. of Indian Affairs, Letters Received, GD #36853, RG 75 (Federal Archives, San Bruno, California):

Sir.

I have the honor to address you this communication in the best interest of the Indians and further from the fact I have noticed in quite a number of newspapers of the day statements in relation to the present semi-religious Indian excitement as to the coming of the Indian's messiah and the present residence of the Prophet—and the point where the Messiah is to appear.

While Special Census Agent of the Indians for Nevada I learned of the whereabouts of this Prophet—and I deem it not inappropriate for me to address your Hon. Office upon this and state briefly a few facts that came under my observation. First—It is true that most of the Indians are believers in the coming of the Messiah early spring. The Prophet resides in Mason Valley, Esmeralda County, Nevada close to the Walker River Reservation—his name is not Johnson Sides at Reno but Captain Jack Wilson known among all Indians by the Indian names of We-vo-kai and Co-we-jo an intelligent fine looking Indian of about 35 years of age who goes into trances or seemingly so from 12 to 14 hours in presence of large numbers of Indians upon invitation of Prophet—upon his recovery he relates to them what he has seen. He tells them he has been to heaven and that the Messiah is coming to earth again and will put the Indians in possession of the country—that he has seen in heaven a heap of Indians some of which are dressed in white man's clothes—he counsels the Indians not to disturb the White Folks saying that the blanket—or Rabbit skin that was put over the moon by the Indians long ago will soon fall off and then the moon which is now on fire will destroy the whites. The Messiah is to appear on Mount Grant which is a very large mountain and is estimated about 16 miles south of the Walker River Agency buildings and on the west side of the Lake. Here is where the first Indians appeared according to their belief. I visited this mountain last September in performance of my duty as Special Census Agent of Indians. This mountain is held as a sacred mountain to the Indians and on top they allege they can see foot prints of the first Father Numenna if I may be permitted to suggest I would recommend that all the Indians be permitted to visit this mountain as I am satisfied they will only send delegations from each tribe for the purpose of ascertaining the truth of the Prophesy the Indians of Nevada expect delegations from most of the tribes north and northeast—and Sitting Bull is expected. The only fear the Nevada Indians have is that the government will interfere with troops. I think if the Indians are let alone on the various agencies the whole thing will die away. All of the Indians here do not believe in the Prophet although Josephus the chief at Walker Lake thinks maybe so Co-we-jo is a prophet for the reason that he went twice to this Prophet to consult about water as it had no rain and Walker River nearly dry up and upon each occasion the Prophet predicted rain which really came and saved their crops hence their belief in this Prophet.

Capt. Dave of the Nevada Agency and Jo-sephus of Walker River are better posted upon this Indian craze than any other Indians in Nevada. They are truthful intelligent and reliable and would very much like to see their Big Chief the Commissioner. Capt. Dave was very anxious to see you at the time of your last visit to the Nevada Agency in Nevada but he never knew of your coming until you had gone as Agent Sears did not tell of your presence. Outside of their present religious craze these Indians could give your office a great deal of information the way things are managed at the Nevada and Walker River Agencies that are not always learned by US Inspectors of a few days visit no odds how good and vigilant the Inspector may be. Would it not be a good idea to endeavour to get this Prophet Co-we-jo with these Indians to visit Washington it might have a tendency to quiet this craze, if the visit is held out to them as one of business not relating to the excitement or to interfere with his prophecies.

(4) 29 November 1890, C. C. Warner, U.S. Indian Agent, Nevada Agency to Hon. Comm. of Indian Affairs, Washington, D.C., Letters Received, GD #37260, RG 75 (Federal Archives, San Bruno, California):

Sir.

Noticing from reports to your Dept. as also to Gen'l Miles that they (the reports) seem to be entirely erroneous, as to the "Original Messiah"—creating so much disturbance. I presume to address you believing that I have arrived at the true origin.

I have lived in Nevada 28 years—have been familiar with all Nevada Indians and while an officer of Volunteers fought them. The originator of all this trouble is a Pah-Ute by the name of Jack Wilson who is now near the Walker Lake Reserve.

It has been reported to Gen'l Miles by someone at Los Angeles that Johnson Sides (a Pah-Ute on this Agency) was the Messiah and that he had been seen at or near the Rosebud Agency, passing as such. I have for years known Sides and he has never been far away from the Pyramid Agency and I have seen him almost daily, and today, for the past month or more.

And further the cause of all the trouble among the Cheyennes, Kiowas, Pawnees,

Arapahoes, and other Indians I believe to be caused by a visit of 34 Indians containing representatives from most of these and the effected tribes, which visit was made to this fellow Jack Wilson about Apr. or May last. I saw the delegation while en route and know that they did pay this visit—had dances, etc.—and I recognized among them some Bannocks.

I expect within a few days to go to the Walker Lake Reservation when I will see and talk with this man Jack Wilson and those of his followers for he has some among the Walker Indians when I can give you further information will do so.

I have a plan which I believe will effecually [sic] break up and stop the whole trouble with light expense and without army assistance. And my plan is indorsed [sic] by intelligent Pah-Utes who are most decidedly against the whole fanaticism. I have the honor to be -

(5) 1 January 1891, John S. Mayhugh, Elko, Nevada to His Excellency Benjamin Harrison, President of the United States Washington, D.C., Letters Received, RG 75 (Federal Archives, San Bruno, California):

Dear Sir:

I have the honor to address you in view of the present troubled condition of the Indians of Nevada and elsewhere. While the Indians of Nevada both in and off the Reservations seem to be peaceable upon the surface yet there is a great deal of uneasiness and an unusual number of dances—this has been caused more or less by visiting delegations of Indians from several tribes, particular Fort Hall—I think a little timely diplomacy among the Indians of Nevada (and adjoining Territory, Utah also Fort Hall) — they might be kept from joining hostile tribes in any uprising among the whites or amongst themselves. Resident Indian Agents have not sufficient influence over their particular if they dislike them and the average Indian looks upon an Indian Agent as a kind of go between them and the Government.

While I was Special U.S. Census Agent for Indians of Nevada last summer and fall I found a great deal of dissatisfaction among the Indians at the three Reservations all of which facts are reported by me to the Census office and I presume they found their way to the Indian Office and are there on file. These communications were separate and apart from the Census taken by me and were not entered in the Census Book. These communications I most respectfully refer you to as they show their condition and doubtless have had a great deal to do in causing their present uneasiness.

I have resided in this State for 30 odd years and have been among the Indians more or less the entire time. I think I am not saying too much when I say, I think there is hardly an adult Indian in the State of Nevada but what knows me, either personally or by reputation and I believe I have more influence over them than any one individual in Nevada, as I have been always their friend in and out-of-office. I was U.S. Indian Agent at Western Shoshone Agency, Nevada, my term of office expiring during President Cleveland's administration.

Believing I can be of service to the Government and the Indians during this present crisis I most respectfully request that I be appointed U.S. Special Indian Agent or U.S. Inspector (during the present trouble) for Nevada and adjoining Territories for the purpose of visiting the Indians both in and off the Reservations— hold talks with them and point out to them that the interests, and welfare of their people will be best served by them, remaining true and faithful to the Government and by discountencing [sic] all dances and hostile movements, etc.

I have had Indian messengers from Fort Hall visit me some time in October saying Major George, Big Jim and other headmen wished me to come and have a talk with them on some very important business but as a matter of course I did not go not having any official authority. I am well acquainted with quite a large number of the headmen. I have since learned they wished to talk to me about the Messiah craze as they knew I had been to Walker Lake and knew all about Cowejo, the Indian Prophet, and had been at their sacred mountain known as Mount Grant.

I have the honor at present to hold a Commission from you as Special Agent of Allotment of lands to Indians. Dated October 3rd 1890—but I have never been ordered to duty. I presume for the reason that the Indian Office has been too busy with the pending Indian difficulties—I therefore thought that in the meantime until the Indians were restored to their normal conditions that I might exercise the duties of U.S. Special Agent or Inspector for the purpose above mentioned after which I could take up the duties of my present appointment. Notwithstanding their present unsettled conditions, Indians visit me from the different parts of the State wishing to know if I am going to give them land soon.

All of which is respectfully submitted to your favorable consideration.

(6) 6 February 1891, C. C. Warner, U. S. Indian Agent to Hon. Commissioner of Indian Affairs, Letters Received, RG 75 (Federal Archives, San Bruno, California):

Sir:

I enclose you these clippings for your information. Showing how silly rumors are started here by people who should be more sensible—There is not the **slightest** foundation or cause for the scare as you will see an adjacent newspaper says— Hawthorne is but a few miles from the Walker River Reserve — Some foolish leaders thought they saw a chance to get a Military Post.

P.S. I go to the Walker River Reserve tomorrow., C. C. W.

(7) 17 August 1891, C. C. Warner, ARCIA 1891:298-305, Letters Received, RG 75 (Federal Archives, San Bruno, California):

The Messiah—In conclusion I desire to call your attention to the so-called Messiah. The originator of this craze is one of my Pah-Ute Indians. His name is Jack Wilson, and like all such cranks he is a fraud, but a pretty smart fellow. He achieved his notoriety by telling the Indians that he would invoke the Great Spirit and bring rain (after there had been two years of drouth [sic]), and it so happened that his promised invocation was in the commencement of our severe winter of 1889-1890, during which time it stormed almost incessantly from October to April. His success was rapidly spread abroad, and from that time on he has had many followers. Many Indians from distant tribes have been here and are now visiting him, and from eighty to a hundred been to see him during the past six months. They generally pass through these headquarters, and usually come with letters from their respective agents accrediting them. These visits do no good, and I would suggest caution in agents giving such letters. This is the whole story of the Messiah craze in a nut-shell.

(8) 19 August 1891, C. C. Warner to First Lieut. Johnson at Fort Hall Agency, Letters Received, GD #33874, RG 75 (Federal Archives, San Bruno, California):

Jack Wilson, the so-called "Messiah," is a Pah-Ute Indian, but does not live on the reservation, and of course I have no jurisdiction over him or other Indians from various agencies who visit him, without special authority....

About two weeks ago the Indians in this vicinity did have a big dance in Wadsworth but it is nothing unusual for them to have their dances at this time of the year. The Indians in this vicinity were all preparing to go to California to pick hops, and had this dance in honor of their departure. They had a general "round up" as it were.

These Indians always have dances just before and after harvest, and therefore no significance is attached to them.

(9) C. C. Warner, U.S. Indian Agent to S. G. Fisher, U.S. Indian Agent, Letters Received, G.D. #33874, RG 75 (Federal Archives, San Bruno, California):

Sir:

Your letter of the 13th instant, inquiring about Casper Edsen, Little Raven and Red Wolf, duly received. In reply will state that these Indians arrived here on the 1st instant and stopped with Capt. Dave, chief of my police, for one day only. Casper Edsen, the interpreter, told me that they were on a kind of vacation, and simply wanted to see this section of the country. He appeared to be quite intelligent and spoke the English language fluently; and upon the strength of your recommendation I gave them pass-ports to Walker River reserve; also recommended them to the Div. Supt. of the C.P.R.P for passes back to Ogden.

I have since learned that their sole mission was to visit the "Messiah," and if I had known this in the beginning would not have permitted them to go to Walker River reserve, or at least would not have given them any recommendations. Jack Wilson, the so-called "Messiah," is a Pah-Ute Indian, but does not live on the reservation, and of course I have no jurisdiction over him or other Indians from various agencies who visit him, without special authority.

In my opinion these visits do no good, and I think it would be best for all concerned if the agents of distant tribes would curtail this visiting privilege, or better still abolish it altogether, except in very extreme and extenuating circumstances.

About two weeks ago the Indians in this vicinity did have a big dance in Wadsworth, but it is nothing unusual for them to have their dances at this time of the year. The Indians in this vicinity were all preparing to go to California to pick hops, and had this dance in honor of their departure. They had a general "round up" as it were.

These Indians always have dances just before and after harvest, and therefore no significance is attached to them.

I remain,

(10) 5 September 1891, Frank Campbell, American Falls, to Hon. Commissioner Indian Affairs, Washington, D.C., Letters Received, RG 75 (Federal Archives, San Bruno, California):

Dear Sir -

There is no doubt but that the Messiah Craze has its headquarters at Walker River Indian Reserve Nev. The cause of its spreading so generally among Indians is the hope that these people have that some power greater than themselves may arrest and crush the oncoming flood of civilization that is destined soon to overwhelm them. Should the excitement become active again among tribes east of the Rocky Mts I would advise that delegations be forwarded to Walker Lake Reserve to see for themselves. Sitting Bull requested some office to accompany him in a search for the New Messiah—Had the situation been understood and his request granted no doubt good would have come of it. I was resident Farmer and Indian Agent upon the Walker River Reserve from 1862 to 1872 but since then have not been among those Indians.

(11) 12 October 1891, C. C. Warner, United States Indian Agent, Pyramid Lake Nevada Agency to James Mooney, Esq., Bureau of Ethnology, Letters Received, RG 75 (Federal Archives, San Bruno, California):

My Dear Sir: Your letter of September 24 in regard to Jack Wilson, the "Messiah," at hand and duly noted. In reply will say that his Indian name is Ko-wee-jow ("Big Belly"). I do not know as it will be possible to get a photo of him. I never saw him or a photo of him. He works among the whites about 40 miles from my Walker Lake reserve, and never comes near the agency when I visit it. My headquarters are at Pyramid lake, about 70 miles north of Walker. I am pursuing the course with him of nonattention or silent ignoring. He seems to think, so I hear, that I will arrest him should he come within my reach. I would give him no such notoriety. He, like all other prophets, has but little honor in his own country. He has been visited by delegations from various and many Indian tribes, which I think should be discouraged all that is possible. Don't know what the "Smoholler" religion, you speak of, is. He speaks English well, but is not educated. He got his doctrine in part from contact, living in and with a religious family. There are neither ghost songs, dances nor ceremonials among them about my agencies. Would not be allowed. I think they died out with "Sitting Bull." This is the extent of the information I can give you,

(12) 27 August 1892, C. C. Warner to ARCIA 1892:319-28, Letters Received, RG 75 (Federal Archives, San Bruno, California):

The Pah-Utes both on and off the reservation have been quiet, tractable, obedient and industrious. The white settlers in this section of the country depend almost entirely upon Indian labor, and the Indians are fast becoming proficient in farming and stock raising.

The Messiah craze—I am happy to report this craze as having almost subsided in its cradle.

(13) 5 December 1892, C. C. Warner to ARCIA, Letters Received, G.D. #44805, RG 75 (Federal Archives, San Bruno, California):

Sir.

from newspaper and other sources of information I sometime since became suspicious that the "Messiah" Jack Wilson was using an evil influence among foreign Indians which might result in a spring uprising among the Indians, his influence among my Indians does no harm but I was fearful of its results abroad. Hence I sent to my farmer in charge at Walker River to get at the real existing facts and report them to me that I might advise you should there be any danger from this source. The enclosed is a copy of his report:

(14) 22 November 1892, N. Hammond, Farmer-In-Charge of the Walker River Reservation to C. C. Warner, U. S. Indian Agent, Letters Received, RG 75 (Federal Archives, San Bruno, California):

Sir:

In the case of Jack Wilson, the "Messiah," I have made a thorough investigation and find there is nothing in the rumor of the Messiah and his followers holding holding [sic] "Ghost dances" in this section. I have investigated the matter closely. Jack Wilson is now in Mason valley about 40 miles from here on a rabbit hunt and seemingly happy, he advises his people to be good, and do nothing to offend the whites as the whites are their friends and they cannot get along without them as they give them plenty of work and pay them money for their labor. There have been several delegations from Eastern tribes to interview the "Messiah," some are pleased and some are not. He is not pleased with their visits and does not advocate "Ghost dances" here or among other tribes. These Indians have a big dance or pow wow (such as I have indorsed as being harmless—C.C.W.) two of three times a year lasting four or five days and are pleasant and harmless. I have attended several and see no harm in them. They are not on the "war-path" and do not want to fight but want peace at all times. You can rely on what I have written as facts. The "Messiah" was raised in Mason Valley and Pine Grove where he has worked most of his life for David Wilson, an extensive rancher and from whom the "Messiah" took the name of Wilson. Should you desire any further information please let me know or I refer you to Edwin Dyer or to David or George Wilson of Mason Valley. They are reliable men and well acquainted with the Messiah and his habits.

Shall keep myself posted in the matter and should there be any changes will advise you at once.

(15) 21 August 1893, C. C. Warner to the ARCIA 1893:206-11, Letters Received, RG 75, Federal Archives, San Bruno, California):

The Ghost Dance is "fanaticism is a thing of the past." The strongest weapon to be used against the movement is "ridicule."

(16) 25 May 1912, Letter from Assistant Commissioner of the BIA Abbot to Mr. C. H. Asbury, Special Agent to Nevada Indians, 811 South Virginia Street, Reno, Nevada (Inter-Tribal Council of Nevada Archives, Reno):

Sir:

Enclosed herewith is a clipping from which you will see that it is alleged that the Nevada Indians are reviving the ghost dance. Please give the Office the benefit of any information you may have on this subject, returning the enclosed clipping with your report.

(17) 4 June 1912, C. S. Asbury, Indian Agent, Reno, Nevada to Superintendent S. W. Pugh, Schurz, Nevada (Inter-Tribal Council of Nevada Archives, Reno):

Dear Sir:

I have a letter from the Office dated May 25th in which a clipping is enclosed from some Eastern paper in which it is alleged that the Piutes in Nevada are reviving the ghost dance that caused so much disturbance among the Indians over twenty years ago, requesting me to report any information I have or can secure on this subject.

I feel convinced that this is a pipe dream, but in order to make an authentic report I would like to have you inquire among your Indians and write me at your earliest convenience.

(18) 7 June 1912, S. W. Pugh. Superintendent, Walker River School, Schurz, Nevada, to Spl. Agt. C. H. Asbury, Reno, Nev. (Inter-Tribal Council of Nevada Archives, Reno):

Dear Sir:

I have your letters of the 4th instant. I have talked with two different Indians who ought to know regarding the reported revival of the Ghost Dance and I am satisfied there is nothing in the report at all. I have no doubt some would like to revive it but do not think they would attempt it.

Lats [sic] spring they had a dance at Mason which was such a rotten affair that I refused to allow them to follow it with a dance here, so we have had none of the reservation for two years. Am planning to allow them to have one this fall in connection with a fair, but unless it is a vasy [sic] improvement over any they have ever had in the past 15 years it will be the last one while I remain here. I informed both Jack Wilson and Tom Mitchell after the one last spring that there would be no more in Mason valley without first obtaining my consent.

Now I would be glad if your would take advantage of this opportunity, if it suits your convictions, to express yourself regarding their regular dances and the medicine men.

According to my lights, after 15 years of studying the matter of the main evils affecting these Piutes, I would rate their importance as follows:

Much money is being well spent fighting the liquor problem, but it is the least harmful of all. Opium is doing much more damage, with insufficient law covering the traffic, apparently. U.S. Commissioner Fairbanks, at Yerington, turned down a case for us last Monday, and I cant conceive of a way to make a case any stronger.

As bad as the the [sic] Ghost Dance was (and it should not be permitted), it was never as powerful to these Piutes as either their customary dance or the medicine man, both of which continue without interference so far as the Department is concerned, probably because they think they have some resigious [sic] significance. This is no longer true of the dance.

The only power the medicine men claim to have is of supernatural, but when this type is without exception the most worthless and vicious of the tribe it needs no discussion or recognition.

There is this difference between the ghost dance and their regular dance: the former was a spiritual perversion absolutely, while the latter has completely lost whatever religious features it ever had (unless possibly to a very few of the very old), while it is morally rotten from alpha to omega and is the finest breeder of tuberculosis conceivable. If either dance has any claim to tolerance because of spiritual association it is the ghost dance, though I certainly don't recommend it.

If the Department or the Eastern Indian Lovers want to do something really great along this line let them go after the medicine men and their regular dance. The rest will be easy.

(19) 8 June 1912, Special Indian Agent C. H. Asbury to Commissioner Indian Affairs, Washington, D.C. (Inter-Tribal Council of Nevada Archives, Reno):

Sir:

Upon receipt of the above letter of May 25th, I wrote to the Superintendent at Walker River Reservation who has charge of the Valley where Jack Wilson lives, and is in better position to know the truth of the alleged ghost dance than any other person. I also wrote to Superintendent Oliver at Pyramid Lake, who is in close touch with and has the confidence of the Piute Indians there. I have also been among the Piute Indians in this Section continuously and feel convinced that there was no foundation to this report. I am now in receipt of letters from both Superintendent Pugh and Oliver, denying the existence of such dance.

Superintendent Pugh takes occasion in his reply to call attention to the very demoralizing influences of the social dance that has been indulged in by the Indians on his reservation and the adjacent valley, saying that he has forbidden the dance on the reservation for some time past, and now being in charge of the valleys above he will endeavor to prevent the dance there, unless a decided reform is made in their management. He holds that their dance at present has no religious significance, but is made the occasion for the most immoral and degrading practices.

I will continue to make inquiries regarding the ghost dance, and should anything of interest be learned I will make further report.

It may be of interest to the Office to know that Jack Wilson is still held in reverence by Indians in various parts of the country, and he is still regarded by them as a great medicine man. Just a few weeks ago when the Wild West show carrying Indians from various places made a stand here, I met an old man and his son from the Cheyenne Reservation who were waiting for the train at the Station to go out to see Jack Wilson for a day and overtake the show a day or two later.

I return clipping herewith,

(20) 1912 Letter of Indian Agent S. W. Pugh to the Commissioner of Indian Affairs (In Forbes 1967:176-77):

Jack Wilson, who will be remembered as the "Messiah" who originated the "Ghost Dance" craze about 25 years ago, which spread to Indians all over the West and Middle States, lives in Mason Valley and is subject to this Reservation. He has been wanting for some time to come to this Reservation to live and I would like to have him as he is still a power among his people and could be used to excellent advantage if here. He is a very intelligent Indian, and peaceably inclined apparently, but has some propensities that could be turned to better advantage under environments on the Reservation. These people will follow him anywhere, and he has advanced ideas which, as stated above, could be turned into valuable aid if located here, whereas, in his present environment, influenced by some other Indians with vicious tendencies, and with some whites with no laudable ambitions with regard to Indians, his leadership is more or less perverted.

He and a few of his following came over here on February 1st and they were here several days and came in to see me about land matters. I tride [sic] to show them that all available agricultural land was alloted, but they insisted that there was still land unallotted near the north end of the Reservation. But to satisfy them I agreed to go to the place with them. So we appointed February 8th as a day to meet there. The land in question is about 15 miles from the Agency, but on the Reservation, I took the map and showed them the corners &c. There were about thirty of them, all from Mason Valley. Then they insisted that I gave them allotments there anyway. Each wanted 40 acres to the head of the family. Even Jack Wilson, with his superior intelligence, and with very friendly feelings toward me, could not see why I could not issue them the deed allotments anyway. So you can see what simplemindedness I have to contend with. I explained to them that so far as I knew the only transfer of land an Indian could make was to a child of his who had not allotment. Otherwise, the only course that could be pursued would be for an allottee, if living, of his heirs, if allottee was dead, to relinquish their title and then it could be done, and that a number would prefer to do that, in the interest of their own people, rather than have it sold to whites.

(21) 31 August 1914, C. H. Asbury, Special Indian Agent to Supt. Wm. H. Wisdom, Cantonment, Okla. (Inter-Tribal Council of Nevada Archives, Reno):

Dear Sir;

Three of your wards have just called at my office en route to visit the Masiah [sic] of twenty od [sic] years ago to pay their respects to him and possibly to get some inside information on the old "Ghost Dance." The interpreter, Left Hand, called first to inquire the way to find Wilson and we asked him to bring the other men, "Heep-o-Crow" and "Woods" up to the office. We had a pleasant visit with them and they asked that I write you to tell you that they were getting along well and would start right back home from here after visiting a few days with Jack Wilson, the profit [sic].

A newspaper man discovered them and will have a story about them in the morning. I will enclose a copy though it may be embellished somewhat as things have to be made readable.

(22) 3 September 1914, C. H. Asbury, Special Indian Agent to The Commissioner of Indian Affairs, Washington, D.C. (Inter-Tribal Council of Nevada Archives, Reno):

Sir; -
    I enclose herewith a clipping which may be of interest to the Office as showing that the influence of Jack Wilson the "Messiah" of twenty five years ago is not dead. The news paper report is somewhat colored but they had to fill space.
    These Indians came through here on their return last night going directly home though they had tickets to San Francisco and return and I suggested they should not miss the good opportunity to visit the coast but they seemed to think they did not want to get further from home.
    They mention a ceremonial dance that is to be held the 15th of this month, some form of the old Sun dance. They expressed some intention of having the old Ghost Dance in connection with the meeting already planned.
    So far as I could learn there is no special significance to the dance to be held but I have written to the Superintendent there along this line. Should this prove to be any thing requiring attention it may be well that I be not known as have give any information which would probably prevent my getting at another later time should the occasion arise.
    I am enclosing two small 'fotos of Jack Wilson which we happen to have.

(23) 3 Sept 1914, Special Indian Agent C. H. Asbury to Supt. Wm. H. Wisdom, Cantonment, Okla. (Inter-Tribal Council of Nevada Archives, Reno):

Dear Sir; -
    Your wards who have been visiting the Paiute Masiah [sic] started home, leaving here this morning at 1.35 and will probably reach home before this letter reaches you.
    We suggested to them that they go on to San Francisco as they had the tickets and the time and cost would be but little more but they were not interested in San Francisco and hastened back to carry the message from our famous fellow paiute.
    The agent here collected 50 cents per ticket as a validation fee which may be according to the rules but I see nothing in the contract on the ticket providing for such fee and do not believe it is right.
    It may be advisable to take this up with the selling road to recover the amount for them if possible. I am enclosing the receipt taken from the agent here.
    I understand that they expect to have a big ceremonial dance the middle of this month and may, at that time, indulge in the old Ghost dance that Jack may have taught them. We understand that they planned to have such dance.
    This may be of interest to you but as a matter of policy it will be as well for you not to give me as authority as it might prevent my getting such information in the future if occasion should arrise [sic].
    The Indians spoke kindly of you and seemed contented, and proud of their efforts at farming and use of their land.

(24) September 1914, Telegram of E. B. Merritt, Assistant Commissioner of BIA to Dr. Hubert Hailman, Superintendent of the Walker River Reservation (Inter-Tribal Council of Nevada Archives, Reno):

OFFICER ADVISED (TWO?) ARAPAHOE INDIANS FROM OKLAHOMA VISIT-ING JACK WILSON, GHOST DANCER AND MESSIAH, AND WILL HOLD DANCE TODAY. ADVISE OFFICE FULLY OF FACTS SURROUNDING DANCE AND WHETHER ATTEMPT IS BEING MADE TO REVIVE MESSIAH PROPAGANDA

(25) 16 Sept 1914, E. B. Merritt, Assistant Commissioner of BIA to Mr. Calvin H. Asbury Special Agent, Education #97301 (Inter-Tribal Council of Nevada Archives, Reno):

Mr dear Mr. Asbury:

The receipt is acknowledged of your letter of September 3, 1914, enclosing a clipping and certain photographs, and reporting upon the revival to a certain extent of the influence of Jack Wilson, the "Messiah" of twenty-five years ago, and the ghost dance. You mention the trip to Reno of two Arapaho Indians of Oklahoma to visit Jack Wilson in Mason Valley.

The Office gathers from your report that there is no necessity for any official action in regard to the visit of these Indians, at least at this time. It suggests, however, that you ascertain, if practicable, the nature of the dance held by these old Indians on the 15th of September and advise the Office generally of the circumstances concerning the same, together with any recommendation which you deem advisable.

If the dance is held with a view to the revival of the old ghost dance and "Messiah" craze throughout Indian tribes of the country you should promptly advise this Office in order that steps may be taken to counteract such a revival.

The matter will be taken up also with the Superintendent in charge of Walker River.

(26) 21 Sept 1914, Special Indian Agent C. H. Asbury to The Commissioner of Indian Affairs, Washington, D.C., Education #97310-14 "Referring to Jack Wilson and the Ghost Dance" (Inter-Council of Nevada Archives, Reno):

Sir:

Referring to Jack Wilson, the former "Messiah" and to the Ghost Dance, it is my opinion that there is no special attention necessary, at this time, but I wrote, believing that the Office would be interested to know that he still exercises an influence over distant Indians and that these visitors had or expressed their intention of having a dance at their home. The dance referred to, was to take place at Cantonment, Oklahoma, and I wrote to Supt. Wisdom along the same lines that I wrote to the Office; and if any special dance is held, or has been held, he will, no doubt, be in position to report particulars.

(27) 8 October 1914, Letter to Miss. L. Corwin, Stewart, Nevada (Inter-Tribal Council of Nevada Archives, Reno):

Dear Miss. Corwin:
Enclosed herewith please find two photo films of Jack Wilson which you loaned me for the official use of this office. I thank you for the same.

(28) 14 October 1914, Hubert V. Hailman, Supt. and C. D. Agent, Walker River School, Schurz, Nevada to Commissioner of Indian Affairs, Washington, D.C. (Inter-Tribal Council of Nevada Archives, Reno):

Sir: -
Replying to Office Telegram of September 13th and under above caption, where to say that this message came while I was away from the Reservation. I made as thorough an investigation as conditions here would permit and have been unable to learn of two Arapahoe Indians from Oklahoma visiting Jack Wilson, ghost dancer and Messiah. I sent the Judge of Indian courts to Yerington a few days after receiving this telegram and on his return he advised me that there had been two Navaho Indians visiting Jack Wilson; that these Navaho Indians presented Jack Wilson with beaded moccasins and gauntlet gloves and that these two Navaho Indians came to see Jack Wilson regularly about once every twelve months.
I am unable to learn of any attempt being made to revive the Messiah propaganda. I was advised by several Indians that a dance was held about or before the filing of your telegram and prior to the Indians starting into the mountains to gather pinenuts and that it is customary to hold this dance every year before the Indians go to gather pine nuts; and that dance is held as for luck. Aside from this dance I am unable to learn of any other being held in the Mason Valley or among the Paiute Indians under my supervision.

(29) 27 December 1914, Letter from G. W. Ingalls, The Continental Hotel, San Francisco, CA (Inter-Tribal Council of Nevada Archives, Reno):

My Dear Van,
I have been on my new book nearly a week and may be here until 1st.
Met several representatives of Eastern and Coast publishers—Tomorrow one of the largest of Boston's Educational firms—May I kindly ask you to give me the names of the 3 Indians who came from Oklahoma last summer with their interpreter from Carlisle or Haskell, Ka. Please give the date and name of the tribe and and [sic] of their superintendent and if you get word after their return if they had a Ghost Dance and how many days and how many engaged in it and what was the name of the Chief or medicine man who conducted it and if as Wevoca told me there were any Indians got married at the Ghost Dances and how long they lasted, i.e., how many days and if danced all night and day with usual or former excitement—If any photographs of the men or the dance on their return please loan me photo.
Wevoca told me he authorized I think 15 days and he gave them some feathers and paint and they brought him to me presents he did not say what....

(30) 28 December 1914, Letter to Major G. W. Ingalls, San Francisco, Calif. (Inter-Tribal Council of Nevada Archives, Reno):

Dear Sir:

In reply to your letter of December 27, 1914, will state that the names of the Indians, who made a pilgrimage to Jack Wilson, were: Heep-o-Crows, Woods and Rudolph Left Hand. They were of the Arapahoe tribe and the agency at that point is Cantonment Indian Agency, Cantonment, Oklahoma. The name of the superintendent is William H. Wisdom. Rudolph Left Hand was a Carlisle student. The Indians left Reno on September 2, 1914, on their return trip to the Agency. They were in Mason Valley about one week previous to that. We have no other information in this office, relative to this prilgrimage [sic] and I do not know what the result was on their return to their Agency. You can doubtless secure the information by writing to the Agency at that point, relative to the dance, that was held there and the number engaged in it and in the ceremonials that were held. Personally, I remember seeing some feathers and some paint, that Jack Wilson gave the Indians, as good medicine; other than this, I will not be able to give you any information.

I am glad that you are enjoying your trip to the city and hope that you are successful with the publication of your book,

(31) 2 May 1916, C. H. Asbury, Special Indian Agent to Col. S. E. Day, Carson City, Nevada, Written by his clerk, John Pohland (Inter-Tribal Council of Nevada Archives, Reno):

Dear Mr. Day:

Jack Wilson has been in the office upon two different occasions to complain that he is being deprived of the use of his land in Mason Valley, which was allotted to him about the time the railroad was built in that Valley. He alleges that he gave the papers to Bill Wilson to keep and that Bill claims that he had burned them up. The land in question, on which he says he has spent $475 in cash and considerable work, is now enclosed in the Wilson Ranch run by Archie Brown. My files fail to disclose any facts as stated above, but appear to show that there was some correspondence as to making efforts to secure a filing from Jack at a later date. He seems to think that you may know something about the matter and if so I would be glad to hear from you in the matter. If Jack has any rights that are being withheld from him, we certainly want to render him every assistance possible in recovering them.

(32) 2 May 1916, C. H. Asbury, Special Indian Agent, Reno, Nevada, to Mr. R. Dyer, Schurz, Nevada, Written by his clerk, John Pohland (Inter-Tribal Council of Nevada Archives, Reno):

Dear Sir:

Jack Wilson has been in the office upon two different occasion in the past six weeks to see about some land which he alleges was alloted to him. He claims that he received papers for the same and that he gave them to Bill Wilson to keep for him. Since then, he has asked Bill Wilson for these papers, but Bill says they have been lost or burned up. The Wilson estate is now being handled by Archie Brown, who has included in a fence the land claimed by Jack Wilson. Jack claims that he has spent $475 on that land. This land is located somewhere near Nordyke. He says that you are acquainted with the circumstances of his receiving the land. He will probably see you personally in a few days on this same matter. I have no date in my files as to this case and would be glad to have you write me fully as to any knowledge you may have of the matter. Mr. Asbury has been almost constantly in the field for the past seven or eight months and is now in Utah and Idaho, consequently I am looking into this matter in his absence. If Jack Wilson has any rights to land in Mason Valley and this land is being withheld from him, we desire to see that his rights are vindicated. He alleges that he received the papers and gave them to Bill Wilson at the time the Copper Belt railroad was being built, though I do not know the exact year.

I am enclosing self-addressed envelope and would be pleased to receive any information that you can give me.

(33) 4 May 1916, R. C. Dyer, General Merchandise Schurz, Nev., to John Pahland [Pohland], Reno, Nev. (Inter-Tribal Council of Nevada Archives, Reno):

Dear Sir,

I received your letter of May 2, 1916 and note what you say in regard to Jack Wilson land. I never knew of him having any the Wilson Bros. at Nordyke Nev gave him use of some land he claims I never seen any papers of his land this land was under there ditch and I think they took it up from the State.

(34) 11 May 1916, C. H. Day, Adjutant-General's Office, State of Nevada, Carson City to Mr. John Pohland, Clerk to S. I. Agent Reno, Nevada (Inter-Tribal Council of Nevada Archives, Reno):

Dear Sir:

If you can state the Township, Range, No. of Section and part of section from the records of your office, or correspondence on file, I can inform you if there was an entry made in the U.S. land office here for Jack Wilson, Pahute. Otherwise I can suggest no course except to wait for Mr. Asbury's return or to write to the Indian Bureau at Washington.

Respectfully,

(35) 12 May 1916, C. H. Asbury to Col. S. H. Day Carson City, Nevada, Written by his clerk, John Pohland (Inter-Tribal Council of Nevada Archives, Reno):

Dear Sir:

Replying to yours of the 11th, will say that I have no information in my files that Jack Wilson ever applied to the government for land. He thought you had some information on the subject, so I took the liberty of addressing you in the matter. I also wrote to Mr. Dyer at Schurz and am in receipt of a reply in which Mr. Dyer states that Jack never had any land of his own as far as he know, though the Wilson

Bros. gave him the use of some land. This appears to be also Mr. Asbury's under-standing of the matter. As soon as I can give this case further attention, I will wrote to the Wilson Bros., or refer the case to Supt. Lawshe of Schurz, who it seems is in charge of the territory in which this alleged allotment is supposed to be. I think it would be well to shift this case thoroughly and dispose of it finally.

Thanking you for the interest manifested,

I am -

(36) 15 May 1916, C. H. Asbury, Special Indian Agent, Reno, Nevada, to Mr. Jack Wilson, Mason, Nevada, Written by his clerk, John Pohland (Inter-Tribal Council of Nevada Archives, Reno):

Dear Sir:

Since you were in the office two weeks ago, I have made an effort to find out something definite as to land which you claim in Mason Valley, but without success. Mr. Asbury has no knowledge of your ever having made a filing on any land. Mr. Day apparently has no knowledge of the matter either, but signified his willingness to look up the matter in the land office if he were supplied with the description of the land you claim. Mr. Dyer does not know of your ever having title to any land, but says that the Wilson Bros. allowed you to use some of their land. As this matter probably comes under the supervision of Supt. Lawshe of Schurz, as I believe this is territory over which he has jurisdiction, I am writing him all the information I have in the case and it might be well to consult him in the matter.

Regretting my inability to give you anything more definite, I am,

Yours truly,

(37) 15 May 1916, C. H. Asbury, Special Indian Agent, Reno, Nevada, to Supt. H. D. Lawshe, Schurz, Nevada, Written by his clerk, John Pohland (Inter-Tribal Council of Nevada Archives, Reno):

Dear Sir:

Jack Wilson, the famous Indian Messiah of the 90's, whose home is in Nordyke, in Mason Valley, has been in the office several times during the past two months inquiring about the status of his (?) land. Upon the first occasion, he was accompanied by Billy Sheep of your reservation, who is a relative. Jack claims to have taken up an allotment and that he had a paper relative to it, though he couldn't say positively it was a patent, and that about the time the railroad was built into Mason Valley, he gave his papers to Bill Wilson for safekeeping and that Bill Wilson now informs him that the papers have been burned. Jack claims to have made an outlay of $475 in cash in improving the land and that the Wilson Ranch has it included in their fences. The Wilson Ranch is now managed by Archie Brown, some relative of the Wilsons by marriage. He asserts that he made a request for some hay cut off this land and that Brown made reply to the effect that he could have hay for $10.00 per ton.

I wrote to Mrs. Ashbury in regard to this matter and Mr. Asbury informs me that he has no knowledge that Jack ever had an allotment. Col. S. H. Day of Carson City, a friend of the Indians, does not know definitely of the matter and has offerred [sic] to look up the records in the land office, if I could give him the location of the land. I also received a reply from R.D. Dyer of Schurz, as follows:

...I never knew of him having any [land]. The Wilson Bros of Nordyke, Nevada, gave him use of some land he claims. I never seen any papers of his land. This land was under their ditch and I think they took it up from the State.

I looked the matter up in our files and it seems that Mr. Asbury wrote Mr. H. V. Hailman, on March 18, 1914, he being then superintendent of Walker River, asking him to look into this same case and if Jack did not have legal title to land there, to file him on land that was still open to entry and was suitable, if such could be found, this office rendering such assistance as was practicable. I can find no reply to this suggestion in our files, nor any indication that any action was taken.

Upon referring this matter to Mr. Asbury recently, he suggested that as the case came in your territory, it would probably be proper to refer it to you for such attention as you might see fit to give it, and a personal interview on the ground with the parties concerned will be much more satisfactory than for me to try to handle this matter further by mail. As you are probably aware, the Wilson family have in the past taken some interest in Jack Wilson, the Indian, especially when he was a young man. It is possible that he used this land through the indulgence and the kindness of this family and that he never acquired any legal title to it. However, I was of the opinion that it would be well to ascertain how and why he had spent the $475 he alleges he expended on the land in question and also, if possible, the nature of the papers he entrusted to Bill Wilson.

I am simply calling your attention to the case for such action as you may deem it worth and am writing Jack Wilson to that effect, as per copy herewith.

(38) 17 May 1916, Letter to Col. S. H. Day, Carson City, Nevada (Inter-Tribal Council of Nevada Archives, Reno):

Dear Sir:

I have been unable so far to make my contemplated trip to Topaz and places in Carson Valley, but hope to do so within the next two weeks. I will write you a few days prior, so that if any Indians have any matters to take up with me, they will have an opportunity.

In regard to the Jack Wilson case, I have written the Superintendent of Walker River, in whose jurisdiction that alleged allotment is located, fully of the case and informed Jack of my action, so that he can consult the Superintendent further. Being on the ground, this course will be more satisfactory, than to try to handle the matter by correspondence. I am greatly in doubt, however, that Jack ever filed on any land and that the land he occupied was simply by permission or the indulgence of the Wilson Brothers.

(39) 27 November 1916, C. S. Asbury, Special Indian Agent, Reno, Nevada, to The Commissioner of Indian Affairs Washington, D.C., #558. re: "Alleged activity of Jack Wilson, Wovoka, the Messiah" (Inter-Tribal Council of Nevada Archives, Reno):

Sir:

The Office will recall that Wovoka, who was at the bottom of the ghost dance and Messiah religious craze, lives in this locality. We have had occasion to refer to him occasionally in former correspondence. This was the subject of (Office letter: Ed-Law & Order 45953—12 PHL, dated May 25, 1912, to which I replied on June 8, 1912. It was also the subject of my letter of September 3, 1914 and of Office letter: Education 97310-14, dated September 16, 1914.

About the first of last July, Jack Wilson, the Messiah, visited the Shoshoni Reservation in Wyoming. I had him call at the office there and had quite a talk with him. He claimed to be just visiting the Indians at various places, but I heard among the Indians that he was referred to as a "big medicine man," but I could not learn of any particular activity on that tribe. He told me that he had been in Oklahoma a few months before and that he was especting [sic] to go to Oklahoma from there. I heard since coming here that he had recently returned from Oklahoma. Whether he has been there all this time, or not, I have not learned.

Just a few days ago, Bishop Hunting of the Episcopal Church of Nevada, called at the office and said that a report had reached him that Jack Wilson is now engaged in promoting the use of peyote with its attendant ceremonies. He says that it is reported that Jack claims that the use of this drug fosters the understanding of the Christian religion and that he is thus reaching a class of Indians who have to a greater or less extent adopted Christianity. The bishop is naturally very much interested and hopes that this may be investigated and stopped, if such report is true. It appears that he has already made a date to visit the Pyramid Lake Reservation, about Christmas time, when the Bishop fears that he may introduce this drug among the Paiute Indians of that reservation.

So far as we know, the Indians of this section of the country have never used peyote. They probably have all the other bad habits in the catalog and if there is anything that we can do to forestall this additional vice, it should be done.

It may be appropriate at this place, to say that Jack Wilson has been exceptionally free from the use of whiskey, opium, etc., and that his talks to the Indians in this locality have been along the lines of temperance, morality and industry and we are reluctant to believe that he is engaged as alleged, though just what particular thing he is doing among these Indians visited, we don't know. Jack is a mercenary fellow and it may be that his visits are purely for his own financial needs, as he is still able to collect considerable money from the Indians visited, for his work as a "big medicine man." I have made some inquiry among the Indians here, but without learning anything of interest as to his activities. I have known Jack Wilson somewhat for a number of years and up till recently, he has very seldom left Mason Valley, where he lives and works on ranches, just as the other Indians of the locality do. He very seldom visits even the Walker River Reservation, which is in close proximity to his home and so far as I can learn, he has never visited Pyramid Reservation, which is but a short distance. It may be that the Bishop is unduly alarmed, but knowing Jack's influence and power with these Indians, especially the Arapahoes, it will probably be worthwhile to cause some investigation to be made, probably through Mrs. Larson's office. It might be possible for someone by acting promptly to ascertain whether of not he brought back with him from Oklahoma a supply of peyote. It is alleged that he brought back an abundant supply of gold coin.

(40) 11 December 1916, E. B. Merritt, Assistant Commissioner of BIA to Mr. J. D. Oliver, Supt. Nevada School, 1-17156, Ed-Law and Order 134188-16, FHD #558 (Inter-Tribal Council of Nevada Archives, Reno):

Mr. dear Mr. Oliver:
        There is inclosed herewith a copy of a letter from Special Agent Asbury relative to the proposed visit of Jack Wilson, the Messiah, to your reservation and the possibility of his introducing among your Indians the use of an article known as peyote, and which the Office is making every effort to suppress.
        You should give careful consideration to this matter and be on the look-out for Wilson, and if he visits your reservation observe his actions and endeavor to offset his influence if he attempts to get the Indians to use peyote.
        Please submit a report on this matter at a later date.

(41) 17 January 1917, Lorenzo D. Creel, Special Supervisor, 31 Gazette Bldg., Reno, Nevada, to Commissioner of Indian Affairs, Washington, D.C. (Inter-Tribal Council of Nevada Archives, Reno):

My dear Mr. Sells:
        Enclosed please find two photographs of Jack Wilson, the "Messiah" of Ghost dance fame. They were taken the latter part of December, 1916, and are very true to life. I have learned considerable of his early and later history through the Wilson family of Nordyke, Nevada, about and upon whose ranch he has always made his home.
        I am steadily gaining in weight and my health appears to be up to normal. While I wish that the work I am engaged in could be moved a little faster, yet I feel that we are making very substantial progress, as you undoubtedly hear through Colonel Dorrington.

(42) 26 January 1917, E. B. Merrit, Assistant Commissioner of BIA to Mr. Lorenzo D. Creel, Special Indian Agent, Reno, Nevada (Inter-Tribal Council of Nevada Archives, Reno):

My dear Mr. Creel:
        The Office acknowledges receipt of your letter of January 17, 1917 inclosing photographs of Jack Wilson, the "Messiah," and thanks you for the same.

(43) May 12-13, 1917, Inspector L. A. Dorrington, Section II 5-9, Law and Order, "Uses of Peyote and Mescal," (In Stewart 1977:221-22):

There is absolutely no evidence indicating that either peyote or mescal is used on the reservation or that the Indians know anything about it. There was a persistent rumor last winter to the effect that Jack Wilson, the "Messiah," was going to visit the reservation during the Christmas festivities and that it was his intention to introduce peyote at that time. The matter was given careful consideration and inquiry. I "got a line" on Jack and learned that he was at his home near Mason and from most reliable authority learned that he was expected to visit Nevada (Pyramid) Reservation. Later, and before the time of his contemplated visit Jack was seen at Carson, Nevada, and in discussion with him it was learned that he did not intend to visit the Nevada Reservation as reported. He informed me that he would be leaving within a few days for Montana; that he had intended visiting the Nevada Reservation but his plans had changed. However, that did not prevent me from going to the Nevada [Pyramid] Reservation and remaining for several days during their festivities solely for the purpose of making sure that Jack was not there. He did not visit the reservation and did not leave this section as he had informed me he would. Since that time considerable has been seen of him and opportunity to study him and his activities has been afforded. He is more or less in the "lime light" and has been the subject of considerable correspondences in the past.

As already stated, Jack Wilson resides in Mason Valley near the village of Mason, Nevada, a small mining town about four miles southwest from Yerington, Nevada. He is the "Messiah" and the originator of the "Ghost Dance." He appears to attract little attention from the Indians in this locality but apparently has considerable influence among distant tribes and he seemingly keeps in close touch with them; that he is corresponding with certain individuals in Montana, South Dakota, Wyoming and Oklahoma. It is also learned that some few Indians from a distance have called upon him at his home. It is further learned that even delegations have paid him a visit. They no doubt left more or less disappointed in what they found as he lives in purely Indian custom. He resides with four or five other Indian families, who are squatters on land in the vicinity of Mason. His house consists of roughly boards divided into two rooms, the probable cost of which does not exceed $80.00. He owns or possesses a team, buggy and harness valued at about $250.00. He lives purely Indian customs with very little household effects. They sleep on the floor and from all appearances also use the floor as their table for eating. He is also known as a "medicine man" and practices some among his people but most of the time is believed to be spent visiting the distant and more prosperous tribes and individuals from whom he procures large sums of money, also valuable Indian handiwork which he afterwards sells for good sums. This seems to be his almost entire source of income. It was learned that upon a recent trip to Oklahoma he raised about $400 in cash, besides valuable gifts from Indians and whites. Upon his return he wore a $15.00 new Stetson hat which had been given to him on the trip. I was informed that he had received a call from a certain Indian in South Dakota who sent him $50.00 to pay railroad fare, requesting that he go at once for the purpose of treating the Indian's daughter; that Jack replied stating that he was too busy to leave at that time but that he would use the money anyway, and that he did.

Jack Wilson is a very dignified and striking Indian. He is about sixty-five years of age and of good stature, weighing about 185 pounds. From all accounts he has always been friendly with the whites. He never speaks of his religion and apparently has no conception of the effect it would have or has had among the Indians in various localities. A recent picture of Jack, taken by myself is attached. It cost me the sum of one dollar, that is, Jack make a "touch" for that amount after the picture had been taken, informing me that he was very much in need of a dollar that morning.

After careful inquiry I am satisfied that Jack Wilson does not use peyote or mescal, nor has he encouraged its use by others. In fact, it is learned and believed that he is very temperate in his habits; that he is constantly advising the Indians to abstain from the use of all drugs and intoxicants.

He sends his own relatives to the Carson Indian School and advises others to do likewise.

(44) 19 July 1938, Joseph W. Wilson, Elko, Nevada to Miss Grace Dangberg, Minden, Nevada (In The Grace Dangberg Field Composition Notebook, Nevada Historical Society, Reno):

Dear Grace:

I have found your article on Jack Wilson very interesting and entertaining, and have no suggestions or changes with the exception of two or three pencil notations which I have made on the margin. These are not corrections but merely the suggestion that word or a sentence be added to clarify the meaning.

Your article has emphasized the religious side of Jack, which I think is fine. There was one side of Jack I also remember, and that is that while he was good at heart and desired to do good he, at times, was roguish in his methods, rather a delightful rogue I would say.

I will be delighted to get a copy of the magazine containing the story.

(45) 19 August 1938, Joseph W. Wilson to Miss Grace Dangberg, Minden, Nevada (In The Grace Dangberg Field Composition Notebook, Nevada Historical Society, Reno):

Dear Grace:

I have read your introductory remarks on the letters to the prophet and found them very interesting. I have made some comments in pencil on the typewritten pages, but thought perhaps it would be better to give more detail in a letter on some of the points which I have suggested slight changes.

On page 3 you state that Jack went alone on all these journeys with reference to his eastern trips. This is incorrect because Jack took a boy who he said was his nephew on each of the two trips which he made to Oklahoma. The boy was about 18 or 20 years of age and had attended the Carson Indian School. He, therefore, had sufficient education to purchase the tickets and to act as an interpreter, although Jack understood English quite well.

I spent considerable time with Jack from 1906 to 1916 and in all that time I don't think I ever heard him use the word "dam" [sic] or any other swear word.

I happened to be present at the time Jack returned from his first eastern trip. Jack was very much elated and my memory of Jack telling of his meeting with the Indians was that there was (sic) immense crowds and he said, "Me stand up from sun up until sun down, shaking hands all day. Me pretty tired. Five big Indian chief lay `em $20.00 in my hand. Me like em that way shakin' hands. Me think that a pretty good way shakin' hands."

Along about 1907 Jack used to get $5.00 per eagle feather whereas I note you merely mention $2.50. It is, therefore, probably that Jack raised on his price as his fame increased.

I think one important point not noted in your remarks was the psychology which Jack used in his letter writing. The letters to Jack were from Indians who were always asking Jack to make it rain more and to cure their people who were ill with diseases or imaginary diseases. Therefore, when Jack wrote a letter to the patient he would always insist that his own letter close with the statement that "we have lots of rain here and my people are all very well and happy."

The letters which you have from the Indians were found in a cellar which was constructed by Jack for the purpose of keeping vegetables and other supplies. When he moved away he left the letters to-gether with perhaps old clothing which he considered of no value.

At one time I figured that Jack received about $35.00 per month in eastern money, Indian gloves, moccasins, or other presents. One time he received a buckskin shirt nicely decorated with beads.

I trust the above remarks will be of value to you.

APPENDIX E.1

Additional Government Letters and Reports

(46) 28 October 1891. N. Hammond to C. C. Warner (RG 75. Nevada Walker River Indian Agency, Box 315 "Farmer to Asbury, etc." Bound Volume, Federal Archives, San Bruno, California):

Dear Sir—Josephus has been informed that there are several Indians coming over from Wadsworth to kill Jack Wilson, the Messiah. The names of the Indians are Natches, Lee Winnemucca, one Indian from Quinn River, some unknown. One from the Sink of the Carson named Johnson. Also one from Humboldt named Humboldt Natches. Josephus is anxious for you to retain these Indians and not allow them to come over here, and wishes you to write to him in person in relation to the matter.

(47) 22 November 1902. N. Hammond to C. C. Warner, Indian Agent, Wadsworth (RG 75. Nevada: Walker River Indian Agency. Box 315. "Farmer to Asbury, etc." Federal Archives, San Bruno, California):

In the case of Jack Wilson, "the Messiah," I have made a thorough investigation and there is nothing in the rumor of the "Messiah" and his people holding "Ghost dances" in this section. I have investigated the matter closely, and thoroughly. Jack Wilson is in Mason Valley on a rabbit hunt, and seemingly happy. He advised his people to be good, and do nothing to offend the "whites," as the white people, as a general thing are their friends, and they cannot get along without them, as they give them plenty of work and pay money for their labor. There have been several delegations from "Eastern" tribes to interview the "Messiah." Some of them pleased with interview and some are not. The "Messiah" is not pleased with their visits and does not advocate "Ghost dances" here or among other tribes.

These Indians have a big dance or "pow wow," as they call it, two or three times a year. Their "pow wow" generally lasts four or five days, and they are seemingly pleasant. I have attended several and see nothing wrong in their dances. They are not on the "war path" and do not want to fight, but want peace at all times. You can rely on what I have written as facts. The "Messiah" was raised in Mason Valley, and Pine Grove, where he has worked most of his life for David Wilson a large rancher, from whom the "Messiah" took his name. Anything more you wish to know about the "Messiah" please let me know. Should you desire any further information concerning Jack Wilson will refer you to Edwin Dyer or David or Geo. Wilson of Mason Valley. They are reliable parties and well acquainted with the "Messiah" and his habits. I shall keep myself posted in the matter, and should there be any change, will notify you at once.

(48) 19 December 1911. From Walker River Agency Superintendent S. W. Pugh (RG 75. Box 316. fy 1909-1916. "Official and Unofficial Correspondences." Federal Archives, San Bruno, California):

To: Jack Wilson, Indian, Mason, Nev.:

I have been told by some of the Indians here [Schurz] that you were talking about having a dance there soon. I think they have made a mistake, but I thought best to write you and tell you that there will be no dance there now and if you have made that arrangement you will please tell the Indians there will be no dance there. I wrote you before that all that country was now under my charge and any time you want to do anything of that kind you must first talk about it.

(49) 21 August 1912. From Walker River Agency Superintendent S. W. Pugh (RG 75. Box 316. fy 1909-1916. "Official and Unofficial Correspondences." Federal Archives, San Bruno, California):

To: H. Pilkington, Yerington, Nevada:

Indians inform me that you white people are planning to give them a big feed and prizes for races &c., and they expect to have a dance in connection with them &c., and it seems that you are one of the prime movers in the affair...From all accounts, the dance held last year at Mason by the Indians was the rottenest affair of the kind in the history of Indian dances. You have admitted the inability of the community to control the constant drunkenness and debauchery among the Indians there and yet you will encourage such gathering among them. You may be working for the financial interest of your town but it is my duty to protect these Indians, so I thought it advisable to notify you that I will not permit those Indians to participate in the proposed games there. I wish your town and community unlimited prosperity but I am informing the Indians that they can not participate in those games. We will have them later down here.

(50) 22 August 1912. From Walker River Agency Superintendent S. W. Pugh (RG 75. Box 316. fy 1909-1916. "Official and Unofficial Correspondences." Federal Archives, San Bruno, California):

To: Jack Wilson:

I guess you got my letter that I wrote to you a few days ago. I find that the intention is to have a dance there so I wirite [sic] again to tell you that there will NOT BE ANY DANCE THERE AND I EXPECT YOU AND JACK BOVARD TO [word? word? word?] they do not let them try. If they do there will be some of the leaders arrested. I expect to be there myself. I have promised the Indians a dance and good time here this fall but have told you before that there will none there because they get too much whiskey. I have my instructions from Washington and intend to carry them out. You can tell these Indians not to dance.

(51) 26 August 1912. Superintendent J. D. Oliver of the Nevada Agency Training School, Wadsworth, Nevada, to S. W. Pugh of Walker River School (RG 75. Box 316. fy 1909-1916. "Official and Unofficial Correspondences." Federal Archives, San Bruno, California):

Relative to the proposed dance at Yerrington [sic], will say that I do not expect any of the Indians from this [Pyramid Lake] reservation to take any part in the "Fandango," if one should be held.

(52) 28 August 1912. Superintendent J. D. Oliver of the Nevada Agency Training School, Wadsworth, Nevada, to F. F. Fairbanks, Mayor of Yerington (RG 75. Box 316. fy 1909-1916. "Official and Unofficial Correspondences." Federal Archives, San Bruno, California):

Beg to advise that I received a wire from the Commissioner this morning saying "I disapprove of Indians gathering for the purpose of holding dances as give their ancient and barbarous customs." So it would seem to leave no doubt that the dance contemplated Monday night [Labor Day?] should not be permitted...I am satisfied that you were prompted by nothing but good motives in planning this, but I believe you will agree with me that nothing would have been gained by having had it and it won't affect your program much.

(53) 28 August 1912. Walker River Agency Superintendent S. W. Pugh to "Jack Wilson, Ind., Mason, Nev.," (RG 75. Box 316. fy 1909-1916. "Official and Unofficial Correspondences." Federal Archives, San Bruno, California):

Dear Sir:

Beg to advise that I received a telegram from Washington this morning disapproving of your dance on Labor Day. So you will see that they do [sic] not have it. The rest of the program is alright.

I understand that you told the Indians last Sunday that the Indians were the same as in jail and that you would do as you please up there. I wrote you before that you Indians had been placed under the charge of this Agency, and you know that the Indians there are drinking and using opium and doing things that are wrong and I am trying to help you stop such things but if you want to work against me I will have to take the matter up with you. I expect you to work with me. You wanted land here and I thought it would be a good thing as we could [sic] the work together, and help each other, I have been holding land for you and wrote you long time ago to come over, but if you do not come pretty soon I will give it to some one else.

You know yourself that last year your people got into lots of trouble at a dance at Mason. So I don't want any more such things there. We can have them here and have no trouble.

(54) Accessed 11 December 1916 (RG 75. Reno Land Allotment Heirship Case Reviews, Box 3. Federal Archives, San Bruno, California):

There is inclosed herewith a copy of a letter from Special Agent Asbury relative to the proposed visit of Jack Wilson, The Messiah, to your reservation and the possibility of his introducing among your Indians the use of an article known as peyote, and which the Office is making every effort to suppress.

You should give careful consideration to this matter and be on the look-out for Wilson, and if he visits your reservation observe his actions and endeavor to offset his influence if he attempts to get the Indians to use peyote.

(55) 9 October 1917. Superintendent of the Walker River Agency and School Robert E. Burris (RG 75. Box 248A. Carson Indian School Correspondence, Walker River 1902-1906, Federal Archives, San Bruno, California):

As to Alice Wilson, mentioned in yours of October 3, I have to state that she is married so I will not consider her in my round up.

(56) 15 October 1917. James B. Royce, Superintendent of the Carson Indian School (RG 75. Box 248A. Carson Indian School Correspondence, Walker River 1902-1906, Federal Archives, San Bruno, California):

In regard to Alice Wilson, I understand that she is married to Andrew Vidovich. I am just in receipt of a letter from his sister in which she is very much concerned about Andrew. She states that she understands they were married Indian fashion and not legally married. She also states that Andrew is only nineteen years of age and has a legal guardian, and for that reason he cannot secure a license. She desires that Andrew be sent back to school and compelled to remain at school until he is twenty one. If you are at Yerington any way soon, I wish you would investigate the matter. While at school, Andrew was one of the best boys we had. He is a good worker and a first class carpenter, and if he could be induced to attend school longer he could prepare himself for a good position.

(57) 20 November 1922. Letter from the Superintendent of the Walker River School and Agency to Mrs. Etta J. Shipley, Field Matron, Yerington, Schurz Nevada (RG 75.

Walker River Agency, Box 303. Correspondence 1922 and 1923. Federal Archives, San Bruno, California):

> In regard to Jack Wilson, he name is not on the roll. He says his wife has an allotment there.

(58) 28 November 1922. Letter from the Superintendent of the Walker River School and Agency to Mrs. Etta J. Shipley, Field Matron, Yerington, Schurz, Nevada (RG 75. Walker River Agency, Box 303. Correspondence 1922 and 1923. Federal Archives, San Bruno, California):

> Jack Wilson is not entitled to a pass. He neither lives here nor is on our Roll. The fact that his wife is interested [in living?] here does not give him any rights here so far as passes are concerned and you may so advise him. The agreement which these people have with the railroad company provides that only these Paiute Indians resident here are entitled to passes.

(59) 11 October 1963. Letter from Paul J. F. Schumacher, Regional Archeologist, San Francisco, California, to Mrs. Helen Davis Wellington, Nevada (Box 4:29 "Wilson, Jack," Margaret M. Wheat Papers #83-24, Special Collections, University of Nevada–Reno Library):

> Dear Mrs. Davis—Mrs. Margaret M. Wheat has requested that I write you concerning the Wilson site near Yerington, Nevada. This 5 acre site is located just east of the ranchhouse in Nordyke, 7 miles from Yerington, Lyon County, Nevada. It is approximately 250 feet east of the paved county highway, along the northeast side of Mill Ditch. Mrs. Kay Bunn, owner of the Nordyke ranch, Box 825, Yerington, Nevada, owns the property on which the Wilson site is located.
>
> In this area in 1890 was a Paiute known as Jack Wilson because he had grown up in the home of David Wilson. He listened attentively to family readings of the Bible, making interpretations to suit himself, and soon came to believe himself the Indian Messiah. Jack was a sincere, kindly, full-blooded Paiute, but he taught his tribesmen that the white men would suddenly disappear from the face of the earth and that all the land would again belong to the Indians. The Ghost Dance was the climax of ceremonies that would bring this to pass. So much faith was placed in these prophecies that tribal leaders from far and near came to offer gifts, which he accepted gravely and in profound silence. Restlessness among the tribes spread east of the Rocky Mountains and climaxed in trouble when the white men did not disappear on schedule. The outbreak of the Sioux in 1890, which resulted in the killing of Sitting Bull and the massacre of Wounded Knee in South Dakota, are directly attributed to Wilson's teachings.
>
> The 10´ X 6´ wood and mud semi-subterranean hut in which Wovoka lived is still standing although some of the roof mud has collapsed. The Nevada State Museum has an exhibit case containing some of Jack Wilson's clothing and a photograph of his hut made by Lowie in the early 20th Century. It is the same hut. It is located on what is locally known as the Mac Wilson Place or Ranch. During Wilson's days it was a hay ranch with a few cattle and mules. Wovoka or Jack Wilson worked for the Wilson family and acquired the family name. The original [David] Wilson house burned to the ground in the late 19th Century—probably ca. 1895. Apparently Wovoka never lived in the family house, just in his hut. The present white frame 2 & 1/2 story ranchhouse belonged to Senator Stewart of Nevada and was moved from its original site in Virginia City to the Wilson ranch in 1900-1902.
>
> The Wilson Ranch is known as the Nordyke Ranch and contains 1100 acres. It is mostly a hay operation. The Wovoka hut is just east of the ranchhouse. Jack Wilson, a Paiute Indian, known to the Indians as Wovoka was born in Mason Valley in 1858. After the death of his father he was taken into the household of a farmer David Wilson who lived near Yerington and given the name of Jack Wilson.

Wilson originated the Ghost Dance after having a revelation from the heavens. His fame spread to other Indian Tribes. Bannocks came to one of the first dances held near the Walker Reservation in 1889. Cheyennes and Arapahos later sent a delegation to learn the Ghost Dance and took gifts to Wovoka, headdress, trousers, etc. Wovoka sent gifts of gaming sticks, pinion nuts, rabbit skin robes, and sacred red paint (red ochre) in return.

Wovoka preached "Peace and Harmony" to the Indians. However, the Plains Indians tended to use the Ghost Dance to unite the tribes to regain their lost lands from the white man. Wovoka died September 1932 at 74 years of age.

From this you can see the great importance of this original mud and wood hut. I hope that some interested group would provide funds to place a strong cyclone fence around this important site. I believe Mrs. Bunn would be willing to grant permission to fence in this small area around the hut. It would take approximately 50 to 60 feet of cyclone fence to protect it properly. I wish you success in this worthy endeavor.

The Messiah Letter

(Mooney 1896:780-81)

1. Arapaho version, written down by Casper Edson, August, 1891, following a visit to Wovoka. Purported to be "the genuine official statement of the Ghost dance doctrine as given by the messiah himself to his disciples."

> What you get home you make dance, and will give (you) the same. when you dance four days and (in night) one day, dance day time, five days and then fift, will wash five for every body. He likes you (flok) you give him good many things, he heart been satting feel good. After you get home, will give good cloud, and give you chance to make you feel good. and he give you good spirit. and he give you (al) a good paint.

> You folks want you to come in three [months] here, any tribs from there. There will (be) good bit snow this year. Sometimes rain's, in fall, this year some rain, never give you any thing like that. grandfather said when he die never (no) cry. no hurt anybody. no fight, good behave always, it will give you satisfaction, this young man, he is a good Father and mother, dont tell no white man. Juesses was on ground, he just like cloud. Every body is alive again, I dont know when they will [be] here, may be this fall or in spring.

> Every never get sick, be young again, — (if young fellow no sick any more,) work for white men never trouble with him until you leave, when it shake the earth dont be afraid no harm any body.

> You make dance for six (weeks) night, and put you foot [food?] in dance to eat for every body and wash in the water. that is all to tell, i am in to you. and you will received a good words from him some time, Dont tell lie.

2. The Messiah Letter: Cheyenne version: Dictated by Black Short Nose to his daughter, ca. 1891, following an August, 1891, visit to Wovoka:

> When you get home you have to make dance. You must dance for four nights and one day time. You will take bath in the same morning before you go to yours home, for every body, and give you all the same as this. Jackson Wilson likes you all, he is glad to get good many things. His heart satting fully of gladness, after you get home, I will give you a good cloud and give you chance to make you feel good. I give you a good spirit, and give you all good paint, I want you people to come here again, want them in three months any tribs of you from there. There will be a good deal snow this year. Some time rains, in fall this year some rain, never give you any thing like that, grandfather, said, when they were die never cry, no hurt anybody, do any harm for it, not to fight. Be a good behave always. It will give a satisfaction in your

life. This young man is a good father and mother. Do not tell the white people about this, Juses is on the ground, he just like cloud. Every body is a live again. I don't know when he will be here, may be will be this fall or in spring. When it happen it may be this. There will be no sickness and return to young again. Do not refuse to work for white man or do not make any trouble with them until you leave them. When the earth shakes do not be afraid it will not hurt you. I want you to make dance for six weeks. Eat and wash good clean yourselves [The rest of the letter had been erased].

3. The Messiah Letter: Mooney's free rendering:

When you get home you must make a dance to continue five days. Dance four successive nights, and the last night keep up the dance until the morning of the fifth day, when all must bathe in the river and then disperse to their homes. You must all do in the same way.

I, Jack Wilson, love you all, and my heart is full of gladness for the gifts you have brought me. When you get home I shall give you a good cloud (rain?) which will make you feel good. I give you a good spirit and give you all good paint. I want you to come again in three months, some from each tribe there (the Indian Territory).

There will be a good deal of snow this year and some rain. In the fall there will be such a rain as I have never given you before.

Grandfather (a universal title of reverence among Indians and here meaning the messiah) says, when your friends die you must not cry. You must not hurt anybody or do harm to anyone. You must not fight. Do right always. It will give you satisfaction in life. This young man has a good father and mother. (Possibly refers to Casper Edson, the young Arapaho who transcribed this message for the delegation.)

Do not tell the white people about this. Jesus is now upon the earth. He appears like a cloud. The dead are all alive again. I do not know when they will be here; maybe this fall or in the spring. When the time comes there will be no more sickness and everyone will be young again.

Do not refuse to work for the whites and do not make any trouble with them until you leave them. When the earth shakes [at the coming of the new world] do not be afraid. It will not hurt you.

I want everyone to dance every six weeks. Make a feast at the dance and have food that everybody may eat. Then bathe in the water. That is all. You will receive good words again from me some time. Do not tell lies.

APPENDIX G

Nine Ghost Dance Songs of the Northern Paiute
(Mooney 1896:1052-55)

1. Nuva ka ro'rani

Nuva ka ro'rani!
Nuva ka ro'rani!
Nuva ka ro'rani!
Nuva ka ro'rani!
Gosi'pa' havi'ginu',
Gosi'pa' havi'ginu'.

The snow lies there - **ro'rani!**
The snow lies there - **ro'rani!**
The snow lies there - **ro'rani!**
The snow lies there - **ro'rani!**
The Milky Way lies there,
The Milky Way lies there.

2. Dena' Gayo'n

Dena' Gayo'n, De'na ga'yoni,
Dena' Gayo'n, De'na ga'yoni,
Bawa' doro'n, Ba'wa do'roni,
Bawa' doro'n, Ba'wa do'roni.

A slender antelope, a slender antelope,
A slender antelope, a slender antelope,
He is wallowing upon the ground,
He is wallowing upon the ground,
He is wallowing upon the ground,
He is wallowing upon the ground.

3. Do' Ti'mbi

Do'ti'mbi, Do'timbi-na'n,
Do'ti'mbi, Do'timbi-na'n,
Ti'mbi bai'-yo, Ti'mbi ba'i-yo-a'n,
Ti'mbi bai'-yo, Ti'mbi ba'i-yo-a'n.

The black rock, the black rock,
The black rock, the black rock,
The rock is broken, the rock is broken,
The rock is broken, the rock is broken.

4. Pasu' wi'noghan

Pasu' wi'noghan,
Pasu' wi'noghan,
Pasu' wi'noghan,
wai-va wi'noghan,
wai-va wi'noghan,
wai-va wi'noghan.

The wind stirs the willow,
The wind stirs the willow,
The wind stirs the willow,
The wind stirs the grasses,
The wind stirs the grasses,
The wind stirs the grasses.

5. Pagu'nava'

Pagu'nava'! Pagu'nava'!
Tungwu'kwiji! Tungwu'kwiji!
Wumbe'doma'! Wumbe'doma'!

Fog! Fog!
Lightning! Lightning!
Whirlwind! Whirlwind!

6. Wumbi'ndoma'n

Wumbi'ndoma'n, Wumbi'ndoma'n,
Wumbi'ndoma'n, Wumbi'ndoma'n,
Nuva'ri'p noyo'wana', Nuva'ri'p noyo'wana',
Nuva'ri'p noyo'wana', Nuva'ri'p noyo'wana'.

The whirlwind! The Whirlwind!
The whirlwind! The Whirlwind!
The snowy earth comes gliding,
The snowy earth comes gliding,
The snowy earth comes gliding,
The snowy earth comes gliding.

7. Kose' wumbi'ndoma'

Kose' wumbi'ndoma',
Kose' wumbi'ndoma',
Kose' wumbi'ndoma',
Kai-va wumbi'ndoma',
Kai-va wumbi'ndoma',
Kai-va wumbi'ndoma'.

There is dust from the whirlwind,
There is dust from the whirlwind,
There is dust from the whirlwind,
The whirlwind on the mountain,
The whirlwind on the mountain,
The whirlwind on the mountain.

8. Dombi'na so'wina'

Dombi'na so'wina',
Dombi'na so'wina',
Dombi'na so'wina'.
Kai'-va so'wina',
Kai'-va so'wina',
Kai'-va so'wina'.

The rocks are ringing,
The rocks are ringing,
The rocks are ringing,
They are ringing in the mountains,
They are ringing in the mountains,
They are ringing in the mountains.

9. Su'ng-a Ro'Yonji'

Su'ng-a Ro'Yonji', Su'ng-a ro'yon,
Su'ng-a Ro'Yonji', Su'ng-a ro'yon,
Su'ng-a Ro'Yonji', Su'ng-a ro'yon,
Pu'i do'yonji, Pu'i do'yon,
Pu'i do'yonji, Pu'i do'yon,
Pu'i do'yonji, Pu'i do'yon.

The cottonwoods are growing tall,
The cottonwoods are growing tall,
The cottonwoods are growing tall,
They are growing tall and verdant,
They are growing tall and verdant,
They are growing tall and verdant.

Appendix H

Tibo'o Remember

1. "An Indian Medicine Man," Anonymous, Lyon County Public Library, Yerington, Nevada.

When the first white men settled Mason Valley, Nevada, many years ago, there were many Indians living there. They were wild as is only natural and they made several attempts to crush the new inhabitants but as must happen they failed.

Among those Indians there was one named Jack Wilson. He was the medicine man of the tribe and he was famed far and wide for his great ability. Among the early settlers ther [sic] were two brothers named Wilson. It was from these brothers that Jack Wilson derived his name.

Jack was a large man and phisicaly [sic] he was perfect. He was far more intelligent than the ordinary Indian, and he used this intelligence coupled with their ignorance to better himself.

Jack came peacefully to the settlers and stayed with them a large amount of the time, in this way he learned many of the ways of the white men.

It was not long after the settlers had gotten their homes build [sic] that Jack made his first move to raise his position among his people. He went to the camp and making a great show he said to his followers: "Come with me and I will show that the white mans gun cannot kill me." Now as we look at in one way it was the gun that had taken the Indians land away from them, if it had not been for the gun the whites would have had met defeat. So they held the gun in great fear, and even though they trusted their medicine man and believed in him they could not match him with the gun. It was for this reason that his speech met with loud jeers from the group of Indians. He took them toward Pizen Switch but on the way they met two white men, both of whom had shot guns with them. To his followers Jack said in a low voice: "I will have these two men shoot at me." And to the two men: "White men I am not afraid of your guns." At the white mens jeer he answered: "To prove it to you I will let you shoot at me you can not kill me." So the white men agreed to this. All preparations were made and the tribe of Indians were well out of the way. Jack stood up and one of the white men shot at him. We, who cannot see it cannot realize the amount of suspense that the Indians went through. They had great faith in their medicine men but they thought that white mans God was stronger. Can we blame the red man for worshipping him when he stood up before the weapon which they looked at as sudden death, not even flinching? When the shot struck Jack instead of falling dead, as all expected, he stood there and calmly told them to shoot some more. This was repeated three times, and after each shot he would calmly shake a little shot out of the leg of his pants. To the Indians this meant very much, it made Jack Wilson a God in their eyes. To-day if a white man would do that we would think nothing about it; it would be merely a trick, that is all it was then but it served the purpose: it made Jack Wilson a great man.

After this the medicine man's name was spread far over the country.

Once later than the experience that has just been related the Medicine Man made ice come down the river on the fourth of July. It came about as follows: Jack told the Indians that he could make ice on the river, this time there were only a very few that disbelieved but they all went down to the river to see him do it. He told all them to go into the river and stay there until he told them to come out. They all obeyed his orders, and in a short while he told them to come out, and when they had reached shore there were several blocks of ice laying there. George Wilson still says that the ice was stole out of his ice house.

After this Jack was very popular, nearly every day saw him at the post office where he received wonderfull [sic] presents nearly every day, these presents he would sell.

Jack is still living to-day and though he is still Medicine Man his one-time power is gone. As the Indians became more civilized they found him out, therefore to-day he doesn't amount to much with the Indians.

2. G. W. Ingalls, pp. 954-55, In Sam P. Davis, ed. *History of Nevada,* Vol II:

About 1890 an Indian known as Jack Wilson, a large, fine-looking Indian of the Piute tribe, began giving ghost dances out in the timber and in the open spaces in the woods and creating quite a stir among the Indians, but he did not receive the support that he expected here. So he went East and through his agents communicated with the Sioux Indians, and started the last Indian war, known as the Ghost Dance War. This Indian Jack was raised in the family of David Wilson where the old-fashioned custom of reading the Bible, and having the family prayers twice a day obtained. He evidently listened closely to the story of the Messiah and, being a very bright Indian boy, at the age of about 17 was employed by a sleight-of-hand performer going through the country to work over this section with him as an assistant. Through this employment, he learned many mysterious tricks, and so it was a very natural sequence to his early impressions that he should constitute himself the Indian Messiah. At the age of about 28 years, he started these ghost dances before mentioned. His promises made to the Indians that after they begun [sic] the war there would be a resurrection of all the Indians who had previously died, and they would join in the battles and drive the White man out of the country, formed the inspiration for their actions. This same "Messiah" now receives prominent Indians from the Middle West and Montana, who give him many presents and treat him with great consideration when they come. He accepts these attentions with great dignity and in profound silence.

3. Irma Wittacre, "History of Mason Valley," Lyon County Public Library, Yerington, Nevada.

Jack Wilson, an old Indian in Mason Valley was called the Indian profit [sic]. The Indians would all go to him to find out when it was going to rain. He would set aside a certain day for the Indians to come and see him. One day he took the shot out of the shells and when the Indians came he told them that they could shoot at him and kill him, they believed him. He also told them another day that he could make ice float down the river, he hired some people to take some ice up above them and when the Indians came to drop it in. They also believed this. They have got over this superstition now. They are being educated now and taught better ways of living. The White people have also.

4. Irma Wittacre, "The History of Lyon County," Lyon County Public Library, Yerington, Nevada.

An Indian by the name of Jack Wilson who was raised in the family of David Wilson went among the Piute tribe and tried to cause trouble. He made them think he was some kind of a God and had come down from Heaven to rule over them. He was bright and a great many of the Indians believed in him. But the majority did not believe in him so he did not succeed very well in making trouble.

5. Irma Wittacre, "Untitled," Lyon County Public Library, Yerington, Nevada.

In 1890 a young Indian by the name of Jack Wilson came into prominence. He started giving lessons in Ghost Dances but these did not cause enough excitement so he went east and communicated with the Sioux Indians through his agents and started the last Indian war called the Ghost Dance war.

6. John Henry, "An Old Settler's Story," Lyon County Public Library, Yerington, Nevada.

In about 1890 Jack Wilson, the chief of the Piute tribe, tried to stir the Indians up to revolt but the Indians did not have any shot so he hade [sic] them think that he loaded his gun with shot which was sand but he tricked them and put real lead into his gun. Then he went out in the hills and killed jack rabbits. They though [sic] he was doing it with the sand. Then he loaded their guns with lead, or at least they thought he was loading them with lead, but he didn't load them at all. Then he stood out about two hundred yards from them and let them shoot. After they each took a shot at him he tore holes in his shirt and then he told the Indians that they had made the holes with their guns. When they saw the holes in his shirt they thought that he was immortal and could not be killed. Then he told the Indians that he was such a great man that he could make ice in the middle of summer. It is not known where he got the ice, but he got a wagon load and went up the river about a mile and threw the ice in. When the ice floated by the waiting Indians, they saw it and of course that was proof that he was a great man. The Indians were about ready to revolt one time but they finally calmed down and the trouble was forgotten. If he had had an other man as good as he was it wouldn't have been a very hard job to have stirred the Indians to war on the white people in the valley, which were very few at that time.

7. Cora Sayre (1977:42), "Memories of Smith Valley."

I do remember some Indians from earlier days.... Dr. Joe was a medicine man before Jack Wilson, who was the famous "Wovoka." Dr. Joe was killed by Potato Pat because Pat's wife was doctored by Dr. Joe before she died.

8. Alex Miller, Interview, 1986.

I hear the Wilsons raised him. They were Methodists. Educated him and so he became a religious leader. Like Billy Graham, in his class. So when Wovoka preached a lot, the whites outlawed him.

I guess he's got an organization backing him, too. A revolutionist. Why? Cause he wants the land back. Before the white man came, there was lots of fish, deer, antelope. White man spoiled everything.

My wife [Laura] told me about his miracles. She said he allowed people to shoot at him. Here's how he did that. He took the shells out and left the powder. One of those Wilson boys said, 'Can I shoot you with my gun?' 'Course Wovoka said, No!

A couple of times he came to Wellington. One time he was with a couple of Indians to buy a watermelon from my mother-in-law, Mrs. Dickinson. I guess she overcharged and so he refused to pay. Threatened to send a flood and throw the watermelons field into the [Walker] river. She said, "Go ahead!"

My wife used to tell me stories about Wovoka. I guess he would allow Indians to shoot at him by taking the shell out and leaving the powder. But when one Wilson boys said to shoot with my gun, Wovoka said no. Those Wilson boys took the ice from the storehouse to make other Indians believe.

9. Claude Keema, former Sheriff, Lyon County. Interview, 1968.

He taught them to live with the whites, not to take over. If they had listened, then there wouldn't have been that Sioux Uprising. This community owes it to him to put up a commemorative stone at Schurz, where he's buried.

10. Luther Caton, former pastor, Assembly of God Church, Yerington Indian Colony. Interview, 1968.

I read Bailey and Jack Wilson is a big phony. Stetson hat and magpie feathers and ghost dance shirt, his Wilson Canyon prophecy on July 4th; the ice floating in the river....

11. Clark J. Guild (1967:230), "Memoirs of Careers with Nevada Bench and Bar, Lyon County Offices, and the Nevada State Museum."

I had a stepfather-in-law named William Powers in Yerington, who used to dance with Jack Wilson, Wovoka, the great Indian prophet from Nevada, who used to bring the tribesmen from Oklahoma and different places and have dances in Mason Valley. I was personally acquainted with Jack, too. And I've seen some of the dances. But my stepfather-in-law, Bill Powers, learned to talk Paiute. And Jack had given him, in his life-time, his buckskin suit and several other very splendid articles of Indian make. Bill donated those to the museum.

Jack got his training in a peculiar way. He lived with the Wilson family, who were at the south end of Mason Valley as farmers — Joe Wilson and his wife and Billy Wilson (Joe and he owned the Nordyke flour mill) and Mack Wilson. And they were churchgoing people, and Jack, living with them, they insisted on him going to Sunday school. And he learned a great deal about the Bible and he made use of it. In one sense of the word, he was a fraud. He'd bring these people together, you know, and he'd perform miracles for them and he learned it out of things that he was taught out of the Bible. But he misconstrued the Bible in many instances. But he did a marvelous job. He did marvelous things and made quite a collection from these people that would come to visit him.

12. Guild (1967:274-276), con't.

I knew Jack Wilson, a Paiute Indian, as a very young man, particularly when I was on those survey crews in Mason Valley, because we camped at each ranch that we were surveying.... We camped at the Wilson Ranch. The Wilsons—David Wilson first settled in Pine Grove, and his sons, J.I. and Bill and Mack all moved to Mason Valley and took up ranches in what we called the Plummer district.

Jack Wilson, a Paiute Indian, took up his residence with the Wilson family. They were quite religious and they made Jack go to Sunday school, and he learned a great deal about the Bible, and he was a good Indian dancer. They had many different kinds of dances. His reputation got out some way or other to the Oklahoma and to the Dakota Indians and they used to come to visit him. And he'd pull these gags on them that he was calling the spirits out, and so on, and they'd bring him presents.

My wife's stepfather, Bill Powers, could talk Paiute and used to dance with Jack. And Jack made him a present of a buckskin suit that one of these Indians had brought him from the plains.

A man by the name of Ed Dyer, who lived in Yerington and ran a store, was a great friend of Paiutes, could speak Paiute, and he did a lot of business with them— and they were fond of him, and he of them. (Afterwards, Dyer moved to Fallon, where his oldest son, Edward, was head of the Carson-Truckee Irrigation District for many years, just retired a year or two ago, and the other son has a ranch there—the other two sons now dead.) Well, anyhow, Ed Dyer also could talk Paiute, as could Bill Powers, and they always attended these dances, and I had occasion to attend one or two of them just as a spectator. It was quite a sight to see — they were serious in their dancing, and they were good dancers, light on their feet and kept good time.

By the way, the suit that he gave Bill, Bill gave to his son, Jack, my brother-in-law. Before he died, he gave it to Jack, and then Jack brought it to the museum, and we have it in the Jack Wilson Wovoka case there at the museum. It's the one that was given to him, and he wore it. We have a lot of other things of his there at the museum.

The story was that one of the few groups of people to come from Oklahoma, or someplace, to this ranch at the mouth of Wilson Canyon, the Mack Wilson ranch, and the river froze over, and some way or other, Jack had schemed around where he had tied some catfish to a string in an opening of the place where this was froze over. And then he gave them a demonstration of how the spirits would help him fish. I don't remember—Bill told me—he had these fastened on a wire loop some way so that when he'd put his pole down with a hook, he could just take one up at a time, and he had these Indians just mystified, see? Talking Paiute all the time, and singing, see, and making them a present of the fish. He had about a dozen of them. Well, they just thought that was the most wonderful thing in the world. They believed it—they didn't investigate that thing, you know; they had faith in Jack. He did things like that—similar to that to these people that come and visited him. They loaded him down with bead presents and everything you could think of. I don't suppose there was an Indian in the United States as popular as he was. He wasn't a fighting Indian; he was one of these preaching Indians.

13. Mr. Newcombe (In Davidson 1952:47).

Jack and I were close friends, I considered him a sly ole boy; he was smart, no question about it. He could sure get a kick out of a good joke.

I was the telegrapher at Mason, Nevada, the place where Jack sent and received his messages from those that thought he was a great medicine man. One day Jack came into the office to mail one of his customary small packages of red ground-up rock to an Indian patient. Jack would send the packages, collect $15.00 and promise to make them well. This day I had a message for Jack so I read it to him. The message said, "Father Wovoka—you no make my wife well no more—she dead now."

Jack laughed and laughed and laughed and then said, "Well, we all have to die sometime."

14. Riley, In Davidson (1952:46).

If revelous behavior meant having a good time, then Wovoka was always one to show the folks a good time. Once Wovoka gathered together many members of his flock and on a hot summer day predicted snow and ice. In the meantime, a helper would drive an ice truck with a few hundred pounds of cold storage ice up the river aways and deposit it. Then in the middle of Wovoka's ceremony, the ice would come floating by amid much rejoicing.

15. Joseph I. Wilson, In Davidson (1952:46-47).

He was raised by David Wilson whose name he took and it was then that he learned to do slight of hand tricks. He used these in order to work miracles with the Indians and they regarded him as a Messiah. On one occasion he said that he would cause it to rain and Indians came from all over the United States to witness this miracle. There was much speculation whether he could do it or not and there had been much betting among Indians and white people both. The great day finally came and it did rain a few drops, which probably saved Jack's hide. It is said that if it had not rained the Indians would have killed him. Another time their Messiah told them that he was bullet proof and that it was impossible to kill him. He fixed up some blank cartridges and gave these to the Indians. Then he stood up and let them shoot at him. After they had fired the gun he shook out some powder which he had concealed in his shirt and convinced the Indians that he was bulletproof. To this day many prominent Indians from the east and Middle West seek his advice and treat him with great consideration.

Wovoka promised the Indians a good time if they would come down by the river near Yerington to a big meeting. It was a hot summer day, yet he told the Indians that he could make ice on the river. And sure enough, he did! He walked into the river aways and picked out a big chunk of ice in his hands that all might see it. This meeting lasted three days. He also told the people that they would all go to heaven.

Wovoka loved to play tricks on us boys, and have fun when a trick was played on himself. If this means revelous behavior,. then Jack sure was a good one for it. An example of this was the time Jack drove into town with part of a load of ore and gave it to my brother. The ore was valued in gold content at two hundred to four hundred dollars per ton. My brother asked him where he got it; he replied, "Someday I tell you, maybe; not now." My brother could not get him to tell where he had discovered it, so finally my brother came down to the flour mill and got me to try to get Jack to tell where he had found the ore. Finally I got Jack to promise to show us where the ore came from. In the meantime, word got around to the whole town about Jack's greatest discovery. The morning we set out toward the mountain that supposedly contained a strike, we noticed that half the town was following our tracks. No one ever found anything worthwhile that day. When we later asked Jack about it, he would just stare at us.

However, I guess some of his tricks paid off, or at least made him famous, like the time Jack (Wovoka) went back to Oklahoma to see some Indians; he returned with about twelve hundred dollars. Jack told me of his visit and said, "The sun come up, the sun go down, three times; all the time I stand and shake my hands. People keep putting money into my hands; the chiefs put twenty dollar gold pieces."

16. Fieldnotes of Karl Fredericks, Reporter for **NUMU YA DUA**, The Tribal History of the Yerington Paiute Tribe.

Walker McKay also recalled an incident at the Wilson Ranch. His uncle was working there, the head of the hay pitching crew. McKay's uncle told Jack Wilson that if he didn't start pitching hay right he would end up sticking someone with the pitch fork. Jack Wilson struck him with the pitch fork. Walker McKay's uncle jumped off the hay wagon and started chasing after Jack. Jack was able to run fast enough stay just out of reach. They ran and ran up and down the river bank near where the men were pitching hay....

One old Indian by the name of Hudson George ran to the Wilson house and told Mr. Wilson that Bill Wise was going to kill that Indian. By the time Mr. Wilson arrived, both men were exhausted and tongues were hanging out. Bill Wise told Mr. Wilson to get a gun, he was going to shoot Old Jack Wilson.

McKay also recalled an incident when Wovoka showed the Blackfeet and Sioux that guns would not hurt him. Well, it is said that Wovoka had already shot holes in his shirt. Wovoka also placed shot inside of his shirt at the belt line. He looked around for loaded a shotgun with powder and had an assistant shoot at him. The Blackfeet and Sioux were amazed at this act of bravery.

Mr. Wilson owner of the ranch Jack worked on asked Jack if he would let him shoot at Jack with a 30-30 rifle.

Walker McKay also recalled when four Indians from either Montana or South Dakota came to the McKay Ranch. The Indians asked if they could buy breakfast from the McKays. They cooked breakfast from the four Indians. The Indians came to Mason Valley looking for Wovoka. They were pretty upset. It seems everything Wovoka had told them on their first trip to Nevada was nothing but lies. They spent four days in the valley looking for Wovoka. They never did find him. It's a good thing, too, because if they did find Wovoka, they would have killed him!

17. Tim McCoy, McCoy-McCoy Tapes, No. 6:12-16. Quoted with permission of Ron McCoy.

And in talking to General Scott one time I said, what about this Wovoka, what about the messiah? What became of him, where is he? And General Scott said, I don't know. Well, I said, do you think he's still alive? Still, he said, I don't know. Haven't heard of him, no one has mentioned him, no one has thought about him in a long time. Well, that was all I needed. I said to myself, I'm gonna find that injun if he's alive. So from different Indians I picked up a bit of information here and there and I found out he had come from that Mason valley down in Nevada, so I took it upon myself to dig him out. I got down into that country, found that he had been on the Pyramid Lake reservation, and there's where I found him. I ran him down, dug him out, forgotten man, nobody knew him, and he never knew but what something might happen to him, you know, so no one mentioned him, that's why no one would say that's where the great messiah was. So he was hidden out, you might say. And I got hold of him.

Q. How'd you find him?

By tracing him down from on injun to another. I finally found where he was on Pyramid Lake and I took an interpreter with me and I went right out to see him. And he was quite reluctant to talk until after I'd explained to him that nothing was going to happen to him, that I wasn't there to drag him in, that all I wanted to know was to have him tell me, and that all of these Indians who came to see him, among them the Arapahoes and some of the Sioux, had been my friends. And that I wanted to carry a message back to the Arapahoes about him. And the upshot of the whole thing was that after quite some time I gained his confidence and he told me his story. He also gave me some of his paint, he still had some of the medicine paint, and told me his story, all about how he'd died and went to heaven.

Q. What'd he say?

Well he said, long time ago he had, wasn't very well, sort of sickly when he was young, and he working for a whiteman called Wilson and that's where he got his whiteman name Jack Wilson. That his name he took was Wovoka because his father's name was Wovoka. His uncle was Winnemuka natcha, the great Piute chief. He told me he was born about the time of the great treaty at Fort Churchill, and that would point him up into his early 80s. And that he had this vision, he fainted, he said he died, and went up to heaven and he met the great spirit and the great spirit told him that one time he'd sent his son down on the earth to tell the white men to live at peace and teach them a big religion, but the white men put his son to death. Now, he was going to send another messiah down to the injuns, and that he would be the one. And he gave him this song, or these songs as he had it, and this dance, and if they would sing these songs and dance this dance for so long, then this great miracle would happen. This great cloud would come over the earth, and on it would be all the injuns who had ever died, mounted on their war ponies, and the buffalo, and the elk, and the antelope would all come back. And this cloud would cover the earth, cover all the whitemen and the injuns would have all this country again. And so he came down to earth and he began to preach, telling the Indians that they must live at peace but dance this dance, sing these songs, until they brought about this great miracle. But to live at peace, everybody must be at peace. And that was his story.

...You have that picture of me taken with the messiah when I first knew him, and then I have another picture, about 40 years later, when I stood beside the grave of the messiah, up in Yearington Nevada, where he died. I brought him over, I was up making a picture in northern California, up near Bishop, Mulner Lake was where it was, and it was winter time again, and I'd brought this bunch of Arapahoe Indians over there with me and I thought it would be a great thing for them, something that they would really appreciate, if they could see the messiah. And so I wangled it and sent a car clear up to Pyramid Lake, with a message from me, that I was there and that I had some Arapahoes who had been ghost dancers and that they would like to meet the great man. We'd bring him down there and look after him. So, as I say, I sent this car up there for him and brought him down. I kept him there for a couple of days...that car was first class transportation. He's on the maharajah's elephant by that time. So he came. And I had a room fixed there for him. And he brought an interpreter, his nephew or grandson, I think it was his nephew.... And I brought these Arapahoes out to meet him. I'll never forget this night. He sat there as tho he were Queen Victoria in a chair at the end of the room, and these Araphaoes came one by one, they had every bit of reverence they would have had it been the Pope giving an audience to them. They were so embarrassed, they were so awed, that they wouldn't even look up at him. They kept their heads down. But when they came up to him, and I introduced each of them by name, and you know that those guys were slipping $5 bills into his hand....

Q. He was accepting it...?

Oh, he was taking every bit of it, Billy Graham had nothing on him, to say nothing of Amy Semple McPherson, saying "and I don't want to see any of those $1 bills in there, either." The Indians were coming up with their heads bowed, mind you, these great big strong looking fellows with their braids wrapped in otter skin, and they come up to this great man, this Piute, chunky looking old man sitting there without batting an eye, the king of all that he surveyed—and they'd come up and bow their heads and then put a $5 bill in his hand. He made a pretty good haul off all those injuns, because I had a lot of Arapahoes. So the next day, before I sent him back, I'd gotten everything I wanted out of him and he'd met the Indians and the Indians were happy and they were gonna take the message...all those messages were a goin' back to Wind River.

Q. What sort of message did he give them?

Well he told them all about live at peace, and be good people and all that sort of thing.

Q. Did he tell them the cloud would come?

Oh no, that was finished. Nobody dared ask him any questions, they didn't say, "what do you mean telling us that a cloud was coming over?" Oh no, they were still frightened of the medicine man, and they still are. Don't fool yourself. It's like putting a hex on you. He might put a hex on them and by the time they got home their grandchildren might be dead, even if they'd died of small pox.

18. Walter Cox, Former Publisher of the *Mason Valley News*. Interview, 1988.

Wovoka was older when I knew him. "Good morning, Jack," I'd say when I saw him. That's around 1921. He spoke very good English, you know. Don't talk "hogadai," "I'm hungry." Or "Pahmu," "Give me a smoke!" He'd be standin' in front of the bank, wearing a hat that was brought to him from the Midwest—because Joe Wilson is the President [of the bank]. He'd come to town in the afternoons standing there, check out the scene. Quiet. Best human impression of a wooden Indian I ever seen. Oh, he was the only kind of individual that shook up the Army and Washington, D.C. Somebody today should. And I don't know about the Navy.

Tim McCoy came through Yerington overnight and I took him to the graveyard to Wovoka's headstone. No flowers decorating it that time....

No, I don't think he was after money. What I heard was that he had revelation and went to Heaven which made it a peace and friendship religion. Actually a new dance. It was the Sioux who made it out to be a war dance.

One story I can tell you, this one is true. A Mormon came to Schurz to convert him, and Jack refused. He [Wovoka] sent his friend to steal his shirt from the clothes line. That was like a chastity belt [re: the Mormon holy undergarment]. With buttons and insignia on it. You see, Jack Wilson confused the bullets with evil. Well, and so that left the Mormon holding his pants!

I know he died. I heard he had VD. And I was sure as hell teed off my own newspaper never ran it [the story of Wovoka's death]!

APPENDIX I

Anthropologists (and Others) on Wovoka

He has been denounced as an imposter, ridiculed as a lunatic, laughed at as a pretended Christ, while by the Indians he is revered as a direct messenger from the other world, and among many of the remote tribes he is believed to be omniscient to speak all languages, to be invisible to a white man (Mooney 1896:764).

In January, 1892, there was great religious excitement among the Indians, Jack Wilson on the Walker reservation claiming to be the Messiah. Piutes and Washoes, and even Dakota and Montana Indians gathered, but the prompt action of Natches and agents averted trouble (Wren 1907:307).

He taught that the whole human race was of one kindred, and particularly that the Indians of the several tribes were all brothers and must give up tribal warfare and all thought of warfare with the whites (Mooney 1911:175).

In the "Ghost Dance" of the Paviotso of Nevada (a ceremonial religious dance connected with the Messiah doctrine, which originated among that people about 1888 and spread rapidly among other tribes, through the agency of the pretended prophet, one Wovoka, a medicine-man who had lived among whites), hypnotic trances were frequently induced to enable the Indians to converse with their dead relatives, who were, it was said, to return to them, and sweep the earth clear of the whites in a great Armageddon (Spence 1917:782).

Wovoka, the son of Tavibo, was responsible for the "Ghost-dance" religion and prophecies, perhaps the most important from a political point of view in the history of the relations of the Whites and Indians. This creed he nurtured among the Paviotso of Nevada about 1888. It spread rapidly until it embraced all the tribes from the Missouri to the Rockies and even beyond them. Wovoka (who was also known to the Whites as Jack Wilson), like other native prophets, declared that he had been taken into the spirit-world, where he had received a revelation from the god of the Indians to the effect that they would be restored to their inheritance and united with their departed friends. They were to prepare for this event by practicing song-and-dance ceremonies given them by the prophet. During these dances many of the Indians fell into a condition of hypnotic trance and intense excitement usually prevailed. The movement led to an outbrak in the winter of 1890-91. It has now degenerated into a mere social function (Spence 1917:382, Vol. 10).

Of the two great messianic movements that appeared among the western Indians toward the close of the last century, that of 1890 is best known for the extent of its influence, culminating as it did in the last desperate conflict and ultimate subjugation of the Plains Indians. Although it had its origin among the Northern Paiute (Paviotso) of western Nevada, in its home its result was hardly more than to add to the body of esoteric lore, but its eastward and southward spread among the Plains Indians and those of the Southwest was accomplished with great rapidity and inflammatory effect. It disappeared as rapidly as it came, leaving few traces of its presence.... (Spier 1927:43).

During the latter part of the nineteenth century a messianic cult known as the Ghost

Dance Religion and emanating from the Northern Paiute, was diffused among the Indians of the western United States in two distinct waves, one about 1870, the second about 1890. That the dead would return and peaceful and prosperous conditions be re-established if the Ghost Dances were permitted was the essential doctrine of both movements. The second movement, that of 1890, instigated by Jack Wilson (Wovoka), is well known for its far-reaching political and psychological effects upon native life. Of the earlier movement which began in 1870, little is known save that it was originated by an older relative of Jack Wilson (Gayton 1930:57).

The accounts are far from satisfactory and even these were not with some difficulty. A number of informants claimed not to remember the dance at all or stated that they had heard of it, but vaguely. It seems unlikely that this should be attributed to reticence due to emotional associations; perhaps there is rather a reluctance to admit having been duped. Or again, informants may really be correct in insisting that their attitude was one of skepticism. The Ghost Dance may have been a non-spectacular affair which made little impression on them. Yet this would be singular in view of the fact that the whole movement had its inception among their Nevada congeners (Kelly 1932:179-80).

The doctrines of the son [Wovoka] do not seem to have differed materially from those of [Tavibo] the father (Lesser 1933:53).

The doctrines of Wovoka, as revealed in what he told Mooney of his vision experience, and in the message he gave the Cheyenne and Arapaho, are clearly doctrines of peace. In only one region where the Ghost Dance was taken up was this aspect forgotten. The western Dakota...transformed the doctrine from one of peaceful faith and hope, into one of war (Lesser 1933:59).

The first dancing among the Paiute involved not trances. But the people of the various Nevada reservations made their own interpretations of Wovoka's purpose and doctrine; they spread the word that Christ had come, and that people should dance. Wovoka never claimed to be the Son of God; he sincerely believed he was a prophet with a divine revelation to impart (Lesser 1933:54).

The dances held in connection with the Ghost Dance movements of 1870 and 1890 were not shamanistic performances. There is evidence that the prophets of both movements, with the possible exception of Wovoka, were not shamans until after they had ceased to lead dances to bring about the return of the dead. In the minds of the Paviotso, there is no connection between those dances and the shaman's performance (Park 1938:45).

Wovoka, the leader of the 1890 Ghost Dance movement, was well known in his later years as a shaman with unusually strong power for curing disease. At the same time, his counsel was often sought in other matters. Clearly, he wielded greater influence over the Paviotso than did any of the contemporary chiefs; but in spite of this unofficial recognition and the great prestige that he enjoyed among his people, Wovoka was not looked upon as a chief nor did he ever claim the title (Park 1938:67).

As to the origins of both the 1870 and 1890 Ghost Dance movements are traced to the Paviotso, it may be of interest to estimate the position in the society of the various leaders of these movements. Four prophets who announced the imminent return of the dead and held dances to facilitate that event are distinctly remembered today; possibly there were others. At the time that they preached their doctrines, the prophets were not shamans, i.e., they did not have power to cure. But all, of course, had visionary experiences and, therefore, were apart from normal individuals. Apparently when a messiah declined in favor, because of his inability to bring about the promised resurrection, he acquired power to cure disease. Several of these prophets became powerful doctors in their later years and were much in demand for their curative abilities (Park 1938:69-70).

The social position of the prophet is rather difficult to reconstruct on the basis of present conditions alone. Evidence suggests, however, that Ghost Dance leaders did not become chiefs; in fact the vested interests of the chief and the well-established shamans were the source of the strongest opposition. In spite of this resistance, the prophets appear to have exerted considerable influence and caused a great flurry of excitement for short periods; then followed a marked decline in public interest when they failed to produce results. At least two prophets later regained much of their earlier prestige through the demonstration of great power in curing. One of these, Wovoka, was a powerful and influential figure among the Paviotso. He was held in high esteem by members of all the bands, and five years after his death, he was spoken of by nearly all Paviotso with admiration and respect. Perhaps some of the influence he enjoyed in later years among his own people can be traced to the demand by other Indians for his advice on religious matters (Park 1938:70).

Many other leaders who sought to restore the ways of their ancestors, but with little permanent effect, arose from time to time, but it was not until the late 1860s that Tavibo, a Paiute of Mason Valley, Nevada, practiced his beliefs. Dying in 1890, Tavio left a son, Wovoka, then about fourteen years of age, who later followed the teachings of the father, which had a far-reaching effect and ultimately resulted in the Ghost Dance religion which, far from a part of the Paiute belief, practically met its end in the disgraceful masssacre of the Sioux at Wounded Knee, South Dakota, in 1890 (Hodge 1956:12-13).

[Mooney describes Wovoka as a] rather weak personality, which makes him an exception among the prophet figures we know. His teachings, which showed little or no hostility towards the white man, were not very revolutionary either.... His message even contained all sorts of elements in conformity to the white men's ideals.... For Wovoka's teaching became the object of far-reaching reinterpretation.... The Dakota Sioux went further in this. Reinterpreting this originally pacifistic doctrine inspired them to armed battle.... (Kobben 1960:120).

An Indian prophet told them [Plains Indians] that he had experienced visions which indicated that all the Indians, dead as well as living, would be reunited upon a regenerated earth to live a life of happiness again, free from the Whites, misery, disease, and death. This package of prosperity was so attractive to the depressed, oppressed, repressed, and suppressed personality of the defeated Plains Indians, that they became converted to the new religion in droves. They actually thought a transformation of the world was about to take place and discussed the dates when it was supposed to happen (Driver 1961:536).

A resurgence of the Ghost Dance began in 1889, led by another Paiute messiah by the name of Wowoka [sic] (or Jack Wilson). The doctrine was the same as that of the first Ghost Dance. Wowoka asserted that he had visited the spirit world while in a trance, and that he had seen God. God directed him to instruct the living Indians that they should be good and love one another, that they must live peacefully and return to the old ways, and that they were to sing certain songs and hasten the millennium by dancing. If they did these things, the white men would disappear and the living and dead Indians would be united in a renovated world where all would live in happiness in deliverance from misery, death, and disease (Spencer and Jennings 1965:499).

In the case of Wovoka we have left to us accounts of his message which if anything are even less authentic than the words of Wodziwob which have filtered down to us

(Dangberg 1968:6).

The claim that his visions were "messianic" cannot, however, be substantiated by anything that he himself said.... (Dangberg 1968:10).

Some of the Dakota distorted Wilson's ideas into a hope of earthly resurrection, but for most of the Plains ground, including the Dakota near Prince Albert, the Ghost Dance furnished an **apologia** for the life they were forced to lead at the end of the nineteenth century. Their nostalgia for the virile, independent, aboriginal culture was assuaged by the expectation of resuming that culture after death. At the same time, the forging of a new reservation culture was facilitated by Wilson's approbation of a modified Euro-American pattern. The Ghost Dance was thus an adjustment movement that crystallized into a religion (Kehoe 1968:302).

It is virtually impossible to find a cult movement anywhere that does not contain at least some important elements from antecedent religious system (Walker 1969:250).

The Ghost Dance of 1890 was the revelation of a Paviotso messiah, partly a mixture of borrowed Christian notions with early Indian cults, and partly the authentic vision of the messiah. The fantasy of a new heaven on earth and the miraculous reappearance of dead ancestors and leaders as helpers was a response to the disintegration of Indian cultures under the pressure of the advancing white frontier (La Barre 1970:44).

[The successors to Pope of the Pueblo Revolt in 1680 were] Wabokieshiek, or "White Cloud," the Winnebago-Sauk Prophet of the Black Hawk War, the Delaware Prophet of Pontiac's conspiracy (1762), Tenskwatawa, twin brother of Tecumseh, and the well-known "Shawnee Prophet" (1805), Kanakuk, the Kickapoo reformer (1827), Smohalla, the Sokulk dreamer of the Columbia (1870-1885), Tavibo, the Paiute, Nakaidoklini, the Apache (1881), Wovoka, or Jack Wilson, the Paiute Prophet of the Ghost Dance of 1889, and...Skaniadariio, or Handsome Lake," the Seneca teacher (La Barre 1970:89).

It was the great Ghost Dance of 1890, however, that provided the crashing climax to the collapse of the American Indian culture. Tavibo, the messiah of the Ghost Dance of 1870, is said to have left a son when he died, a boy named Wovoka, "The Cutter." Some students doubt the relationship, but the two messiahs did come from the same area. As an adolescent boy, Wovoka is thought to have witnessed the ceremonies in Tavibo's tule reed wickiup, and he certainly saw the many visitors from all over the West who came reverently to hear the prophet's revelations. Like many other Paiute, Wovoka worked for the white ranchers of Mason Valley in Nevada. He became attached as a ranch hand to the very religious family of David Wilson, from whom he learned some English and at least a smattering of Christian theology. He also got from them the name Jack Wilson, under which he had almost legendary fame all over the west. Even far-off tribes knew he was omniscient, spoke all languages, was invisible to white men, and was direct messenger from the Great Spirit (La Barre 1970:229).

...and of these [the Sun Dance and the Peyote Cult], the Ghost Dance, as the movement symbolizing the greatest degree of cultural resistance and "nativistic feeling," was the specific ritual that entirely disappeared (Opler 1971:283).

This was the Ute Ghost Dance, in which the living were enjoined to prepare themselves by returning to the old ways. When this prophet died, Jack Wilson, a Paiute leader of the new revelation, sent his personal messenger to teach the Ghost Dance religion to the Utes. The Paiute's prophet stated that the Ute ancestors would return from the West in real bodily form and that there would be a great cyclone in which the Whites would perish.... [He] set the time within the next year so that the Utes waited expectantly, though many doubted the possibility (Opler 1971:283-84).

The Kuyui group was one of the bands which denounced the Ghost Dance theory. It believed the shamans were curers rather than prophets. It did not believe in Jack Wilson's prophecy. Its belief was that rain making was shamanistic and not prophetic (Harner 1974:92).

Wovoka's teachings were a curious blending of Christianity and native religious belief and practices. How this amalgamation took place is a mystery and the detail of their coming together may never be fully known (Johnson 1974:44).

Wovoka's influence, however, failed to extend to the Paiute of Oregon and to the Shoshoni of eastern Nevada, where the Indians resorted to warfare, or to the Paiute of eastern California and adjoining Nevada where the crisis, which came later (1860-1865) was quickly settled (Steward and Wheeler-Voegelin 1974:79).

The threat of white invasion to Paiutes in all parts of the territory was a different matter. Yet the reaction for the Indians was by no means uniform. Some followed Wovoka, the Prophet, whose religious formulaes were designed to expel the whites and restore native conditions (Steward and Wheeler-Voegelin 1974:304).

Tavibo, the prophet, arose in Mason Valley in about 1869, and his more famous son, Wovoka, preached in this area in the 1890s (Steward and Wheeler-Voegelin 1974:77).

Wovoka taught that the time was coming when the whites would be supernaturally destroyed and all dead Indians would return to the earth. The herds of game animals would also be restored, and the old way of life would flourish again on a reconstituted earth in which there would be no more sickness or old age (Overholt 1978:171).

Jack Wilson is said to have made the clouds come for the purpose of shade, to have made blocks of ice float down Walker River in mid-July, to have freed himself from jail by causing lightning to rip open the jailhouse, to have engaged in competition with other doctors of other tribes, and, as his well known to anthropologists, to have predicted the future (Olofson 1979:14).

He was then told that the dead would return and with them the old, happy wilderness life, provided that the Indians tirelessly devoted themselves to round dances.... (Hultkrantz 1979:152).

Jack Wilson prophesied that a time would come when all Indians living and dead would be reunited on a regenerated earth, in aboriginal splendor, forever free of death, disease, poverty, and non-Indians.... (Moses 1979:298).

...the new religion of Jack Wilson enjoined all Indians to love one another, to regard themselves as members of one family, a chosen people, and never to fight, cheat, and steal (Moses 1979:298).

When speaking of the Ghost Dance we usually refer to the movement that was started in 1889 by a Paiute living in Mason Valley, Nevada, Wovoka ("the cutter") or Kwohitsauq ("big rumbling belly"), 1858-1932. He was also known as Jack Wilson, a name given to him by his white employers, a farming family bearing this name. He was the son of Tavibo, a man who apparently took part in the Ghost Dance of 1870. Wovoka may have been influenced by his father. It is in any case striking that his message did not basically deviate from the gospel of the first Ghost Dance.

Wovoka had charismatic gifts. He could suck out diseases from his sick tribesmen, and he possessed the power of causing rain and snow. Sometimes he relapsed into deep tances, and in consequence of one such trance, or more probably a whole series of trance experiences, he was called by the Supereme Being to prophesy a reunion betwen the living and the dead. The exact wording of the message seems to have varied. While in 1892, after the Sioux Ghost Dance disaster, Wovoka told James Mooney that people would gather in the other world, provided they lived righteous lives and danced the round dance given to him by the Lord, he had a more active message of the coming of the blessed realm to this world in letter addressed to Arapaho and Cheyenne visitors (August 1891). The basic tenets were the following: the dead are arisen and are on their way to this earth, conducted by a spirit in a cloud-like appearance. The game is returning. There will be peace with whites. There was also talk of the whites disappearing from Indian grounds. It is quite probable that Wovoka's message was more revolutionary than eschatological from the beginning, but that he tempered it down after the military campaign against the Sioux.... (Hultkrantz 1981:266).

Wovoka's dramatic vision during the eclipse excited the Paiute. There was nothing novel in Wovoka's practices, though his message stressing peace and accommodation to Euroamerican patterns and his Christian-like promise of reunion with the dead in heaven differed from the former prophets' emphases. The young man's fervency, coupled with his tall, strong appearance, reputation for good character, and shamanistic techniques, brought him an immediate following. Songs were composed conveying allusions to his vision. The Paiute danced frequently (Kehoe 1981:311).

Wovoka believed that all Indians—living and dead—would be reunited in a world paradise, where Indians would be eternally free from poverty, disease and death. Wovoka prophesied a great cataclysm whereby whites and their ways would be swept away, inaugurating an Indian millennium. All of this would be hastened by the continual per- formance of the "Ghost Dance," a religious movement which spread rapidly among numerous western tribes (Moses 1985:336).

Dancing, peaceful Indians awaiting their divine redemption did not sell newspapers, so journalists surfeited the country with stories about Indians dancing themselves into frenzies as they awaited reinforcements from the risen dead. No journalist and no official of the Indian service ever traveled to Mason valley to hear the Prophet's unadorned message. Instead, misunderstanding of Wovoka's religion (of peace and love) significantly contributed to the Dakota disaster that ended at Wounded Knee, South Dakota (Moses 1985:342).

By any standard, Wovoka, the Ghost Dance Prophet, was one of the most significant holy men ever to emerge among the Indians of North America (Moses 1985:348).

Although Wovoka would have disavowed the honor of being the Indian Messiah, his identity underwent a metamorphosis in the minds of the faithful from the Paiute Prophet to the Indian Messiah, and finally to the inviolate Christ. By the time the Plains tribes began their investigations of the new religion, Wovoka had ascended to such spiritual heights that his visitors, by some accounts, approached him with averted eyes. Wovoka, however, never said he was the messiah, claiming only to be a prophet of God. Indeed, this fact was recorded by John S. Mayhugh, former agent at the Western Shoshone reservation in Nevada, and the allotment officer of the Nevada tribes. Mayhugh, who knew Wovoka, wrote that the Prophet foretold the coming of a Messiah who would appear on Mount Grant near the Walker River agency. Mayhugh's accurate message never became the prevailing view, and even today Wovoka is usually referred to as the "Indian Messiah" (Moses 1985:340-41).

In 1887.... Like Wodziwob, Wovoka preached that if the people danced the traditional Round Dance and prayed the Whites would be removed, their dead relatives would return and native resources would be restored.... (Fowler and Liljeblad 1986:460).

Although this last resurgence of the Ghost Dance as a religious movement did not last long, was mostly disregarded in the Great Basin even at that time, and was completely forgotten in the 1980s, the songs associated with it were remembered. In the absence of other choreographic types, the Round Dance as well as its musical style, assumed a devout character that it had presumably never had before (Liljeblad 1986:647).

Both the Ghost Dance and the Peyote religion taught the value of peaceful inter-tribal relations. Both taught that Jesus is a living God, who can appear, anytime on earth (Stewart 1986:675).

Wovoka's Ghost Dance, then, called for both accommodation to Whites and the strengthening of the Indian community. It called for adjustment to odious conditions in this world, the here and now, so that eternal happiness could be achieved in the "other world" in the future (Jorgensen 1986:662).

The second wave of the Ghost Dance was initiated by the Indian laborer Wovoka in 1890. During a solar eclipse he had an attack of fever and heard his fellow tribesmen make a loud noise to drive away the monster that devoured the sun. Then he had the following vision: When the died, I went up to heaven and saw God and all the people who had died a long time ago. God told me to come back and tell my people they must be good and love one another and not fight, or steal or lie. He gave me this dance to give to my people (Drijvers 1987:295-96).

WOVOKA (c. 1856/8-1932), Paiute religious prophet and messiah of the Ghost Dance of 1890; also called Jack Wilson by white settlers. Although he often referred to himself as Kwohitsauq ("big rumbling belly"), after his paternal grandfather, he was given the name Wovoka (or Wuvoka, "cutter") by his father, Tavibo ("white man"), who was reported to have trained his son in Paiute shamanistic practices. Tavibo had been an active participant in the 1870 Ghost Dance led by the Paiute shaman-prophet Wodziwob. Central tenets of this earlier Ghost Dance were related to the later teachings of Wovoka, which in turn lead to the Ghost Dance movement of 1890. Among these earlier revelations was the prediction of the return of the ancestral dead. This imminent return was to be assisted through the practice of a round dance, which would also effect an earth cataclysm and so result in the removal of white men.

In addition to Paiute shamanic practices and the Ghost Dance of 1870, Wovoka was influenced by his contact with Skokomish Shakers, Mormons, and other Christians. The Puget Sound Shaker religion of the Skokomish leader Squ-sascht-un (called John Slocum by whites) was primarily concerned with healing. It combined native shamanistic and Christian religious practices. These Shakers produced twitching-ecstasies and trances that sometimes lasted for days. Wovoka's later teachings were also similar to Mormon doctrines regarding the rejuvenation of the American Indians, the radical transformations in the earth's terrain, and the return of the Messiah. Moreover, Paul Bailey indicated in his biography of Wovoka (1957) that the famous Plains Ghost Dance shirt bears a resemblance to Mormon holy garments. Finally, after his father died, Wovoka was hired by a white family named Wilson. This position brought him into close contact with Presbyterian Christianity, which involved Bible reading, moral exhortations, and pietistic stories about Jesus.

Around 1888 Wovoka is reported to have undergone his first deathlike trance-journey to heaven. From this point his teachings were derived from conversations with the ghosts of the dead. Wovoka's oral revelations were associated with the ritual performance of the round dance, which promoted moral and spiritual renewal. His teachings were transmitted by means of syncretic mythology and dramatized through the skillful use of his personal symbols.

Wovoka's foremost revelation came in a deathlike coma experienced while he was suffering from scarlet fever during the solar eclipse of 1889. During this trance-coma Wovoka related that he saw God on a transformed earth where Indians and game animals abounded. Wovoka's messages increasingly focused on the presence of the Messiah, a role he himself gradually assumed. His mythology centered on the imminent revival of deceased Indians, who would be reunited with their living kin in an earthly paradise. His description of the fate of whites varied. He predicted that they would be either swept away by the cataclysm or amalgamated into the restored humanity. Many of these doctrines, such as the transformed earth, were more fully explicated by Wovoka's disciples, who disseminated the Ghost Dance in the years following 1889.

The later Ghost Dance, similar to that of the Ghost Dance of 1870, was a kind of round dance that lasted for five nights. Men and women, their fingers intertwined, shuffled sideways around a fire, dancing to the songs that Wovoka received from the dead. While the Paiute participants themselves did not go into a trance, Wovoka did occasionally journey in a trance state to the ghosts, who assured him that Jesus was already on the earth with the dead, moving about as in a cloud. Moreover, along with their remonstrations against lying, drinking, and fighting, the dead said that Indians should work for the whites and have no more trouble with them.

Wovoka's personal power-symbols were typical of native shamanic practices. Along with his sombrero he used eagle, magpie, and crow feathers and red ocher paint from the traditional Paiute holy mountain (now called Mount Grant). As with so many visionary symbol systems, their meaning is not fully known, but Wovoka often incorporated these symbols into his teaching so as to foster belief in his messianic role among his followers.

Wovoka went somewhat into hiding when news of the Wounded Knee massacre of 1890 reached him. He vigorously condemned the misunderstanding of his teachings, especially as reflected in the Lakota armed resistance. He also denied any influence in the development of the Ghost Dance shirts. He later reemerged as the continuing leader of the much diminished Ghost Dance. He readjusted his predictions of imminent earthly transformation, explaining that Indian ritual and ethical behavior had not conformed properly to his visions. Wovoka died on 20 September 1932 in Schurz, Nevada; his death was preceded a month earlier by that of his wife, Mary, his companion for over fifty years.

More is known of Wovoka than of other similar religious figures, but he can be seen as part of a larger revivalistic movement of the period. Various tribal groups, caught in the death throes of their traditional cultures and the inescapable morass of government reservation policy, responded to Wovoka's revelations from a variety of motivations that mediated between their present distress and their future hopes. Wovoka's injunctions against warfare, immoral behavior, and some traditional medicine practices enabled many who participated in the Ghost Dance to begin the psychic transitions needed to respond to the changing circumstances of life. Most important in this connection was Wovoka's orientation away from exclusive tribal recognition toward a pan-Indian identity (Grim 1987:486-87).

In 1889, well after the [1870] Ghost Dance religion as transformative movement had died among most California, Oregon, and Great Basin societies, a second Ghost Dance movement was started. Wovoka ("the cutter"; also known as Jack Wilson), a Northern Paiute from Mason Valley, Nevada, received a series of visions instructing him to revive the Ghost Dance religion. Redemption rather than transformation was Wovoka's message, but interpretation of his message varied outside the Northern Paiute area (Jorgensen 1987:543).

It began in the state of Nevada when a Paiute Indian named Wovoka had a vision that the white man would disappear from the face of the earth in a cataclysmic event: the earth would turn over, taking all the white men with it. All the old Indians who had died, as well as the buffalo, now all but extinct, would return to live the old way of life. Wovoka claimed that in his vision he visited with these spirits of the deceased Indians and they taught him a dance that would bring about the destruction of the whites. Wovoka preached to other tribes that it was useless to fight with the white man anymore, for soon this cataclysm would be upon them and they would disappear (Powers 1987:496-97).

Wovoka's teachings strongly opposed warfare with the Whites (Zanjani 1988:121).

Jack Wilson's creed was distorted among the Lakota, becoming a millennarian movement yearning for utopia instead of the Paiute prophet's sensible guide to a clean, honest life. Distorted, the Ghost Dance seemed to fail the Lakota (Kehoe 1989:39).

Additional Anthropologists (and others) on Wovoka

From information just received from Mr. James Mooney, who has seen the Payute prophet in person, I present the following biographic facts, with reference to this personage.

As near as can be ascertained, Jack Wilson is now (1893) thirty-five years old. He was called after the family name of David Wilson, the white farmer who brought him up in Mason Valley, Nevada, after the demise of his father. In the same valley, about thirty miles from the capital, Carson, he resides now. His stature nearly reaches six feet, which is more than the native Payute generally attains, and this magnitude of bodily proportions may have contributed to his success. He is a *full-blooded* Indian and was married in his twentieth year; no other language but Payute is spoken by him, and he is but imperfectly acquainted with English. There is no doubt that his religious teachings rest on a well-ordained religious system, and, in spite of the numerous false reports that are spread about him, he does not claim to be either God or Jesus Christ, the Messiah, or any divine, superhuman being whatever. "I am the annunciator of God's message from the spiritual world and a prophet for the Indian people," is the way he defines the scope of his work among men. The first revelation he received of God himself took place about four years ago, after he had fallen asleep. God admonished him to work zealously among his fellow-men in promoting good morals and delegated special powers to him to this effect. Thus he considers himself a messenger of God appointed in a dream, and has, on that account, compared himself to St. John the Baptist. When he had that dream he thought himself to be in heaven (Albert S. Gatschet 1893:111).

Jack Wilson could bring rain. At Sweetwater, five Sioux came to see him. As soon as they arrived he took a magpie-tail feather from his hat. He waved it in front of his face. Right away the clouds came up in the sky. Rain started to fall. When Jack stopped waving the feather the clouds went away (Park 1934:108).

By 1888 an interesting development took place among them [Northern Paiutes], which became famous throughout Indian country. Everyone who has read any Indian history has heard of the Ghost Dance, yet few remember that it started among the Northern Paiute. In fact, it began some forty miles northwest of Walker Lake...There lived a young man known as Wowoka [sic], which means "the cutter." He supported himself, as other Paiute did, by working on a White ranch, while he camped with his family in a brush-covered Indian house near by. In 1888 there was an eclipse of the sun, at a time when Wowoka was ill with fever. He "went out of his head" as the Whites would put it or, as the Indian[s] say, he "died for time." In that state, he had a dream or a vision about the life of the Indians in this changing time. This is how he told about it:

"When the sun died, I went up to Heaven and saw God and all the people who died a long time ago. God told me to come back and tell my people they must be good and love one another and not fight or steal or lie."

That was how a peaceful man thought of solving his peoples' difficulties. He wanted them to be at peace with everyone, even the Whites. In his vision, God gave him a special dance, to make his people happy. It was the regular round dance, which we have described, where men and women step sidewise in a circle, hand in hand.

Wovoka said they must dance it for five nights in succession, singing the songs he had dreamed. They were sung to the usual slow music of the Basin and their words were poetic, though brief.

The wind stirs the willows,
   The wind stirs the grasses
The whirlwind, the whirlwind
   The snowy earth comes gliding,
   The snowy earth comes gliding.
The rocks are ringing
   They are ringing in the mountains.

Wovoka taught that if people went through this dance at intervals, decorating themselves with a sacred point he had and if they lived rightly for the rest of the time, everyone
on earth would be happy. The Indians would live as they used to do, the White people would
disappear, all dead Indians would return and there would be no more death nor disease. He
did not tell his people to fight. He preached only that they should be good and hold the
dance, which was really a religious ceremony. His doctrine spread, for there were many
Indian tribes who wanted the old days to return. Some of these were fighters, like the
Arapaho and the Sioux. The Sioux, particularly, took up the dance with excitement and
added more to it than Wowoka had preached. In the end, their dancing brought about a
battle with the Whites and the Ghost Dance became known all over the country as a warlike
ceremony. It was never that in the Basin. There it continued for a few years and finally it was
dropped, though there are old people who can still sing the songs. The Paiute turned to
more practical ways of getting on under the new conditions (Underhill 1941:62-64).

Jack Wilson could bring rain. At Sweetwater [California], five Sioux came to see him.
As soon as they arrived he took a magpie-tail feather from his hat. He waved it in front of
his face. Right away the clouds came up in the sky. Rain started to fall. When Jack stopped
waving the feather the clouds went away (Park 1934:108).

To this may be added another cause [of Wounded Knee]—the spread Eastward of the
Ghost Dance religion, originated in Nevada in the late eighties by a deluded Paiute Indian
named Wovoka (Watson 1943:207).

Most of the familiar traits of the Ghost Dance complex, the resurrection of the dead,
the removal of the whites, the re-establishment of the old order of life, and survival
through compulsory belief and participation in the movement, were known to the Navaho.
The most widespread and significant element was the reported return of the dead (Hill
1944:523).

[Wovoka] could at will go to heaven by way of the Great Dipper and the Milky
Way...This was one of Jack's claims to supernatural power, according to Robert Dyer (Dangberg
1957:287 n.13).

Ghost Dance doctrine was compounded of ancient Northern Paiute and Northwest
Plateau beliefs in a periodic world renewal that could be brought about by ceremonies
(usually group dancing), combined with Christian teachings of the millennium and the
second come of Jesus Christ. The dance taught by Wovoka was the ordinary Paiute round
dance, performed by individuals holding hands and circling by stepping sideways. New
songs were composed. According to Wovoka, instructions were received from supernatural
powers, especially Jesus, during periods of trance or unconsciousness. Faithful dancing,
clean living, peaceful adjustment with whites, hard word, and following God's chosen
leaders would hasten the resurrection of dead relatives and the desired restoration of the
"good old days" of Indian prosperity. During world renewal whites would be quietly removed.
Although variations on the above doctrine later developed, these basic Ghost Dance teachings remained remarkably stable (Stewart 1980:180).

His research into the history of the spread of the ghost-dance, and his pilgrimage, at
the end of 1891, to Wovoka, the Paiute prophet who lived on Walker Lake reservation in
Nevada, convinced Mooney that the dance was a ceremony of peace and brotherhood, a
movement of cultural revitalization among desperately poor, nearly hopeless peoples (Hinsley
1981:216).

This movement, which was founded on a hope that the whites would soon be elimi-
nated through some supernatural agency and that dead Indians would be resurrected and
with their still-living relatives restored to the old way of life...(Overholt 1982:11).

Wovoka believed that all Indians—living and dead—would be reunited in a world paradise, where Indians would be eternally free from poverty, disease, and death. Wovoka prophesied a great cataclysm whereby whites and their ways would be swept away, inaugurating an Indian millennium. All of this would be hastened by the continual performance of the "Ghost Dance," a religious movement which spread rapidly among numerous western tribes (Moses 1985:336).

By any standard, Wovoka, the Ghost Dance Prophet, was one of the most significant holy men ever to emerge among the Indians of North America (Moses 1985:348).

A Northern Paiute sheepherder and shaman named Wovoka on the Walker River reservation had fallen ill, it appeared, and during the solar eclipse had had a vision in which he was transported to heaven. There, God had shown him a radiant world where there were no whites and where all the dead Indians and the former huge herds of buffalo and wild game were still alive. This happy world, Wovoka was told, was already coming through the heavens from the west toward America. By adopting certain prayers and practices, the Indians still on earth would be lifted in the air as the new world met and rolled over the present one, obliterating it and driving the white men back across the ocean to where they had come from. The Indians would be lowered to an eternal life of abundance and peace among their returned ancestors, relatives, and friends in the new world. Charged with conveying to the Indians what he had seen and been told, Wovoka after his vision had returned to earth as a Messiah who would rescue the tribes for their despair and suffering.

The religion he preached was a pacifistic one, based in large part on tenets of Christianity. To deserve the new world, which was to arrive in the spring of 1891, his Indian audiences were admonished not to fight among themselves or with white men, but to be honest, peaceful, and chaste and to follow a moralistic code of conduct closely resembling that of the Biblical Ten Commandments. Specifically, Wovoka taught the Indian prayers, songs, and a special dance they were to perform at certain intervals that would enable them to receive advance glimpses of the wonderful new world that was approaching. To convince his visitors, like the Sioux, that he was, indeed, a Messiah speaking the truth, he used his shamanistic powers and knowledge to perform deeds that appeared to be miracles (Josephy 1990:15-16).

Wovoka's vision transformed dry ghosts back into moist souls, a form in which they were retrievable to consciousness and life (Vander 1997:74).

According to modern-day Indian informants, he went on a journey to the other world where he met "The Messiah" (Christ) who told him that the spirits of the dead were going to return to earth and that the earth was going to be a happy place again. The Messiah gave Wovoka a "dance of welcome" to dance in order to welcome the returning spirits... Wovoka did not see God, but "The Messiah" (Christ), and Wovoka did not claim he went to Heaven as Mooney implies by saying he went "up to the other world." Rather, he went along a path bordered by flowers to the other world (Kersten Jr. n.d.:4-5).

The Prophet's Death

1. "INDIAN MESSIAH'S CAREER IS RECALLED WITH DEATH OF JACK WILSON AT YERINGTON," *Reno Evening Gazette* (4 October 1932):

PIUTE WHOSE STRANGE GHOST DANCE AROUSED TRIBES OF ENTIRE WEST TO FRENZIED OUTBURSTS AGAINST WHITES BURIED AT SCHURZ.

The Indian prophet, Jack Wilson, Wovoka, whose fanatic doctrines symbolized by the ghost dance spread like wildfire among Western Indians in the late '80s, died unnoticed in his hut near Yerington this week and was buried in a sandy grave at Schurz near the shores of Walker lake.

The excitement created by the spread of Wovoka's doctrines, which included a belief that the red men were to be restored to their inheritance and reunited with their departed friends, led to a frenzied movement which was partly to blame for the Sioux outbreak in the badlands of South Dakota in 1890.

IS REMEMBERED

Old-timers here remember Wovoka, or Jack Wilson as he was commonly known, as an unusually ambitious Indian, hailed by his brothers as a second Messiah.

"Magic" worked with the aid of a bullet-proof vest, white men's pills and some good "breaks" in the weather made him the most influential figure of his time among the Indians. So great was his influence, in fact, that representatives of the bureau of Indian affairs were sent here from Washington in an effort to get him to cease his activities, but Wovoka hid in the buck brush until they had departed and then resumed where he had been interrupted.

Born about 1857, before the first white family came to Mason valley, Wovoka was the son of Tavibo, the prophet of Mason valley, and when the father died, the son was left to carry on his work. By nature of a solitary and contemplative disposition, he showed no promise that he even remembered the work of the other prophet, and it was not until he was over thirty years old that he began spreading his fantastic doctrine among his people.

In the interim he had been adopted by the David Wilson family who bestowed upon him the name Jack Wilson, by which he is commonly known among the whites. From his association with the Wilson family he gained some knowledge of English, together with a confused idea of the white man's theology.

STARTS IN 1888

It was in 1888 that Wovoka first launched the doctrine that spread among the Indians in the late '80s and was held responsible for serious Indians wars, notably the Sioux outbreak. Wovoka was ill with a fever, and during that same time there was a total eclipse of the sun. The prophet went into a three day trance, according to the story, and when he recovered, he told his people he had seen the great spirit, and that the great spirit had told him that the people might recover their land and the whites disappear if they would live properly and if they performed the ghost dance.

"WENT TO HEAVEN"

Wovoka, in later years, had this to say: "When the sun died, I went up to heaven and saw the great spirit and all the people who had died a long time ago. He told me to come back and tell my people they must be good and love one another and not fight or steal or lie. He gave me this dance to give my people."

Mrs. George Wilson, with whose husband the prophet was raised, said today she recalled the time when he became the Messiah.

"Not long after an eclipse of the sun," she said, "Jack called a big dance to which hundreds of Indians came. The dance was held below Missouri flat, near what is now the Cordry ranch. Throughout the dance Jack remained in his tent in what he said was a trance. He was there for three days and nights, and during the day all we were permitted to see was his back. At the end of the third day, he arose and came out with a gun, which he handed to another Indian who fired it at him. The bullet took no effect, and the Indians hailed him as a messiah."

POWERS DOUBTED

The action is said to have been largely characteristic of his workings and it let many to doubt his real sincerity. Placing of ice in the river in mid-summer to prove to Indians his prophetic powers and other similar acts caused him to be discredited in many sources.

There are those, however, who have talked with him intimately, and who have not doubt of his sincerity, at the first at least. They claim Wovoka really thought he was endowed with prophetic vision and that he believed he could help his people to wrest from the white man the land which he believed was rightfully theirs. It is noteworthy that he distrusted the whites as they distrusted him and was loathe to talk with persons other than those of his own tribe.

HAD GREAT INFLUENCE

That the Indians believed in his completely is evidenced in the wide-spread adherence to his doctrine. Although the ghost dance custom lived for only a decade in Nevada, he continued to exert great influence over Indians in other sections, and for many years continued to receive gifts of moccasins, beads, shawls and money. In return he sent from Mount Grant red paint for them to decorate their bodies and eagle feathers which carried his blessing.

The department of archeology, anthropology and ethnology at the University of California has displayed great interest in the ghost dance and other tribal customs peculiar to Nevada Indians and made several calls to Wovoka to travel to Berkeley to explain his powers. He heeded none of the calls, and many of the secrets invaluable to research workers, were buried with him.

In the true mein of the tribal daughter, Mrs. Alice Vidovich of Sparks, Wovoka's daughter and only surviving relative, would give no information as to the declining years of her father's life. With her husband Jerry [sic] Vidovich, Southern Pacific employee in Sparks, she is the owner of a well-kept modern cottage, and on the surface she is truly Americanized. But she retained the old Indian belief that whatever secrets Wovoka possessed should remain with him, and said today she did not wish to discuss her father's life or his powers.

FIRST GHOST DANCE

The first ghost dance took place on the Walker lake reservation in January of 1889. Hundreds of Indians gathered about the scene of the dance, which had been cleared of grass. Wovoka stood in the center of the cleared space while the Indians gathered around him in silence, and led the dance until late at night. The next day the dance continued, but he was not there, and on the third day the prophet lay perfectly motionless while the tribesmen continued their movements. All the next night and until sundown the following day the dance went on, until the medicine man gave orders to the crowd to disperse.

NO MUSIC

Without music, even the beating of the tom-toms, was the dance conducted by the Indians in Nevada. The Piutes danced in the cleared circle four nights and until the morning of the fifth day, ending the performance with a general waving and shaking of blankets, this act being designed to dispel evil influences and drive sickness and disease away from the dancers. Despite the subsequent development of the custom there were no trances among the Piute dances, early day ranchers who have witnessed the dance say.

Other tribes took up the dance and within a short time it had spread as far East as Missouri. The religious frenzy it aroused, aggravated by local grievances, led to numerous disturbances, of which the Sioux outbreak was the most noteworthy.

The dance as performed outside of Nevada was more frenzied but was an elaboration of the dance first projected by Wilson.

The funeral services held as Schurz were simple and in no way indicated the great place that the man once held in the council of the Indians. Following his death the body was taken from the Indian camp at Yerington to a home in Schurz where it was kept during the night, while the Indian men and women kept up the customary "wailing." The following day the body in the coffin was taken to the Indian burying ground and lowered into the freshly dug grave, while scores of Indians stood around with bowed heads.

Rev. H. H. Enig, Indian missionary at Schurz, recited a short prayer, and the Indians then departed for their homes.

Whether a special marker will be placed over the grave has not been decided. It is in the family plot in the Indian burial ground, but Indians at Schurz and vicinity have indicated that it will represent no special shrine of worship for them, although they all admit, even the young ones, that Wovoka once was the most powerful Piute of the tribe. Of late years he has acted as a medicine man, but failing health caused him to become very inactive recently.

2. "AN INDIAN PROPHET'S PASSING," *Reno Evening Gazette* (6 October 1932):

Known only to a few white persons as an Indian of note and by them his importance hardly realized, Jack Wilson, Piute medicine man and prophet, who died near Yerington this week, once caused grave anxiety to this government. Credited by some authorities with being the originator of the real ghost dance and by others with have revived it after it had been originated by his father, Tavibo, during the 'seventies, he began teaching it in 1889 in Mason Valley in this state as a prelude to bringing the Indian dead to life and restoring to the tribes the control of their ancient lands. His teachings became the basis of a sort of new Indian religion. The dance and the doctrine spread rapidly and its misinterpretation caused the battle of Wounded knee, South Dakota, in which a body of Sioux clashed with regular troops. It was a religion of peace, as Wilson taught it, but at Wounded Knee, its perversion led to the death of at least two hundred warriors, women and children among the Indians—some say a hundred more—and thirty-one soldiers.

Part of the Indian world in America seems to have been in a mental condition to receive the "revelation" that Wilson offered, and by 1890 delegations were visiting his tepee in Mason Valley from tribes of the Arapahoes and the Cheyennes on the east, and from as far as the Pacific Ocean in Southern California, while to the north Indians in Idaho sought to learn the new religion and at length it reached the Sioux. The Arapahoes accepted it, especially the doctrine of peace. With the Sioux it took another form. Wilson is said also to have predicted that the white man would disappear, though he disclaimed the spirit of hostility, but the Sioux, led by Sitting Bull, Red Cloud and others, angered at a recent reduction in rations and a long course of what they charged was injustice, used his peaceful religion to arouse dissatisfaction against the Whites. Sitting Bull, who had been leader at the battle of Little Bighorn in 1876, where General Custer was killed and his entire force wiped out, and who was chief votary for the ghost dance of Wilson, was among the first to fall while resisting arrest in the new movement. By January 16, 1891, the trouble was over.

While all of this was going on Wilson was living quietly in his little hut in the Mason valley, receiving delegations from distant tribes and occasionally receiving visits from distinguished white students on American Indian life. The later generally agreed that Wilson did not counsel violence but only kindliness and peace. Like many other prophets, however, he was to see his religion perverted to warlike ends by those who adapted it to their own purposes.

3. Letter from Alida C. Bowler, Superintendent of Carson Indian Agency, Stewart, Nevada, to John C. Harrington, Ethnologist, Smithsonian Institution, Washington, D.C., 15 December 1938. Inter-Tribal Council of Nevada Archives (#739).

Dear Mr. Harrington,

We were very much interested in your letter of November 8 inquiring about Jack Wilson who started the Ghost Dance. I find that he died in Yerington, Nevada, September 29, 1932 at the age of 74. The death record gives uremic poisoning as the cause of death. By going through the files of old newspapers in Reno, I was able to find that the *Reno Evening Gazette* had a front page account of him on October 6 and an editorial a couple of days later. We have copied these two newspaper accounts and are sending you copies, so that you can see the information that they gave. Apparently the other Reno paper took no notice of his death.

I have made some inquiry about him and think I will be able to get more information for you later. I have the name of a woman on our Walker River Reservation who is supposed to know quite a bit about him, but I have not been able to get over there to talk to her. I did talk to Jim Vidovich, our Indian police from Reno whose brother, Andrew, is married to Jack Wilson's step-daughter. Jim Vidovich is not a man that I had ever suspected would be particularly interested in this sort of thing. He does not even speak any Indian language. However, he was very enthusiastic in telling me about Jack's power. He told of trips that Jack made back into the middle west where he had conferences with other medicine men and his power was always greater than theirs. It seems that he was considered a powerful Indian doctor by everyone in this region and even white people went to him for help. Once a white farmer in the vicinity of Yerington who was depending on rain rather than irrigation found his crops burning up and went to Jack who made it rain on that man's farm only and his crops were saved. This same white man had a neighbor whom he disliked and he asked Jack if he could make the neighbors crops burn. Jack told him that he was perfectly able to do this, but that he would not do it. I am sure that as I get opportunities to inquire around, I will be able to get a good many more stories about him and his life.

I asked Jim Vidovich whether he thought Andrew's wife would be willing to give information about her step-father. He says that she never liked to talk about things like that and he doubts very much if a person could obtain much information from her. That family is now living in Saceton, Arizona, where Andrew Vidovich is employed as carpenter in the Indian Service. I have not yet been able to learn the meaning of Jack's Indian name nor how it was pronounced, but will try to get information about that and send you later.

Appendix K

"I Remember Jack"

(Remembrances of Wovoka
by Yerington Paiute Tribal Members)

ROSIE BROWN (b. 1905)

After Jack Wilson got his power, he used to go up to Pine Grove. White guys would tease him there. They'd say, "Jack, why don't you make it rain? It's hot up here. It's July, and we're going to roast." Well, so all Jack said was, "Uh-huh!" And he laughed.

'Cause, Jack, you know, has many feathers that can do many things. Like make it rain or make the wind blow. So one day, after they said that to him, Jack went up there and stood up one of his magpie feathers. It was a nice day, and pretty soon it started to cloud up. Rain started pouring down, in a little while, it washed out cabins, horses, and cows, down the canyon. So those men who teased him, they begged Jack Wilson to make it stop.

Jack was always showing his buha. Another time he made icicles in his hands. My mother said she saw him do this. First he prayed, which he did a lot of. And after Jack put his hands, palms up, and little icicles formed, the people began eating the ice from his hand. Another thing my mother said he did—When he had certain things to do, like doctoring someone, Jack would call his Indians together and they would have big circle dances. Three of four circles would be going, one circle in another.

Another thing about him—Jack Wilson used to sleep a lot. Sometimes he would sleep half a day or longer. While he was sleeping, it was said he went to Heaven. Indian Heaven, you know, it's just the same as white man's Heaven. And people would sing special songs that he taught them while he slept. This would bring him back to earth, and he would wake up again.

I know Jack Wilson spoke of Heaven, but I never heard him pray. People say he believed in the Bible, but he wasn't even educated, so how could he?

ANDY DICK (b. 1887)

The early dance was in Sweetwater [Valley], at the Walley Ranch, near Paddy Conway's place. That was a Pine Nut dance, you know. Jack, he put ice in the water, told all to wash in the creek afterwards. So they did. [It was a] Two night dance there. 'Course I was just a little fellow, then. [I'd] Play with the little fellows and sleep in the morning....

I know one summer, Jack put up a dance. In Wellington. No food during that dance, no, Sir! Jack, he called that "Indian dance." Rained 4-5 nights, by God. Rains like hell, but he keeps right along, keeps right along. Indians [came] from back East. They came that time, too. Some of his relations from Schurz, they came, too. Yeah, two times they came to Smith Valley like that.

I also heard about a big circle dance in Yerington. Don't know if that one was a Pine Nut dance, though, but Jack, he gives Buckaroo Sam a stick. Just like his Hand Game stick, that kind. Jack cuts a piece of willow [or bone?] that's the size of your finger, gives it to that other fellow. And Jack's song goes through that stick [bone?] to Buckaroo Sam's mind. 'Cause he's just as good [singer] as Jack, that fellow, you know. Yes, Sir! Buckaroo

Sam sings same songs while Jack goes to sleep.

Another time, there was a dance in Nordyke. When he warns of the ice in July....

Dances, Big Time, that's all [we call them]. But some bad ones come in from the East, tryin' to kill him. You see why you can't? 'Cause Jack's got more power than they [do].

Last dance I hear about was in Schurz [Walker River Reservation]. No more after that. 'Cause you see why? Jack, he don't wanna. Don't wanna sing no more. He's gonna make those fellows good over there. And Jack, he don't pray in Schurz, either. Don't say nothing like that [praying]. Says, "We'll have good fun. Pine Nut time. Then we go home." That's all he says.

Yeah, Jack's dances just called "dances." Like that one in Smith Valley, at Irene's [Thompson] place. Fall time of the year, and it starts to rain, by God. But he makes it all night. Yeah, I'm a little fellow then. So I run inside my dad's tent. Jack, he sings, and everybody dances all night long in the rain.

At East Walker, Jack was walking along one time and he stumbled over a log. Shot himself in the neck—with his own 12 gauge shot gun. That's way before I'm married. So Jack, he sings, and he dances for his self. Gets well, too, by God.

Another time, near Campbell Ranch, the Pittman Ranch, near the foot of the hills, Jack chased the rabbits toward the drivers. And they shot, alright, but their shots don't hurt him. 'Cause bullets bounce off his head. Same way at the Gallagher Ranch, back of Campbell Ranch, another rabbit drive, some crazy guy shot him. But he's not hurt.

Another time, George DeCroy shot Pat Wilson. Shot him in the head. At John Hardie's place, somebody else shoots Pat Wilson, at sundown. Shot him in his stomach. That was a rabbit drive, too, but he [Pat Wilson] never say nothing. 'Cause he's not hurt. Must have been just like Jack, huh? Got his own power!

And I know at East Walker, too, Wutsikopa shoots Pat Wilson. He was running behind him [Pat] and he fell, and Pat is accidentally shot. Wutsikopa belongs to Yerington, East Walker bunch. Pat's shot in the head, so his brother put a white blanket down and took the bullets out. Next day, his brother was O.K. Jack just puts his hands on Pat Wilson's head and all those shots come out.

Jack Wilson doctors his own way, you see. With his head. Nobody gives him that power, either. Same as my father.

Yeah, good man, Jack Wilson. Good Headman. He knows the country. Jack's just the same as any preacher. Talks to God.

I'll tell you how they [Jack and Pat Wilson] die: Tom Mitchell's doing that to them both.

RUSSELL DICK (b. 1923)

I myself have had two visions of Wovoka.

The first time, I was walking from Smith Valley to Mason Valley, and at Wilson Canyon, with the sun coming up, his face showed to me on the rocks. That was about 1968.

The second time, I was sitting in somebody's house and next to me was a man in a black suit. I asked my partner if he saw him, too, but he said he didn't.

NELLIE EMM (b. 1906)

Mother said that Jack had an old horse, but when Jack got on it, he put his feather on its mane and they flew over the sagebrush. His [horse] name was Wuchubai?A.

Jack's father's name was Numuraivo-O. He had a long beard which he trimmed by plucking the hair with two nickels.

This story was also told to me by my mother. She was about the same age as Jack Wilson. About 84 years old when she died.

My mother said that Jack Wilson went up to the Wabuska Hills to get his power. Way up on top there's a ridge with a V on it. By the white spots; the white dirt was used to make plaster. There's a road going up around the back of the mountain. Jack was a young man when he went up there, and at that spot, there's big rocks. Yeah, Jack Wilson had to go up there. He had to stay up there three nights and three days. I guess there were caves up there for them [medicine men] to stay in. From the lower end, from the road, you can see the spot. His father [Numuraivo-o] instructed Jack what he was supposed to do [up there].

Jack had to take a young horse with him, a horse that has never been ridden. And after he stayed up there for three nights and three days, the power that he was to possess came to him, with its special songs, too. Jack Wilson's father said, "When you are ready to come down, tie an eagle feather around the horse's neck and then put one on each of your arms. Tie them at the elbow. After you do this, you get on that horse that has never been ridden and you're going to fly off the mountain." Well, so he flew down over the big rocks and the big bushes. Landed on the high peak in Wilson Canyon. This is the place where his power and his medicine is. This is how Wovoka got his power.

Jack Wilson also controlled the power in Wilson Canyon. Whenever someone was sick, they would ask Wovoka for help, and he would then call this power, his medicine from that mountain in Wilson Canyon.

My husband called Wovoka in for my sister who was shot and he put his feather in the wound and the blood was drawn into the quill. My sister also had pneumonia at the time, so this was only half a cure. She died two years later, of lockjaw. Because I don't think Wovoka took out all the buckshot.

This was on 4 October 1927. Here's how that happened....

We were working at the Old Grock's place, picking potatoes. Coming home from work, and my husband asked me to come to Yerington. To watch the gambling with him. I said, No! Because I had my baby's clothes to wash. (Hadn't washed for a week. My mother used to baby sit for me when I washed clothes.)

Well, when we got home, my sister was sitting in the back of a Model T. In blankets. She was in the back with my mother and a friend. Nobody knew that [BM] had a 45 pistol loaded in the car. In the old times, he [her husband] had a bag hanging beside the seat. So he asked me to go [get it] again and again I said, No! Well, [BM] grabbed his gun and he accidentally shot my sister on the right side. Under her arm, by the waist. The bullet came out her back. I didn't even realize what happened. I was so confused, I didn't even remember where I put my baby. Then I went around the car to hold my sister. Asked her, Where she was shot? "In my arm," she said. When I looked and I saw blood squirting out her side. Just like a faucet. We all started then toward the house. It was only about 10 feet away. I took my sister inside. When we were in school, we were taught not to expose ourselves to the cold weather, so that's why I wanted to get her inside the house. While we were walking to the house, my mother went around the car to my husband. She pushed his hand down. Told him not to do that. He was pointing the gun at my back, you see. While I was helping my sister inside the house.

Mother then went after Dr. Reese [the contract physician]. I and my step-father, in the meanwhile, put my sister down on the bed and cleared out her wounds with Lysol and water. Wiped them with clean clothes. After we finished, I went over to [Sheriff Claude] Keema's place to call for the doctor. But when I got there, they said they didn't have a telephone. So I told Mrs. Keema what I had done for my sister, and Mrs. Keema said that's really all you can do. Mrs. Keema then gave me some more clean clothes. I went home [Yerington Indian Colony] and made more fire. Just waited for the doctor.

When Dr. Reese got there, he gave my sister some morphine pills for the pain. That's when they found out that [BM] was on drugs, too. That's probably why he shot my sister. 'Cause she was also on drugs. She said she didn't feel anything. I went outside and I prayed. Raised my hands and I said, "God, it wasn't intended for her. It was for me. Jesus, please save her life. Don't make her have pain. Heal her wound." I prayed real hard, I don't remember what else I said.

After I went back inside the house, my sister sat up. They put a blanket behind her head and she went to sleep. The next day my husband went after Jack Wilson. He was an old man then. He came and he doctored my sister. Jack had some eagle feathers. He put one of them on her wound, then he sucked on the feather. You could see the blood coming through the feather. Blood went into Jack's mouth and he spit it out again.

Later, after he had done this a number of times, Jack sat down. He said she has a chipped bone. Piece of bone from her rib. Said he was going to take it out. And that piece of bone was about as big as a liver. After Jack spit it out, he showed us. Then he put it in the palm of his hand and rubbed his hands together. Sang one of his medicine songs. When he opened his hands, the sliver of bone had disappeared. My sister got well, and in two weeks, she was again walking.

After Jack doctored my sister, he sat around and joked with us. Jack was sure a funny man. Visited a while, then he went home.

Jack Wilson was just another Indian to me. My second husband [Brady Emm] used to live with him. Brady was born in Jack's house in Mason, you know. Jack Wilson is his cousin-grandfather. One time, Brady got into a car accident, and Jack took [extracted] the windshield that was in Brady's mouth from that car accident with his feather. Didn't even have to suck it out, either.

Here's how Jack Wilson died:

He got with a woman from Fallon. This was after his first wife, Mary, died. Jack was fooling around and he caught V.D. Long time ago, Numus didn't know those kinds of sickness.

Anyway, my mother was in the Pine Nut Hills when she heard that Wovoka died. She didn't believe that. My mother says she can't believe he'd ever die. She's seen his miracles, that's why. "How could he die? He was such a smart man." That's wha she always said.

HAZEL QUINN (b. 1899)

Jack Wilson was born in Smith Valley. His father was named "Indian White Man." His father was a medicine man and his son was just like him. Jack Wilson healed everything. He could control the seasons, the winter, and thunder, too. Why he can even make the rain come. Those thick clouds would just start to gather up! 'Cause that's how he was, a real smart man.

From then on the news got around and he started to get better and better and more well known all over. And if anything happened to somebody, like they got sick or got shot and needed doctoring, they would go to Jack. If someone got shot with a gun and had internal bleeding, Jack Wilson sucks out the blood. The blood don't stay inside a person that was shot. Later, the patient would get well. Jack sings only five songs, no more. He sings five songs to doctor each patient. Yes, sir, he was a real powerful man.

Later on he used to be around Schurz. (He was really from Smith Valley, you know, and he moved here to Yerington.) And he can show people his power and how he can use it.

When he went from place to place he would hear people make fun of him. There was a time at a place called Circle in Smith Valley, and the men saw him coming and yelled at him. They were saying, "There goes the Rainmaker!" So Jack Wilson showed them that he was a rainmaker. He made the rain come to only that place where the men were haying. It rained and it rained, no one could travel through there because the place was all plugged with water. There's no lie about everything he could do. This was Jack Wilson.

Later on he came to a place called Ma-tah. This was where he made his home. And this was where he started the dances. People came from all over to dance.

He talked to the people when they gathered to dance. There used to be lot of Indians in those days. Nowadays, there's not that many. There was one big mountain where he gathered his people. They gathered below to hear him talk of the coming vision of a horse that was to appear on top of the mountain. There were thousands, maybe two thousand people, to hear Jack Wilson talk, and show his power, and listen to the stories that were coming to pass. He wanted to show the people because some people didn't believe his miracles.

He said in five days a horse will appear on the mountain top. And sure enough a beautiful white horse appeared on top of the mountain. The horse was so beautiful, it was the color of snow. My mother told me this. She saw it happen! It was before my time.

Jack kept talking to the people, same time motioning the horse to come down. So slowly it came, taking its time. Once in a while it would stop, too. It would neigh once in a while, too. And that horse was so beautiful. When it was coming, it looked like its hooves weren't even touching the ground. My mother thought to herself: What kind of animal would understand him? My mother had good eyes when she saw all this. Yeah, that horse was so beautiful. Jack kept motioning to the horse to come down. And when he started to come down from the mountain, every once in a while it would swing its neck and neigh softly. But Jack kept begging him to come closer and see your children. 'Cause they had already sprinkled the ground with water where the horse was supposed to stop and stand, you see. To meet his children. Yeah, my mother said the horse was really beautiful.

So pretty soon the horse came to a stop. He looked at the big crowd of people and he swung his head and neighed again, then he stood still while Jack talked to him. Jack told the crowd to watch the heavy cloud. "Watch it closely," he told the crowd. Then a heavy cloud started to move towards them, coming closer, closer.... It came right on top of the horse. It was bringing rain for the people to drink! And all the people drank from a cup that time. The horse, he stood still. Every once in a while he would neigh, too. Jack, he said to the horse:

"Slow down my little one. Don't be impatient. Your children haven't taken a good look at you yet."

Jack told the people, this horse has pity on you and wishes you all abundance. The horse neighed again. He said, "Take it easy before you depart from your children. Before you leave your children in good faith. You will go back on your journey in a peaceful way."

Now that horse finally departed back onto his journey. He was going along slow, trotting along part of the time, and his hooves looked like they weren't even touching the ground. My mother said this. It was a beautiful sight, she said. The horse went up the mountain and he disappeared. My mother said there was no lie to this. This was Jack Wilson's power.

So after all this happened, Jack set up a dance. He said, "We will dance for five nights." This was in reverence of the horse for coming down from the mountain to see his children. People came from all the country to dance. Lots of people, not like nowadays. In those days, everybody dances. When they say they're going to dance nowadays, just a handful dance, and the rest of the people just watch on. In Jack's day, when they dance they make a big circle....

So the Indians danced for five days. Jack Wilson sang all the songs for those nights. There were some real intelligent men among the crowd. They caught on to those songs fast and took turns singing. My mother has seen all this.

And when Jack lost one son, he made rain fall down to earth and covered all the footprints of the places where the boy had traveled. It rained for five days. Meaning [that] everywhere his footprints were, [they] would all disappear with him, and everything would be alright again. Jack said this will be the truth. There was a big flood those days when it rained. It rained and it rained. People lost their little dwellings, because those days nobody had wooden houses. It rained and it rained, destroyed everything. One old man by the name of Tom Mitchell went out to see and to talk to Jack about the rain. He said, "Jack, Why are you doing this? Our children are freezing. Why don't you take it easy. We don't have any homes. What are we going to do?" So Wovoka said in a few more days it will stop raining.

This was what Jack done: ordered the rain to come and cover the tracks of his son that died.

That's the story about Jack, Jack Wilson. Where Jack used to live I think they are going to fix it up (Interview by Dorothy Nez and Winona Holmes, 12 March 1974, Yerington Paiute Tribal Archives).

FRANK QUINN (b. 1902)

There used to have a lot of rabbit drives there across the valley when I was a little boy. The Indians used to gather together and plan where and when to meet. They used to have Indians dances, too. That was the best part of it. Jack used to go all over to the rabbit drives. There's one incident I would like to tell you about.

I guess somebody didn't like him and took a shot at him, intending to kill him. I saw this, because I was with the gang. I was just a little boy, then, bringing the team of horses for them. Anyway, when Jack got shot he was hollering at everybody and moving his hands up. He was standing there and he said, "Boys, I've been shot!" And another thing, he asked for a handkerchief, too. You know the old time blue and white kind men used to wear around their neck in those days? When Jack stood up, there was an ant nest, so he stood up there [on it] and he put the handkerchief on the ground. When he did that he unbuckled his belt and pulled out his shirt and his shirt was full of holes. And then he took off his shoes. Laid them right there. He shook himself off, shook off all the shells, and he stood there and he said: "Boys, you see all these bullets were
intended to kill me." Then he picked up the bullets and he wrapped them up and he

passed them around to the men to see. When he pulled off his shirt, you could see where the bullets hit. There's lots of red spots on his body, too.

That's the kind of man he was. If it was just an ordinary man, he'd be a dead man. But nobody knows how it happened or who did it. They did try to find out later. But Jack knew all right, he didn't want to say nothing.

This is all I can say about him. When that was over, everything is quiet, nothing goes on. They tried to plan for an Indian dance at one time, but a bunch of drunks came around. So now the people don't plan anything like that. Never used to be like that, though.

[Also] He doctored when he was asked. His wife lived at the Yerington Indian Colony. She died at the south end, and so Jack, he moved to the north end. He moved in with his grandson and his grandson's wife.

Taivos called him "Rainmaker." They're afraid of him. He was supposed to be a "Big Man." But they all know him. When he lived here [Mason Valley], [Taivo] people would come to see him on business. Even when he lived at the Wilson Ranch they came there to see him (Interview by Dorothy Nez and Winona Holmes, 12 March 1974, Yerington Paiute Tribal Archives).

CORBETT MACK (b. 1892)

Jack Wilson's name is Muhu-bit, Owl. Maybe he says this all the time, maybe that's how he gets that name. Jack, he lives with his father all the time, across from Nordyke, small lumber house. Jack's father? Call him Numuraivo-o, "Indian [Northern Paiute]-White man." 'Cause you know why? He's stolen from this country. Soldiers, they drive him out of his own country in that [Pyramid Lake] War to make a home elsewhere. They do that to a lot of Indians, you know. Afraid of them Indians, that's why. Too many in one place. Don't know where Numuraivo-o's sent to, either, but, anyway, he comes back.

Yeah, he was stolen before Jack is born. Blind when I first came to know him. And he had a wife back there. Soldiers, they forced him to marry, you see. Lonesome, I guess. So when he comes back here, he's with that wife. I know I call that old man gunnu-u [father's father], grandfather. He's a doctor, too, a witch, sa-ab. Jack Wilson's father doctored the old man's sister after she stole a baby off one Ay-taya [Italian]. Only thing was, Numuraivo-o made her worse. So she died, but my father can't do nothing to him, 'cause they related. That's Big Mack, my old man. His sister, she was the one that died that way. That's the only [bad] thing I ever heard about Jack Wilson's father.

He lives at Nordyke all the time when I know him. Camps near his son, 'cause Jack Wilson, he lives by Bill Wilson and Joe Wilson. Works for those Taivos all the time. But they don't raise him, Jack Wilson's own father raise him. Father and his mother raise him. Never did know what they call Jack Wilson's mother, though. She dies first, then 2-3 years later, her husband, Numuraivo-o dies. That's before [the death of] Wodziwob [1870 Ghost Dance Prophet],'cause they're way older than Wodziwob. They're like my grandmother.

And Jack Wilson has got two brothers, Pat Wilson, and Toyanoga-a. They're both full [blooded]. Toyanoga-a, he was married to Nelson Charles's mother—before she had him. He's the youngest. Anyway, he dies young, some kind of sickness. But I used to know Pat Wilson real good. He dies before his wife [Annie]. Pat gets along real good with his wife all the time, only thing though, he's a heavy muhu [opiates] man. Steady user, I tell you. He uses that all the time. And Pat's way older than me, 'cause he's already married when I know him. I know him. Work with him and his wife at Mencarini's Ranch all the time, in Smith Valley. Pat Wilson's a real Old-Timer, you know, but he uses that muhu all the time, anyway. And Pat, he likes his whiskey, too. Wine or whiskey.

I used to come to visit Jack Wilson in Mason all the time. That's after that dope business is all cleaned out. They get alone good always, Jack's people. Nowadays, though, seems like

brothers don't get along so good, but them days, everybody's a brother. 'Cause that was Old Indian way—everybody's your cousin-brother.

Same way with his kids, they're full [blooded] too. Jack's oldest daughter is older than me. They call her Lucy, or Josie, or Poosie, or Tusi. She's about the same age as Mamie [Dick c. 1887]. Lucy was married to Pete Penrose. She don't use no dope; only that second one [daughter], Ida, ?ayidi-I, she does. She's the one using muhu, you know. You see why? 'Cause she's married to one guy that's doing that. But I don't think Jack Wilson ever says anything to Ida about that either. Don't try to bawl her out for using muhu, 'cause he's not that kind of guy. Yeah, he talks sense, you know. How to make a living.... But he never did say about whiskey, dope or wine. 'Cause he knows young people won't mind him.

Last one [daughter], though, she's not full [blooded]. She's a nomogwet [half-Paiute]. That's Jack Wilson's youngest girl, Alice. She belongs to Simpson. You see why? Jack Wilson, he used to work for Old Man Simpson. Same as his wife does, too. I know he's been working for Simpson in Smith Valley a good long time, irrigating, haying, all that kind work, 'cause he used to live up there [Smith Valley] a long time ago. Yes, sir, before he move[d] down here. So George Simpson, he makes a "friend" with the Indian. He sneak on her. George or Joe Simpson, I'd say, 'cause that girl looks mostly like George Simpson when she laughs. But George, he's got a wife, so he can't claim her. Good man, though, Jack Wilson. He says she's his daughter. Names her, too, by God. Most people are not like that, you know. They don't say "my daughter," they just name them. That's the way some of them Old-Time Indians are. And that's early days ago, partner, when his [Old Man Simpson] father's still living. Old Man [Dan] Simpson always has to hire the Indians all the time. That's why all them Simpson boys like the Indians, so they can sneak on them.

Jack's partner with Big Mack, you know. Visits him all the time, brings him food, pine nuts, kuha . . . I know I call Jack Wilson's wife pithu-u [aunt] and I call Jack hai-i [father's brother], but I don't even know how we're related. Smith, that's where Jack has his camp. That's where my father bought a lumber house from him. It's a big wood house, Jack Wilson gives it to my father on account of how he can't move it. You see why? He wants to move back to Missouri Flat, Nordyke, where he stayed for a good many years before, by Bill Wilson's ranch, where he can do ranch work, ploughing job...anything the boss tells him to do. That's why when Jack was working for Simpson, he wants a [lumber] house. So he builds it. Bigger than a tent, but it wasn't that good. So when the old man bought that lumber house from Jack Wilson, we just get our two horses and we moved it.

Jim Wilson's the one told me about Jack Wilson's powers. Said, Long time ago, there was no snow and everything was drying up. So Jack Wilson called for a willow basket and water filled up that basket, and he gave it to the people to drink. I know that's what I'm always hearing, what Jim Wilson's always says. Says that Jack Wilson can make it rain. He says the river was dry, no snow in the winter and people were suffering for water. Digging in the snow for water but they can't get any. No, so! And so Jack Wilson, he put a willow basket there and it filled up. Lots of people drink out of it, too, I hear. In Mason Valley.

Sam Leon told me that one time, Jack Wilson worked for Dan Simpson and he digs up a tree. Small tree, you know. Jack Wilson can pack that on his shoulder. But when it starts to rain, Jack, he don't even get wet. And that tree, it's still up there [in Smith Valley]. Over where Fred Fulstone lives.... Jack's clothes didn't get wet, either, so I kind of think, maybe he makes that rain himself?

Those miracles, they're before my time. Once there was no water in the river, and so I guess Jack puts a pot down. Water came down, his pot fills up, and everybody that's thirsty, they can drink. Jack's also got power to make it snow. Winter snow, you know, so there can be lots of water for those pine nuts [to grow]. Big Mack says how he once made ice float in the river in the days when there wasn't any ice. Said Jack Wilson also lays down all night long alongside his dead grandson, and by morning, by God, that boy's back, well again. Big Mack says how he borrowed a man's gun one time and he cocked it. No Indians could shoot that gun. Only Jack could. Says one time at a rabbit hunt, someone got shot full of shells. It was an accident, and so Jack, he goes and gets a tarp and he puts the man on it. Cures him, all right. Those shells just fall straight out.

Yes, sir, Jack Wilson has a strong mind. He believes in God. Believes in Jesus, too, but he don't talk [preach] about Jesus. Jack Wilson don't never do that. I never did hear him tell the Indians about that kind of story.

And he don't talk much about himself, either. I know that, 'cause sometimes, we come down to Nordyke and stay 1-2-3 days. Jack, he don't talk about nothing, then. Him and the old man, they tell one another about something, that's all, but nothing about the real Indians. Just about people, that's all. That's all they ever talk about.

Another thing the old man tells me about Jack Wilson—he's a huviya-u, a singer. Puts up dances all the time. And that's before he's a doctor. You see, Jack Wilson's a powerful man before he's a doctor. Got some kind of Old-Timer song that only those real Old Timers can sing, only thing is, I can't get his song. I know him, but I just can't get it.

My mom and the old man been to his dances, too. Not my grandmother, though. My grandmother's a funny woman. She never gets in there where there's fun. My grandmother's a hard-working lady, she just likes to stay home. Don't want to look at nothing. A lot of old ladies, they're like that, you know. And those dances Jack Wilson had, they're in Smith Valley. He puts up those dances to cause storms in the winter, so there can be more food to grow for the Indians. Indian food, that's why. And they can have those dances any time of year. After a while, we don't hear about any more dances down here, so I kind of think Jack Wilson puts them up in Schurz.

I know one dance was across the highway from where Irene Thompson lives. In the brush. I remember that dance. Foreign Indians with a tub came, and they beat it and hop around in their loin cloth, nearly naked. But that's not a Pine Nut Dance. Jack Wilson's dance that time, you see, was just to show these fellows around here how those other Indians dance, that's all. I got tired, but I saw those guys dancing. They put paint their face, white paint. Face and on their chest, too. They don't use a pole, though, to dance around it. And they're real good at their dance. Never stay in one place for very long, and they don't fall down, neither. Yeah, they dance good. Everybody's there, too. All them Smith Valley Indians come down to Jack Wilson's place. October, sometime in October, that's when they're doing that. Before the cold. One I'm talking about now was on the other side of that Central Store, 'bout a half mile away. And Taivos, they don't go into that night time dance. Daytime dance, maybe, not nightime dance. Ghost Dance? I never heard of that kind.

And I don't know how many days, nights, they stay. Dance a couple or three nights, get tired, and them fellows wanna go back. Jack Wilson's the only one with beads in his moccasins.

Another time, way up to Wellington, when I'm small, I remember a dance. Same people coming in here. Bannocks, from Idaho, and Indians from Utah, Colorado Indians, too. Bannocks, you know, they got bows and arrows, so any Taivos want to watch, they got to back up when they dance in Smith Valley, 'cause they're afraid they're going to turn them [arrows] loose. But they [Bannocks] don't do that. Just to make believe, you know. They dodge around, lay down there, that's what them Bannocks are doing. Just like that's a war. Showing these Indians from around here how they do it when they go to war.

Another kind of people that came down here to Wellington we call ?ad siva, Cheyenne. They got a Mohawk hair cut—sides are all bald and the center is long and tied. I know we make a pine nut soup for them. But Bannocks, they don't wanna gamble when they do that kind of dance. Just play football and that woman's stick game, too. Show that to them Bannocks, too, only thing is, they won't try to play is handgame....

The only time I seen Jack to show his power was during a Big Time in Smith Valley. That time, people were also coming down here. Bannocks from Idaho.... They came over to visit and dance. I'm a young guy yet, never went to Stewart. Four, maybe five years old, that's why I remember. And Jack Wilson, he's a powerful man, I guess. You see why? Them [Bannock] fellows, when they went away, they want to shake his hand. And they're getting pretty shakey when they do, I tell you, by God. But Jack Wilson, he just laughs about it. Just sits there and laughs, 'cause it's his power that's doing that to them. Shakes them all over, you see, and they feel scared or something. And by God, he can also load up his pipe with Indian tobacco and point it to the sun. Suck on it and it's going to light, too, By the Sun! That's the only time I seen what he's doing.

Jack don't work, though. Visitors, they can bring money to him. They're his friends, you know, ones [who] come down here to visit him. They're the ones he sends feathers to. Also he goes out [travels]. I don't know how many times he traveled to Idaho, but each time he comes back home with money. Goes to California, all through that State. And Jack, he takes Pete Penrose [son-in-law] on his first trip—to Idaho. He can take Tommy Cyphers [from Carson City] with him, too, 'cause they're related. I don't know how many times he went over there to Oklahoma, either. Twice, I kind of figure. Yeah, twice. Just visits around, I guess. Maybe they call him, huh? To visit. Well, anyway, he likes to go all around to see the country. Yeah, Jack Wilson, he's the only one like that. Travels around.

And he comes back here with a lot of them Navaho blankets. Nobody around here don't give him a lot of presents like that. Friends, long way, they're the ones doing that. You see how? Jack Wilson can treat them right and they give him something. This Indian around here don't treat him right. Don't give him present, 'cause they ain't got nothing good!

But I never see that Jack Wilson's rich. Oh, he might have a little money, 'cause you know them Old Timers, they always got a little money. They can hang on to what little money they make all the time, them Old Timers. Only thing is, Jack Wilson, he also makes his money doctoring.

You see, he don't doctor when he's in Smith Valley. He starts late. And Jack Wilson, he's the best doctor around here. Pretty powerful man, I tell you, Mike. 'Cause I know him. Wears his hair long, like a woman's hair. But he cuts it when his wife dies. Yeah, so he starts in to doctor late. Before I'm married. Starts in Mason. And that was when [David?] Wilson leased his ranch to an Ay-taya [Italian], and there was no more work for Jack down there, so Jack moves to Mason and starts to doctor.

But nobody's afraid of Jack Wilson, 'cause he's a good guy. He can put his hands on a sick person, cure that way. I know when my mother was hurt, Jack tried to doctor her. Tried to take that sickness out of her. That was only a little cure, but he can't make it. Told the old man, "I ain't got too much of that kind of power. You better get another doctor for that."

No, I don't think he can stop an eclipse. You gotta stay home when that eclipse comes. Stay in your house, 'cause you can't hid from it. And you gotta put your coat on if you're outside. I never seen anybody's praying when that kind of thing happens, but I'm working with all Taivos all the time. No Indians around.

Yeah, Jack has power on his arms, and he can cure that way. I know he's just starting to get power the real way when he died. You know how he dies? Tom Mitchell. He b.s. him. Says, "We can put our power together and help the Indians." But he's only b.s.ing him. So Jack, he loses his power and he dies. I know I'm afraid of him [Mitchell]. Every time I see him walking along, I give him $1.00....

And I don't see where the hell I am when Jack Wilson dies. Even the old man don't come to his funeral. End of his life, you know, Jack's living at that Indian camp in Yerington. Both his daughters already gone by sickness.... And there was an Earthquake when Jack Wilson dies. 'Cause he says [prophecies] so, you see. Says, "If I go a long ways from here, I'm gonna shake the ground for you." Well, so Jack Wilson, he died and was buried in Yerington. And that earthquake, shakes pretty hard that time, I tell you. Pretty nearl looks like those trees over by Central Store [Smith Valley] gonna shake over. I know when we hear that earthquake, we just stay there on the ground. You stand up, it makes a fellow pretty much think maybe he's gonna fall over. Makes you pretty shakey, partner, I tell you. Jenny Joe, she lives with that Chinaman who runs the laundry in Smith. She's from Bishop or Hawthorne, and they found her crawling near a ditch, speaking the Bible. Nobody else was praying, though. We don't do anything like that when the earthquake comes. So I guess it's true what Jack Wilson says. How when he gets to that different country, he's gonna shake this earth!

HOWARD ROGERS (b. 1903)

I remember Jack. You know I never heard that name Wovoka until 1938, when we first moved up here [Campbell Ranch]. Jack, Jack Wilson, that's how they speak about him all the time.

Stands straight all the time. Got straight cut hair [above the ears] like that. Wears regular shoes. Also moccasins, Levis, jean or suit pants. But he's always wearing a black suit coat. And any kind of shirt. Oh, and he owns a hat like nobody else does. And he wears it, too. No, I never did see him wearing Indian jewelry or beaded things, but I did hear Indians used to send him things from Idaho—blankets, shawls and money.

One funny thing about him—I never seen him do a day's work!

He's living in Mason when I first came to know of him. South of town. Only Indian family there. Got his wife, and his daughter Ida, and her hubby, and their kids. I know Jack raised Archie and Andrew and Inez [Penrose] because their mother died. You could always see him at the Mason store. Any kind of time of day, you can see him there.

They called him a medicine man, and he could make 'em well, too. Indians from around here, they all looked up to him. They respected Wovoka. Most doctors have to use their lips and mouth to suck illness out a person's body. Not him. Wovoka don't use his mouth. Just his hands. People used to go to him and say that when he put his hands on your sore parts, it felt like

someone was sucking or pulling on that. Only thing was, he charges too much. Say, around ten dollars. And he stops at midnight. Most of them Indian doctors go all night. Not Jack Wilson. He goes only half a night. But I never saw him doctor nobody.

Wovoka? That comes from cutting wood. I guess 'cause he does that, you see why? Lots of wood always: Su wivi?qa-A. Wika is one, and more than one is wivika-a.

Yeah, he's famous, alright. 'Cause he's a doctor. Got powers just like the others. One time, though, some white people made fun of him. Said he put ice in the river. But the Indians, they believe him. Yeah, he just says it to do it, 'cause that's his power, you know. Another time, his brother Pat got shot. That was at a rabbit drive. Wounded, you know. With beebees. So Jack spread out his canvas and lays him out. Tapped him with his hand and the shot fell right out! And I know that's true, 'cause I was a little guy then.

Sure he's bulletproof! Lots of those people were like that.

You know, you don't even have to be a powerful man to make it storm. Just so long as you don't make fun of it [the weather], that's all.

No, me and Lena didn't go to his funeral. We heard he died, but our car had poor tires. I heard he just got sick and died.

LENA ROGERS (b. 1904)

My mother was doctored by Jack Wilson and she got well. Why is he famous? Because he's doctor. But he's a nice, friendly man. Related to my grandfather some way. Usually you're afraid of those doctors, you know, 'cause they can witch you. So you tell your kids to be scared of them. To talk nice to them. But not Jack, though. He's a real nice old man.

Yeah, I'd say he was bulletproof. Beebees can bounce off him and his shirt will be full of holes. No, he doesn't talk about Jesus, though. He's just like us. Talks like us common people. Not like Taivo preachers, either. Yeah, I'd say he's just like anybody else.

CHESTER SMITH (b. 1915)

I remember Jack Wilson. I was 8 or 9 and I used to stay with him. He used to give us kids a quarter to go to the movies.

His house was at the "Y," that fork in the old road that used to run down the center of this [Yerington Indian] Colony. Never heard the name Wovoka, though. Just Jack. I heard he had a Indian name, but I can't tell you that. But I know he's got a horse and a buggy because we can ride Jack's horse—bare back. Has a barn for his horse and buggy, too. Where Harvey [Conway] lives. Across from the road from the ex-cop [Jack] Dalton. Jack and Mary sleep on the floor. Just like the rest of us!

I believe he went to the White Hills in Mason for his buha. Then he used to get lots of letters, they called for him to come to Oklahoma. So he'd pack up his suitcase and we'd take him to the railroad back here in Mason—the old Copper Belt to Wabuska, and from there, he'd go to Hazen, near Fernley. He didn't have to pay anything, either. Schurz prearranged for all that free transportation.

He'd leave with one suitcase and when he'd come back, he'd have four suitcases, all of them filled with all sorts of things: beads, beaded moccasins, buckskin dressed clothes.... He'd lay it all out to show us because Indians back then don't use a table like nowadays, they put everything on the floor, spread out some canvas, you know. Or if they have a sheet, they put everything on that sheet.

Jack Wilson had a good home. One big bedroom. Later on, another room got added on.

And people would come from here to ask him to doctor them. Charged five dollars and up I hear. Only thing was, Jack never touched the money. They always gave that to his wife, Mary. She does all the talking [interpreting] for him, too.

I think I even saw two Ghost Dance. One was up in Missouri Flat. Jack got all painted up with white chalk and red paint that time. There was a barn fire, and he preached, but I don't remember anything he said. Too young that time. Not interested in anything like that.

Another time he had a Ghost Dance under the light at the Colony. I was also a young guy, then. Jack got all painted up again. Taivos came to see him, but they got scared. They just got in their 1929 Fords and they left when he started dancing around. They were afraid of him.

I heard he died of v.d. Body was left in his house for three days. He tried to doctor himself but I guess he couldn't cut it. Guess his spirit wasn't with him any longer.

IRENE THOMPSON (b. 1911)

Everybody calls him Jack Wilson. He used to call me tocho-O, granddaughter, only I don't even know how we're related. Oh, he talks to me in our language, alright. But I never heard him talk English. I'm hanging around his place all the time because I used to play with his granddaughter, Elizabeth [Bender]. She lives with him, you know. Afraid of him? Why I should I be? He's just another nice old man to me. Jack! You know what his Indian name means? Chopping up something or breaking up something. Maybe stove wood. I know my grandfather always used to talk to Jack. His name is Tom Mitchell, and he's got just as much power as Jack. My grandfather used to dress in a suit all the time, too. Just like Jack. Only thing was, Jack, when he walks to town, he's always dressed up with his buckskin gloves.

I heard what my grandmother told me about Wovoka:

One time, a long time ago, during the Pine Nut Dance I guess, and all the Yerington people were down there at Schurz, 'cause you how they always have a Big Time long time ago. Anyway, somebody ran over one of his kids, and Jack, he got mad. Makes the wind come up. Blow everybody's house over. Indian houses don't have a floor, you see. So I guess he just blew those houses away.

I know I believe that part. Because my grandmother was there. Not my real grandmother, she was blind; Indian-way [classificatory] grandmother. And my grandmother said she was scared to death. Jack made a big fire, she said. And after all that wood went down [burned], I guess Wovoka had something special in his hands, 'cause when he rolled up his sleeves he had red charcoals under there.

Yeah, Jack Wilson did that. And he never got burned. That's when the wind started blowing.

Dennis Bender's mother had that accident [suicide?]. His other daughter, Andrew Vidovich's wife, what's her name? Oh, yeah, they call her Pozi?niyu, "Patchquilt." 'Cause she's making quilts I guess. She's one of them [illegitimate children], you know. Her sister also had one of those kind—with an Ay-tayay [Italian], but she died when that girl was seven years old. And here Alice claims she's Jack Wilson's real daughter!

His wife? She's a Pit River Indian. Spoke good Paiute, though. Jack used to go to Idaho they say. He always used to say, "I'm a Bannock Indian."

Another time, I heard Jack's wife Mary was from Schurz, Mono Lake country.

I also remember an old Indian from Oregon. Jack Sundown was his name, and he used to come down here every summer for Wovoka's healing powers. Jack Sundown was a real good rodeo rider. Spent two weeks with Jack in the summer. They'd sit together on a blanket and Wovoka would talk and pray for Old Sundown. Well, it seems that Jack Sundown never came back here anymore. Horse fell on him and killed him.

Jack Wilson was a different kind of medicine man. He would sit down beside you whenever he doctored. Others would dance in a circle around their patient, praying.

Once he was doctoring an Indian [Numu] lady named Elsie. Seems she had a bad chest cold. Jack was leaning over her, you know, doctoring her, when her husband Stanley came home. Stanley thought that Old Jack Wilson was trying to take over his woman, so he started beating up on Old Jack. Gave him a good licking, too. Afterwards Jack Wilson told everyone: "I had to stop doctoring that old lady. Almost got me killed!"

To me, Jack's just a regular fellow. I wasn't afraid of him. Why should I be? He's just another old man: Jack. That's how I'm always thinking to myself: "Just another old Indian man. So what's so special?" Nice old man, though, so he must be a Christian. Maybe he is the second Jesus. I don't think so myself. But I know he don't preach and holler around like my father-in-law, George Decroy did at the [Yerington Indian] Colony. You know, hollering around in the morning about us doing this and that. And he's always neat when he comes to town. Jack Wilson wears beaded gloves with fringes, moccasins, his black hat all the time. But lots of old Indians also dress like him. I know my grandfather did. I'd see Jack walking to Yerington and he was always dressed up like that.

He lived in a cabin by the tree he planted at the north end of the Yerington Indian Colony when I was married. I don't ever go inside there, though, I just stand by the door. It was a lumber house. And Jack talks in Paiute. Dennis Bender takes care of him, and Robert Minkey lives with them, too, but what I hear is, those two brothers don't get along so good. Oh, and Catherine [Bender], she does all the cooking. They all sleep in the same house.

When he died, many people thought Wovoka will come back again.

Alice Wilson Vidovich, Andy Vidovich and Peg Wheat on Paul Bailey

Tape 74, February 1966, Margaret M. Wheat Papers #83-24, Special Collections, University of Nevada–Reno Library. Transcribed and edited by Michael Hittman.

Tape 74. Part 1: Side 2.

ANDY: And, Alice, gee, I'm proud of her people: Her mother and her father was just so darn good to me. I don't know, I just feel so—I didn't have my father and my mother too long, but they were everything in the world to me. And when I married her, believe me, she was, they were really good. Alice said that her mother wanted me [laughs]. I guess maybe she did? Because I was willing to work. And I never let my family starve. I couldn't do that, so, she thought the world of me, her mother did. Dad [Wovoka], too. And that's the reason I honored them very much. Among the finest people I ever known.

Yeah, so, I've got the right to be thankful for what I have got. And I've got Danny [nephew] here, and his family. So, I don't know what any other contentment [besides] what I have now.

...

Yeah, that old Paul Bailey stuff, though, that got me. Darn it, I'd like to kick the head off of him!

(Alice laughs.)

PEG: Yes, let's all get together and do it!

ALICE: Oh, I never cried so much in all my life. I'd stay, I'd cry nights. And feel so bad.

ANDY: She got in with Dad, you know, one day, and they was going to do everything. Made up her mind that she'd let, you know, and maybe that's about the only gateway to bring out right, you know? Some body to get the truth? Truth overcome all things, they say.

PEG: This is true, it will!

ANDY: I could turn around and talk for three, four days about the Old Man [Wovoka]. But the thing is, I know Alice'd shut me up pretty quick, so I don't.

PEG: But you'd tell all the real fine things to goad him on.

ALICE: Sure! He [Wovoka] was a good man, that's all I could say about him. Kind, he'd help *every*body. I don't care who he is! And he didn't charge a penny, either.

ANDY: Wanna talk nice to you, and he'd talk. If the other way, he'd walk away.

ALICE: [And] Never was cross us kids. Never! Only when we were naughty he'd switch us on our legs. But we deserve it, 'cause we all have to have that.

PEG: This is important to grow up right.

ALICE: I would [can] still feel it on the leg [laughs]! He never hit us on our head, or body, only on our leg with the switch. And he didn't do that very often. Just once in a great while.

ANDY: I told her she was lucky, because out at Stewart [Institute], they not only had those blacksnakes [describes J.D. Oliver, disciplinarian, who used a hose with ball bearings and buggy whip on little kids, whom he tortured on a platform or at a whipping post to which their hands were held up, stretched and placed in cuff; larger kids were beaten with the blacksnake]. Cut you up in pieces! [Describes three kids who got away and an old Indian tracker who found them, and how the kids were then punished in the same manner. Alice recalls the jailhouse in which they gave those kids bread and water after whipping them, and which others tried to burn down.]

Tape 74. Part 2: Side 1.

ANDY: Oh, [and] they make me sick when they hurt him. I can take that man's [Bailey's] head off! You know, when you see those things, you know, you have to believe it. 'Cause I know, my poor woman there, she don't wanna say anything, for fear it's gonna be different, and this and that.

...

Yeah, He's [God is] just everything! He's the maker of all things. [So] Why couldn't he [Wovoka] understand? You know, what make me sick these days? They say those Indians are savages; they and they this and they this. Well, we live off the land. And we didn't have to go through these big mines, and this and that. And gather gold, and go crazy up on it. Why didn't we have a religion that's just as good as our white brothers? Why couldn't we?

PEG: You did, and it was better!

ANDY: Now there's over 700 different religions in the United States, and each one profess to be the *true* religion. It makes me sick! And the Indians, they were savages, they don't know what religion is. They don't do this. And then they have a hard time making inroads to baptize the Indians, because the Indians had their own [religions]. Why, sure! And they believed in it, too! They had faith, where the white man would fall down in different things!

(Both agree with Wheat's claim that there was no hell in "Indian religion.")

ANDY: [After also agreeing with notion of the incompatibility of evil with a good and just God] I wonder about these different [Euro-American] religions, and all this and that. [They say:] "Andy, what make your folks so far away from God? Because you don't understand our Bible?" And all this and that. And won't listen [But] I know doggone well, when I read that Bible, when I get sick, that that ain't gonna make me well! But in our own belief, and in our own faith, we had men that we live with that took care of that. And when that prayer is put through, [if] it's a good prayer, it would heal a person! But a White man's prayer would hit that ceiling and bounce back! That's about as far as it got!

Alright, so, the thing is, when a person tries to reason this out, that's something. But I'm gonna tell you something; I'm gonna tell Alice is this: When I went through those terrible operations in Arizona, I wasn't supposed to live. I had only about 36 more hours to go. And my gall bladder was all busted, it went through into my system. Album [sic] was all in that blood. And they had to give me eight cans of ether to put me away [sleep]. And I was in terrible condition. And they thought I wouldn't come out of it. And they thought I was a drinking and a smoking man, and everything. But I'm gonna tell you something, believe me, and I wonder about it:

I remember when they wheeled me from the operation table—I was under the operation for about four hours: on Armistice Day. They took me into that place where, that room, I was to stay; in that big hospital. Light came on, I seen those windows; and I seen everything. Even though I was out, and mind you, I see things! And who did I see?

ALICE: You was delirious, that was all!

ANDY: You could say "delirious"; you could say the dream. You could say everything. But I say to this day that I've seen it! I seen the Great Master come through dimensions; in that hospital. And I know just exactly like he looked, as he looked. And there's no pictures today that has a resemblance of the Great Master! There ain't nothing there to compare with. Alright! And back of Him was who? Was the old man [Wovoka]! See? And they talked. I remember the Great Master looked at me like this, and I was sitting up, and I looked at his face so close, to see if there was any turning point in his face where he, which he was gonna say, if I was gonna live or die or anything like that? But there wasn't. But I remember her dad says: "My son: You have been a good man." And he said to me: "You have loved your family. And cared for them." And he says, "You're gonna live." And I went right through dimensions on the other side—just as if that wall was made out of paper. Or made out of [?].

And I remember, I don't know how long I lay there? Alice says I lay there four days before I came to. She was in the room when I came to. I told her afterwards what happened.

ALICE: Well, he was in that delirious stupor, you know; from that ether. That's why he wasn't in his mind when he "went through."

ANDY: I didn't have that in my mind!

(And after they quarrel)

ANDY: Here's the thing: I could see it right here, just as if—

ALICE: You must have! Because that's not—

ANDY: You see, now there it is. People wouldn't believe it! They can't visualize it, you know what I mean? It's something that you can't see. You know, you can't believe it. Well, but I could believe it. Because I seen it, and seems like it was so real. And it didn't fool me, you know what I mean? It wasn't like looking at that dead wall there. But the thing is, now, he [Wovoka] spoke, and that's the last I ever seen [of him]. So that's a connection with the Great Spirit, so the Indian must have had something.

(Following Wheat's comment "There's more than meets the eye," and how there's help when you need it, he agrees, then implies that he, too, must have **booha** or shamanic power, insofar as he always knew when his wife or son were sick, and how his employers thought he was crazy when he insisted upon being let off work early to return home.)

ANDY: [But] Bailey [laughs], he just made fun of it. He ride the fence. He [Wovoka] did do it, and then he didn't do it. By golly, Bailey, I'd like to—Bailey was a good man, and he was a just man. And if he'd told the truth, oh, he'd have been a *wonderful* man. He just done it wrong! But the thing is, what I'm trying to do is to set it right! To show that man [Wovoka] was a wondrous man, and he was a good man. Yes, he was, there's no question about it! And the Great Spirit must have had the blessing for him, like he gave to nobody [everybody] else. The Great Spirit had gave it to the White folks, all the way on through. Moses had it; everybody had it. All the disciples had it. But why couldn't it be for the poor American Indian? Why couldn't it be?

(Wheat agrees. Stressing "The Plan," and how it's for everyone, Indians included, how the majority "can't see it," only the great teachers can; and how they are misunderstood at one time or another, still, they survive and rise above misunderstanding.)

ANDY: [In agreement] I know poor Alice don't like to mention lots of these things, for the fear that it would naturally make him look bad, and all this and that; and take away the blessing for Danny [nephew]. And all this that. And his children that are coming up. She wanna leave them a nice road. But the things is, now, to set that good thing right. The truth will have to be brought out! That's the reason why I brought these little happenings out—to show that it was the truth. And everything else.

ALICE: But you couldn't say what Bailey said about him was true!

ANDY: No, that's what I say: He [Bailey] set it apart from the truth! And it takes truth, Alice, to bring that back. You know what I mean? To kill it! [Because] You can't make wrong right. Nobody can! It's once done, it's wrong, that's all. But you take people today, they do things, they cover up and cover up. But still it's wrong. It's still wrong. The more they try to cover up, the worse it gets. Bailey, he's just one of those fellows that think they can do these things, make money, and all this and that. And he just breaks those things. And he know darn well in his heart he was doin' wrong. Oh, shucks, that's quite a thing. And that's the reason it really have to be put in to place, in order to make it right. And make him honorable, you know. As he had right to be made honorable. I just, I don't how people could do these things. Because—

PEG: Wovoka is honorable! If there's anybody who's not honorable, it's Bailey. Nobody will ever change Jack Wilson! He was a great guy! But Bailey has put a very unhappy light on the whole thing, because he just doesn't understand. You don't change Jack Wilson, Jack Wilson's great. And I think that anybody who ever came into contact with him realized his sincerity, his kindness; his desire to help people. And his ability to help people. I think he was fabulous. I'm glad I know somebody who knew him. I'm very proud of this! I think he was a fabulous man! And if he had the strength, and ability, to make people well, I think this is absolutely wonderful! And I believe it! I believe it! Just as strongly as I believe anything. There have been others that could do this, too.

ALICE: OH, YEAH!

PEG: All down through the line.

ALICE: He's not the only one. But he happened to be the goat.

PEG: You're right. Alice! People are writing things about Jesus since always that have always not been true.

(Andy then discusses "the Pope of Rome's" removal of the "tinge of killing Christ" from Jews, "lots of whom" he notes supported Jesus, and how it was "the Sanhedrin religion" which should be blamed for the Crucifiction. "To make money. Like today!" And how if Jesus walked the streets today, he would "set right" the Communists and different religions who operate for money.)

PEG: If Jesus walked the streets today, He would be treated in no different terms than Paul Bailey did to Jack Wilson. Because they just don't understand! But I wouldn't worry about it. The people who knew him, Jack Wilson, I mean, love him. And the worst thing in the world, the hardest thing to bear, is to be unjustly accused. But that is exactly what Jesus died before he stood before the council. And he didn't raise a voice; in self-defense. It was the strongest defense in the world!

(Andy's comment that Wovoka was a great man.)

PEG: He was among these people who were having a hard, hard time.

(Wheat then comments about starving Indian women who appeared outside the Virginia City mines with baskets begging for leftover bread and undrunk coffee. Andy agrees.)

PEG: [So] The people needed a leader. He [Wovoka] was wise, he was serene. He never got mad at anyone. I don't think he ever got mad.

ALICE: No, he was always kind.

ANDY: No, he was a wonderful man.

PEG: Serene above all these troubles! I would like to tell the story about the great part of him. And I don't know if you can denounce Bailey and get away with it. I don't know if it will help things. I think the thing to do, is to tell the wonderful things. Like when you [Andy] were hurt. [And how] People came to him for solid advice, and he gave it with dignity.

ANDY: And there's no pay for all the things he ever done. Because I don't think there's anybody could pay for what he done. Not enough money to pay, even if they had a billion dollars!

PEG: People bring gifts, because they love him.

ANDY: Yeah, because they loved him.

PEG: Not a pay thing.

ANDY: From their hearts.

(Wheat then discusses a newspaper clipping from 1911: A return visit by Arapahoes, bearing gifts, in exchange for which Wovoka gave red paint and feathers.)

ALICE: And herbs!

ANDY: And that Indian tobacco. Gee, I sure liked it. You take those Arapahoes and everybody, those Cheyenne: By golly, they really loved him!

PEG: People came from far—to bring gifts.

ANDY: And he [also] give them good teaching—just like Alice said. Those Gros Ventre Indians, that time when they started that peyote. [Actually] It was the White folks that start that. They make beautiful teepees. Oh, the most beautiful things! You ever see them? With paintings all over it—was just out of this world! But they started that religious sect among them, they use that peyote, you know. They go into that dream land, and all that stuff. So they were starting it that time, and like he says, them Gros Ventre Indians came up from up there in Wyoming, and they come on down to see him. Where did he get that wisdom? He didn't know what peyote was! Any more than anything! And that fellow handed it to him, he looked at it, and he told him: "No, no! Don't use that! That is no good for your people!" He said it make your mind drift away, and all this and all that. Oh, he'd get into something, not good for you. Get the habit, it won't do you no good. [So] Where did he get the wisdom to understand to know that it was no good? Alright! But that's something.

[Same as] He said opium is no good. Why I tell you, that man, he had it! So, he must have had some guiding spirit in order to do those things, you know what I mean?

Now, they started it [peyote] up among Indians up there—Poor fellows, they can't break away from it. They started it here for a little while, and they had these people walking around like coyotes: On their hands and two legs! But he [Wovoka] told his people what to do: Be honorable, and all this and that.

[So] Them were the things. I think if White folks would have more men like him, instead of been preaching for money, and all this and that; being a little closer to God; and gave the same—Well, I don't like that word "power," to do these things—

ALICE: Wisdom!

ANDY: —wisdom! And knowing how to do these things, and this and that, our country would be better off.

(He then complains about children killing their mothers and fathers, and burning draft cards, and about blacks taking over.)

ANDY: Why, if they had a man like the Indians had, you know what I mean? Then I think it would do the world more good.

(A long complaint by him against preachers who have nice homes and worry more about the color of their cars, then hardly even preach at all: an hour on Sunday morning, another on Sunday night, eight hours a month.)

ANDY: Poor Jack: When he talked to his people, about these things, he didn't charge them no penny. For his healing. [Or] For his herbs. It was all free of charge. I remember he used to have to go and get his own wood. And he'd chop it; haul it in. And he'd go to work to buy food for his family. And he'd work hard. Pitch hay, believe me. And he was getting, was supposed to be one of the top men, old as he was, and he was making about $4 a day.

ALICE: Four dollars, nothing! Dollar and a half!

ANDY: Dollar and a half. Two dollars for building a stack.

ALICE: Dollar and a half for stackers, and dollar a day for the other people that pitch hay and put it on the wagon.

ANDY: And so you see on that meager earnings he supported his family. Of course, Alice's mother had to go and wash clothes and work, too. They worked together.

ALICE: And then my mother raised 13 children! But it's not her children: Other children that were motherless, that their mother had died, my mother picked up. That [Warren] Emm's mother. See, their mother got killed: The horse run away and killed both of them. Some way, I don't know, that's the way I got told; I don't know what happened. Anyway, Emma and Wichiri—"Willy," we call him—my mother went, and they came up and raised them.

ANDY: They didn't have no welfare them days.

ALICE: They [her parents] took care of them! And then when they grew up, [since] Mother raised them, and Emma took care of my sister's children while they were coming; then when she got little older, she got married and she had children of her own. And then Wichiri stayed with us. I always call him "Uncle Wichiri." And when I was a little girl, they would say, even in the winter time, if I hear somebody hollering, coming, you know, from town or somewhere, they would just holler, just to hear what I would say: In Indian. And then I'd ask mother if I was awake during that time. They'd probably holler outside. And I would say, "Listen," I'd say to my mother. "Listen: Uncle Willy is coming with a big watermelon," I would say. In winter time [laughs]...

Tape 74. Part 2: Side 2.

(Following a seeming break in continuity)

ALICE: Five! There's Henry and Jess. And James. And the Burbanks. She [her parents] took them [in]. And Dad and Mother raised them, as their own. They'd take care of them. Kids work, you know, bringing in wood. That stuff. But it was hard kicking for my mother and Dad to feed all them.

ANDY: So good and great, I tell you.

PEG: Where were you living then, Alice?

ALICE: Smith Valley. Of course, I was born at Day's Ranch, Smith Valley; near Colony [District]. Biggest ranch they had was Day's Ranch. That's where I was born.

That's where all these happenings were, where my mother raised all these kids. And they worked hard, both of them.

ANDY: And they moved to Nordyke, and from Nordyke into—

ALICE: Mason.

ANDY: —Mason!

PEG: There's a little house at Nordyke left, isn't there?

ANDY: That's right! A little cellar, ain't it, Alice?

ALICE: No! There's nothing left! We lived on that side there, we lived on that side of Nordyke there. Let's see? The south side. [And] There used to be a big orchard there, and we live on that side there: on a little ravine, like, on top of the hill. And that's where we were raised. Right there. And the people, Mr. and Mrs. Joe Wilson, and Billy Wilson. Dad worked in the mill.

ANDY: He used to take care of flour and—

ALICE: Flour mill. And he used to, my Dad would sack the flour, and the barley. Not barley, the grain. Then he used to count all the wheat that come in. He knew everybody in the valley, then he'd say: "So-and-so bring 14 sack or 15 sack of wheat." And he'd have it in his mind. And then he would tell Billy Wilson, then he'd [Billy] put it down on the paper. And then he would say: "Well, so-and-so brought so much wheat," and then Billy would put it down. And just how many sacks of flour he had sacked that day. And he had it [all] in his mind. He never had a day of school, but he knew how to count. And he told Billy, and then Billy would write it down. That's the way he made his living, right there.

My mother would work for Billy Wilson's wife, then next day he [she] worked for Mrs.—Joe Wilson's wife. And it was back and forth like that. And that's where we lived: on the other side there.

PEG: The west side of the highway?

ALICE: Yeah, on the west side. Well, as you going to Wilson Canyon, it's that side there.

(Wheat then inquires about her older brother who was said to have fallen under a wagon and was killed.)

ALICE: I don't remember. I don't know. They never said. But my little brother, him and I are the two different [blood] kind. And he died—he was about 6 years old when he died, my little brother.

(Then following Wheat's repeated inquiry about a wagon accident.)

ALICE: No, he just took sick and he died, that was all! Nice little boy. He looked something like [nephew] Harley: Brown hair. He was younger than me.

(Wheat, however, persists in the previous line of questioning about her older brother's death.)

ALICE: Could have happened, I don't know anything about it. You see, I don't know, I was so young, at that time I don't know very much. But I know that Hazel's mother, well, his [her] mother, the wagon ran away, they said, and something happened to him [her], and they were instantly killed, the two: husband and wife.

(Then to Wheat's suggestion that the two deaths might be confused or conflated.)

ALICE: Could be? They could have mixed it? And then my mother took them [in]; took Willy and Emma—Willy was the oldest.

ANDY: That teacher's grandmother; that teacher's mother?

ALICE: This is [Warren] Emm's mother!

ANDY: That fellow teaches at Fernley.

ALICE: He's a teacher out there: Warren. That's his mother; it was his mother that my mother raised. My mother fed her and clothed and anything. She stayed with Mother till she got married. And then Willy keep on living with us. And I always call him "Uncle Wichiri." Wichiri is "Willy" in Indian. I don't know why they love me so much. I guess it's something, and they always say, we'll holler out in front of the house, you know, and if I'm awake I'd hear it, and tell mother like this: "I hear Uncle Willy coming with watermelon!" Even if it was wintertime, she'd say I was, I'd say: "Listen, listen: That's Uncle Willy coming with watermelon. Wichiri is coming with watermelon!"

And they'd laugh. You know, when I come back from Arizona, I went to Yerington, and I saw them there: Him and Emma was walking down the street. And I said, "Emma!" And then they both grabbed me and said: "My poor little sister." And a few years after that they both died: Willy went first, then Emma last. And they always call me, **Pozina**. Means "rabbit kidney." If they were eating rabbit, I'd crawl all over everybody and ask for it. That was my speciality! They just let me do anything, I guess, because there were so many of us. They'd be eating, and I was the littlest. My brother and I was the smallest in the family. So, whatever we asked [for], we got.

And then Aunt—Ana Wasson—took me away from my mother when I was 15 months old. She raised me right up here.

...

No, I didn't stay with my mother, I stayed with my aunt. Right up here [Schurz] by the graveyard; beyond the graveyard. And then she used to take me down here, and Bob Dyer used to hold me and carry me around. And tell everybody that I was his daughter! [But] He just said that, you know. And there used to be a big platform there in front of his store—was facing the [railroad] track, and Indians'd sit along this, and people would go down when the train stop; people get out and walk around.

ANDY: That was when Goldfield started in.

ALICE: Oh, yeah! I was a little teensy weensy girl. I don't remember very much of it, but they used to give me nickles, they'd give me their lunch. Like that. I guess I looked so pitiful, that they give me their lunch.

(Wheat suggests they dressed her like a "little old lady," and how cute she must have looked.)

ALICE: Well, could be, you know? I didn't know how I was dressed, only that my aunt, **Tuzeeqama**, that she used to make clothes for me. And more likely she did dress me like a little old lady!

I was a pitiful little thing, I guess, 'cause my mother said I was so tiny, so little, underfed, because I was a seven month baby. And if it wasn't for this woman my mother was working for—

See, it was the third of July, and she was expecting a big company: People coming from San Francisco. And she [Wovoka's wife] moved some bedsteads from downstairs upstairs, then she'd bring the others downstairs. And she overdid herself. [So] On Fourth of July morning, two o'clock, well, I was born. Mother couldn't show up to work, to help her, so she [employer] sent down a man: To see if my mother was alright. Then Mother told her we had a little baby girl, and we don't know if she's gonna live or not. She's only a seven month baby. Of course, she came down and took me over—over to her house. And I stayed with her, my mother, for a long time. And they raised me on cow's milk. And now I just hate cow's milk! I don't like 'em!

[So] That's how it happened. I was only a 7 month baby. Well, I guess if it was 8 months, I guess I'd have been dead!

(Wheat inquires about the two ladies living together who raised her.)

ALICE: Yeah! Two old ladies: One was an old maid, and the other was married to Johnny Jones. And I was the only baby there. Mrs. Johnny Jones didn't have any children, and Aunt Tuzeeqama just adopted me. And she raised me till I was able to go to school. But she said she didn't have enough money to buy my clothes, so I could go to school, so she brought me back to my mother. My mother was living in Nordyke, and then they moved to Mason. And then Mother worked for some lady owned that Mason Hotel. She worked there, and then I went to the public school there. Yeah, I went to public school there, and then from there, my niece didn't want to go to school, so she said, well, then she got a cousin down here; her name was Mary Mason. She says, "You'll go faster if you go to an Indian school." So, we decided we'll go to Stewart. And, so, that's how we got there. In 1913.

(Wheat questions their respective ages; says she was born in 1908.)

ALICE: Well, my mother said I was born 1902, so, I'm a little older than you are.

(Wheat then asks for the age of her son Harlyn at Wovoka's death.)

ALICE: 24 years old! He was 24, when he died in China.

(Wheat rephrases her question, asking whether or not Harlyn Vidovich was four or five at the time of Wovoka's death.)

ALICE: Oh, yeah, he was about six years old, or something like that.

(Wheat comments, then, that he therefore had a chance to know his grandfather.)

ALICE: Oh, yes! That's why he always said "Grandpa can't say fish!" He was just a little boy about so big.
        [And] Yes, I remember [Wovoka]. But he was never mean to anyone; he always has kind word for everybody. And I don't see how, if he was living, and if I read that story to him that Paul Bailey wrote, I think he would have just died! Die of shame, you know, thinking he never did those things. Oh, I don't know what he'd do. But I think Paul Bailey is, I think is the lowest type of white man to run down a poor old—Oh, of course, he just think that it's just, oh, they're just Indians, and that's all. Nothing! You see, that's the way some people think. And they act it, too! I don't know. But I say, We're human beings, just like anybody else, Indians.
        Of course, the Indians in Montana, I mean, the Sioux, suffered more than we did, Nevada Indians. All along the line. They suffered more. They killed them, and do everything to them. And lie about things, and so on. Of course. I guess this was the last stand they made. And made all these terrible things—lies—about my Dad.
        [Because] He wasn't anything extra. He just used his common sense, that was all. Even then, you see, a lot of people, you know, well, they think, they think, I don't know: Like Bailey said he went out and had somebody shoot at him. And he wore a bulletproof vest. Well, how does Indian know anything about that? Indian don't know anything about that! And then salting the mine with gold—Where would he get the gold to salt the mine with? Well, gosh, that's unreasonable. [So] I don't know. To me, his book is just—out of whack, that's all. Of course, it makes it real bad, you know, for us. Maybe the government will take his word more than others? And maybe they might say that Jack Wilson was a bad man?

(Then to Wheat's "No chance!" reply,)

ALICE: Well, I hope not! And then it says that Dad took these people to Sacramento and up and Oregon, to give them work. And then he collected tithes from them. And Dad never done that! The only person who done that was Johnson Sides! He's the one take them to Sacramento and Oregon. And he [Bailey] said that he joined the Quakers, the Shakers, or something.

ANDY: The Shakers. He don't know anything about the Shakers!

ALICE: And, Dad, he never believe—Well, he believed there was a supreme being, but he never went toward this church or that church. Or any other church! He had his own belief.

ANDY: And he [Bailey] said the Mormons—

ALICE: Were closer!

ANDY: He said that he must have heard about the Mormon religion, or something.

ALICE: Oh, something like that!

ANDY: Because his teaching were so close to the Mormons.

ALICE: Yeah! That's what Paul Bailey said; in that book. Oh, it just, honestly, it was disgusting! To me it was, oh, I could have just throw that book! But, of course, there's millions of books out. And he sold them, either $10 or $5 apiece?

ANDY: $10 apiece!

ALICE: $10 apiece, I think? Because that's what we paid for ours: $10. Little red book.

(And after Wheat again attempts to console her with the notion that the same thing has happened to every great man, who nonetheless rise above it, and how justified though was her hurt, she, too, should just "rise above it," because "people don't take this seriously,")

ALICE: Yes, but they're reading it in schools! I know [somebody's boy] asked me the other day, and it was embarrassing to answer those questions he asked. [Because] They got it in school over there in Hawthorne, and he says he's been reading it. He asked me about it, and I said: "Well, I guess Paul Bailey is satisfied that he wrote that kind of story about my father." That's what I said. It's kind of very, very embarrassing. To me it is. And I just feel like to run and hide.

PEG: Don't!

ALICE: Oh, I wouldn't! But it just make you feel that way.

PEG: If he were my father, I would be proud. Beat my chest.

ALICE: Well, I do, I do. But, you know—

(Wheat then reminds her that even after the President speaks, people will criticize him, their attempts to demonstrate superior intelligence, etc.)

ALICE: Yeah, that's very true. But, still, you know, they had mixed him up with this big South Dakota deal, where Custer was killed. And that's what Paul Bailey said: That my boy had paid for that [breaks down and cries].

PEG: Very crude wording!

ALICE: [sobbing] And Andy, when [Bailey] asked about it, and Andy told him, I guess, 'cause I know I didn't. And I didn't ask him. And I know one of the ladies, Mrs. [?] said: "You give him permission to write that!" And [sobs] I didn't! [Because] That really hurt! She came right out, she said you had given him permission to write it; I said I didn't. I told her right out. And I said, if I had give him permission to write it, I'd have asked him for the money that he sold it for! Or, I would ask him to let me read before it's gone into the the public hand. That's what I told her. But she said, "You told him that you give him permission," and I didn't! [Because] If I did, I would ask him to let me read it first before the copy went out into public. But he just went right ahead; didn't even say—Well, I guess he thought I was just a dirty old Indian! And it really hurt deep [cries again].

[while sobbing] And I told Andy, if that man ever come around me to say anything, I think I'd just pull his eye out! But I know I wouldn't do it, but, still, I feel that way. I feel that mean toward that man. [Sobs] That was a dirty, dirty trick. I've read another book of his. The name of the book is *Wakawa*. He's an Indian man from Idaho. And he was supposed to be a big man, too. Oh, [but] he run him down, just like he did run down my dad.

(Wheat then requests some of the "real fine gentle things" Wovoka did.)

ALICE: Oh, he's always kind to everyone. My Dad was kind! And if you come to his house, he would say, "We don't have much, but if you want to eat what we've got, you're welcome!" That's what he always says. And he's always kind to everybody. I've never seen that man mad. Or say a unkind word to anybody. He's always kind to everybody. And then people from all over would come and talk to him ask for advice.

(Wheat questions whether she ever saw this.)

ALICE: Yes!

(Wheat next asks her about Wovoka's house.)

ALICE: Well, we had a little cabin, and it had floor on it. Then we had a little kitchen. And we had a big room—Oh, pretty near big as this room. And then we have a little kitchen in there; that's where we eat and cook. But this is where we have sleeping quarters here; we stayed in this room, and it had a big stove in there. That's where we live! We didn't have anything, we were poor. Poor little old cabin, just like anybody else, any other Indian. [And] We had benches, and we sit around and talk—benches that I guess Dad built. And we then had a little table in our kitchen, and we'd all eat in there. That's the way we lived. We wasn't—just like any other Indian. You've been to a home of Indians—like ours!

(Wheat comments on their functional simplicity.)

ALICE: Yeah, that's it! Just as plain as anybody! Yeah, that's the way it was in our home: We didn't have very much, we didn't have hardly anything; we just live from day to day. Of course, Dad had, when he worked, he always save his money for winter. And that's when he buy a little extra. You know, like canned food. He liked canned peaches, and [so] he always buy peaches. And Momma would dry a lot of fruit—Like somebody would give her apple, Mrs. Sheirone was quite—my mother would wash for her and help her out, and then she'd give her some fruit; like peaches, plums. And then she'd take it home and dry it. For winter. She would even dry fish. She worked for Mrs. Dick [?]. She was a Strosnyder, Mrs. Dick was; she worked for her. And Mr. Dick used to bring her liver. And the head. And my mother would always make strips of meat out of the cheek: She'd cut it small pieces, and she would dry it; then she would hang it up. And then if we go pine nutting, well, she had food. And he would bring the tripe, the whole thing, then we'd go down to the river and wash it.

       We didn't have—and what little few dollars Mother earn, and few dollars Dad earn, well, they saved that for winter use when they can't work. [So] That's the way we lived. We didn't live like some people

(Polka music interferes; difficult listening.)

ALICE: They were five cents a yard at that time. Then she [Mary Wilson] would buy enough to put little lace, those little embroidered lace, around our winter, I mean, our Sunday dresses. And she always kept it clean: Mother was very clean, I could say that much for her. And we always dressed nice. If it wasn't gingham, this percale [?], they were five cents a yard. We always dress like little old dolls, I guess? Well, that's the way she dressed us. And we always had plenty to eat. If we had fried potatoes, that's all we had, there was plenty of it, we ate plenty of it. If we had eggs, well, she never cook one egg, or two eggs to a person; she would maybe break [?], she fry potato: she had a big pan like I have. [And] She'd fill that up with fry potatoes, and she'd fry it. And then she would beat up two or three eggs, and then she'd mix it with this. And that's the way we would eat our eggs—Every one of us would have eggs, on account of

(Tape runs out.)

APPENDIX M

On Wovoka

Eileen Kane, Final Report, NSF Summer Field Training Project in Anthropology: 1964. University of Nevada Ethnographic Archive #3. Desert Research Institute, Reno. Special Collections, University of Nevada–Reno Library, pp. 39-44.

The most historically distinctive and really aberrant of the Mason and Smith Valley Indians doctors was Jack Wilson, whose Paiute name, **Wy"kotyhi**, meaning a "cutting or chopping instrument," has been corrupted in historical reference to "Wovoka" which has no meaning in Paiute, and which is not known to Wilson's relatives and followers. Wilson has been credited with being the inciter of the 1890 Ghost Dance, which supposedly resulted in the death of Sitting Bull. Yerington Indians know nothing of this, saying that Wilson taught them no new dances or songs, but merely used the ones which had been traditionally used since aboriginal times. The dance which he used in Yerington was the same circle dance which is the basis of the several seasonal-oriented celebrations. He was, however, an excellent singer, and remembered for the beauty which he brought to traditional music. Indians of Yerington are unaware that Jack Wilson is known at any distance outside their valley: his role in the spread of the so-called "Ghost Dance" is completely unknown to them.

Jack Wilson was born in approximately 1861, a son of **Nymytaipo?o**, or "white Man-Indian," also called **Pa-na**, and a mother whose name or character no one can recall. Wilson's father worked on the white Wilson ranch between Nordyke and Smith and from this family he took the name which he passed on to his only two offsriping [sic]: Jack, and Pat, born about 1880. According to the only popular book published on Jack Wilson, *Wovoka, the Indian Messiah*, by Paul Bailey, Jack was raised by the white Wilson family and was taught to speak and read English by his white "brothers," the Wilson boys. According to the older Indians of Yerington, and the early white residents, Wilson could scarcely speak English: according to Sheriff Claude Keema, his uncle Irving had to read all of Wilson's mail for him. Wilson was not raised with the white family, but merely, in the practice of the day, lived with his own ranch-hand parents in a hut on the employer's land. As a boy and young man, Jack Wilson had no particular power, and his brother Pat never did gain any. Wilson fashioned leather articles and ropes to supplement his living as a sporadic ranch hand. Later, he was able to persuade Indians to harvest the little grain which he would plant, and haul it to the white Wilson's mill. He was also frequently given gifts of money or food by Indians who deemed it an honor to visit him. Whites who knew him, including Sheriff's [sic] Lee Litell and Claude Keema, felt that he was quite adept at turning a situation to his own profit, and usually garnered the choicest plots of land for pine-nutting.

Jack Wilson married before the age of twenty-two, to a woman whose name local Indians can't recall and she was apparently not from this area, although she was Paiute. He had two daughters, Rose and Ida. The former, his favorite, had three children: Andy, Archie, and Inez, and died in her early thirties. His stepdaughter, Alice Wilson Vidovich, was the daughter of Wilson's wife and a white rancher, George Simpson: she presently is a Mormon and refuses to discuss her father's life.

Wilson's father acquired his Indian name from being taken by white soldiers, for a period of time, for some unknown reason: he was supported by Jack, as the oldest son, in his later years, and died, blind, at over one hundred years of age. If it is true, as Lowie claims (p. 193) that Wilson's father was the instigator of the first Ghost Dance of 1870, local people know nothing of it.

Wilson lived most of his life in the Mason-Smith Valley area: he lived for periods of time in a hut near the old mill at Nordyke, dying in a tent in the Yerington Indian Colony, by the present church, in 1931. He dressed as other ranch hands did, although he was frequently pictured in a black suit and hat: for dances, he wore a fringed and beaded buckskin suit and hat with a feathered headdress.

Wilson exerted a considerable political leadership in the Yerington area: he organized the pine nutting expeditions, sending runners and scouts into the mountains, and frequently "speaking for" the group. He was described by most informants as an extremely intelligent, even shrewd man. He also frequently led dances and prayer meetings.

It is interesting to note the amalgamation of aboriginal Indian and Christian beliefs which are present, not only in the mythological Paiute tales, such as the comparison of Wolf and Coyote with Cain and Abel, but also the very apparent influence of Christianity in the essentially nativistic tenets of Jack Wilson. Wilson preached that there was a heaven, to which all good Indians would go: death was therefore not a cause of grief: he preached that a good life on earth, with acceptance of the inequalities of white ways, would result in an Indian land of happiness, in the afterlife. Wilson knew this because he had visited heaven in several trance states which he had. His two major miracles involved the use of both baptismal and communion elements.

Wilson's mist [sic] prestigious and famous exploit was the floating of the ice down the Walker River, although their [sic] are varying versions of this event. Andy Dick, the oldest Indian in Yerington, had been told that the ice floated down the river on a summer noon, in accord with a prediction made by Wilson. Nellie Emm's mother, Mattie Paddy, saw the ice fall from trees, to be eaten by the Indians as communion feast, after which he bathed in the river, as a baptismal rite. This variation is particularly interesting since "Sister Emm" is one of the staunchest members of the Assembly of God Church in the Yerington Colony. Corbett Mack agrees with her account but sees no Biblical analogies. Jack McGowan, a local white resident, now deceased, reportedly once told a neighbor that his grandfather, one of the white Wilsons, had aided Wilson by floating the ice down from a higher point on the river: he also once dynamited the river, and the flying fish were attributed to Wilson.

Both of Wilson's two major miracles involve a prediction of the event: his second publically witnessed supernatural feat occurred, as prophesid [sic], on the fourth night of a five day dance (the number is typical of Ghost Dances) when a white horse came slowly over the mountain, through the air, in close proximity to a large white cloud. The cloud was seized by Indians and eaten, after which bathing in the river again occurred: the horse was eventually returned to his heavenly home.

Wilson also effected a number of cures: his medium was apparently eagle feathers, and his cures were accomplished, like most by a laying of hands; however, informants recall distinctly that he also "prayed to God:" accounts of other doctors say that they chanted or danced or made conspicuous of their medium, such a the prominent smoking of tobacco.

Wilson's indefinable powers, which cannot be traced to any specific source, and which was the basic cause of his position of leadership, was taken from him by Tom Mitchell, although Wilson was considered to be a "smart man," he was deceived and overpowered by Mitchell, who suggested that they pool their power and have double curate agents for the Indians: Wilson agreed, and Mitchell then seized ALL the power. Wilson rapidly became senile, and died shortly thereafter, in 1931, although people still sought him for curing until immediately before his death. Mitchell, who had witched most of the local doctors, soon lost this doubled power to Ben Lancaster, thus bringing to an end a flourishing era of Indian doctors.

Wilson, in public fashion, predicted an earthquake upon his demise: this came to pass as an indication of Wilson's power, according to informants, although the Mason Valley News reports no tremors in 1931.

The effect of Wilson's death was tremendous on the local populace: frequently before, Wilson had entered trance states and had communed with the dead in heaven, this time, however, he made no such claim prior to his unconsciousness. People refused to believe that a man of such power could be dead: Nellie Emm said that both she and her mother still believe that Wilson is alive, but waiting for opportune moment to appear.

The attitudes toward Jack Wilson were quite ambivalent: white informants, except for two, felt that while Wilson's seeming chicanery was admirable in its success, he nevertheless exploited the Indians in his reception of gifts, money, and food. (Whites, however, were unaware that it was a standard practice for a doctor to be paid.) Many of the local white apparently ridiculed Wilson, several claiming that they had helped him in the performance of his miracles. The widespread reading of Paul Bailey's *Wovoka* has increased the impression that Wilson was a charlatan, and has caused great resentment among the Indians. Two white informants felt that Wilson took positive, although ineffective, action against fear and disease, and that this in itself was a source of solace and well-being to ailing Indians; one of these informants was an eighty-five year old man who knew Wilson personally.

Little attention was paid to Wilson among the white populace; no note was made in the local paper, although, by 1931, names of prominent Indians was [sic] occasionally found in obituaries: few white residents can recall when he died.

Local Indians, however, have a strong feeling for Wilson: most claim his as relative, and do so accurately. There is still a strong belief in his power, and somewhat of a reluctance to discuss him with outsiders.

Bibliography

Aberle, David F.
    1959   "The Prophet Dance and Reactions to White Contact." **Southwestern Journal of Anthropology** 15:74-78.

    1966   **The Peyote Religion Among the Navaho.** Aldine Publishing Co., Chicago.

Angel, Myron (ed.)
    1881   **History of Nevada: With Illustrations and Biographical Sketches of its Prominent Men and Pioneers.** Thompson and West, Oakland.

Bailey, Paul
    1957   **Wovoka, The Indian Messiah.** Westernlore Press, Los Angeles.

    1970   **Ghost Dance Messiah: The Jack Wilson Story.** Westernlore Press, Tuscon.

Barber, Bernard
    1941   "Acculturation and Messianic Movements." **American Sociological Review** 6:663-69.

Barnett, H. G.
    1957   **Indian Shakers: A Messianic Cult of The Pacific Northwest.** University of Southern Illinois Press, Carbondale.

Barney, Garold D.
    1986   **Mormons, Indians and the Ghost Dance Religion of 1890.** University Press of America, Latham, Md.

Beach, Margery Ann
    1985   "The Waptashi Prophet and the Feather Religion: Derivative of the Washani." **American Indian Quarterly** 9(3):325-33.

Briggs, Marion P., and Sarah D. McAnulty
    1977   **The Ghost Dance Tragedy At Wounded Knee.** Smithsonian Institution, Office of Printing and Photographic Services, Washington, D.C.

Carroll, Michael P.
    1975   "Revitalization Movements and Social Structure: Some Quantitative Tests." **American Sociological Review** 40:389-401.

    1979   "Rejoinder to Landsman." **American Sociological Review** 44:166-68.

Chapman, Arthur I.
    1891   "Report of the Secretary of War." Vol. 1:191-94, Washington, D. C.

Clemmer, Richard O., and Omer C. Stewart
    1986   "Treaties, Reservations, and Claims," pp. 525-57. In **The Handbook of North American Indians: Great Basin,**Vol XI, ed. Warren L. d'Azevedo. Smithsonian Institution, Washington, D.C.

Colby, General L. W.
    1895 ·   "Wanagi Olowan Kin" ("The Ghost Songs of the Dakotas"). **Nebraska Historical Society** 1(3):131-50.

Coleman, Michael C.
1985   Presbyterian Missionary Attitudes Toward American Indians, 1837-1893.
            University Press of Mississippi, Jackson.

Dangberg, Grace
1957   "Letters to Jack Wilson, The Paiute Prophet." Anthropological Papers, Number
            55. Bureau of American Ethnology. Bulletin 164, pp. 279-96.

1968   Wovoka." The Nevada Historical Society 11(2):1-53.
File   Field Composition Notebook. Nevada Historical Society, Reno.

Davidson, Robert Nathaniel
1952   "A Study of the Ghost Dance of 1889." M.A. Thesis, Department of Sociology
            and Anthropolgy, Stanford University.

Davis, Sam P. (ed.)
1913   The History of Nevada. Vol 1. Elms Publishing Co., Reno.

Dobyns, Henry F., and Robert C. Euler
1967   The Ghost Dance of 1889: Among the Pai Indians of North-Western Arizona.
            Prescott College Press, Prescott, Arizona.

Dorinson, Joseph, and Joseph Boskin
1988   "Racial and Ethnic Humor," pp. 163-93. In Humor in American: A Research
            Guide to Genres and Topics. ed. Lawrence E. Mintz. Greenwood Press,
            Westport, Conn.

Drijvers, Han J. W.
1987   "Vocation," pp. 294-295. The Enclyclopedia of Religion, ed. Mircea Eliade.
            MacMillan Publishing Company, N.Y.

Driver, Harold
1961   Indians of North America. The University of Chicago Press, Chicago.

Du Bois, Cora
1939   "The 1870 Ghost Dance." Anthropological Records 3:1. University of
            California, Berkeley.

Dyer, E. A.
Mss.   Wizardry - The Jack Wilson Story. Special Collections, University of Nevada
            Library, Reno.

Erasmus, Charles J.
1961   Man Takes Control: Cultural Development And Economic Aid. The Bobbs-
            Merrill Company, Inc., New York.

Egan, Ferol
1972   Sand in a Whirlwind: The Paiute Indian War of 1860. Doubleday & Company,
            Garden City, N.Y.

Euler, Robert C.
1966   "Southern Paiute Ethnohistory." Anthropological Papers, No. 78. University of
            Utah, Salt Lake City.

Fletcher, Alice C.
1891   "The Indian Messiah." Journal of American Folklore 4:57-60.

Forbes, Jack D.
1967   Nevada Indians Speak. University of Nevada Press, Reno.

Ford, Velma
    1976   "History of Lyon County," pp. 135-40. In **Nevada—The Silver State**, Vol 1. Western States Historical Publishers, Carson City, Nev.

Fowler, Catherine
    1986   "Subsistence," pp. 64-97. In **Handbook of North American Indians: Great Basin**, Vol XI, ed. Warren L. d'Azevedo. Smithsonian Institution, Washington, D.C.

Fowler, Catherine S., and Lawrence Dawson
    1986   "Ethnographic Basketry," pp. 705-737. In **The Handbook of North American Indians: Great Basin**, Vol XI, ed. Warren L. d'Azevedo. Smithsonian Institution, Washington, D.C.

Fowler, Catherine S., and Sven Liljeblad
    1986   "Northern Paiute," pp. 435-465. In **The Handbook of North American Indians: Great Basin**, Vol XI, ed. Warren L. d'Azevedo. Smithsonian Institution, Washington, D.C.

Fowler, Don D.
    1966   "Great Basin Social Organization," pp. 57-74. In **The Current Status of Anthropological Research in the Great Basin: 1964**, ed. Warren L. d'Azevedo, et al. Desert Research Institute, Social Sciences and Humanities Publications, No. 1. Reno.

    1986   "History of Research," pp. 15-30. In **The Handbook Of North American Indians: Great Basin**. ed. Warren L. d'Azevedo. Smithsonian Institution, Washington, D.C.

Fowler, Don D., and Catherine S. Fowler (eds.)
    1971   "Anthropology of the Numa: John Wesley Powell's Manuscripts on the Numic Peoples of Western North America, 1868-1880." **Smithsonian Contributions to Anthropology**, No. 14. Washington, D.C.

Gaster, Theodor H.
    1969   **Myth, Legend and Custom in the Old Testament: A Comparative Study With Chapters From Sir James Frazier's Folklore in the Old Testament**. Harper & Row, New York.

Gatschet, Albert
    1893   "Report of an Indian Visit to Jack Wilson, the Payute Messiah." **Journal of American Folklore** 6:108-111.

Gayton, A. H.
    1930   "The Ghost Dance of 1870 in South-Central California." **University of California Publications in American Archaeology and Ethnology**, No. 28. Berkeley.

Ginzburg, Louis
    1909   **Legends of the Bible**. The Jewish Publication Society of America, Philadelphia.

Gottwald, Norman K.
    1985   **The Hebrew Bible: A Socio-literary Introduction**. Fortress Press, Philadelphia.

Greenway, John
    1969   "The Ghost Dance." **American Mercury** 83:42-47.

Grim, John A.
1987   "Wovoka," pp. 486-87. **The Encyclopedia of eligion**, ed. Mircea Eliade. MacMillan Publishing Company, N.Y.

Guild, Clark J. (1887-1971)
1967   **Memories Of My Work As A Lyon County Official, Nevada District Judge, And Nevada State Museum Founder**. Oral History Program, University of Nevada, Reno.

Hall, Joseph H.
1987   **Presbyterian Conflict and Resolution on the Missouri Frontier**. Studies in American Religion, Vol. 26. The Edwin Mellen Press, Lewiston, Maine.

Handleman, Don
1979   "The Development of a Washo Shaman." **Ethnology** 4:444-64.

Harner, Nellie Shaw
1974   **Indians of Coo-Yu-ee Pah (Pyramid Lake): The History of the Pyramid Lake Indians in Nevada**. Western Printing and Publishing, Sparks, Nev.

Hattori, Eugene Mitsuru
1975   "Northern Paiutes on the Comstock: Archeology and Ethnohistory of an American Indian Population in Virginia City, Nevada." **Occasional Papers (#2), Nevada State Museum**, ed. Donald R. Tuohy and Doris L. Rendall, Carson City.

Hedrick, B. C.
1971   "Quetzalcoatl: European or Indigene?" pp. 255-65. In **Man From Across The Sea: Problems of Pre-Columbian Contacts**, ed. Carroll L. Riley, J. Charles Kelley, Campbell W. Pennington, and Robert L. Rands. University of Texas Press, Austin.

Herzog, George
1935   "Plains Ghost Dance and Great Basin Music." **American Anthropologist** 37:403-19.

Heschel, Abraham J.
1962   **The Prophets**. The Jewish Publication Society, Philadelphia.

Hill, W. W.
1944   "The Navaho Indians and the Ghost Dance of 1890." **American Anthropologist** 46:523-527.

Hittman, Michael
1970   "Drug Addiction and the Rejection of Peyote in Smith and Mason Valleys, Nevada." 69th Annual Meetings of the American Anthropological Association. San Diego, California.

1973a   **"Ghost Dances, Disillusionment and Opiate Addiction: An Ethnohistory of Smith and Mason Valley Paiutes**. Ph.D. Dissertation, Department of Anthropology. University of New Mexico, Albuquerque.

1973b   "The 1870 Ghost Dance at the Walker River Reservation: A Reconstruction." **Ethnohistory** 20(3):247-78.

1984   **A Numu History: The Yerington Paiute Tribe**. The Yerington Paiute Tribe, Yerington, Nevada.

n.d.   **Nomogweta: The Life-History of Corbett Mack, Northern Paiute.**

Hittman, Michael, ed.
    1982-84   **Numu Ya Dua** ("Northern Paiute Speaks"). Tribal Newspaper of the Yerington Paiute Tribe, Yerington, Nevada.

Hodge, F. W.
    1956   "Foreword," pp. 11-13. In **Drummers and Dreamers,** by Click Relander. The Caxton Printers, Ltd. Caldwell, Idaho.

Hultkrantz, Ake
    1979   **The Religions of the American Indians.** University of California Press, Berkeley.

    1981   **Belief and Worship in Native North America** (ed. Christopher Vecsey). Syracuse University Press, Syracuse.

    1986   "Mythology and Religious Concepts," pp. 630-40. In **The Handbook of North American Indians: Great Basin,** Vol. XI, ed. Warren L. d'Azevedo. Smithsonian Institution, Washington, D.C.

    1987   "Ghost Dance," pp. 201-206. In **Native American Religions: North America,** ed. Lawrence E. Sullivan. MacMillan, N.Y.

Ingalls, G. W.
    1913   "Indians of Nevada, 1825-1913," pp. 20-132. In **The History of Nevada.** Vol 1, ed. Samuel P. Davis. Elms Publishing Co., Reno.

Johnson, Edward C.
    1975   **Walker River Paiutes: A Tribal History.** Walker River Paiute Tribe, Schurz, Nev.

    1986   "Issues: The Indian Perspective," pp. 592-600. In **The Handbook of North American Indians: Great Basin,** Vol XI, ed. Warren L. d'Azevedo. Smithsonian Institution, Washington, D.C.

    1987   "Wovoka Brought Pride To Indians." **Native Nevadan** 23 (12):14.

Jones, Osakie W.
    1899   "Legend of the Ghost Dance." **Journal of American Folklore,** Vol. 284-86.

Jorgensen, Joseph
    1985   "Religious Solutions and Native American Struggles: Ghost Dance, Sun Dance and Beyond," pp. 97-128. In **Religions, Rebellion, Revolution: An Interdisciplinary and Cross-Cultural Collection of Essays,** ed. Bruce Lincoln. St. Martin's Press, New York.

    1986   "Ghost Dance, Bear Dance, Sun Dance," pp. 660-72. In **The Handbook of North American Indians: Great Basin,** Vol XI, ed. Warren L. d'Azevedo. Smithsonian Institution, Washington, D.C.

    1987   "Modern Movements," pp. 541-45. **The Enclycopedia of Religion,** ed. Mircea Eliade. MacMillan Publishing Company, N.Y.

Kehoe, Alice B.
    1968   "The Ghost Dance Religion in Saskatchewan, Canada." **Plains Anthropologist** 13 (1):296-304.

    1981   **North American Indians: A Comprehensive Account.** Prentice-Hall, Inc. Englewood Cliffs, N.J.

    1989   **The Ghost Dance: Ethnohistory and Revitalization.** Case Studies in Anthropology, Holt, Rinehart and Winston, N.Y.

Kelly, Isabel T.
 1932   "Ethnography of the Surprise Valley Paiute." **University of California
               Publications In American Archaeology and Ethnology**, Vol. 31. Berkeley.

 1938   "Northern Paiute Tales." **Journal of American Folklore** 51:368-438.

Kerstein, Earl W., Jr.
 1961   **Settlements and Economic Life in the Walker River Country of Nevada and
               California.** Ph.D. Dissertation, Department of Geography, University of
               Nebraska, Lincoln.

 n.d.   "What Happened to Wovoka (Jack Wilson)?" Knack, Martha C., and Omer C.
               Stewart

 1984   **As Long as the River Shall Run: An Ethnohistory of Pyramid Lake Indian
               Reservation.** University of California, Berkeley.

Kobben, A. J. F.
 1960   "Prophetic Movements as an Expression of Social Protest." **International
               Archives of Ethnography** 44:117-64.

Kroeber, Alfred L.
 1904   "A Ghost Dance in California." **Journal of American Folklore** 17:32-35.

 1925   **Handbook of the Indians of California.** Bureau of American Ethnology, No. 78.
               Government Printing Office, Washington, D.C.

La Barre, Weston
 1970   **The Ghost Dance: The Origins of Religion.** Doubleday and Company, Garden
               City, N.J.

Landsman, Gail
 1979   "The Ghost Dance and the Policy of Land Allotment." **American Sociological
               Review** 44:162-66.

Lanner, Ronald M.
 1981   **The Pinion Pine: A Natural and Cultural History.** University of Nevada Press,
               Reno.

Lanternari, Vittorio
 1965   **The Religions of the Oppressed: A Study of Modern Messianic Cults.** Mentor
               Books, N.Y.

Lauben, Reginald, and Gladys Lauben
 1976   **Indian Dances of North America.** University of Oklahoma Press, Norman.

Lesser, Alexander
 1933   **The Pawnee Ghost Dance Hand Game: Ghost Dance Revival and Ethnic
               Identiry.** Columbia University Press, N.Y.

Lewis, I. M.
 1971   **ECSTATIC RELIGION: A STUDY OF SHAMANISM AND SPIRIT POSSES-
               SION.** Routledge, London.

Liljeblad, Sven
 1986   "Oral Tradition: Content and Style of Verbal Arts," 641-59. In **Handbook of
               North American Indians: Great Basin**, Vol. XI, ed. Warren L. d'Azevedo.
               Smithsonian Institution, Washington, D.C.

Linton, Ralph
    1943   "Nativistic Movements." **American Anthropologist** 45:230-240.

Logan, Brad
    1980   "The Ghost Dance Among the Paiute: An Ethnohistorical View of the Documentary Evidence, 1889-1893. **Ethnohistory** 27 (3):267-289.

Lowie, Robert
    1924   "Notes on Shoshonean Ethnography." **American Museum of Natural History, Anthropological Papers**, No. 20. New York, N.Y.

Mair, Lucy P.
    1958   "Independent Religious Movements in Three Continents." **Comparative Studies in Society and History** 1:113-136.

McCoy, Tim (with Ronald McCoy)
    1977   **Tim McCoy Remembers The West.** University of Nebraska Press, Lincoln.

Miller, Christopher
    1985   **PROPHETIC WORLDS.** Rutgers University Press, Rutgers.

Miller, David
    1959   **GHOST DANCE.** Duell, Sloan and Pearce, N.Y.

Miller, Jay
    1983   "Basin Religion and Theology: A Comparative Study of Power (**Puha**)." **Journal of California and Great Basin Anthropology**, Vol 5:66-86.

Mooney, James
    1896   "The Ghost Dance Religion and the Sioux Outbreak   of 1890," Fourteenth **Annual Report (Part 2) Of The Bureau of Ethnology To The Smithsonian Institition, 1892-1893,** by J. W. Powell. Government Printing Office, Washington, D.C.

    1911   "The Indian Ghost Dance," pp. 168-86. Address, **Proceedings and Collections of the Nebraska State Historical Society**, Vol. 16.

Moses, L. G.
    1979   "Jack Wilson and the Indian Service: The Response of the BIA to the Ghost Dance Prophet. **American Indian Quarterly** 3(3):295-316.

    1984   **The Indian Man: A Biography of James Mooney.** University of Illinois Press, Urbana

    1985   "The Father Tells So! Wovoka, the Ghost Dance Prophet." **American Indian Quarterly** 9(3):335-57.

Nash, Philleo
    1937   "The Place of Religious Revivalism in the Formation of the Intercultural Community on Klamath Reservation," pps. 377-441. In **Social Anthropology of North American Tribes,** ed. Fred Eggan. University of Chicago Press, Chicago.

Neihardt, John G.
    1932   **Black Elk Speaks.** Washington Square Press, N.Y.

Olofson, Harold
    1979   "Northern Paiute Shamanism Revisited." **Anthropos** 79:11-24.

Opler, Marvin K.
 1971   "The Ute and Paiute Indians of the Great Basin Southern Rim." In **North American Indians In Historical Perspective**. ed. Eleanor B. Leacock and Nancy O. Lurie. Random House, N.Y.

Overholt, Thomas W.
 1974   "The Ghost Dance of 1890 and the Nature of the Prophetic Process." **Ethnohistory** 21 (1):37-63.

 1978   "Short Bull, Black Elk, Sword, and the `Meaning' of the Ghost Dance." **Religion** 8:171-95.

Park, Willard Z.
 1938   **Shamanism In Western North America: A Study In Cultural Relationships**. Northwestern University Press, Evanston, Ill.

 1941   "Cultural Succession in the Great Basin," pp. 180-203. In **Language, Culture and Personality**, ed. Leslie A. Spier, et al. Sapir Memorial Publication Fund, Menasha, Wis.

Phister, Lt. Nat P.
 1891   "The Indian Messiah." **American Anthropologist** 2:105-8, o.s.

Poldervaart, Arie
 1987   **Yerington Paiute Grammar**. ed. Tupou L. Pulu, Bilingual Education Services, Achorage, Alaska.

Powers, William K.
 1987   "Indians of the Plains," pp. 490-499. **The Encyclopedia of Religion**, ed. Mircea Eliade. MacMillan Publishing Company, N.Y.

Ricketts, Mac Linscott
 1987   "Tricksters," pp. 167-170. **The Enclycopedia of Religion**, ed. Mircea Eliade. MacMillan Publishing Company, N.Y.

Riddell, Francis A.
 1960   "Honey Lake Ethnbography." **Nevada State Museum Anthropological Papers**, No. 4. Carson City, Nev.

Ring, Kenneth
 1984   **Heading Toward Omega: In Search of the Meaning of the Near-Death Experience**. Quill/William Morrow, N.Y.

Sayre, Cora (1897-)
 1971   **Memories of Smith Valley**. Oral History Project, Mary Ann Miller, Interviewer. University of Nevada, Reno.

Shimkin, Demitri B.
 1942   "Dynamics of Recent Wind River Shoshoni History." **American Anthropologist** 44(3):451-62.

Slagle, Al Logan
 1985   "Tolowa Indian Shakers and the Role of Prophecy at Smith River, California." **American Indian Quarterly** 9(3):353-74.

Smith, Morton
 1978   **Jesus the Magician**. Harper & Row, San Francisco.

Smith, Timothy B.
  1911-12   "Recollections of the Early History of Smith valley," **Nevada Historical Society**,
                   Papers, Third Biennial Report. Carson City, Nev.

Sockman W. Ralph
  1963   "What is a Methodist?" pp. 121-30. In **Religions In America**, ed. Leo Rosten.
                   Simon & Shuster, N.Y.

Spencer, Robert F., and Jesse D. Jennings, et al.
  1965   **The Native Americans**. Harper & Row, N.Y.

Spier, Leslie
  1927   "The Ghost Dance of 1870 Among The Klamath of Oregon." **University of
                   Washington Publications in Anthropology** 2:2.

  1935   "The Prophet Dance of the Northwest and its Derivatives: The Source of the
                   Ghost Dance." **General Series in Anthropology**. No 1., Menasha, Wis.

Spier, Leslie, and Wayne Suttles, and Melville J. Herskovits
  1959   "Comment on Aberle's Theory of Deprivation." **Southwestern Journal of
                   Anthropology** 15:84-88.

Steward, Julian
  1938   "Basin Plateau Aboriginal Sociopolitical Groups." **Bureau of American
                   Etnology**,Bulletin 120. Washington, D.C.

Steward, Julian, and Erminie Wheeler-Voegelin
  1974   **Paiute Indians III: The Northern Paiute Indians**. Garland Publishing Inc., N.Y.

Stewart, Omer C.
  1939   "The Northern Paiute Bands." **University of California Anthropological
                   Records**, Vol. 2, Berkeley.

  1941   "Culture Element Distributions: XIV, Northern Paiute." **University of
                   California Publications in American Archaeology and Ethnology**, Vol. 40.
                   Berkeley.

  1944   "Washo-Northern Paiute Peyotist: A Study in Acculturation." **University of
                   California Publications in American Archaeology and Ethnology** 40(3).
                   Berkeley.

  1971   "The Peyote Religion and the Ghost Dance." Paper presented at Nineteenth
                   Annual Meeting, American Society For Ethnohistory.

  1977   "Contemporary Document on Wovoka (Jack Wilson) Prophet of the Ghost
                   Dance in 1890." **Ethnohistory** 24(3):219-23.

  1986   "The Peyote Religion," pp. 673-81. In: **The Handbook of North American
                   Indians: Great Basin**, Vol XI, ed. Warren L. d'Azevedo. Smithsonian Institution,
                   Washington, D.C.

Thornton, Russell
  1986   **We Shall Live Again: The 1870 and 1890 Ghost Dance Movements as
                   Demographic Revitalization**. Cambridge University Press, Cambridge.

Trafzer, Clifford E., and Margery Ann Beach
  1985   "Smohalla, The Washani, and Religion as a factor in Northwestern Indian
                   History." **American Indian Quarterly** 9(3):309-24.

Unrau, William E.
  1985   "Charles Curtis: The Politics of Allotment," pp. 113-38. In **Indian Lives: Essays on Nineteenth- and Twentieth-Century Native American Leaders,** ed. by L. G. Moses and Raymond Wilson. University of New Mexico Press, Albuquerque.

Utley, Robert
  1963   **Last Days Of The Sioux Nation.** Yale University Press, New Haven.

Valentine, Charles A.
  1960   "Uses of Ethnohistory in an Acculturation Study." **ETHNOHISTORY** 7:1-27.

Walker, Deward S., Jr.
  1969   "New Light on the Prophet Dance Controversy." **ETHNOHISTORY** 16:245-255.

Wallace, A. F. C.
  1956   "Revitalization Movements." **American Anthropologist** 58:264-81.

  1970   **The Death and Rebirth of the Seneca.** Alfred A. Knopf, N.Y.

Weber, Max
  1947   **The Theory of Social and Economic Organization.** Oxford University Press, Oxford.

Whiting, Beatrice B.
  1950   "Paiute Sorcery." **Viking Fund Publications in Anthropology,** No. 15. N.Y.

Wier, Jennie
  File   Field Notes. Nevada Historical Society, Reno.

Wilson, Bryan R.
  1973   **Magic and The Millennium: A Sociological Study of Religious Movements of Protest Among Tribal and Third-World Peoples.** Harper and Row, N.Y.

Worrell, Estelle Ansley
  1979   American Costume 1840-1920. Stackpole Books, Harrisburg, PA.

Worsley, Peter
  1957   **The Trumpet Shall Sound: A Study of 'Cargo Cults' In Melanasia.** Shocken Books, N.Y.

Wren, Thomas
  1907   **A History of the State of Nevada: Its Resources and People.** The Lewis Publishing Company, N.Y.

Zanjani, Sally S.
  1988   "The Indian Massacre That Never Happened." **Nevada Historical Society Quarterly** 30(2):119-29.

Supplemental Bibliography

d'Azevedo, Warren L.
    1986   "Introduction," pp. 1-14. In **The Handbook of North American Indians: Great Basin**, Vol. XI, ed. Warren L. d'Azevedo. Smithsonian Institution, Washington, D.C.

Clifford, James, and George E. Marcus
    1986   **Writing Culture: The Poetics and Politics of Ethnography**. University of California Press, Berkeley.

Festinger, Leon, Henry W. Riecken, and Stanley Schachter
    1956   **When Prophecy Fails: A Social and Psychological Study of a Modern Group that Predicted the Destruction of the World**. Harper & Row, New York.

Glancy, Diane
    1993   "Jack Wilson or Wovoka and Christ My Lord," pp. 11-17. In **Firesticks: A Collection of Stories**. University of Oklahoma Press, Norman.

Grinnell, George Bird
    1891   "The Messiah Superstition." **Journal of American Folklore** 4:61-66.

Hinsley, Curtis M.
    1984   **The Smithsonian and the American Indian: Making a Moral Anthropology in Victorian America**. Smithsonian Institution Press, Washington, D.C.

Hittman, Michael
    1992   "The 1890 Ghost Dance in Nevada." **American Indian Culture and Research Journal** 16(4):123-66.
    1996a   **Corbett Mack: The Life of a Northern Paiute**. University of Nebraska Press, Lincoln.
    1996b   "Ghost Dance," p. 223, "Wovoka (Jack Wilson)," pp. 700-702. In **Encyclopedia of North American Indians: Native American History, Culture, and Life From Paleo-Indians to the Present**, ed. Frederick E. Hoxie. Houghton-Mifflin, Boston.

Hulse, James W.
    1989   "Reformers and Visionaries on Nevada's Frontier," pp. 56-72. In **East of Eden, West of Zion: Essays on Nevada**, ed. Wilbur S. Shepperson. University of Nevada Press, Reno.

Hultkrantz Ake
    1993   Review of **Wovoka and the Ghost Dance** by Michael Hittman. **American Indian Culture and Research Journal** 17:528-29.

Jensen, Richard E., R. Eli Paul, and John E. Carter
    1991   **Eyewitness at Wounded Knee**. University of Nebraska Press, Lincoln.

Josephy, Alvin M., Trudy Thomas, and Jeanne Eder
    1990   **Wounded Knee: Lest We Forget**. Buffalo Bill Historical Center, Cody, Wyo.

Kane, Eileen
    1964   "Field Report: Summer 1964" (Ethnographic Archive #3). Desert Research Institute, Reno. Special Collections, University of Nevada–Reno Library.

Kersten, Earl W., Jr.
n.d.   "What Happened to Wovoka (Jack Wilson)?" Mss. in possession of the author.

Kroeber, A. L.
1948   **Anthropology**. Harcourt, Brace & World, Inc., New York.

Mooney, James
1907   "Ghost Dance," pp. 491-92. In **Handbook of American Indians North of Mexico**, ed. Frederick Webb Hodge. Smithsonian Institution, Bureau of American Ethnology, Bulletin 30.

Moses, L. G.
1987   "James Mooney and Wovoka: An Ethnologist's Visit With the Ghost Dance Prophet." **Nevada Historical Society Quarterly** XXX:131-46.

Osterreich, Shelley Anne
1991   **The American Indian Ghost Dance, 1870 and 1890: An Annotated Bibliography**. Bibliographies and Indexes in American History Number 19. Greenwood Press, Westport, Conn.

Overholt, Thomas W.
1982   "Seeing is Believing: The Social Setting of Prophetic Acts of Power." **Journal for the Study of the Old Testament** 23:3-31.

Park, Willard Z.
        Field Notes. In possession of Catherine S. Fowler.
1934   "Paviotso Shamanism." **American Anthropologist** 36:98-113.
1937   "Paviotso Polyandry." **American Anthropologist** 39:366-88.

Powell, John Wesley
1971   **Anthropology of the Numa: John Wesley Powell's Manuscripts on the Numic Peoples of Western North America, 1868-1880**, ed. Don D. Fowler and Catherine S. Fowler. Smithsonian Contributions to Anthropology 14. Smithsonian Institution, Washington, D.C.

Sandos, James A.
1993   Review of **Wovoka and the Ghost Dance** by Michael Hittman. **American Indian Quarterly** 17(3):408-9.

Shepperson, Wilbur S., ed.
1989   **East of Eden, West of Zion: Essays on Nevada**. University of Nevada Press, Reno.

Siskin, Edgar E.
1983   **Washo Shamans and Peyotists: Religious Conflict in an American Indian Tribe**. University of Utah Press, Salt Lake City, 1983.

Smart, James R.
1980   "Emile Berliner and Nineteenth-Century Disc Recordings." **The Quarterly Journal of the Library of Congress** 37(3-4):423-40.

Smith, Anne M. Cooke
1939   "An Analysis of Basin Mythology." Ph.D. diss. in Anthropology. Yale University, New Haven.

Steward, Julian
1936   "Myths of the Owens Valley Paiute," pp. 355-440. **University of California Publications in American Archaeology and Ethnology** 34:3.
1943a   "Culture Element Distributions 23: Northern and Gosiute Shoshoni," pp. 263-392. **University of California Publications in American Archaeology and Ethnology** 8:3.

1943b   "Some Western Shoshone Myths." **Anthropological Papers Number 31. Bureau of American Ethnology**. Bulletin 136, pp. 249-99.

Stewart, Omer C.
1937   "Northern Paiute Polyandry." **American Anthropologist** 39:368-69.
1944   "Washo-Northern Paiute Peyotism: A Study in Acculturation." **University of California Publication in American Archaeology and Ethnology** 40:63-142.
1980   "The Ghost Dance," pp. 179-187. In **Anthropology on the Great Plains**, ed. W. Raymond Wood & Margot Liberty. University of Nebraska Press, Lincoln.

Tedlock, Dennis
1979   "The Analogical Tradition and the Emergence of a Dialogical Anthropology." **Journal of Anthropological Research** 35(4):387-400.

Underhill, Ruth
1941   **The Northern Paiute Indians**. Sheridan Pamphlets #1. Education Division of the United States Office of Indian Affairs. Haskell Institute Printing Office, Lawrence, Kansas.

Vander, Judith
1997   **Shoshone Ghost Dance Religion: Poetry Songs and Great Basin Contest**. University of Illinois Press, Urbana.

Vizenor, Gerald
1990   **Interior Landscapes: Autobiographical Myths and Metaphors**. University of Minnesota Press, Minneapolis.

Watson, Elmo Scott
1943   "The Last Indian War, 1890-91—A Study of Newspaper Jingoism." **The Journalism Quarterly** 20:205-19.

Wheat, Margaret M.
Margaret M. Wheat Papers #83-24. Special Collections, University of Nevada–Reno Library.

Wier, Jeanne Elizabeth
1987   "The Mission of the State Historical Society" (Address given before the Academy of Science in 1905). **Nevada Historical Society Quarterly** XXX(2):86-92.